Cannabis Law

A Primer on Federal and
State Law Regarding Marijuana,
Hemp, and CBD

BARAK COHEN, EDITOR | WITH MICHAEL C. BLEICHER

AMERICAN**BAR**ASSOCIATION

ABA Publishing

Cover design by Amanda Fry/ABA Design

Printed in the United States of America.

25 24 23 22 21   5 4 3 2

A catalog record for this book is available from the Library of Congress.

Discounts are available for books ordered in bulk. Special consideration is given to state bars, CLE programs, and other bar-related organizations. Inquire at Book Publishing, ABA Publishing, American Bar Association, 321 N. Clark Street, Chicago, Illinois 60654-7598.

www.shopABA.org

Contents

Chapter 6

Chapter 7

Chapter 11
Insurance Considerations for the Cannabis Industry...............................167

Chapter 12
Bankruptcy 183

Chapter 13
Regulation of Cannabis-Containing Products in the U.S. Food
and Beverage Supply...199

Editor's Note

Authorities differ as to the correct spelling of "marijuana," with some laws and regulations substituting an "h" for the "j." This treatise uses the more common and generally accepted spelling "marijuana" throughout. Substitutions of this spelling in quotations from sources that use "marihuana" have not been noted.

Similarly, there is some confusion over the terms "cannabis" and "marijuana." Both marijuana and its non-psychotropic cousin hemp are varieties of the cannabis plant. Thus, some marijuana is cannabis, but not all cannabis is marijuana. Nevertheless, authorities, including some of the authors of the chapters of this book, often conflate these terms. In most instances, context clarifies these blurred lines, and the editor has further attempted to make clear these references where context fails to do so.

In doing so, the politics that underlie these terms should be acknowledged. With good reason, some commentators and participants in the cannabis industry have rejected "marijuana/marihuana" as historically derogatory. Even so, the decision has been made consciously to prioritize clarity in the use of these terms in the legal analysis that follows.

Preface

There is no denying that, over the last two decades, by any measure (commercial accessibility, range of products, revenues, state legalization, and seriousness of efforts at federal legalization, to name a few), the cannabis industry has grown by leaps and bounds. That undeniable fact is reflected implicitly and explicitly in every page of this treatise, which was born of that breathtaking growth.

Explicitly, it is reflected in numerous financial statistics. For example, according to one source, the total combined legal sales of medical and adult-use marijuana alone are projected to reach an impressive $30 billion by 2025.[1] It is further expressly reflected in the many ways that the industry monetizes cannabis. For example, the industry broadly includes both recreational and medicinal marijuana, CBD products, hemp products, foods and beverages, core services (such as cultivation), and ancillary services (supportive technology, e-commerce, advertising, etc.).

Implicitly, the budding diversity of the many legal questions implicated by these multidimensional business efforts inherently reflects an industry that grows increasingly complex. In fact, it underlines that the "cannabis industry" is not one industry; it is many. As such, the legal needs relating to cannabis have become more sophisticated. Cannabis businesses may now require expert transactional advice, for example, relating to filings with the U.S. Securities and Exchange Commission. They may require advice related to the regulation of food and beverages by the U.S. Food and Drug Administration, as well as bankruptcy advice, representation in litigation relating to the myriad lawsuits that successful businesses face every day, trademark and patent counseling, and the list goes on.

This treatise aims to address these diverse legal questions by offering high-level overviews of the law, from a federal and general state level, with a particular focus on the concerns that cannabis businesses face. This goal is unique. This is the first multi-practice legal primer that responds to the key questions faced by the cannabis industry, which has advanced to where there is significant demand for such guidance.

In the pages that follow, you'll find advice from authorities with deep expertise in their respective practice areas. These lawyers and experts

---

1. Chris Hudock, *U.S. Legal Cannabis Market Growth* (Sept. 8, 2019), https://newfrontier data.com/cannabis-insights/u-s-legal-cannabis-market-growth/.

include not only U.S. lawyers but also Canadian practitioners with analysis regarding their domestic legal regime, a highly regulated market with demonstrated appeal to U.S. businesses and investors, as well as Dr. Stephen M. Ostroff, Former Deputy Commissioner for Foods and Veterinary Medicine, U.S. Food and Drug Administration.

Our hope is that this advice will offer initial guidance to dedicated practitioners, both in-house and from outside law firms, who provide legal services to cannabis businesses or to businesses that are considering entering the cannabis industry. Only by ensuring that these businesses receive superior legal counsel can we, as lawyers, help promote the responsible and profitable growth of what is surely one of the most promising industries in the United States today.

Acknowledgments

Many people deserve thanks for their roles in this book's creation.

First and foremost, I thank my family (Lore, Big A, and Batmanninja-pirate) for putting up with the many early, late, and weekend hours that I spent working on this book. Your support was critical. I particularly want to thank Lore, who urged me to follow through with the initial idea.

Also deserving gratitude is my extended Perkins Coie family, without whose support that initial idea would never have taken definite form. I'd particularly like to thank Michael Bleicher and Hanna Mullin, who spent hours editing, compiling, and offering suggestions that, ultimately, became this book. Rebecca Gordon also generously shared her time offering advice from her own editing experiences, and, in fact, helped connect me with my publisher, the American Bar Association. Thank you also goes to the many firm lawyers (as well as the lawyers and specialists from outside Perkins Coie) who contributed chapters to the book and put up with my editorial pestering and dunning e-mails. The final product reflects your collective expertise and legal acumen.

I'm very grateful for the support of my clients. When I started representing clients involved in or seeking to become involved in the cannabis industry, it was difficult to find dependable legal resources to help guide me as I responded to the new questions and issues I faced. This primer, a first of its kind, was born of the challenge of trying to educate myself regarding the legal nuances of a new, multifaceted, and increasingly sophisticated industry. My clients trusted me to help navigate them across the shifting topography of this poorly mapped legal landscape. The experience inspired me to edit and compile this book in order to help provide legal guidelines to an industry that matures and grows daily.

Last but not least, thank you to the American Bar Association, and especially my editor John Palmer, for your willingness to take a risk on a novel idea, patience with deadlines, and responsiveness addressing my editorial questions.

1

Basic Issues: The Tension between Federal and State Law and Policy

Barak Cohen and Michael Bleicher

1. Introduction

Cannabis businesses face unique risks because significant, unresolved tension exists both between federal and state regulation of cannabis and between black-letter law and actual enforcement. These discrepancies are intertwined. For example, federal law purports to criminalize marijuana although several states have decriminalized marijuana, but federal laws criminalizing marijuana are not consistently enforced, and state-level legalization regimes often have significant restrictions, carve-outs, or ambiguities of their own.

This chapter explains key aspects of the federal–state tension, as well as conflict between the law as it is written and the law as it is enforced. By way of mapping this tension, this chapter reviews the relevant definitions relating to cannabis regulation. Second, it sets forth the history and current state of play pertaining to cannabis regulation at the federal level. Third, it offers some general observations and insights of value to cannabis law practitioners.

2. Definitions

The legal vocabulary surrounding cannabis regulation often differs from how cannabis terms are used in the lay context. Understanding the terminology is crucial to understanding the regulatory landscape.

- **Cannabis, marijuana, and/or marihuana** refer to the plant *Cannabis sativa L.* Under U.S. federal law, it is categorized as a controlled substance equivalent in seriousness to narcotics such as heroin, LSD, and cocaine. As noted below, specified portions of the cannabis plant are not illegal under U.S. law. The primary psychoactive ingredient in cannabis is the chemical compound tetrahydrocannabinol (THC), which is responsible for the substance's intoxicating ("high"-inducing) effect.
- **Cannabinoids** refer generally to various chemical compounds found within the cannabis plants. There are more than 100 known cannabinoids, which can be extracted from cannabis and used as additives in foods, beverages, dietary supplements, personal care products, and drugs. It is possible that many cannabinoids may offer health benefits.
- **CBD** refers to cannabidiol, currently the most popular cannabinoid for commercial applications. CBD does not have the same intoxicating properties as THC, nor does it generate psychoactive effects in humans. CBD can be sourced either from marijuana or hemp (see next). Depending on how CBD is sourced, it may still be treated under federal law as a controlled substance. CBD is gaining popularity because it is non-psychoactive; easily added to foods, beverages, and supplements; and may possess numerous health benefits.
- **Hemp** refers to the fiber of a distinct variety of cannabis that is generally legal under federal law. It is useful for industrial applications, such as textiles and paper manufacturing, and as a source of CBD. Hemp contains only a negligible amount of THC and may be used to create CBD. The most important distinction between hemp and marijuana is the THC content; federal law requires a plant to contain under 0.3 percent THC to be classified has hemp. Plants with more than 0.3 percent THC are classified as marijuana.

3. Overview of Law and Regulation

3.1 Federal Law and Enforcing Agencies

From a high level, the cannabis industry implicates a small number of federal agencies that oversee a variety of interlocking laws and regulations. These laws and regulations are addressed in greater detail in subsequent chapters.

3.1.1 U.S. Congress and DOJ

U.S. Congress introduces, votes on, and potentially passes federal cannabis legislation. For the time being, Congress is broadly unable to agree on legislation decriminalizing cannabis, codifying policies of nonenforcement, or facilitating cannabis business at the state-legal level, but there are signs of gradual movement toward some or all of these outcomes. **U.S. Department of Justice (DOJ)** chooses whether or not to enforce federal cannabis legislation passed by Congress. In other words, some of the tension just described—between what the law technically says and how it is actually enforced—stems from whether the DOJ chooses to enforce laws on the books.

3.1.2 U.S. Food and Drug Administration (FDA)

The FDA regulates and enforces legislation pertaining to the safe manufacture and sale of products containing cannabis and cannabis derivatives (e.g., CBD). To date, the FDA has only sent warning letters for egregious marketing claims; it has not taken actual enforcement action. The FDA recently issued its determination that CBD is not generally recognized as safe (GRAS), a decision with implications for how CBD may be legally added to foods, beverages, and cosmetics.

The FDA has not yet approved CBD or any other cannabidiol (whether derived from hemp or marijuana) as a food additive, and the agency has concluded that CBD is not GRAS for use as an additive in human or animal food, beverages, or dietary supplements under the federal Food, Drug, and Cosmetic Act.[1] The FDA has approved CBD as a drug for use in an antiseizure medication, Epidiolex.

3.1.3 Federal Trade Commission (FTC)

The FTC regulates unfair and deceptive practices. Through authority granted by the FTC Act, the FTC has sent independent warning letters and undertaken independent enforcement actions relating to misleading or deceptive marketing of CBD products. The FTC has also joined the FDA in warning letters relating to CBD products.[2]

3.1.4 U.S. Department of Agriculture (USDA)

USDA is responsible for issuing or approving state-level plans for growing and transporting hemp. Although the 2018 Farm Bill guaranteed interstate shipment of hemp, the guarantee did not take effect until October 2019, when the USDA published an interim final rule specifying rules and

---

1. *See* 21 U.S.C. §§ 301 *et seq.*
2. *See* 15 U.S.C. §§ 41 *et seq.*

regulations for domestic hemp production. Agencies issue interim final rules when it is in the public interest to promulgate an effective rule while keeping the rulemaking open for further refinement, generally because there is compelling justification or little controversy regarding the rule. This particular interim rule will be operative for two years (until November 1, 2021).

3.1.5 U.S. Department of Treasury (Treasury)

The Treasury has recognized legitimate banking with the cannabis industry by issuing guidelines for banks to do business with the industry. The Treasury's Financial Crimes Enforcement Network (FinCEN) has most recently issued guidance regarding provision of financial services to customers engaged in hemp-related businesses.

The Treasury has taken steps to facilitate cannabis industry banking despite the CSA's prohibitions. As of this writing, there are at least 8,610 depository institutions that provide financial services to the marijuana industry (the most controversial aspect of the cannabis industry from the perspective of federal law) according to FinCEN. Banking services are critical: they facilitate more, and larger, transactions (it is difficult to move large quantities of cash); discourage criminality (cash businesses are vulnerable to money laundering); and make it easier to conduct business safely (cash businesses are easier to steal from). Lack of access to banking services poses a significant problem as the legal cannabis industry continues to grow rapidly and exponentially; it is expected to be worth $30 billion by 2025.[3]

FinCEN has issued guidance as to how financial institutions servicing state-legal marijuana businesses can remain compliant with federal regulations, but some banks are still reluctant to enter the market.[4] This reticence is due to the fact that it is not unambiguously legal to bank cannabis businesses generally; banks are also concerned that supporting marijuana businesses while marijuana remains explicitly illegal under the CSA can theoretically be characterized by prosecutors as aiding and abetting or money laundering. Such characterization could be the case even with respect to marijuana businesses that are otherwise legal at the state level.

Additionally, the **National Credit Union Administration (NCUA)** has issued guidance to credit unions, announcing that federally insured credit unions may offer financial services to legal hemp businesses, a promising step toward legal banking for the broader cannabis industry.

---

3. Iris Dorbian, *New Cannabis Report Predicts Legal Sales to Reach Nearly $30 Billion by 2025* (Sept. 24, 2019), https://www.forbes.com/sites/irisdorbian/2019/09/24/new-cannabis -report-predicts-legal-sales-to-reach-nearly-30-billion-by-2025/#459fba651121.

4. *See* FinCEN Guidance on BSA, *Expectations Regarding Marijuana-related Businesses* (Feb. 14, 2014), https://www.fincen.gov/resources/statutes-regulations/guidance/bsa -expectations-regarding-marijuana-related-businesses.

4. Cannabis and Hemp: Enforcement

Because federal regulation and enforcement of cannabis currently struggles to keep pace with market realities, state-level legalization, and divided political opinion, it is broadly contradictory and often ambiguous.

4.1 DOJ

The DOJ does not enforce the CSA as to marijuana in states where it is decriminalized and the law is otherwise followed. Regardless of marijuana's legality under the CSA, federal prosecutors have "wide latitude in determining when, whom, how, and even whether to prosecute for apparent violations of federal criminal law."[5] Formerly under Presidents Obama and Trump, the DOJ exercised this discretion for more than ten years in states where such marijuana is legal and the conduct does not implicate some other criminal prohibition, such as violent crime.

This remarkably consistent nonenforcement policy has been clarified in a series of memoranda and public statements issued by Attorneys General in both the Obama and Trump Administrations. In 2009, President Obama's then-Attorney General issued the Ogden Memo, which stated that prosecutors should "not focus federal resources . . . on individuals whose actions are in clear and unambiguous compliance with existing [state] laws providing for the medical use of marijuana."[6] Four years later, and in the wake of additional state decriminalization initiatives, Obama's DOJ reaffirmed and clarified this guidance in the 2013 Cole Memo, which directed prosecutors not to prosecute marijuana offenses (medicinal or recreational) in states where it is legal and well-regulated, unless on federal property or other federal law-enforcement priorities, such as gang activity, are involved.[7]

The Trump Administration continued a hands-off approach in state jurisdictions with legalized marijuana and settled expectations related to the same. The Sessions Memo, issued in 2018, delegated enforcement decisions to local prosecutors, even in jurisdictions where marijuana is legal.[8] In his confirmation hearings, Attorney General William Barr confirmed that he would continue this federalist approach, saying, "To the extent people are complying with the State laws, [DOJ isn't] going to go after that."[9] Although Barr indicated that he personally favors enforcing the CSA, he

---

5. U.S. Attorneys' Manual, § 9-27.110.

6. *See* U.S. DOJ, Memo on Investigations and Prosecutions in States Authorizing the Medical Use of Marijuana (Oct. 19, 2009), https://www.justice.gov/archives/opa/blog/memorandum-selected-united-state-attorneys-investigations-and-prosecutions-states.

7. *See* U.S. DOJ, Memo on Guidance Regarding Marijuana Enforcement (Aug. 29, 2013), https://www.justice.gov/iso/opa/resources/3052013829132756857467.pdf.

8. *See* U.S. DOJ, Memo on Marijuana Enforcement (Jan. 4, 2018), https://www.justice.gov/opa/press-release/file/1022196/download.

9. *See* Transcript of Confirmation Hearing (Jan. 15 & 16, 2019), https://www.congress.gov/116/chrg/CHRG-116shrg36846/CHRG-116shrg36846.htm.

stipulated that he did not intend to "upset settled expectations" and reliance on previous nonenforcement at the state level.[10]

Congress has included riders along with each budget passed since 2014 (known as the Rohrabacher-Farr and Rohrabacher-Blumenauer amendments) that use spending to compel a continuance of DOJ's nonenforcement strategy. The riders prohibit DOJ from spending federally assigned funds on preventing states from implementing their own laws legalizing medical marijuana.

4.2 FDA and FTC

The FDA's enforcement of its CBD-related regulations and positions has likewise been markedly less aggressive than the letter of the law. FDA enforcement activity to date has focused on concerns that marketing of CBD products' health benefits may be deceptive, but its responses to these issues has been remarkably toothless and ambivalent. The FTC has voiced similar concerns and joined in a small number of FDA warning letters, as well as recently actively pursuing independent enforcement actions, but only against a handful of companies for marketing claims that are alleged to be particularly overreaching and unsupported.

From 2015 to date, the FDA sent 88 warning letters to 62 different companies for deceptive marketing regarding the therapeutic qualities of CBD (e.g., "contains CBD oil to alleviate anxiety"). The FTC also joined the FDA in three warning letters sent in 2019. All of these letters targeted egregious offenders that made irresponsibly extreme and unsupported specific claims regarding the health benefits of CBD, and none of these warning letters resulted in enforcement actions.[11] For example, such claims included:

- "For Alzheimer's patients, CBD is one treatment option that is slowing the progression of that disease."
- "CBD successfully stopped cancer cells in multiple different cervical cancer varieties."
- "CBD may be used to avoid or reduce [drug] withdrawal symptoms."[12]

---

10. *Id.*

11. *See* Review of the FY2020 Budget Request for the FDA, Hearing Before the Subcomm. on Agriculture, Rural Development, Food and Drug Administration, and Related Agencies of the S. Comm. on Appropriations, 116th Cong. (2019) (statement of Scott Gottlieb, Comm'r, Food and Drug Admin.), https://www.appropriations.senate.gov/imo/media/doc/03.28.19–FY20%20Gottlieb%20Testimony.pdf.

12. *See* FDA News Release, Statement from FDA Commissioner Scott Gottlieb, M.D., on new steps to advance agency's continued evaluation of potential regulatory pathways for cannabis-containing and cannabis-derived products (Apr. 2, 2019), https://www.fda.gov/news-events/press-announcements/statement-fda-commissioner-scott-gottlieb-md-new-steps-advance-agencys-continued-evaluation.

The two agencies' general approach to enforcement in this area indicates recognition that CBD has gained widespread acceptance, and that the agencies generally regard the substance as a benign (and possibly beneficial) substance. The FDA is seriously considering easing restrictions on hemp-derived CBD but plans to do so via a rulemaking process, which will likely take multiple years to complete.

4.3 Treasury

Generally speaking, banking in the cannabis industry is "quasi-legal." The federal government tacitly permitted banks to support the industry, and even provides official guidelines for how banks can provide financial services to cannabis businesses, but this support is technically illegal under federal law.

5. Proposed and Pending Federal Legislation

There are various pending efforts to legalize aspects of the cannabis industry federally, which have been pending as far back as 2013, enjoy significant support, and have repeatedly been proposed—but none have yet passed.

5.1 Decriminalization

Two bills pending as of January 1, 2021, the Marijuana Opportunity Reinvestment and Expungement (MORE) Act and the Strengthening the Tenth Amendment Through Entrusting States (STATES) Act, reflect competing approaches to decriminalizing marijuana: top-down regulation versus a federalist decision to leave matters up to the states themselves. The MORE Act would resolve the current stalemate by affirmatively decriminalizing marijuana at the federal level, allowing states to enact their own marijuana policies, and instructing federal courts to erase prior convictions for marijuana offenses.[13] The House passed the MORE Act on December 4, 2020, the first time that a chamber of Congress has approved legislation ending the federal prohibition against marijuana. The MORE Act's approach would offer immediate clarity regarding marijuana, facilitate lucrative interstate commerce, and help address concerns regarding social equity and the cannabis industry.

In contrast, the STATES Act formalizes the DOJ's current ad hoc policy of not enforcing CSA where cannabis is legalized and regulated, without requiring Congress to decide formally whether cannabis should be legal at the federal level.[14] A bipartisan bill, the STATES Act would prohibit federal

---

13. *See* MORE Act, S. 2227, 116th Cong. (2019), https://www.congress.gov/bill/116th-congress/senate-bill/2227/text.

14. *See* STATES Act, H.R. 2093, 116th Cong. (2019), https://www.congress.gov/bill/116th-congress/house-bill/2093/all-info.

enforcement of CSA's cannabis provisions in states that have legalized and regulated marijuana. This would effectively remove risk of federal enforcement against marijuana operations conducted in states with legalization regimes. Despite bipartisan backing, the STATES Act has stalled in both houses of Congress. More progressive members of Congress fear it does not address social equity issues relating to enforcement, and more conservative members are opposed to decriminalization generally.

5.2 Banking

Another pending bill, the SAFE Banking Act, does not address cannabis legality directly but instead facilitates cannabis industry banking, thereby supporting state-legal cannabis businesses without taking a federal position on cannabis legality. The SAFE Banking Act would protect financial institutions and entities that insure cannabis business in states that have legalized these activities. The bill implicitly acknowledges that cannabis industry growth has outstripped federal regulation; in attempting to facilitate state-level commerce without touching the "third rail" of legalizing the substance itself, the bill resembles the STATES Act and current DOJ policy. This gradualist approach is probably the most politically expedient in the short and medium term, and we expect legislation along these lines to have greater chances of success than sweeping decriminalization efforts. However, as with the MORE and STATES Acts, the legislation appears to have stalled, in this case after being passed by the House of Representatives in September 2019. The SAFE Banking Act's provisions subsequently became part of the Health and Economic Recovery Omnibus Emergency Solutions (HEROES) Act, a Covid-19 relief bill that was passed by the House in May 2020 but ultimately rejected by the Senate.

5.3 Looking Forward

The 2018 Farm Bill exemplifies the form cannabis legislation likely must take to be successfully passed: federalist, gradualist, and clarifying uncertainty that has become inexpedient or unsustainable to ignore. As noted earlier, the Farm Bill legalized hemp at the federal level but allowed states to choose to prohibit hemp.

Accordingly, the Farm Bill contained several elements we see repeated in other pending legislation. First, it took a federalist approach by freeing states to be more restrictive, something that helps to lower controversy lingering around cannabis legislation. Second, it clarified and standardized federal law in a manner consistent with marketplace realities because demand for hemp and hemp-derived CBD was extant. Third, it facilitated interstate commerce through this clarity: pursuant to directives in the Farm Bill, interstate shipment of hemp was guaranteed by the USDA in October 2019. Although the details differ, we see elements of these approaches in the MORE, STATES, and SAFE Banking Acts, each of which would clarify expectations to facilitate economic growth. In light of significant questions regarding the disparate effects of policing on communities of color, future federal cannabis legislation should also address social equity and the racist impact of the War on Drugs.

6. States

States regulate cannabis and hemp idiosyncratically, differing from both the federal government and each other. Practitioners should not assume that states track federal cannabis regulation, that states with more liberal approaches to decriminalizing marijuana are similarly tolerant of CBD, or that states that prohibit recreational marijuana also outlaw CBD.

For example, both California and Washington state have broadly legalized industrial hemp and recreational marijuana, in stark contrast to federal law.[15] However, both states currently prohibit the addition of CBD from any source to food, beverage, or dietary supplement products. (Both states prohibit CBD as a food additive unless and until the FDA decides that CBD is safe for such purposes.) In contrast to these states, Texas, which has taken a hard line against legalizing recreational marijuana, *does* permit hemp-derived CBD as an additive to foods, beverages, and dietary supplements.[16] And as of this writing, Idaho, Mississippi, and the District of Columbia continue to outlaw industrial hemp altogether.[17] Given this patchwork, state-by-state analysis of cannabis and hemp law is crucial.

With respect to enforcement of cannabis laws, most states have analogous bodies to the federal entities listed earlier. Again, a state-level review is crucial on a case-by-case basis. In addition to state assemblies that regulate cannabis and hemp legality, many states' departments of public health take active roles in proscribing whether or to what extent CBD may be added to foods, supplements, and/or drugs. For example, the Colorado Department of Public Health and Environment and California Department of Public Health have each issued substantial guidance on this topic.

7. Afterword

Although federal bills addressing the disjunctions in cannabis law—both between federal law as-written and as-enforced, and between state and federal law—appear to have stalled in Congress, all trends point toward gradual but continuing legalization. More states are approving bills legalizing hemp

---

15. *See* Adult Use of Marijuana Act, AB-64 (CA); 2013 Wash. Sess. Laws 28 (Marijuana) (WA); WASH. REV. CODE § 69.50 (2013) (Uniform Controlled Substances Act)—Marijuana Provisions in Article 3 (WA).

16. *See* Texas H.B. 1325.

17. *See* NCSL, State Industrial Hemp Statutes (Feb. 25, 2020), https://www.ncsl.org /research/agriculture-and-rural-development/state-industrial-hemp-statutes.aspx.

and/or marijuana, including long-time holdouts.[18] And at the federal level, the contours of two approaches for resolving the current tension are taking shape: either codifying the DOJ's current policy of nonenforcement or positively legalizing cannabis. By the time this treatise goes to press, the landscape may have changed further—even if only slightly—as the country shifts slowly toward legalization in all states.

---

18. For example, South Dakota, one of the few states that had continued to prohibit hemp even after it was legalized at the federal level, legalized hemp in April 2020. *See, e.g.*, Lisa Kaczke, *Industrial Hemp Becomes Legal in South Dakota after Noem Signs Bill*, Argus Leader (Mar. 27, 2020), https://www.argusleader.com/story/news/politics/2020/03/27 /industrial-hemp-becomes-legal-south-dakota-after-noem-signs-bill/5058216002/.

2

Transactional Considerations

Danielle Fortier

1. Introduction

As cannabis regulatory regimes mature, the cannabis industry has transitioned from primarily mom and pop operations to big business. Along with this transition, significant transactions, such as mergers, acquisitions, joint ventures, and initial public offerings (IPOs) have become increasingly common.

Since 2012, the number of strategic merger and acquisition (M&A) deals increased by 3,000 percent and the median deal value rose by nearly 800 percent: 2019 saw 425 companies participate in 428 deals, with a median deal size of $12.5 million. Whereas financial buyers and investors were almost nonexistent in the cannabis industry prior to 2014, private equity funds were involved in 30 deals in 2019, with a median deal size of $8 million. Furthermore, 314 companies raised a total of $2.82 billion from venture funding across 356 transactions, with a median financing size of $2.31 million.[1]

In the years to come, the numbers of deals and players are not likely to rise as dramatically as they have since 2010; however, deal making is beginning to reach a critical mass, and industry participants and potential participants will continue to seek new investment opportunities, avenues for

---

1. Data regarding deal activity, size, and change over time comes from Pitchbook Data, *Investments over Time*, https://my.pitchbook.com/search-results/s26959744/overview _tab (last visited Apr. 8, 2020). In 2019, according to *Forbes*, at least ten venture capital firms funded 12 or more deals, with four of the ten funding 20 deals or more. Javier Hasse, *Even as Overall Deals Declined, VC Investments in Cannabis Nearly Doubled over 2019*, FORBES (Jan. 28, 2020), https://www.forbes.com/sites/javierhasse/2020/01/28/vc-in -cannabis/#4ce2f465a8c9.

growth, and exit options. In the realm of financial sponsors, a group of private equity firms are beginning to focus on medium- and longer-term investment in the cannabis industry. Venture capital firms, some with celebrity sponsors,[2] are also backing cannabis startups and looking for high-growth opportunities in the industry. As these investors build their assets under management or prepare for exits from their investments, mergers and acquisitions, financings, and IPOs can be expected to continue apace.

In the marijuana space, with more states now legalizing, if not welcoming, the sale of recreational and medical marijuana, companies (including those in extraction and manufacturing, as well as dispensaries) are increasingly focused on success as multistate operators (MSOs). For some MSOs, growth has come organically, through repeated licensing applications and an ability to operationalize licenses efficiently in new markets. For others, the race for market share has been fueled by strategic acquisitions, as MSOs vertically integrate in order to avoid transporting cannabis across state lines and horizontally integrate in order to capture and build customer loyalty and broader brand recognition.

Generally, as the range of companies involved in the cannabis industry expands, transaction activity is less likely to be siloed among "cannabis companies" only. In 2018 and 2019, several large beverage companies, such as Constellation Brands, entered into the cannabis space in Canada. With more entrants into the cannabis industry—whether repeat financial players, MSOs, or those with expertise in other industries, such as food and beverage or technology—investors and cannabis-related companies will continue to grow more sophisticated in order to secure shares in a dynamic, expanding market.

In addition to the continuing spread of legalization of marijuana (both medical and recreational) across U.S. jurisdictions, a number of key legal developments have contributed to the transaction boom. Legalization of marijuana in Canada resulted in a number of cross-border transactions between U.S. companies and Canadian marijuana producers in 2018 and 2019. The passage of the Agriculture Improvement Act of 2018 (Farm Bill) was also a significant contributor to activity in the cannabis space, as it removed federal restrictions on hemp and hemp derivatives. Changes to state law, such as Colorado's repeal of certain restrictions on entities permitted to own a marijuana business, have further contributed to an increase in

2. Casa Verde Capital, which was founded and is backed by rap artist and producer Snoop Dogg, specializes in seed investments across the "ancillary part of the industry." Connie Loizos, *Snoop Dogg's Venture Firm Just Closed Its Debut Fund with $45 Million*, TECH CRUNCH (Mar. 13, 2018), https://techcrunch.com/2018/03/13/snoop-doggs-venture-firm-just-closed-its-debut-fund-with-45-million/. Former San Francisco 49ers quarterback Joe Montana is also heavily invested in early-stage cannabis companies. Associated Press, *Football Great Joe Montana Joins Investment in Legal Marijuana Operator*, ESPN (Jan. 24, 2019), https://www.espn.com/nfl/story/_/id/25845197/football-great-joe-montana-joins-investment-legal-marijuana-operator.

cannabis transactions.[3] Finally, stock exchange rules have permitted Canadian producers and U.S. companies providing ancillary services (i.e., that do not "touch" the marijuana plant) to register on U.S. stock exchanges.

With these developments, lawyers are increasingly being asked to provide legal advice with respect to cannabis transactions. This chapter provides a high-level overview of key considerations when advising on transactions in the cannabis space. We will primarily focus on private deals, which make up the vast majority of transaction volume in the cannabis industry. We will then briefly address public company cannabis transactions.

2. Private Company Transactions

2.1 Federal Legal Considerations

As discussed in more detail in Chapter 1, at the federal level, cannabis is classified into two legal categories: marijuana and hemp. Participants in the cannabis industry may be involved in the production or sale of hemp, marijuana, or both. Although the Farm Bill paved the way for legal hemp production and sale, marijuana remains a controlled substance under federal law. It is important to inform clients of federal restrictions on marijuana handling if they are considering acquiring or partnering with a marijuana business. Other chapters of this book address federal enforcement of marijuana laws and provide critical context for parties evaluating the risks of transactions with marijuana businesses.

In the transactional context, restrictions on the ability of marijuana businesses to obtain financing and tax deductions are particularly salient.

As described in additional detail in other chapters of this book, many mainstream banks will not provide services to marijuana businesses due to the federal classification of marijuana as a controlled substance. In addition to limiting the ability of marijuana businesses to maintain basic checking and savings accounts and corporate credit cards, this also prevents acquirors from conducting leveraged buyouts (LBOs) where debt is used to finance some or all of the purchase price and may hinder the ability of private equity to use an LBO structure or preferred financing sources in acquisitions of marijuana businesses. Although marijuana businesses have been able to obtain banking services through credit unions, access to the full range of transaction financing remains a challenge and should be considered in structuring cannabis transactions.

On September 25, 2019, the U.S. House of Representatives passed the SAFE Banking Act, which would eliminate potential penalties (such as fines, account termination, or loss of deposit insurance) to financial institutions that provide services to marijuana businesses operating in states that

---

3. Colorado House Bill 19-1090 repealed a provision that prohibited publicly traded companies from holding a marijuana license and a provision that limited out-of-state direct beneficial owners to 15 persons.

have legalized marijuana. The SAFE Banking Act, which, if passed, can be expected to increase the willingness of traditional banking institutions to work with marijuana businesses, is currently under consideration by the U.S. Senate.

Some hemp and hemp-derived CBD businesses have also had difficulty obtaining banking services and financing from mainstream banks due to confusion over the difference between marijuana and hemp and the effect of the Farm Bill on hemp's legal status. If a potential target or counterparty only handles hemp and not marijuana, there should not be any *legal* restrictions on access to banking and financing services. However, discussions with the financial institution and clarification of the nature of the business and effect of the Farm Bill may be necessary.

Other chapters of this treatise address federal tax considerations relevant to marijuana businesses, including the limitation under section 280E of the Internal Revenue Code on tax deductions for business expenses. Potential deductions for transaction-related expenses (for example, transaction bonuses to key employees) can be significant. However, such deductions may not be available in transactions involving marijuana businesses. Parties should also consider the limitations set forth in section 280E when conducting due diligence. An acquiror should confirm that a potential target has not claimed deductions for expenses related to marijuana activities and has kept careful records of deductible expenses arising from other business activities.

2.2 State Regulatory Considerations

Since cannabis is highly regulated at the state level, it is critical to consider regulatory requirements at the initial deal planning stages. Each state will have unique regulatory requirements with respect to cannabis and will usually have different requirements for or restrictions on transactions involving marijuana and hemp. Where a state has legalized both recreational and medical marijuana, there will likely also be different requirements for each. For example, in Colorado, marijuana is regulated by the Marijuana Enforcement Division, whereas hemp is regulated by the Colorado Department of Public Health & Environment. The Marijuana Enforcement Division regulates both medical and recreational marijuana but has separate licensing regimes for each. It is critical for any practitioner advising on cannabis deals to understand what forms of cannabis the parties to the transaction produce or handle and identify the applicable regulator.

Common regulatory hurdles in cannabis transactions include:

- Restrictions on transfer of applicable licenses;
- Restrictions on ownership of cannabis businesses; and
- Reporting requirements for owners of cannabis businesses.

Next, we address each of these in greater detail and provide some examples.

2.2.1 Transfers of Applicable Licenses

Most states do not permit the assignment or transfer of cannabis-related licenses, which means that, in order to use an asset purchase structure, the purchaser would either need to have its own license that can be amended to add additional sites and operations or would need to obtain a new license prior to closing the deal.

In order to avoid the need to obtain a new license, the parties may desire to structure the transaction as an equity acquisition, but should be aware that this structure can also pose hurdles. In some cases, a change of control may require providing updated ownership details to the applicable regulatory agency. This is the case in Colorado, where the parties are required to make a filing that includes the name, address, taxpayer identification number, and ownership percentage of each owner, if the controlling owners of the business are changing.[4]

In contrast, in California, the parties are not able to implement a full equity buyout (i.e., no continuity of ownership) without obtaining a new license.[5] In order to comply with this law, practitioners in California have approached marijuana deals using a two-step equity transfer, with at least one prior owner remaining in place through the first transaction. Given the complications inherent in accomplishing an equity in transfer in California and states with similar regimes, structuring a deal and an equity transfer may not have significant benefits from a regulatory perspective, which the parties should take into account.

2.2.2 Restrictions on Ownership of Cannabis Businesses

Many states restrict who may own a cannabis business. These restrictions range from prohibitions on certain persons with criminal convictions[6] or state personnel[7] owning cannabis businesses to residency requirements.[8]

---

4. Colorado Marijuana Rules § 2-245.

5. CAL. CODE REGS. tit. 16 § 5023(c)(1) ("The business may continue to operate under the active license while the Bureau reviews the qualifications of the new owner(s) in accordance with the Act and these regulations to determine whether the change would constitute grounds for denial of the license, if at least one existing owner is not transferring his or her ownership interest and will remain as an owner under the new ownership structure. If all owners will be transferring their ownership interest, the business shall not operate under the new ownership structure until a new license application has been submitted to and approved by the Bureau, and all application and license fees for the new application have been paid.").

6. See, for example, WASH. ADMIN. CODE § 314-55-040, which assigns points to various criminal convictions of every officer and stockholder of a marijuana licensee and bars licensure of applicants with points in excess of thresholds specified in the Code.

7. See, for example, CAL. CODE REGS. tit. 16 § 5005, which prohibits ownership by anyone charged with enforcing cannabis laws (e.g., district attorneys, police officers).

8. Although Colorado significantly liberalized its ownership to permit investment by investors outside of Colorado and public companies, effective January 1, 2020, C.R.S.

Practitioners should confirm that all owners or potential owners (including equity holders up a corporate chain where the state considers them to be "owners") are permitted.

In addition to the restrictions just outlined, some states also restrict the nature of ownership of certain cannabis businesses. For example, Arizona requires all medical marijuana dispensaries to be operated on a nonprofit basis, and Maine's regulations permit a mix of for-profit and nonprofit medical marijuana dispensaries.[9] When advising on transactions involving medical marijuana producers in these states, practitioners should keep potential restrictions on distribution of profits to equity holders in mind.

2.2.3 Reporting Requirements for Owners of Cannabis Businesses

Many state cannabis regulators require extensive disclosure of ownership details. For example, in California, the Bureau of Cannabis Control requires licensees to disclose details about each holder of an interest greater than 20 percent of the licensee, including his, her, or its ownership stake; interests in any other cannabis business; history of convictions; and certain more limited information regarding other financial stakeholders (such as persons holding less than 20 percent ownership interests or lending money to the business).[10] Furthermore, these requirements extend to ownership interests at entities up the corporate chain from the license holder.[11] Such extensive disclosure requirements may be of special concern for private

---

§ 44-10-308 requires natural persons with "day-to-day operational control" over the business to be Colorado residents.

9. A.R.S. § 36-2806(a) ("A registered nonprofit medical marijuana dispensary shall be operated on a not-for-profit basis. The bylaws of a registered nonprofit medical marijuana dispensary shall contain such provisions relative to the disposition of revenues and receipts to establish and maintain its nonprofit character. A registered nonprofit medical marijuana dispensary need not be recognized as tax-exempt by the internal revenue service and is not required to incorporate pursuant to title 10, chapter 19, article 1."); 22 M.R.S.A. § 2428 (11-A), (13) ("Any of the 8 registered dispensaries that were issued registration certificates as of April 1, 2018 and that are operating as nonprofit entities may convert to a for-profit entity pursuant to this subsection. A registered dispensary established pursuant to subsection 11-A, paragraph A that was not issued a dispensary registration certificate before April 1, 2018 and operates as a nonprofit entity may not convert to a for-profit entity.").

10. CAL. CODE REGS. tit. 16 § 5002.

11. Section 5003(c) of title 16 of the California Code of Regulations provides that "when an entity is an owner in a commercial cannabis business, all entities and individuals with a financial interest in the entity shall be disclosed to the Bureau and may be considered owners of the commercial cannabis business. For example, this includes all entities in a multilayer business structure, as well as the chief executive officer, members of the board of directors, partners, trustees and all persons who have control of a trust, and managing members or nonmember managers of the entity. Each entity disclosed as having a financial interest must disclose the identities of persons holding financial interests until only individuals remain."

equity funds and family offices, which usually prefer to keep ownership details confidential, particularly at the aggregator or fund level.

In light of the foregoing, consider in advance how seeking regulatory approvals, especially in multistate deals, may affect deal timeline and structure. The parties may wish to structure the transaction with an executory period in order to ensure deal certainty prior to seeking regulatory approval, which could take a significant period of time, particularly if the applicable regulatory authority has a licensing backlog. In multistate deals, prepare to coordinate the processes and approvals with multiple regulatory bodies, which may move at different paces.

2.3 Contract Considerations

Prior to drafting the definitive agreement governing your transaction, we recommend considering the following structure, drafting, and due diligence points.

2.3.1 Structure

The regulatory considerations just outlined may impact transaction structure. For example, take a fact pattern where the target is a marijuana grower, the buyer does not have its own grower license in the state where the target is located, and the state does not permit assignment of grower licenses (essentially, the buyer is required to submit its own de novo application) but only requires notice of a change in ownership of a grower. This fact pattern would weigh in favor of doing the transaction as an equity acquisition, particularly if deal timing and speed to closing are critical. On the other hand, if the state treated a change in ownership of the target as an "assignment" of the license (see preceding discussion with respect to California's treatment of changes in ownership), there would not be any additional benefit to structuring the deal as an equity acquisition.

Such regulatory considerations should also be weighed against traditional liability considerations. For example, a potential acquiror may desire to structure a transaction as an asset acquisition in order to limit liability for pre-closing activities (subject to exceptions where applicable law imposes successor liability on asset acquirors). This may be particularly valuable in situations where a target engaged in marijuana or hemp production prior to state or, in the case of hemp, federal legalization. When determining whether to move forward with an asset acquisition, those liability benefits would need to be considered alongside the ability (or lack thereof) to assign and process for assigning required licenses.

In cases where ownership is not possible or creates undue burdens in terms of licensing or disclosure requirements, but a potential acquiror desires to capitalize on the potential financial upside, a minority investment may be the best structure. For example, in California, an owner of 20 percent or more of a cannabis business (defined as an "Owner" in the statute) is required to disclose its investments in other cannabis businesses in annual registrations, whereas a smaller stakeholder would just be listed in the application.[12] Subsection 2.3.5 Minority Investments and Joint Ventures addresses drafting considerations in this context.

2.3.2 Representations, Warranties, and Indemnification

From an acquiror's perspective, robust representations and warranties are vital in cannabis deals. In particular, given the complexity and rapid change of the regulatory landscape for cannabis, a potential acquiror will desire strong, unqualified representations regarding the target's compliance with applicable laws. A potential acquiror should also ensure its definitive agreement contains representations that the target has all appropriate permits and licenses and has complied with all requirements (whether codified or not) of applicable regulatory authorities. Finally, where cannabis products are intended for human consumption, acquirors should consider including representations regarding labeling, FDA compliance, and product liability, though targets may resist or attempt to add exceptions to these.

On the other hand, the target should be careful to tailor representations regarding compliance with laws to the reality of its activities. For example, if a target sold hemp-derived cannabidiol-infused creams prior to passage of the Farm Bill, the target would not be able to represent that it complied with all laws during that period and would want to adjust the look-back period of the representation or add an exception to the representation in a disclosure schedule. Even now, sale of certain CBD-infused products would contravene FDA regulations (as further discussed in Chapter 13) and require an exception to a representation regarding compliance with laws.

As in all transactions, the scope of the representations and warranties will ultimately dictate which party bears the associated risk that such representation or warranty is inaccurate. In the context of cannabis transactions, this often includes risks associated with known illegal activities. Although an acquiror would typically argue that the sellers should be responsible for costs arising from known illegal activity during the pre-closing period (for example, if the federal government were to prosecute recreational marijuana sales), a seller may reject this argument where its business remains illegal at the time of the transaction and the acquiror is knowingly accepting the associated risk.

Over the past several years, there has been a large uptick in the use of representation and warranty insurance (R&W insurance) as a means to reduce risk to acquisition parties. However, at the time of writing this chapter, R&W insurance is of limited value in the cannabis industry. First, R&W insurance typically only provides recovery in the context of unknown risks. An insurer generally will not provide coverage for a known risk, such as a federal enforcement action arising from sales of marijuana in violation of

---

12. Cal. Code Regs. tit. 16 § 5003(c).

federal law. Furthermore, R&W insurers generally will not provide insurance in connection with acquisitions of marijuana businesses, even with respect to unknown risks and breaches of representations and warranties unrelated to compliance with federal law. The R&W insurance market is, however, continually changing, so we recommend consulting with an R&W insurance broker to see what is available if the parties are considering obtaining R&W insurance.

In connection with drafting the representations and warranties, acquirors should also make sure to do sufficient due diligence on the target's operations. In particular, a potential buyer will want to confirm that the representations and warranties in the definitive agreement regarding compliance with laws and proper licensure are, in fact, accurate. Furthermore, in light of the rapid growth of the cannabis industry against a backdrop of legal uncertainty and limited access to traditional financing sources, cannabis companies may not have internal infrastructure typically expected of similarly sized businesses. Therefore, we recommend that a potential buyer carefully review capitalization details[13] and governance practices.

2.3.3 Covenants and Conditions

In light of licensing and other regulatory requirements, many transactions in the cannabis industry will have an executory period, which, in turn, necessitates interim covenants and closing conditions in the definitive agreement.

The parties should consider including tailored covenants to address state licensure requirements. For example, if a buyer is required to obtain a license in order to operate the acquired business post-closing and conditions consummation of the transaction on receipt of that license, the seller will want a covenant requiring the buyer to take the steps necessary to obtain that license. If a license needs to be transferred, each party may desire an interim covenant requiring the other to take the steps necessary to affect that transfer. Buyers may also wish to include interim covenants defining the scope of the target's activities—for example, limiting its expansion into new states or into marijuana (where the target previously only handled hemp)—in order to avoid having a contractual obligation to purchase a business that looks very different legally than initially anticipated.

Given the rapidly changing regulatory landscape for cannabis, parties may choose to condition consummation of a transaction on the state of applicable federal or state laws. From a buyer's perspective, it may be prudent to condition consummation of the transaction on the nonoccurrence of certain unfavorable legal changes (for example, a change in state law that would make the buyer ineligible for a license or cap access to licenses

---

13. Companies may have complex capital structures that have undergone multiple rounds of financing or have high numbers of shareholders. John Bessonette, *Pitfalls to Avoid as Cannabis M&A Takes Off*, LAW 360 (May 8, 2019).

or a step up in enforcement of the federal Controlled Substances Act). Some parties to cannabis transactions have chosen to condition consummation of the transaction on future legal changes. "[B]oth state-legal and federal-legal companies are entering into transaction agreements with closing contingent upon either federal legalization, state legalization or another change in state laws, such as a move from a nonprofit to a for-profit regime."[14] While this approach may permit parties to act quickly upon a changing regulatory landscape, we recommend using caution prior to entering into a definitive agreement for a transaction that may not be consummated for a significant or unknown period of time after execution, as regulatory and financial realities can change significantly and result in one or both parties being unable to meet their obligations.

2.3.4 Dispute Resolution

In determining how to draft dispute resolution provisions of the definitive agreement, we recommend that the parties consider whether the chosen adjudicating body (1) has experience with cannabis transactions, (2) is in a jurisdiction that has legalized hemp and marijuana (and, therefore, is less likely to have a substantive objection to parties' underlying activities), and (3) has previously enforced cannabis contracts. Courts in states that have a longer history of legal cannabis, such as Colorado, may have greater comfort with cannabis transactions, and this should be weighed against traditional venue considerations, such as the extensive experience of Delaware courts with corporate transactions, in determining the appropriate venue.

Certain courts have refused to enforce marijuana contracts for public policy reasons. For instance, in *Polk v. Gontmakher*,[15] the Western District of Washington determined that "the production, distribution, and sale of marijuana remains illegal . . . so any agreement giving Mr. Polk an equity interest in NWCS [Northwest Cannabis Solutions] is illegal under federal law," and declined to enforce a contract granting Mr. Polk an equity stake in NWCS as contravening federal law. Uncertainty regarding court enforcement of marijuana-related contracts has led to expanded use of arbitration in cannabis deals. Although some of the traditional benefits of arbitration (such as reduced costs and quicker timelines) are increasingly less prevalent, requiring arbitration as the parties' method of dispute resolution is one way the parties can avoid having their contracts voided for public policy concerns and ensure they receive the benefit of their bargain.[16]

---

14. *Id.*

15. Polk v. Gontmakher, No. 2:18-cv-01434-RAJ, 2019 WL 4058970 (W.D. Wash. 2018).

16. Cozen O'Connor, *Recent Decisions Impacting Cannabis Contracting and How to Protect Your Business*, JD SUPRA (Nov. 26, 2019), https://www.jdsupra.com/legalnews/recent-decisions-impacting-cannabis-25054/.

2.3.5 Minority Investments and Joint Ventures

In addition to the foregoing drafting considerations, minority investors and joint venture partners should consider carefully defining the scope of the underlying business and negotiating special consent or exit rights. Given the variety of regulatory regimes and legal statuses of cannabis, any investor who does not exercise full control over a cannabis business may wish to contractually limit the scope of permitted business activities. For instance, if, at the time of the investment, the intent is to produce hemp-derived CBD only in State A, which has a well-defined hemp regulatory regime, an investor may wish to ensure that the definitive agreement restricts the business's ability to expand into marijuana activities in State A or any cannabis activities in another state.

If the parties have a plan for business expansion, the parties should carefully define agreed upon expansion conditions (for example, expansion into a state that has legalized recreational use of marijuana, whether or not marijuana is federally legal).

If minority consent rights are not possible, an investor could negotiate an exit right that is triggered if the business expands into activities that are illegal at the state or federal level. The specific terms of the exit right (e.g., whether the stake may be sold to a third party or only the other party, the process for buy back, the price, etc.) would need to be carefully negotiated, but the concept would protect a minority investor from being locked into a business that expands into illegal activities without its consent.

Finally, a minority investor should carefully review any amendment terms to ensure that the negotiated restrictions described earlier cannot be amended out of the contract without its prior written consent.

3. Public Company Transactions

3.1 Disclosure Requirements

Public companies are subject to extensive disclosure requirements, and cannabis companies should carefully consider whether they have the infrastructure, experience, and financial resources necessary to fully comply with Securities and Exchange Commission (SEC) reporting requirements. In considering whether to list on over-the-counter (OTC) markets, companies should weigh the filing and disclosure requirements imposed by the SEC against the incremental capital raising benefit, if any, over private financing arrangements. In many cases, such incremental benefit may be minimal, and a number of OTC-traded cannabis companies have been subject to SEC-imposed trading suspensions for failure to provide adequate disclosure.[17]

---

17. CannaSys., Inc., et al., Order of Suspension of Trading No. 500-1 (Jan. 9, 2020), https://www.sec.gov/litigation/suspensions/2020/34-87926-o.pdf; Applied Biosciences

Since 2014, the SEC has brought several enforcement actions against marijuana companies making false or misleading statements to investors and potential investors.[18] In light of these enforcement actions, the SEC can be expected to scrutinize disclosures made by marijuana businesses. In drafting public disclosures, cannabis companies should make sure to adequately cover any legal uncertainty and risk factors, such as federal prohibitions on marijuana activities and the lack of FDA approval of CBD (including hemp-derived CBD) for human consumption, along with business risks, such as consumer perception of involvement in the cannabis industry.

3.2 Exchange Rules

In addition to the foregoing considerations, listed public companies in the cannabis space face an additional hurdle of complying with applicable securities exchange rules. For example, the major securities exchanges require that listed companies comply with all applicable laws. Therefore, a company growing, handling, or selling marijuana (any activity that "touches the plant") in the United States would not be permitted to list its securities on the New York Stock Exchange (NYSE) or NASDAQ.

These rules do not, however, restrict the ability of companies growing, handling, or selling marijuana in Canada from listing on U.S. exchanges. In fact, there are several Canadian marijuana producers so listed, including Aphria Inc. and Canopy Growth Corporation on the NYSE, and Tilray Inc. on the NASDAQ. Most Canadian marijuana producers listed on U.S. exchanges conducted their IPOs on the Toronto Stock Exchange (TSX) and subsequently listed on a U.S. exchange, but Tilray completed the first IPO of a marijuana business on a U.S. exchange.

With passage of the Farm Bill, we would not expect companies that only grow, handle, or sell hemp and hemp derivatives and not marijuana to face similar securities exchange restrictions. Companies that engage in marijuana activities that are legal at the state level but not at the federal level may list on Canadian stock exchanges or trade on OTC markets in the United States.

Before opting to list on any exchange, in addition to the foregoing, companies should consider the myriad of significant financial and governance requirements imposed by exchanges. At the time of writing this chapter, one cannabis company was slated for delisting from the NYSE, and other

Corp., Order of Suspension of Trading No. 500-1 (Apr. 13, 2020), https://www.sec.gov/litigation/suspensions/2020/34-88627-o.pdf.
18. *Investor Alert: Marijuana Investments and Fraud,* SEC (Sept. 5, 2018), https://www.sec.gov/oiea/investor-alerts-and-bulletins/ia_marijuana.

cannabis companies were at risk of delisting for failure to meet financial and/or governance requirements.[19]

Existing publicly traded companies should also keep the exchange rules in mind when considering potential acquisitions or expansions into the marijuana space.

---

19. Trading of CannTrust Holdings Inc. shares on the NYSE was suspended on March 30, 2020, and an application to the SEC to delist is pending. PR Newswire, *CannTrust Provides Default Status Report*, YAHOO FINANCE (Apr. 9, 2020), https://finance.yahoo.com/news /canntrust-provides-default-status-report-225600867.html; Sean Williams, *Start the Clock: The Cannabis Stock Delisting Countdown Has Begun*, NASDAQ (Mar. 18, 2020), https:// www.nasdaq.com/articles/start-the-clock%3A-the-cannabis-stock-delisting-countdown -has-begun-2020-03-18.

3

Banking and Finance Issues

Dana Syracuse and Sam Boro

1. Introduction

The financial services industry—banks, money services business, credit card companies, and payment processors—historically has been prohibited from working with marijuana-related businesses (MRBs). Despite changes to federal policy, legalization in the states, and technological innovations, federal law still makes it illegal to engage in activities that involve the handling of marijuana or for dealing in money that is the proceeds of the sale of marijuana. As a result, the financial services industry has been wary to engage with MRBs, driving these businesses into the financial shadows and creating very cash-heavy businesses.

Most states in the United States have legalized or decriminalized in some way the production, sale, or use of cannabis-related products in some form, through legalizing medical or recreational use of marijuana, or permitting hemp or cannabidiol (CBD) products to be sold in stores.[1] Because of the rapid growth in the number of MRBs throughout the country,[2] financial institutions in states where marijuana is legal will inevitably be servicing companies that are producing and selling products that are illegal under federal law.

As state laws have changed and the federal government has modified its enforcement priorities regarding marijuana-related products, banks and other financial services companies have become more willing to work with

---

1. *See* NORML Map of State Laws, https://norml.org/laws/.
2. *See* Iris Dorbian, *New Cannabis Report Predicts Legal Sales to Reach Nearly $30 Billion by 2025*, FORBES (Sept. 24, 2019), https://www.forbes.com/sites/irisdorbian/2019/09/24/new-cannabis-report-predicts-legal-sales-to-reach-nearly-30-billion-by-2025/#612ede411121.

these businesses. Nevertheless, there are still significant uncertainties and hurdles in the legal and regulatory landscape.

2. Federal Controlled Substances Act

The federal Controlled Substances Act (CSA) provides the authority for the federal government to regulate the lawful production, possession, and distribution of controlled substances. Under the CSA there are a series of schedules for controlled substances, with controlled substances in Schedule 1 being the most restricted. For controlled substances under Schedule 1, the federal government holds that these substances have a high potential for abuse and have no medical use.[3] Because marijuana is a Schedule 1 controlled substance under the CSA, it violates federal law to produce, possess, and distribute it.[4]

In December 2019, the federal banking regulators issued guidance for financial institutions providing services to hemp-related businesses. This guidance followed the 2018 Farm Bill,[5] which removed hemp and derivatives of cannabis products containing less than 0.3 percent THC (i.e., CBD or other substances that contain or are derived from hemp) as a Schedule I controlled substance under the CSA. The Financial Crimes Enforcement Network (FinCEN) updated this guidance in June 2020, providing clarity on the due diligence financial institutions should conduct to confirm the hemp business's compliance with federal and state laws.[6]

The 2018 Farm Bill directed the U.S. Department of Agriculture (USDA) to issue interim rules to establish a federal licensing regime to allow states to monitor and regulate hemp production. The USDA issued interim final rules in October 2019, establishing the domestic hemp production regulatory program. The interim final rules do not change the status of marijuana as a Schedule I drug under the CSA, and rather merely exempt hemp from the CSA. Farmers that grow plants with THC levels over the legal limit end up with an illegal product. Hemp products that exceed the legal limit may not be used for other marijuana-related products and must be destroyed. Future changes to USDA rules may result in different THC levels receiving exempt status.

Despite hemp-related products being exempt from the CSA, many financial services companies either still refuse to work with hemp-related

---

3. *See* U.S. Dep't of Justice, Drug Enforcement Administration, *Definition of Controlled Substance Schedules*, https://www.deadiversion.usdoj.gov/schedules/#define.

4. Federal Controlled Substances Act, 21 U.S.C. § 812(c), sch. I(c)(10).

5. The Agriculture Improvement Act of 2018, Pub. L. No. 115-334, 132 Stat. 4490.

6. FIN-2020-G001, *FinCEN Guidance Regarding Due Diligence Requirements under the Bank Secrecy Act for Hemp-Related Business Customers*, FinCEN (June 29, 2020), https://www.fincen.gov/resources/statutes-regulations/guidance/fincen-guidance-regarding-due-diligence-requirements-under.

companies or treat such companies as high risk. The CBD industry is booming, but still nascent. Similar to the nutraceutical industry, there are many issues related to health claims made by the sellers of CBD products. For example, the Federal Trade Commission (FTC) has sent warning letters to companies that advertise CBD products because the advertisements contained illegal claims that the products could prevent, treat, or cure certain diseases without scientific evidence to support the claims.[7] With recent statements by federal financial regulators, banks will be more willing to work with hemp-related businesses, but that will not mean in the immediate term that the CBD industry will always have easy access to banking or other financial services. As long as the CBD industry is subject to attention by the FTC for its advertising claims, it is likely that financial institutions will remain wary of taking on these businesses and will require additional due diligence of these companies.

3. Dual-Banking System

Banking in the United States is conducted under a dual-banking system, with bank chartering and oversight powers at both the state and federal level.

At the federal level, a bank may be chartered by the Office of the Comptroller of the Currency (OCC), which is the primary regulator of national banks. Under the National Bank Act,[8] a national bank may take all actions authorized under federal statute as well as all incidental powers necessary to carry on the business of banking as those activities are defined through litigation and OCC decisions.

Alternatively, a bank may be regulated at the state level by a state's bank regulator. In general, state regulators grant to state-chartered banks the same powers granted by the OCC to national banks. A choice in chartering authority determines a bank's primary regulator.

However, state regulation still applies to federal banks in each state, just as federal law applies to state banks. For example, state banks that become a part of the Federal Reserve System will be subject to Federal Reserve supervision. A state bank that does not become a member of the Federal Reserve System will be primarily supervised by the Federal Deposit Insurance Corporation (FDIC).

State bank regulations may supplement federal law, but, in many cases, federal law preempts state bank regulatory frameworks if the laws conflict.[9]

---

7. FTC, Press Release, *FTC Sends Warning Letters to Companies Advertising Their CBD-Infused Products as Treatments for Serious Diseases, Including Cancer, Alzheimer's, and Multiple Sclerosis* (Sept. 10, 2019), https://www.ftc.gov/news-events/press-releases/2019/09/ftc-sends-warning-letters-companies-advertising-their-cbd-infused.

8. 12 U.S.C. §§ 21 *et seq.*

9. *See generally* Barnett Bank of Marion Cnty., N.A. v. Nelson, 517 U.S. 25 (1996).

Federal law can expressly preempt state banking laws or impliedly preempt state law where the structure and purpose of the federal law implicitly preempts state law or where the conflict between state and federal law is such that it would be impossible to comply with both laws.

As a result of the dual-banking system in the United States, practically every state-chartered bank is overseen by a federal regulator and is subject to federal laws applicable to banking. Banks in states that have legalized marijuana to some extent are still subject to federal laws that prohibit dealing with MRBs and in funds associated with activities related to controlled substances such as marijuana.

4. Bank Secrecy Act and Anti–Money Laundering Laws

The Bank Secrecy Act (BSA) requires financial institutions to assist the government in detecting and preventing money laundering through establishing an anti–money laundering (AML) program that includes record-keeping and reporting requirements.[10] The BSA prohibits possessing the proceeds generated from criminal activity, such as the sale of illegal drugs. The federal government can confiscate assets, levy fines, and imprison violators of the BSA. Federal regulators can also exercise administrative oversight and enforcement of financial institutions and their employees and directors for violations of the BSA, including the servicing of MRBs.

The Department of Justice (DOJ) has jurisdiction to prosecute all marijuana-related crimes. In 2013, Deputy Attorney General James M. Cole issued a memorandum (the Cole Memo) that explained that the DOJ's enforcement priorities were geared toward investigating and prosecuting serious crimes, particularly those perpetrated by large-scale criminal enterprises related to marijuana. In furtherance of these objectives, the Cole Memo sets forth the DOJ's priorities when investigating and prosecuting marijuana-related activities and crimes:

- Preventing the distribution of marijuana to minors;
- Preventing revenue from the sale of marijuana from going to criminal enterprises, gangs, and cartels;
- Preventing the diversion of marijuana from states where it is legal under state law in some form to other states;
- Preventing state-authorized marijuana activity from being used as a cover or pretext for the trafficking of other illegal drugs or other illegal activity;
- Preventing violence and the use of firearms in the cultivation and distribution of marijuana;

---

10. 12 U.S.C. §§ 1829b, 1951–1959; 31 U.S.C. §§ 5311–5332; 31 C.F.R. §§ 1010 *et seq.*

- Preventing drugged driving and the exacerbation of other adverse public health consequences associated with marijuana use;
- Preventing the growing of marijuana on public lands and the attendant public safety and environmental dangers posed by marijuana production on public lands; and
- Preventing marijuana possession or use on federal property.

In 2018, Attorney General Jeff Sessions issued a memorandum (the Sessions Memo) that directed all U.S. Attorneys to enforce the laws enacted by Congress and to follow established principles for prosecuting marijuana activities. In short, the Sessions Memo rescinded the Cole Memo and related marijuana guidance. Despite rescinding the Cole Memo, there has been no real-world effect on DOJ enforcement of MRBs or their financial institutions.

4.1 Asset Forfeiture

Banks and other financial institutions are generally not directly involved in the sale, possession, or distribution of their customer's products. Under federal law, a financial institution would be in violation of the BSA when it handles the proceeds of the sale of marijuana products or by otherwise engaging in financial transactions with MRBs because the financial institution is acquiring the proceeds of the sale of the MRB's product, which could be illegal under federal or state law. If a financial institution acquires the proceeds with knowledge that they are derived from the sale of marijuana in violation of federal law, the proceeds could be confiscated by federal authorities, even if the sale is permissible under state law.[11]

Lending to MRBs is also an issue because a state-licensed MRB that sells medical marijuana would still be selling a controlled substance under the CSA. Loans to the MRB for the MRB's purchase of product, real estate, or production materials would require payments by the MRB to the financial institution for the loans. These payments would likely be coming from or be secured by the proceeds of the MRB's business, resulting in the financial institution collecting the proceeds of the illegal sale of a controlled substance. The federal government could require the financial institution to forfeit the proceeds generated from the loan as the proceeds of the illegal sale of a controlled substance.[12]

4.2 Fines and Imprisonment

In addition to the risk of asset forfeiture, engaging in transactions involving the sale of illegal drugs could result in fines or imprisonment under the

---

11. *See* United States v. McIntosh, 833 F.3d 1163, 1179, n.5 (9th Cir. 2016) (noting that the federal government retains the ability to prosecute federal marijuana offenses despite state laws permitting such sale).

12. *See, e.g.*, United States v. Funds Held *ex rel.* Wetterer, 210 F.3d 96, 104 (2d Cir. 2000).

BSA. Bank employees and bank officers could face prison terms for knowingly engaging in financial transactions involving proceeds from federally illegal marijuana businesses.[13] In addition to forfeiture requirements, violations of the BSA can result in a range of penalties, with maximum prison sentences ranging from 10 to 20 years and maximum fines ranging between $250,000 and $500,000 or twice the amount of the transaction, whichever is greater. Civil actions under the BSA may also result in penalties of up to $10,000 or the value of the funds involved in the transaction.[14]

4.3 Bank Regulator Oversight

Federal banking regulators may also impose penalties on banks that work with marijuana businesses. Banks under federal supervision must meet regulators' safety and soundness requirements, including compliance with law.[15] Engaging in business with MRBs that violate federal law could result in administrative actions against the bank, including cease and desist orders, civil money penalties, and orders banning individuals from working in the banking industry.

Federal banking regulators can take action against a bank regardless of state law. For example, in 2016, a small Illinois bank became subject to a consent order issued by the FDIC and the Illinois Division of Banking related to the bank's BSA failures in conducting business with MRBs.[16] The consent order did not directly state that it related specifically to the bank's marijuana business, but it is known that its business with MRBs was the driving force behind the enforcement action.[17] Medical marijuana was legal in Illinois at the time of the consent order, but the subject bank was small and not staffed appropriately to meet the requirements for managing the business with the MRBs. The consent order required the bank to make changes to its AML programs to comply with the BSA, including proper due diligence on customers, and monitoring and reporting suspicious activity.

4.4 BSA Requirements

Despite state legalization and some guidance from the federal government, there is no clear procedure for designing an appropriate AML program for financial institutions dealing with MRBs, nor is there clear guidance on

---

13. 18 U.S.C. §§ 1956(a)(1)(A)(I); 1957(a), (d).

14. U.S. Dep't of Justice, Criminal Resource Manual, Section 2101, https://www.justice.gov/archives/jm/criminal-resource-manual-2101-money-laundering-overview.

15. *See, e.g.,* 12 U.S.C. § 1818.

16. *See* FDIC, Millennium Bank Order, FDIC-16-0016b (Mar. 7, 2016), https://www.idfpr.com/banks/cbt/Enforcement/2016/MillenniumConsentOrder2016.pdf.

17. *See* Kevin Wack, *Marijuana Business Burns Small Illinois Bank,* AMERICAN BANKER (July 13, 2016), https://www.americanbanker.com/news/marijuana-business-burns-small-illinois-bank.

how to set up an appropriate AML program or address how rigorous such a program needs to be. Rather, each financial institution must base its program from the BSA's legal requirements and a risk-based assessment of the complexity, size, and needs of its business, to ensure that the resulting AML program is tailored to the risks the financial institution faces when it takes on MRBs as customers.

Under the BSA, a financial institution must establish and maintain an effective AML program that meets the BSA's five pillars:

- Establish written internal policies, procedures, and controls
- Conduct an independent testing and audit of the institution's AML policies, procedures, and controls
- Designate an AML compliance officer
- Provide ongoing training to relevant employees
- Conduct appropriate customer due diligence

Each pillar is important to an effective AML program and especially so when a financial institution is taking on MRB clients.[18]

4.4.1 Establish Written Internal Policies, Procedures, and Controls

The board of directors and senior management of a financial institution are responsible for ensuring that the institution maintains an effective AML program through appropriate controls, captured in written policies and procedures. The internal controls should be tailored to the size, structure, risks, and complexity of the financial institution. Similarly, internal controls should address the unique risks and compliance requirements of specific lines of business. Accordingly, an MRB program at a bank should be addressed directly and in detail by the written internal policies and procedures, which are developed with the knowledge and involvement of senior management and the board of directors of the financial institution.

The Federal Financial Institutions Examination Council (FFIEC) provides a detailed list of issues that internal controls should address in an AML program. Particularly relevant to an AML program that addresses MRB business, the internal controls should do the following:

- Identify operations, products, services, customers, and geographic locations that are more vulnerable to abuse by money launderers and criminals. Serving MRB customers requires an understanding of the MRB customer's business, including the products that it sells, as well as the state regulatory structure under which the MRB customer operates.

18. *See generally* FFIEC, BSA/AML Manual, *Core Examination Procedures for Assessing the BSA/AML Compliance Program*, https://bsaaml.ffiec.gov/manual/AssessingTheBSAAML ComplianceProgram/01.

- Inform the board of directors and senior management of identified compliance deficiencies and corrective action taken, as well as suspicious activity report (SAR) filings.
- Provide for program continuity, so changes in staffing do not affect the operation of the AML program or the MRB business.
- Provide for adequate supervision of employees that handle making reports of currency transaction reports (CTRs) and SARs or are involved in other activities to implement the financial institution's BSA obligations.
- Train employees to understand their responsibilities under the BSA and the institution's internal policies and procedures.
- Meet all regulatory recordkeeping and reporting requirements, including CTRs and the potentially more complex SAR filing procedures for dealing with MRBs.

4.4.2 Conduct Independent Testing

A financial institution should have its AML program independently tested by its internal audit department, outside auditors, or other qualified independent parties. In general, a financial institution should conduct independent testing every 12 to 18 months, or as commensurate with the institution's risk profile. The audit of the AML program should be risk-based depending on the financial institution's size, complexity, scope of activities, risk profile, geography, and use of technology, and should cover all of the institution's activities. When choosing an auditor, the financial institution should ensure that it chooses an auditor that is experienced in regulations affecting financial institutions' provision of services to MRBs as well as the practical implications of financial institutions onboarding such customers. The audit should be reported to the institution's board of directors to assist management in identifying areas of weakness so the institution can implement stronger controls where necessary.

4.4.3 Designate a BSA/AML Compliance Officer

The financial institution's board of directors must designate a qualified individual to serve as the BSA/AML compliance officer. The compliance officer must have the knowledge, skills, and abilities as well as the time and authority to manage and oversee the AML program and ensure that the financial institution is complying with the BSA and the institution's AML program. The officer must be fully knowledgeable of the BSA and its implementing regulations and must understand the financial institution's products, services, customers, and other risk factors. When a financial institution is taking on MRB customers, it will be important for the BSA compliance officer to have the knowledge, skills, and abilities necessary to undertake supervision of the necessarily more complex AML program.

The person tasked with the BSA/AML compliance officer role must have an appropriate level of authority and responsibility at the financial institution, such that the officer reports to the board of directors and senior management and is able to delegate BSA/AML duties to other employees of the financial institution.

4.4.4 Provide Ongoing Training to Relevant Employees

The financial institution must ensure that relevant employees are trained in aspects of the BSA applicable to the employees' roles and responsibilities at the financial institution, including as it applies to servicing MRBs. The training should include the requirements of the BSA and its implementing regulations, the financial institution's internal AML program. The relevant employees that must receive training include new staff during employee orientation, those employees that have responsibility for compliance with the BSA, the board of directors and senior management that will oversee the BSA compliance officer and the AML program. Each employee should receive training that is tailored to their roles in the institution. For example, a bank teller should be trained on how to recognize large currency transactions and suspicious activities, and those employees that work in providing loans should be trained on red flags for money laundering tied to the lending process. Training should be conducted in an ongoing manner so that relevant employees are provided with knowledge about new developments or changes to the law and the AML program.

4.4.5 Customer Due Diligence

All financial institutions must implement know your customer (KYC) policies and procedures in order to identify and verify the identity of the institutions' customers. Financial institutions must meet customer due diligence (CDD) requirements as part of a written customer identification program (CIP).[19] Certain customers and transactions require enhanced due diligence (EDD) procedures.

The CIP enables the financial institution to form a reasonable belief that it knows the identify of its customers. An effective CIP includes ongoing CDD activities that help the financial institution in identifying the customer; banks must also understand the nature and purpose of the customer relationship to develop a customer risk profile. Ongoing CDD includes monitoring to identify suspicious transactions and to update customer information as appropriate.

---

19. 12 C.F.R. §§ 208.63(b), 211.5(m), 211.24(j) (Board of Governors of the Federal Reserve System) (Federal Reserve); *id.* § 326.8(b) (Federal Deposit Insurance Corporation) (FDIC); *id.* § 748.2(b) (National Credit Union Administration) (NCUA); *id.* § 21.21 (Office of the Comptroller of the Currency) (OCC); and 31 C.F.R. § 1020.220 (FinCEN).

At account opening, CIP procedures will require that the financial institution collect certain information from the customer in order to verify the customer's identity. Such information includes, at a minimum, the customer's name, date of birth (for individuals), address, and an identification number such as a social security number or tax identification number. For corporate customers, the financial institution should also obtain items such as the articles of incorporation and a business license. Based on the financial institution's risk assessment, the institution may require additional information from certain customers in certain lines of business.

Effective CDD policies and procedures will enable a bank to detect and report suspicious activity, avoid criminal exposure for the financial institution from persons who attempt to use the financial institution for illegal purposes, and adhere to safe and sound banking practices. Part of an effective CDD program for financial institutions providing services to MRBs is developing procedures for identifying MRB customers. At account opening, the financial institution's CDD questionnaire should ask questions and require information that will identify the customer and seek information on the customer's activities so that the customer is providing information that would expose its MRB activities. Once identified, requesting additional identifying information from the MRB customer may be necessary. Such information could include information related to the MRB's state license, including information on the MRB's owners, investors, and employees.

As part of its ongoing monitoring activities, the financial institution should determine the extent to which the customer engages in MRB business. For example, is the customer directly selling or producing marijuana or is the customer selling hemp products? As part of this ongoing monitoring, the financial institution should ensure that the customer's activities fit within the financial institution's policies related to servicing MRBs. If a customer is operating in ways that violate the financial institution's policies, then the financial institution may need to terminate the relationship.

FinCEN directs that financial institutions include the following in their CDD of MRBs:

- Verifying with the appropriate state authorities whether the business is duly licensed and registered;
- Reviewing the license application (and related documentation) submitted by the business for obtaining a state license to operate its marijuana-related business;
- Requesting from state licensing and enforcement authorities the available information about the business and related parties;
- Developing an understanding of the normal and expected activity for the business, including the types of products to be sold and the type of customers to be served (e.g., medical versus recreational customers);

- Ongoing monitoring of publicly available sources for adverse information about the business and related parties;
- Ongoing monitoring for suspicious activity, including for any of the red flags described in this guidance; and
- Refreshing information obtained as part of CDD on a periodic basis and commensurate with the risk. With respect to information regarding state licensure obtained in connection with such CDD, a financial institution may reasonably rely on the accuracy of information provided by state licensing authorities, where states make such information available.[20]

Additionally, as part of its ongoing due diligence, a financial institution should consider whether an MRB customer's activities implicates one of the Cole Memo priorities or otherwise violates state law.

Recent FinCEN guidance directs financial institutions serving hemp-related businesses to establish risk-based procedures for conducting ongoing CDD.[21] At its base, a financial institution's CDD responsibilities should focus on the need to identify the risks posed by their customers. This is done by understanding the nature and purpose of the customer relationship in order to develop a customer risk profile, conduct ongoing monitoring, and identify and file SARs. For purposes of ongoing CDD, the financial institution may confirm the hemp business's compliance with state, tribal, or USDA licensing requirements, as applicable, by obtaining a written attestation of licensure or a copy of the license. The financial institution can also seek additional information depending on the financial institution's assessment of the risk the business poses. Such additional information could include crop inspection or testing reports, license renewals, updated attestations, or correspondence with regulatory authorities.[22]

5. Suspicious Activity Report Filing

Financial institutions must file a SAR[23] in the event that they suspect or have reason to suspect that a transaction conducted or attempted by, at, or through the financial institution involves funds derived from illegal activity or is an attempt to disguise funds derived from illegal activity, is designed to evade the requirements of the BSA, or lacks a business or apparent lawful purpose.

---

20. FIN-2014-G001, *BSA Expectations Regarding Marijuana-Related Businesses,* FinCEN (Feb. 14, 2014), https://www.fincen.gov/sites/default/files/shared/FIN-2014-G001.pdf.

21. FIN-2020-G001, *supra* note 6.

22. *Id.*

23. 31 U.S.C. § 5318(g); 12 C.F.R. § 1020.320(a) (banks); 31 C.F.R. § 1022.320(a) (money services businesses).

Federal law prohibits the distribution or sale of marijuana, and so a SAR would generally be required in any transaction involving an MRB. FinCEN has provided specific guidance on SAR filing related to MRBs, including three categories or thresholds for SAR filing.[24]

Marijuana Limited SAR—A Marijuana Limited SAR is filed when a financial institution determines through the exercise of its due diligence that a customer is not engaged in activities that violate state law or raise any red flags as defined in the Cole Memo. The financial institution will state that no additional suspicious activity has been identified related to the MRB's activities and may continue to provide normal services to the MRB despite filing a Marijuana Limited SAR. When a continuing activity report is filed, the financial institution may include the same content as the initial Marijuana Limited SAR, plus details about the amount of transactions related to the account since the previous SAR. If, however, during the time since filing the initial Marijuana Limited SAR, the financial institution identifies changes in activity that could implicate one of the Cole Memo red flags or priorities or violates state law, then the financial institution should file a Marijuana Priority SAR.

Marijuana Priority SAR—A Marijuana Priority SAR is filed when a financial institution determines through the exercise of its due diligence that the MRB may raise one or more of the red flags as defined in the Cole Memo or may not be complying with state laws. The financial institution may continue to provide normal services while further investigation of the MRB related to the SAR filing is conducted.

Marijuana Termination SAR—A Marijuana Termination SAR is filed when a financial institution determines through the exercise of its due diligence that the MRB raises one or more of the red flags as defined in the Cole Memo, is not complying with state laws, or the financial institution has decided not to have MRB customers for business reasons or terminate a relationship with a particular MRB customer. Upon filing the Marijuana Termination SAR, the financial institution will terminate its relationship with the MRB.

5.1 Hemp Business and SARs

As a result of hemp being excluded from the CSA, a financial institution providing services to a hemp-related company need only comply with standard applicable regulatory requirements related to customer identification, suspicious activity reporting, currency transaction reporting, and customer due diligence. In particular, the financial institution need not file marijuana-related SARs for hemp-related businesses. Rather, a financial institution need only file SARs in the normal course if a business or

---

24. FIN-2014-G001, *supra* note 20.

transaction is suspicious.[25] If a business deals in both marijuana-related and hemp-related products, and the financial institution is able to identify which proceeds are tied to marijuana and which are tied to hemp, then the financial institution's marijuana-related SAR filing responsibilities apply only to the marijuana-related portion of the business.[26]

FinCEN has provided examples of suspicious activities for financial institutions to be aware of when servicing hemp-related businesses:

- A customer appears to be engaged in hemp production in a state or jurisdiction in which hemp production remains illegal.
- A customer appears to be using a state-licensed hemp business as a front or pretext to launder money derived from other criminal activity or derived from marijuana-related activity that may not be permitted under applicable law.
- A customer engaged in hemp production seeks to conceal or disguise involvement in MRB activity.
- The customer is unable to or unwilling to certify or provide sufficient information to demonstrate that it is duly licensed and operating consistent with applicable law, or the financial institution becomes aware that the customer continues to operate (1) after a license revocation, or (2) inconsistently with applicable law.[27]

6. Currency Transaction Reporting

MRBs operate cash-heavy businesses due to their lack of access to financial institutions and the prohibitions on many card-type payments to MRBs as merchants. As a result, financial institutions that service MRB customers must ensure that their currency transaction report (CTR) filing procedures are up-to-date and implemented. A CTR must be filed by a bank or money services business when any person transacts (i.e., deposits or withdraws) more than $10,000 in cash per day.[28] An MRB is not eligible for any exemption under the laws governing CTRs.[29]

Additional challenges face financial institutions regarding the filing of CTRs for MRB customers. Carrying and depositing large amounts of cash is dangerous for MRBs due to robbery risks. As a result, there are various armored car services that service MRBs as well as other informal

---

25. Federal Reserve, *Statement on Providing Financial Services to Customers Engaged in Hemp-Related Businesses*, SR 19-14 (Dec. 3, 2019), available at https://www.federalreserve.gov/newsevents/pressreleases/files/bcreg20191203a1.pdf.

26. FIN-2020-G001, *supra* note 6.

27. FIN-2020-G001, *supra* note 6.

28. A CTR is filed on FinCEN Form 8300 (Report of Cash Payments Over $10,000 Received in a Trade or Business).

29. FIN-2014-G001, *supra* note 20.

cash-carrying services that MRBs utilize. Financial institutions should
design their CTR policies to address the potential for inaccurate reporting
or identification when accepting money from MRBs through third parties.

7. Federal Legislation

Proposed federal legislation to make it easier to provide financial services
to MRBs has been floated in several past congresses and has been gaining
support on both sides of the aisle. The bill with the most support during the
current congressional session is the Secure and Fair Enforcement Banking
Act of 2019 (SAFE Banking Act),[30] which passed the House in September
2019 on a bipartisan basis by a vote of 321–103. The bill was introduced
in the Senate and referred to the Committee on Banking, Housing, and
Urban Affairs.[31]

If passed in its current form, the SAFE Banking Act would prohibit a
federal banking regulator from penalizing a bank for providing banking
services to legitimate MRBs. This includes providing cash deposit services
and providing credit to MRBs. Federal banking regulators would be prohibited from (1) terminating or limiting deposit or share insurance of a bank
solely because the bank provides financial services to legitimate MRBs;
(2) prohibiting or discouraging a bank from offering a bank from providing financial services to legitimate MRBs; (3) recommending or encourag-
ing a bank not to offer financial services to an account holder because of
the person's affiliation with an MRB; (4) taking any adverse or corrective
supervisory action on a loan solely because the recipient of the loan owns
an MRB or owns real estate or equipment that is leased or sold to an MRB;
or (5) penalizing a bank for processing or collecting payments for a legitimate MRB. Additionally, under the bill, a bank would not be liable under
federal law or subject to forfeiture of the proceeds of a loan or any other
financial service to a legitimate MRB or its services provider.

The SAFE Banking Act would also modify the SAR filing requirements
for providing financial services to MRBs. The bill directs the Department of
Treasury to provide guidance consistent with the SAFE Banking Act so that
financial institutions are not significantly inhibited from providing financial services to legitimate MRBs.

---

30. Secure and Fair Enforcement Banking Act of 2019, H.R. 1595, https://www.congress
.gov/bill/116th-congress/house-bill/1595/text. *See* American Bankers Association, *Joint
Trades Letter to the House re: Support H.R. 1595, SAFE Banking Act* (Sept. 19, 2019), https://
www.aba.com/advocacy/policy-analysis/joint-trades-letter-to-the-house-support-safe
-banking-act.
31. Secure and Fair Enforcement Banking Act of 2019, S. 1200, available at https://www
.congress.gov/bill/116th-congress/senate-bill/1200. *See* American Bankers Association,
Joint State Bankers Association Letter to the Senate: Support S. 1200, SAFE Banking Act of 2019
(Mar. 6, 2020), https://www.aba.com/advocacy/policy-analysis/joint-sba-letter-to-senate
-support-s-1200.

Finally, the protections in the SAFE Banking Act would also be extended to providing financial services to hemp-related businesses. The bill would direct the federal financial regulators to provide guidance and best practices related to providing financial services to hemp-related businesses.

In addition to bipartisan support in Congress, the SAFE Banking Act has received support from groups of governors,[32] state attorneys general,[33] state treasurers,[34] and banking associations.[35]

The bill does not address every issue related to the provision of financial services to MRBs. For example, the bill does not directly address the Federal Reserve's master account program, which enables a bank to process debit or credit card payments, or other electronic funds transfers. If passed in its current form, further guidance will be necessary to clear up many issues involved in the provision of financial services to MRBs.

8. State Marijuana Banking Innovations

Some states are making efforts to promote state marijuana banking initiatives.

Washington's Department of Financial Institutions (DFI) has been at the forefront of providing a way forward for financial institutions working with MRBs. In 2014, the DFI issued guidance and FAQs for those providing banking services to MRBs. In general, the state's guidance acknowledges that marijuana is illegal under federal law and directs financial institutions to follow federal guidance (e.g., the Cole Memo and FinCEN's guidance). The DFI explains that following Washington's regulations governing MRBs will help a financial institution avoid triggering red flags under federal law.

In Colorado, Governor Jared Polis and the Colorado Department of Regulatory Agencies (DORA) recently released a document called the "Roadmap to Cannabis Banking & Financial Services" (the Roadmap) to provide guidance to state-chartered financial services companies that serve

---

32. Congressman Ed Perlmutter, Press Release, *20 Bipartisan Governors Urge Congress to Pass Marijuana Banking Bill* (June 14, 2019), https://perlmutter.house.gov/news/documentsingle.aspx?DocumentID=4554.

33. National Association of Attorneys General, Letter to Congress re: SAFE Banking Act (May 8, 2019), https://oag.ca.gov/system/files/attachments/press-docs/naag-letter-safe-banking-act-2019.pdf (letter for support for the SAFE Banking Act signed by 38 state attorneys general).

34. National Association of State Treasurers, Resolution re: Advancing Legislation Allowing the States to Provide Banking Services to MRBs (May 17, 2019), https://cdn.ymaws.com/member.nast.org/resource/collection/297F5F58-F244-47A2-8C1F-4EDEF9BBD397/NAST_Cannabis_Banking_Resolution.pdf.

35. American Bankers Association, *Industry Letter to Senate Banking Committee re: SAFE Banking Act (H.R. 1595)* (Dec. 12, 2019), https://www.aba.com/advocacy/policy-analysis/industry-letter-senate-banking-committee-safe-banking-act-hr-1595.

cannabis-related businesses.[36] The Roadmap stated a goal of implementing a plan to increase the number of financial services providers who serve cannabis-related businesses by 20 percent by June 30, 2020. As of this writing, Colorado has not issued a plan. However, the Roadmap explains that to accomplish this goal, Colorado plans to create a regulatory landscape amenable to the development of more financial services for cannabis-related businesses, explore emerging technologies and business models in the financial services industry, and identify opportunities for state legislative and regulatory clarity for state-chartered and -licensed businesses to provide services to cannabis-related businesses.

The Roadmap lists seven strategies that the state will use to accomplish its goal:

1. Establish a working group consisting of senior leadership at DORA to meet monthly to discuss developing a more favorable regulatory structure.
2. Increase transparency of information about cannabis-related businesses, including improved interagency coordination.
3. Engage banking and credit union trade associations to identify areas of opportunity.
4. Encourage innovative technologies to enter the Colorado market, including obtaining legal guidance from the attorney general regarding providing services under the Money Transmission Act and the Trust Companies Act.
5. Provide guidance for state-chartered banks and credit unions that provide services to cannabis-related businesses.
6. Reduce barriers to entry while maintaining consumer protection through evaluating current chartering and licensing requirements.
7. Demonstrate support for a federal solution by submitting letters in partnership with other state bank regulators.

The Roadmap provides a more detailed outline of a state's efforts to encourage the financial services industry as it works with MRBs, but the specific guidance is not very different from Washington state's prior guidance. In particular, Colorado, just like Washington, directs financial institutions to abide by federal law and guidance, with each financial institution making business decisions about serving MRBs through an evaluation of the institution's risk appetite and own internal compliance management abilities. Based on the Roadmap, Colorado intends to issue more specific guidance, including guidance under the state's money transmission laws related to servicing MRBs and guidance about the state's expectations for state-chartered financial institutions under the BSA.

---

36. Colorado Department of Regulatory Agencies, *Roadmap to Cannabis Banking & Financial Services* (Feb. 3, 2020), https://www.colorado.gov/governor/news/polis-administration-unveils-roadmap-cannabis-banking-financial-services.

With respect to California, in 2019 the state Senate passed a bill that would create a Cannabis Limited Charter Banking and Credit Union Law to be administered by the Department of Business Oversight.[37] The bill would create a Cannabis Limited Charter Bank and Credit Union Advisory Board to oversee the provision of licenses and the regulation of cannabis limited charter banks and credit unions. These depository institutions would be formed for the purpose of providing financial services to MRBs. Cannabis limited charter banks or credit unions would be able to issue special purpose checks to account holders that would be valid for specified purposes. These financial institutions would also be able to cash the checks it issues, including by holders of the checks that are not account holders at the financial institutions. The bill also provides for the federal government's removing marijuana as a Schedule 1 controlled substance. In that event, this law would become inoperative.

Nevada is currently beginning a three-year pilot program to allow MRBs and their customers to transact using electronic tokens.[38] Under the pilot program, the Nevada state treasurer will create a pilot program for closed-loop payment processing systems to provide MRBs with a means of paying taxes and to enable customers to make purchases at MRBs.

In 2018, the governor of New York directed the New York Department of Financial Services (NY DFS) to encourage state-chartered banks and credit unions to provide banking services to regulated medical marijuana and industrial hemp businesses.[39] In response, the NY DFS issued guidance that encouraged New York's state-chartered banks and credit unions to support the development of the growth, cultivation, marketing, and sale of industrial hemp and products derived from industrial hemp for research purposes under the state's licensing system. The guidance directs these financial institutions to follow federal law, and to assess and verify the eligibility and authority of the entity under New York law related to industrial hemp.[40]

---

37. California, SB-51 (Dec. 4, 2018), http://leginfo.legislature.ca.gov/faces/billTextClient.xhtml?bill_id=201920200SB51.

38. *See* AB466 (signed into law on June 5, 2019), https://www.leg.state.nv.us/App/NELIS/REL/80th2019/Bill/6890/Overview.

39. New York Department of Financial Services, Press Release, *Governor Cuomo Announces Further Action to Support Development of Medical Marijuana and Industrial Hemp Businesses in New York* (July 3, 2018), https://www.dfs.ny.gov/reports_and_publications/press_releases/pr1807031.

40. New York Department of Financial Services, *Guidance on Provision of Financial Services to Medical Marijuana & Industrial Hemp-related Businesses in New York State* (July 3, 2018), https://www.governor.ny.gov/sites/governor.ny.gov/files/atoms/files/New_York_Online_Lending_Survey_Report.pdf.

9. Identifying a Bank for MRBs

Statistics indicate that it is easier today than it once was for MRBs to find banks to service their transactions. FinCEN tracks SAR filings related to MRBs as well as the number of MRBs in the United States based on SAR records. In the latest update, with data through the end of 2019, FinCEN reports nearly 740 financial institutions providing banking services to MRBs in the United States.[41] The report notes that as of December 2019, 203 banks indicated that they provide banking services to hemp-related businesses, and 142 of these same banks filed marijuana SARs. As a result, FinCEN notes that just under 10 percent of the banks filing marijuana-related SARs are only servicing hemp-related businesses and not marijuana-related businesses. (Accurate data on this point will likely not be possible going forward now that FinCEN has issued guidance that banks no longer have to file marijuana SARS for hemp-related businesses. In light of this guidance, it is likely that more financial institutions will provide banking services to hemp-related businesses.)

FinCEN also reported that as of the end of 2019, it had received over 100,000 marijuana SARs, with roughly 75 percent of those SARs being Marijuana Limited SARs. This statistic indicates that the MRBs receiving banking services are considered by their banks to be complying with applicable law and that the bank will continue its relationship with the MRB. This still leaves roughly 25 percent of marijuana-related SARs indicating a bank's concern about the MRBs practices or transactions, or more often the bank terminating the relationship with the MRB.

10. Payments for Marijuana

It is very difficult for MRBs to accept debit and credit card payments. Payment processors will generally not provide payment processing services to MRBs because such transactions are illegal under federal law. Similar payment issues arise in the context of CBD and hemp due to the ambiguous federal approach to these substances. Despite interim final rules from the USDA, CBD processors and sellers are still treated as high-risk merchants.

Credit card networks, such as Visa and MasterCard, prohibit their networks from being used to process illegal transactions. As marijuana is illegal on the federal level, card networks refuse to process MRB transactions.[42] Cutting off MRBs from accepting debit and credit card payments results in MRBs being cash-heavy businesses.

41. FinCEN, *Marijuana Banking Update*, 1st Quarter, FY2020 (Dec. 2019), https://www.fincen.gov/sites/default/files/shared/291404_1st_Q_FY2020_Marijuana_Banking_Update_Public.pdf.

42. *See* NAFCU, *FAQs: Marijuana Banking for Credit Unions* (Nov. 2019), https://www.nafcu.org/faqs-marijuana-banking-credit-unions.

Many major payment processing companies also prohibit marijuana-related sales. For example, PayPal and Stripe both prohibit the sale of drug paraphernalia.[43] Stripe specifically excludes sales by cannabis dispensaries and related businesses. Square, which generally prohibits its services to be used for the sale of drugs or drug paraphernalia, has recently begun a pilot program to work with certain e-commerce CBD startup companies.[44]

As a result of these issues, MRBs with brick-and-mortar retail presences must accept cash at point-of-sale, provide an ATM on-site, or use a separate system at point-of-sale that enables cashless payments. MRBs and hemp or CBD businesses may also consider engaging a company that offers payment processing services to high-risk businesses and especially to MRBs. As this is an area with a lot of new entrants, MRBs should be cautious of companies offering payment services that do not comply with law.

Some MRBs have attempted to get around the prohibition to accept card payments by conducting illegal factoring. Credit card factoring involves setting up a merchant account that is then used for processing transactions that are different from the original stated purpose of the merchant account. Examples of this include a marijuana dispensary processing card transaction through the dry cleaner next door's merchant account. MRBs should not launder transactions in this way and should be cautious of other actions that aim to evade the restrictions on payments for MRBs.

---

43. PayPal, Acceptable Use Policy, https://www.paypal.com/us/webapps/mpp/ua /acceptableuse-full?locale.x=en_US.; Stripe Restricted Businesses Policy, https://stripe .com/restricted-businesses.

44. *See* Square Editorial Team, *You Can Now Sell CBD Products with Square,* https:// squareup.com/us/en/townsquare/sell-cbd-products-square. *See also* Dan Clark, *Payment Processing for CBD Suppliers: A Q&A with General Counsel Sivan Whiteley of Square,* LAW.COM (Oct. 10, 2019), https://www.law.com/corpcounsel/2019/10/10/payment-processing -for-cbd-suppliers-a-qa-with-general-counsel-sivan-whiteley-of-square/.

4

Employment

Ann Marie Painter, Jeannil Boji, Lauren M. Kulpa, Aimee Raimer, Sara Davey[1]

Federal, state, and local legislatures are continuously reassessing how employers should regulate and respond to cannabis use by employees.[2] This chapter is intended to help employers and their counsel understand the legal issues that may arise when applicants and employees use cannabis products for medical or recreational reasons and the actions the employer may take with respect to cannabis-using job applicants and employees. These topics include background checks and consideration of cannabis-related arrests and convictions in the hiring process; pre-employment drug testing; on-duty use or possession of cannabis products; off-duty use of cannabis products; post-hire drug testing; and accommodating cannabis use. Additionally, this chapter discusses exceptions for certain job positions, employers, or industries for whom state cannabis laws will not apply.

Because many state laws are in a state of evolution, and case law interpreting these state laws is still developing, employers and their counsel should conduct further research on the topics to ensure the information is up-to-date.

---

1. Special thanks to Katherine Hill, Simon Joassin, and Daniel Szewczyk for their invaluable assistance in conducting research for this chapter.
2. Marijuana Moment is tracking more than 1,000 cannabis-related bills for 2020 legislative sessions. *See* Tom Angell, *Marijuana Legislation Tracking—All Bills*, Marijuana Moment, https://www.marijuanamoment.net/bills/ (updated daily); *see also* Jeremy Berke & Shayanne Gall, *All the States Where Marijuana Is Legal—and 4 More that Could Legalize It in November*, BUSINESS INSIDER, (Oct. 6, 2020, 9:29 AM), https://www.businessinsider.com/legal-marijuana-states-2018-1; *Marijuana Law Reform—State Info.*, NORML, https://norml.org/states (last visited Apr. 16, 2020).

1. Federal Law Grants Employers Greater Rights to Regulate Cannabis in the Workplace

Federal law provides the most expansive rights to employers to manage cannabis in the workplace because most cannabis products are illegal under federal law. Cannabis and similar products with a THC concentration over 0.3 percent are Schedule I substances under the federal Controlled Substances Act (CSA) of 1970.[3] Therefore, the possession, distribution, and use of products exceeding this threshold is illegal under federal law. In effect, this means:

- Employers are neither required nor prohibited from testing applicants and employees for cannabis use;[4]
- Employers may strictly enforce "zero-tolerance drug-free workplace policies" (as used herein, this phrase refers to policies that prohibit any on-duty or off-duty use of unlawful cannabis products) and do not risk liability under federal law by taking adverse actions against employees who test positive for cannabis or who use cannabis off duty, even if the employee's use is legal under state law.[5]
- Employers do not risk liability under federal law by refusing to accommodate an employee's current cannabis use.[6]

Although (as of the date of publication) federal law does not protect employee use of cannabis, in November 2019, the House Judiciary Committee approved a bill that decriminalizes marijuana at the federal level. The Marijuana Opportunity Reinvestment and Expungement Act (MORE Act) removes cannabis from Schedule I of the CSA and requires federal courts to expunge prior cannabis-related offenses.[7] The viability of the MORE Act before the House and Senate remains to be seen, however.

To the extent federal law provides some simplicity due to its blanket treatment of cannabis products as an illegal drug, an analysis of federal law is not enough for employers to understand how to address cannabis in the

---

3. 21 C.F.R. §§ 1308.11–1308.15. The CSA defines a Schedule drug as one that has no accepted medical use and that has a high potential for abuse. *See* 21 U.S.C. § 812(b)(1).

4. Note that inconsistent testing practices could run afoul of other employment laws such as Title VII if such practices have a disparate impact on groups who have certain protected characteristics, such as race and ethnicity.

5. However, as discussed later, notwithstanding an employer's ability to avoid liability under federal law, an employer may still be subject to liability under to state law.

6. However, employers may need to accommodate cannabis use under state law. *See* Section 3.4. Accommodating Cannabis Use.

7. Marijuana Opportunity Reinvestment and Expungement Act of 2019 (MORE Act of 2019), S. 2227, 116th Cong. (2019).

workplace. For example, employers must also look to state laws[8] that permit cannabis use to determine whether the employer can take adverse actions (e.g., refusal to hire, denial of promotion, demotion, suspension, termination of employment, and other actions negatively affecting the terms and conditions of employment) against employees for off-duty cannabis use. The answer depends on a review of any one or a combination of the particular state's statutes legalizing cannabis use (either medically or recreationally), employment discrimination statutes and protections, off-duty conduct statutes, and/or case law and other regulatory guidance interpreting the relationship between these laws.

2. Cannabis and the Hiring Process

2.1 Background Checks and Consideration of Cannabis-Related Arrests and Convictions in Hiring Decisions

Employers historically have been able to consider cannabis-related arrests and convictions when making hiring decisions. However, before asking about or considering cannabis-related arrests and convictions, employers must take the following steps to ensure they are permitted to do so.

First, employers must determine whether their state and local statutes include "ban the box" statutes, which prohibit employers from asking applicants about criminal history on an initial job application and may even require employers to wait to ask about criminal history until after the employer has interviewed the applicant or made a conditional offer of employment.[9] And, at least one state has gone a step further and expressly

---

8. As of the date of this publication, the following states have legalized cannabis use for medical and/or recreational use: Alaska, Arizona, Arkansas, California, Colorado, Connecticut, Delaware, Florida, Georgia, Hawaii, Illinois, Louisiana, Maine, Maryland, Massachusetts, Michigan, Minnesota, Missouri, Montana, Nevada, New Hampshire, New Jersey, New Mexico, New York, North Dakota, Ohio, Oklahoma, Oregon, Pennsylvania, Rhode Island, Utah, Vermont, Washington, Washington, D.C., and West Virginia.

9. "Ban the box "statutes vary greatly, and the intricacies of the various ban the box statutes are outside the scope of this chapter. However, the following states have some form of "ban the box" statutes and should be reviewed before inquiring into cannabis-related arrests and convictions: **California**: Cal. Gov't Code § 12952, as amended by A.B. 2845; **Colorado**: Colo. Rev. Stat. Ann. § 8-2-130 (H.B. 19-1025); **Connecticut**: Conn. Gen. Stat. Ann. §§ 31-51i; **Hawaii**: HRS § 378-2.5, as amended; **Illinois**: 820 ILCS 75/1 to 75/99; **Maryland**: H.B. 994; **Massachusetts**: M.G.L. c. 151B, § 4(9), (9.5), M.G.L. c. 6, §§ 171A and 172, and M.G.L. c. 276, §§ 100A, 100C, and 100N, 804 Code Mass. Regs 3.01 and 3.02; **Minnesota**: Minn. Stat. Ann. §§ 364.01 to 364.10; **New Jersey**: N.J.S.A. 34:6B-11 to 34:6B-19, as amended by S.B. S-3306; **New Mexico**: NMSA 1978, §§ 28-2-1 to 28-2-6 (S.B. 96 (2019)); **Oregon**: Or. Rev. Stat. § 659A.360; **Rhode Island**: R. I. Gen. Laws § 28-5-7(6), (7); **Vermont**: 21 V.S.A. § 495j; and **Washington**: RCW 49.94.005

prohibits employers from considering cannabis-related arrests and convictions in the hiring process. In California, employers cannot consider applicants' convictions for most cannabis possession convictions more than two years old.[10]

Second, if employers are permitted to consider cannabis-related convictions and arrests in the hiring process, employers should consider the Equal Employment Opportunity Commission (EEOC) guidance, which states that employers should engage in an individualized assessment of an applicant's criminal history by considering the "nature and gravity of the offense or conduct," "time that has passed since the offense, conduct and/or completion of the sentence," and "nature of the job held or sought" to determine if job relatedness and business necessity warrant exclusion of the candidate.[11]

Employers should also be aware that states are passing or introducing legislation to reduce barriers to employment for applicants with cannabis-related convictions by permitting these applicants to apply for expungement of their records.[12] For example, New Jersey passed a

---

to 49.94.901. The following localities also have similar statutes: **California**: Los Angeles (L.A.M.C. §§ 189.00 to 189.15) and San Francisco (S.F. POLICE CODE, Art. 49, §§ 4901 to 4920); the **District of Columbia** (D.C. CODE §§ 32-1341 to 32-1346); **Illinois**: Chicago (MUN. CODE OF CITY OF CHICAGO § 2-160-054), and Cook County (COOK COUNTY, IL ORDINANCES, §§ 42-31, 42-33, and 42-35(h)); Waterloo City, Iowa (WATERLOO CITY CODE § 5-3-15, Ord. No. 5522); **Maryland**: Baltimore (BALTIMORE CITY CODE, Art. 11 (Labor & Employment), §§ 15-1 to 15-16), Montgomery County (MONTGOMERY COUNTY CODE, Art. XII, §§ 27-71 to 27-75), and Prince George's County (PRINCE GEORGE'S CTY. CODE, Div. 12, Subdiv. 10, §§ 2-231.02 to 2-231.08); **Missouri**: Columbia (COLUMBIA, MO CODE OF ORDINANCES, ch. 12, art. V, §§ 12-90 to 12-94), Kansas City (Ord. No. 180034, CODE OF ORDINANCES OF THE CITY OF KANSAS CITY, MISSOURI, §§ 38-1, 38-104), and St. Louis (Ordinance No. 71074); **New Jersey**: Newark (NEWARK, N.J. REV. GEN. ORDINANCE No. 12-1630 (Ban the Box Ordinance); repealed and replaced by Ordinance No. 14-0921); **New York**: Buffalo (CITY OF BUFFALO CODE, §§ 154-24 to 154-29), New York City (N.Y.C. ADMIN. CODE §§ 8-102 and 8-107(10), (11), (11-a)), Rochester (CITY OF ROCHESTER MUN. CODE (RMC), Ch. 63, Art. II, §§ 63-12 to 63-16), Westchester County (Local Law LL-2018-14, Laws of Westchester County (WCL), § 700.03(a)(10)); **Oregon**: Portland (PORTLAND CITY CODE (PCC) Ch. 23.10 (§§ 23.10.010 to 23.10.100)); **Pennsylvania**: Philadelphia (PHILA. PA. CODE (PPC), ch. 9-3500); **Texas**: Austin (AUSTIN CITY CODE (ACC) §§ 4-15-1 to 4-15-89, Ordinance No. 20160324-019); **Washington**: Seattle (SEATTLE MUN. CODE, ch. 14.17), and Spokane (CITY OF SPOKANE MUNICIPAL CODE (SMC), ch. 09.02, §§ 09.02.010 to 09.02.090).

10. CAL. LAB. CODE §§ 432.7(a)(1) & 432.8.

11. *EEOC Enforcement Guidance*, Consideration of Arrest and Conviction Records in Employment Decisions Under Title VII of the Civil Rights Act of 1964, No. 915.002 (4/25/2012).

12. The following states and localities have enacted "expungement or sealing laws specific to marijuana, decriminalized, or legalized offenses": Arizona, California,

law, that took effect on June 15, 2020 and will resume effect on February 15, 2021,[13] providing for the expungement of certain marijuana-[14] or hashish-related[15] offenses.[16] And, Georgia's First Time Offenders Act permits some first-time offenders to avoid convictions for certain crimes and prohibits employers from refusing to hire a person due to a crime that was discharged under the act.[17] Thus, an applicant would not need to disclose the expunged offense and the expunged offense likely will not be revealed in a background check.

2.2 Pre-Employment Drug Testing

Pre-employment drug testing as part of a conditional job offer is generally permissible under the Americans with Disabilities Act,[18] but some confusion exists regarding pre-employment drug testing in states where cannabis use is legal. Only a few jurisdictions have passed laws expressly addressing the issue. When conducting pre-employment drug testing for cannabis use, employers must first ensure that they are permitted to conduct

---

Colorado, Connecticut, Delaware, the District of Columbia, Hawaii, Illinois, Maryland, Massachusetts, Minnesota, Nevada, New Hampshire, New Jersey, New York, Oregon, Rhode Island, Vermont, and Washington. The Restoration of Rights Project of the nonprofit Collateral Consequences Resource Center maintains a list of these statutes by jurisdiction on their website at http://ccresourcecenter.org/state-restoration-profiles /50-state-comparison-marijuana-legalization-expungement/.

13. *See* L. 2019, c. 269 (providing for expungement) and EO-178 (interrupting implementation until Feb. 15, 2021).

14. "Marijuana" means all parts of the plant Genus Cannabis L., whether growing or not; the seeds thereof, and every compound, manufacture, salt, derivative, mixture, or preparation of the plant or its seeds, except those containing resin extracted from the plant; but shall not include the mature stalks of the plant, fiber produced from the stalks, oil, or cake made from the seeds of the plant, any other compound, manufacture, salt, derivative, mixture, or preparation of mature stalks, fiber, oil, or cake, or the sterilized seed of the plant which is incapable of germination. N.J.S.A. § 2C:35-2 (2013).

15. "Hashish" means the resin extracted from any part of the plant Genus Cannabis L. and any compound, manufacture, salt, derivative, mixture, or preparation of such resin. N.J.S.A. § 2C:35-2 (2013).

16. Pub. L. No. 2019, 2019 N.J. Sess. Law Serv. Ch. 269 (Sen. 4154) (revising expungement eligibility and procedures).

17. *See* Georgia's First Offenders Act (O.C.G.A. § 42-8-63). Other states may have statutes or programs where first-time offenders can qualify for sealing or expungement of convictions which may include cannabis-related offenses.

18. U.S. Equal Employment Opportunity Commission, "The ADA: Your Responsibilities as an Employer," https://www.eeoc.gov/laws/guidance/ada-your-responsibilities-employer ("A test for the illegal use of drugs is not considered a medical examination under the ADA; therefore, it is not a prohibited pre-employment medical examination and you will not have to show that the administration of the test is job related and consistent with business necessity.").

pre-employment drug testing in their jurisdictions[19] and that declining an applicant for a positive drug test for cannabis use will not violate any anti-discrimination or lawful off-duty conduct laws.

Only a limited number of drug testing laws have specific provisions limiting an employer's ability to test for marijuana and/or refuse to hire an applicant for testing positive for marijuana. New York City has the most restrictive statute; it prohibits employers from testing applicants for cannabis, except for (1) applicants who are applying for safety-sensitive positions, (2) applicants whose prospective employer is a party to a valid collective bargaining agreement that specifically addresses pre-employment drug testing, (3) when the employer is subject to pre-employment drug testing regulations or rules promulgated by the federal department of transportation or local department of transportation, or (4) when the employer is subject to a contract or grant of financial assistance from the federal government that requires drug testing of prospective employees as a condition of receiving the contract or grant.[20] Washington, D.C. also restricts the circumstances in which an employer can test an applicant for cannabis. In Washington, D.C., employers may not test applicants for cannabis use until after the applicant receives a conditional offer of employment.[21] After a conditional offer of employment is made, an employer may withdraw an offer of employment if the candidate tests positive for cannabis.[22]

Other states permit pre-employment drug testing, including testing for cannabis and cannabinoids, but restrict an employer's ability to take action in response to a positive pre-employment cannabis drug test. For example, Nevada's statute prohibits an employer from refusing to hire an applicant

---

19. Pre-employment drug testing statutes vary greatly, including whether complying with the drug testing requirements are mandatory or are part of a voluntary program, such as a workers' compensation premium reduction program. However, the following states have some form of pre-employment drug testing statutes and should be reviewed before conducting any pre-employment drug testing: **Alaska**: AS §§ 23.10.630(b), 23.10.655; **Arizona**: A.R.S. §§ 23-493.04(A), 23-493.05; **Arkansas**: A.C.A. §§ 11-14-106(a), 11-14-107(b); **Connecticut**: C.G.S.A. § 31-51v; **Florida**: FL ST §§ 440.102(2), 440.102(4)(a)(1); O.C.G.A. §§ 34-9-412, 34-9-415(b)(1); **Hawaii**: HRS § 329B-5(a), HAR § 11-113-5(a); **Maine**: 26 M.R.S.A. §§ 683(3), 684(1)(A)–(B), 685(2)(A1); **Maryland**: Md. Code Ann., Health Gen. §§ 17-214(a)(6), (b), (h); **Michigan**: MCL 333.27954(3); **Minnesota**: Minn. Stat. Ann. § 181.951, subd. 2; **Missouri**: § 288.045(4), RSMo; **Montana**: Mont. Code. Ann. § 39-2-208(1); **Nevada**: NRS 284.4066; **Ohio**: Ohio Admin. Code § 4123-17-58(C)(5)(a); **Oklahoma**: Okla. Stat. tit. 40, § 554(1); **Rhode Island**: Rhode Island Annotated § 28-6.5-2(a)-(c); **Utah**: U.C.A. 1953 §§ 34-38-3(1), 34-38-8(1); **Vermont**: 21 V.S.A. § 512; **West Virginia**: W. Va. Code, §§ 21-3E-4, 21-3E-9.
20. N.Y.C. Admin. Code § 8-107(31) (effective May 10, 2020).
21. D.C. Code § 32-931(a).
22. *Id.* § 32-931(b)(4).

for testing positive for cannabis; however, the statute provides exceptions for firefighters, emergency medical technicians, and public safety positions.[23] Similarly, Arizona,[24] Delaware,[25] Minnesota,[26] New Jersey,[27] Oklahoma,[28] and Rhode Island[29] all prohibit employers from refusing to hire an applicant who is a registered medical cannabis card holder based on testing positive for cannabis, subject to state-specific exceptions. Arizona, Delaware, Minnesota, Oklahoma, and Rhode Island permit an employer to decline an applicant who used, possessed, or was impaired by cannabis on the premises of the place of employment. As a practical matter, it may be an unusual circumstance when an employer will be able to demonstrate on premises use or impairment, and, thus, the statutes in essence operate to prohibit employers from rescinding job offers to applicants who participate in the state's medical marijuana program for the reason that they tested positive for cannabis use in a drug test.

Even if employers are permitted to conduct pre-employment testing for cannabis, or take action based on a positive marijuana drug test, employers should be wary of inviting discrimination claims. Many states with medical cannabis programs prohibit discrimination based on the fact that a person is a medical marijuana card holder. Conducting a drug test may reveal the applicant's protected status as a medical marijuana card holder, and refusing to hire the applicant because of the applicant's positive drug test may be viewed as a proxy for discriminating based on the applicant's protected status.[30] See Section 3.4 Accommodating Cannabis Use later in this chapter and the following section, Section 2.3 Consideration of an Applicant's Participation in a Medical Cannabis Program or an Applicant's Off-Duty Use of Cannabis, for further discussion on these topics.

---

23. 2019 Nevada Laws ch. 421, AB 132 § 2.

24. A.R.S. § 36-2813(B)(2).

25. 16 Del. C. § 4905A(a)(3)(b).

26. Minn. Stat. Ann. § 152.32(3)(c)(2).

27. N.J.S.A. § 24:6I-6.1(b)(1)–(2).

28. 63 Okla. Stat. Ann. § 427.8(H)(2).

29. 21 R.I. Gen. Laws Ann. § 21-28.6-4(e)(1)(i), (2).

30. *See, e.g.,* Noffsinger v. SSC Niantic Op. Co., LLC, 2018 WL 4224075, at *5 (D. Conn. Sept. 5, 2018) (refusal to hire medical cannabis user who tested positive in a pre-employment drug test was discrimination under state law); Palmiter v. Commonwealth Health Systems et al., 2019 WL 6248350 (Pa. Com. Pl. 2019) (holding an applicant could move forward with an anti-discrimination claim under the Pennsylvania Medical Marijuana Act where the applicant was not selected to be hired due to a positive post-offer drug test despite her being a medical cannabis user).

2.3 Consideration of an Applicant's Participation in a Medical Cannabis Program or an Applicant's Off-Duty Use of Cannabis

Many states with medical cannabis programs prohibit discrimination based on the fact that a person is a medical cannabis card holder.[31] Even without asking directly, employers may learn about an applicant's participation in a medical cannabis program during the screening, interviewing, and background check process. For example, an employer may discover evidence of cannabis use by reviewing an applicant's public social media or may otherwise learn of an applicant's use of cannabis through a voluntary disclosure. Based on this information, an employer may inquire as to whether the applicant possesses a valid medical marijuana card for authorized treatment of a medical condition. If the applicant does not hold a valid medical marijuana card, and recreational use is not authorized, the employer can likely decline to hire an applicant based on that discovery. However, if the applicant does hold a valid medical marijuana card, the employer should check the law in the applicable jurisdiction and consult with counsel before making the decision not to hire the candidate based solely on the fact that the applicant holds a card or participates in a program, as some courts have allowed discrimination claims based on medical cannabis card status to go forward.[32]

Further, the applicant's off-duty use of cannabis (either medical or recreational) may be protected under the state's general lawful off-duty conduct statute. See Section 3.2 Off-Duty Use of Cannabis Products for further discussion on this topic.

---

31. **Arizona**: Ariz. Rev. Stat. Ann. § 36-2813 (B)(1); **Arkansas**: AR. Const. Amend. 98, § 3(f)(3)(A); **Connecticut**: Conn. Gen. Stat. Ann. § 21a-408p(b)(3); **Delaware**: 16 Del. C. § 4905A (3)(a); **Illinois**: 410 ILCS 130/40)(a)(1); **Maine**: Me. Rev. Stat. tit. 22, § 2430-C(3); **Minnesota**: Minn. Stat. Ann. § 152.32(3)(c)(1); **New Jersey**: N.J.S.A. § 24:6I-6.1(a); **New Mexico**: NMSA 1978, § 26-2B-9; **New York**: N.Y. Pub Health Law § 3369(1)-(2); **Oklahoma**: Okla. Stat. tit. 63, § 427.8(H)(1); **Pennsylvania**: PA ST 35 P.S. § 10231.2103(b); **Rhode Island**: R.I. Gen Laws § 21-28.6-4(e); **Utah**: (public employers only) (applies to public employees only) Utah Code § 26-61a-111(2)(a)–(b); **West Virginia**: W. Va. Code § 16A-15-4(b)(1).

32. *See* Callaghan v. Darlington Fabrics Corp., No. PC-2014-5680 (R.I. Super. 2017) (employer discriminated against applicant when it rescinded offer of a paid internship after applicant disclosed she participation in the state's medical cannabis program and would test positive on a pre-employment drug screening); Kamakeeaina v. Armstrong Produce, Ltd., No. 18-CV-00480-DKW-RT, 2019 WL 1320032, at *5 (D. Hawaii Mar. 22, 2019) (permitting an ADA failure-to-hire claim to proceed past the motion to dismiss stage because there was not alleged current drug use where the plaintiff alleged he informed the employer during his interview that he was registered under Hawaii's Medical Cannabis Program, where the employer told the plaintiff that if his drug test was positive it would withdraw its offer of employment, and where the plaintiff said he was "prepared to have the offer taken off the table").

3. Cannabis Use during Employment

3.1 On-Duty Use or Possession of Cannabis Products

As of the date of this writing, no state law requires, and no cases have held, that employers must permit employees to possess, use, or be under the influence of federally unlawful cannabis products on an employer's premises or while conducting business on behalf of the employer. In fact, most statutes legalizing cannabis use expressly state that employers do not need to permit this conduct.[33] Employers are free to adopt policies prohibiting on-duty use or possession of unlawful cannabis-related products or being under the influence of cannabis products[34] and may discipline employees for violating those policies.

3.2 Off-Duty Use of Cannabis Products

Prior to the passage of state statutes legalizing cannabis for medical and/ or recreational purposes, employers could take adverse action against an employee or refuse to hire an applicant based on the applicant's off-duty use of cannabis products. But in states where cannabis use is permitted, the cannabis statutes themselves or the states' general off-duty conduct statutes may prohibit employers from taking adverse action based on off-duty

33. **Alaska (Medical)**: AS § 17.37.040 (d)(1); **Alaska (Recreational)**: AS § 17.38.220 (a); **Arizona**: A.R.S. § 36-2813 (B)(1); **Arkansas**: A.R.S. § 36-2813 (B)(1); **California (Medical)**: CAL. HEALTH & SAFETY CODE § 11362.785(a); **California (Recreational)**: CAL. HEALTH & SAFETY CODE § 11362.45(f); **Colorado**: Coats v. Dish Network, 350 P.3d 849 (Colo. 2015) (Employer may fire employees who test positive for marijuana, even for off-duty use with a valid medical marijuana card.); **Connecticut**: C.G.S.A. § 21a-408a(b)(2)(B), C.G.S.A. § 21a-408p(b)(3); **Delaware**: 16 DEL. C. § 4905A (3)(a–b); **D.C (Medical)**: DC ST § 71-1671.03(b)(1); **D.C. (Recreational)**: (DC ST § 48-904.01(a)(1C); **Florida**: FLA. STAT. ANN. § 381.986(1)(j)(5)(c); **Georgia**: GA. CODE ANN. § 16-12-191(g); **Hawaii**: HRS § 329-122(e)(2)(B); **Illinois (Medical)**: 410 ILCS 130/30(h); **Illinois (Recreational)**: 410 ILCS 705/10-50(b); **Maine (Medical)**: 22 M.R.S.A. § 2426(2)(B); **Massachusetts (Medical)**: 935 MASS. CODE REGS. § 501.840(2)(d); **Massachusetts (Recreational)**: 28-B M.R.S.A § 112, M.G.L. c. 94G § 2(e); **Michigan (Medical)**: MCL § 333.26427(c)(2); **Michigan (Recreational)**: MCL 333.27954; **Minnesota**: MINN. STAT. ANN. § 152.32 subd. 3(c); **Missouri**: Mo. CONST. ART. 14, § 1; **Montana**: MONT. CODE ANN. § 50-46-320(4)(b); **Nevada**: NRS 453A.800; **New Hampshire**: N.H. RSA §§ 126-X:3(II)(a)(2), (d)(2), N.H. RSA § 126-X:3(III)(c); **New Jersey**: N.J.S.A. C24:6I-6.1(c)(1); **New Mexico**: NMSA 1978, §26-2B-9(B)(1); **New York**: N.Y. COMP. CODES R. & REGS. tit. 10, § 1004.18(a)(1), 2014, N.Y. PUB HEALTH LAW § 3369(2); **North Dakota**: N.D.C.C. § 19-24.1-34(2); **Ohio**: OHIO R.C. 3796.28(A)(2); **Oklahoma**: OKLA. STAT. tit. 63, § 427.8(H)(2)(b); **Oregon**: OR. REV. STAT. § 475B.794(2); **Pennsylvania**: 35 P.S. § 10231.2103(b)(2); **Rhode Island**: 21 R.I. GEN. LAWS ANN. § 21-28.6-4(e)(1)(i–ii); **Utah**: UTAH CODE § 26-61a-111(4); **Vermont (Medical)**: 18 V.S.A. § 4474c(a)(3)(B); **Vermont (Recreational)**: 18 V.S.A. § 4230a(e); **Washington**: RCW 69.51A.060(4); **West Virginia**: W. VA. CODE §§ 16A-5-4(b)(2).

34. *But see* Section 3.3 Post-Hiring Drug Testing for Cannabis Use about some state imposed limitations on drug testing to confirm impairment.

cannabis use, and an employer could be subject to liability in these jurisdictions for making hasty hiring decisions.

Thirteen states' cannabis statutes expressly state that employers cannot take adverse action against an employee because of the employee's lawful off-duty conduct related to cannabis.[35] In these states, employers should consider whether the statutes have exceptions, which are discussed later in this chapter in Section 4 Carve-Outs from State Cannabis Laws.

Employees must also consider if applicable state law protects lawful off-duty conduct generally and assess whether those protections would apply to lawful off-duty cannabis use. California,[36] Colorado,[37] Connecticut,[38] Illinois,[39] Massachusetts,[40] Minnesota,[41] Montana,[42] Nevada,[43] New York,[44] North Dakota,[45] and Vermont[46] have lawful off-duty conduct statutes or doctrines. Although these statutes are general and do not expressly mention cannabis, it stands to reason that where an employee lawfully uses cannabis off duty in these states, an employer may not take an adverse action against the employee because of the cannabis use.

However, not all states where there is a lawful off-duty conduct statute or doctrine automatically protect cannabis use. Although Illinois'[47] and

---

35. **Arizona**: Ariz. Rev. Stat. Ann. § 36-2813(B); **Arkansas**: AR. Const. Amend. 98, § 3(f)(3)(A); **Connecticut**: Conn. Gen. Stat. Ann. § 21a-408p(b)(3); **Delaware**: 16 Del. C. § 4905A(a)(3); **Maine**: 22 M.R.S.A. § 2430-C(3) (Medical Cannabis Statute); **Minnesota**: Minn. Stat. Ann. § 152.32 subd. 3(c); **New Jersey**: N.J.S.A. § 24:6I-6.1(a)–(b); **New Mexico**: NMSA 1978, § 26-2B-9; **New York**: N.Y. Pub Health Law § 3369(1)-(2); **Oklahoma**: Okla. Stat. tit. 63, § 427.8(H); **Pennsylvania**: PA ST 35 P.S. § 10231.2103(b); **Rhode Island**: R.I. Gen Laws § 21-28.6-4(e); **Utah**: (applies to public employees only) Utah Code § 26-61a-111(2)(a)-(b); **West Virginia**: W. Va. Code § 16A-15-4(b)(1).
36. Cal. Lab. Code § 96; Cal. Lab. Code § 98.6(a); Cal. Lab. Code § 98.6(c)(2); Cal. Lab. Code § 98.6(d).
37. C.R.S. § 24-34-402.5(1).
38. Conn. Gen. Stat. Ann. § 31-51q.
39. ILCS 55/5(a).
40. Mass. Gen. Laws ch. 12, § 11H.
41. Minn. Stat. § 181.938 subd. 2; Minn. Stat. § 181.938 subd. 3.
42. Mont. Code Ann. § 39-2-313(1)–(2); Mont. Code Ann. § 39-2-313(3)–(5).
43. NRS 613.333(1); NRS 613.390.
44. N.Y. Labor Law § 201-d(2)(b)–(c); N.Y. Labor Law § 201-d(3)–(6); N.D.C.C. § 14-02.4-03(1).
45. N.D.C.C. § 14-02.4-03(1).
46. *In re* Grievance of Hurlburt, 2003 VT 2, 175 Vt. 40, 820 A.2d 186, 193 (citing *In re* Ackerson, 16 V.L.R.B. 262, 272 (1993)) ("In cases where an employer disciplines or dismisses an employee for off-duty conduct, there must be a nexus between off-duty conduct and employment to justify the employer's disciplinary action against an employee for that conduct.").
47. Illinois' recreational cannabis statute expressly amended the general off duty conduct statute, implying the legislature found it applicable to lawful off-duty cannabis use. *See* ILCS 55/5(a).

Massachusetts'[48] statutes have been held to apply to lawful off-duty cannabis use, the Colorado Supreme Court has held that an employer did not violate the lawful off-duty conduct statute by terminating the employment of an employee who lawfully used cannabis off duty.[49] The court reasoned that because cannabis use is unlawful under federal law, off-duty cannabis use was not considered lawful under the federal statute, even though it would be considered lawful under state law.[50] It remains to be seen whether other state statutes protect lawful off-duty cannabis use.

Adding further complexities to the analysis, even though states may have protections for lawful off-duty use of cannabis, 13 states have cannabis statutes that expressly state that employers may create and enforce zero-tolerance drug-free workplace policies.[51] There is scarce case law interpreting how these provisions interact with the anti-discrimination and lawful off-duty conduct statutes.[52] Employers will need to be mindful that the landscape in this area is changing and that courts will be providing guidance on these issues as more employees bring discrimination claims pursuant to the cannabis or lawful off-duty conduct statutes.

3.3 Post-Hiring Drug Testing for Cannabis Use

Many employers voluntarily conduct or are required to conduct employment drug testing in certain circumstances, such as random testing,[53]

---

48. Brown v. Woods Mullen Shelter/Boston Pub. Health Comm'n, 2017 WL 4287909, at *3 (Mass. Super 2017) (holding that the plaintiff had viable claims under the Massachusetts Civil Rights Act relating to being denied access to a homeless shelter due to possession of medical marijuana).

49. Coats v. Dish Network, 350 P.3d 849 (Colo. 2015).

50. *Id.* at 852–53.

51. **Arkansas**: AR Const. Amend. 98, § 3(f)(3)(B)(i); **California**: Cal. Health & Safety Code § 11362.45(f); **Colorado**: C.R.S.A. Const. Art. 18, § 16(6)(a); **Florida**: Fla. Stat. Ann. § 381.986(15)(a); **Georgia**: Ga. Code Ann. § 16-12-191(g); **Illinois**: 410 ILCS 130/50(b); 410 ILCS 130/50(c); 410 ILCS 705/10-50(a); 410 ILCS 705/10-50(c); **Massachusetts**: M.G.L. c. 94G § 2(e); **Michigan**: MCL 333.27954; **Montana**: Mont. Code Ann. § 50-46-320(5)(a); **Nevada**: NRS § 613.333; **Ohio**: Ohio Rev. Code Ann. § 3796.28(A)(3); **Utah**: Utah Code § 26-61a-111(4); **Washington**: RCW 69.51A.060(7); and **Washington, D.C.**: DC ST § 48-904.01(a)(1C).

52. *See, e.g.*, Swaw v. Safeway, Inc., C15-939 (W.D. Wash. Nov. 20, 2015) (employer can terminate employee for using marijuana even if employee is an authorized medical marijuana user and only used marijuana outside the workplace where employer has a drug-free work place policy).

53. Not all states permit random drug testing and practitioners should check their state and local drug testing statutes before conducting such testing. The following states do not permit random drug testing, unless the employee's position is considered "safety-sensitive": **California**: Loder v. City of Glendale, 14 Cal. 4th 846, 878 (1997) (holding that an employer's suspicionless drug testing of all employees regardless of the nature or duties of the position was unconstitutional); **Connecticut**: Conn. Gen. Stat. § 31-51x(b); **Massachusetts**: Webster v. Motorola, Inc., 637 N.E.2d 203 (Mass. 1994) (holding that an

post-accident testing,[54] and testing upon reasonable suspicion.[55] When conducting drug testing for cannabis use during employment, employers must first ensure that they are permitted to conduct a drug test under the desired circumstances in their jurisdiction before conducting a secondary analysis to determine whether taking an adverse action based on a positive drug test for cannabis will not violate any anti-discrimination or lawful off-duty conduct laws.

As discussed earlier in Section 3.1 On-Duty Use or Possession of Cannabis, no state (as of the date of this writing) requires an employer to permit the use of cannabis products on the employer's premises or permit an employee to be under the influence of cannabis products while on duty.

---

employer's random drug testing policy was in violation of state law because it did not distinguish between employees holding safety sensitive position and those who do not); **Minnesota**: MINN. STAT. ANN. § 181.951 subd. 4; **New Jersey**: Hennessey v. Coastal Eagle Point Oil, 609 A.2d 11 (N.J. 1992) (holding that random drug testing is permissible only when the employee is in a safety-sensitive position); **New Mexico**: NM Personnel Board Rules 1.7.8.11(E)(1) (for public employees only); **Rhode Island**: R.I. GEN. LAWS § 28-6.5-1; and **Vermont**: 21 V.S.A. § 513(b).

54. State drug testing statutes vary greatly, including whether complying with the drug testing requirements are mandatory or are part of a voluntary program, such as a workers' compensation premium reduction program. The intricacies surrounding the conditions and requirements of the various drug testing statutes are outside the scope of this chapter. regarding the circumstances surrounding the intricacies of the various ban the box statutes are outside the scope of this chapter. However, the following states have statutes that affirmatively address post-accident testing and should be reviewed before conducting such testing: **Alaska**: ALASKA STAT. ANN. § 23.10.620(c); **Arizona**: A.R.S. § 23-493.04(B); **Arkansas**: A.C.A. § 11-14-106(a)(5); **Georgia**: O.C.G.A. § 34-9-415(b)(5); **Maine**: 26 M.R.S.A. § 682(6)(C); **Minnesota**: MINN. STAT. ANN. §§ 181.951 subd. 5(3), (4); **Missouri**: § 288.045(4), RSMo; **Montana**: MONT. CODE. ANN. § 39-2-208(5); **Ohio**: OHIO ADMIN. CODE § 4123-17-58(C)(5)(b); **Oklahoma**: OKLA. STAT. tit. 40, § 554(3); **Rhode Island**: R.I. GEN. LAWS § 28-6.5-1 (not permitted); **Utah**: U.C.A. 1953 § 34-38-7(1), (2)(b); **West Virginia**: W. VA. CODE, § 21-3E-8(c)(3).

55. State drug testing statutes vary greatly, including whether complying with the drug testing requirements are mandatory or are part of a voluntary program, such as a workers' compensation premium reduction program. The intricacies surrounding the conditions and requirements of the various drug testing statutes are outside the scope of this chapter. However, the following states have statutes that affirmatively address reasonable suspicion testing and should be reviewed before conducting such testing: **Alaska**: ALASKA STAT. ANN. § 23.10.620(c); **Arizona**: A.R.S. § 23-493.04(B); **Arkansas**: A.C.A. § 11-14-104(a)(1); **Connecticut**: C.G.S.A. § 31-51x(a); **Florida**: FLA. STAT. § 440.102(4)(a)(2); **Georgia**: O.C.G.A. § 34-9-415(b)(2); **Maine**: 26 M.R.S.A. § 684(2); **Minnesota**: MINN. STAT. ANN. § 181.951 subd. 5; **Missouri**: § 288.045(4), RSMo; **Montana**: MONT. CODE. ANN. § 39-2-208(4); **New Mexico**: NM Personnel Board Rules 1.7.8.11(C) (for public employees in safety sensitive positions only); **Ohio**: OHIO ADMIN. CODE § 4123-17-58(C)(5)(c); **Oklahoma**: OKLA. STAT. tit. 40, § 554(2); **Rhode Island**: R.I. GEN. LAWS § 28-6.5-1; **Utah**: U.C.A. 1953 § 34-38-7(1), (2)(a); **Vermont**: 21 V.S.A. § 513(c); **West Virginia**: W. VA. CODE, § 21-3E-8(c).

But the difficulty for employers among the growing trend of the legalization of cannabis is determining whether an employee has engaged in on-duty use or possession or has been working under the influence of cannabis products. Unless an employer actively witnesses an employee consuming a cannabis product on company property or while conducting company business, or the employee admits to being under the influence, it is difficult to ascertain whether either of these two factors are satisfied. Prior to the legalization of cannabis use in some states, a positive urine test would have been sufficient to justify the termination of an employee's employment or other adverse action against the employee. However, conducting drug testing to obtain evidence of on-duty use or impairment is not as clear cut as employers may hope, and states have increasingly begun to enact statutory protections regarding employees' rights to use cannabis products, which may further constrict an employer's ability to rely on a positive cannabis drug test to make employment decisions.

Urinalysis, which is the most commonly used drug screening test, is not suitable for detecting cannabis impairment or recent cannabis use because the procedure identifies a THC metabolite that can be present in an individual's system for *weeks* after use—well after any effects of cannabis have worn off.[56] Positive urinalysis results, therefore, do not necessarily indicate current, on-the-job use or impairment.

New methodologies are being developed to determine whether cannabis products have been consumed close in time to testing, including a technique for testing oral fluid that reveals recent marijuana use by registering the presence of THC (not THC metabolites) while at the same time excluding long-past use, and detecting THC in breath via breathalyzers, where THC can stay for two to three hours.[57]

Though the development of tests capable of recognizing recent cannabis use is ongoing, there is currently no test that assesses the level of cannabis *impairment*, that is, what effect a certain concentration of THC has on an individual. Minimal research exists on how cannabis impairs a person's cognitive functions to the point of becoming a safety risk.[58]

---

56. Scott Macdonald, et al, *Testing for Cannabis in the Work-Place: A Review of the Evidence*, 105 Addiction 408 (2010).

57. Maggie Pavlick, *Researchers Create Breathalyzer that Can Detect Marijuana*, Phys. org (Aug. 27, 2019), https://phys.org/news/2019-08-breathalyzer-marijuana.html; Rich Haridy, *Accurate Marijuana Breathalyzers Are Almost Here, but Do THC Levels Even Mean Anything?*, New Atlas (Aug. 28, 2019), https://newatlas.com/health-wellbeing /marijuana-breathalyzers-blood-breath-thc-levels-law-driving/.

58. Michael Kraemer, Burkhard Madea & Cornelius Hess, *Detectability of Various Cannabinoids in Plasma Samples of Cannabis Users: Indicators of Recent Cannabis Use?*, 11 Drug Testing and Analysis 1498 (2019) ("Despite many studies on cannabinoid pharmacokinetics, the proposals of marker cannabinoids for recent cannabis use, and the introduction of mathematical models estimating the time frame between consumption

Because current tests available do not assess impairment, an individual who is being tested could conceivably consume a small dose of cannabis and not be impaired yet may still have THC detected in their breath or oral fluid. Employers should proceed cautiously before acting on the presence of THC in the person's breath or oral fluid without further evidence of impairment, because precipitous actions could subject an employer to a discrimination claim based on the employee's status as a medical cannabis card holder or a claim that the employer has violated the employee's right to engage in lawful off-duty conduct. Moreover, Arizona,[59] Connecticut,[60] Delaware,[61] Illinois,[62] Minnesota,[63] Nevada,[64] New Mexico,[65] New York,[66] Oklahoma,[67] Utah (for public employers only),[68] and Rhode Island[69] all have statutes that require employers to have evidence of impairment prior to taking adverse action against an employee following a positive drug screen.

Because there is currently no widely recognized or accepted definition of "impairment," employers should consider creating their own guidelines, with a close eye on any state-specific guidance,[70] on what the employer considers to be signs of impairment on the job and should train supervisors on these guidelines.[71] Employers should also craft clear procedures to be followed if on-the-job impairment is suspected, such as creating an observation report, removing an impaired employee from duty and having

---

and blood sampling, it is still challenging for forensic toxicologists to estimate the last time of cannabis exposure.").

59. A.R.S. § 36-2813 (no adverse employment actions permitted against medical marijuana users unless they were impaired during work hours or brought/used marijuana in the workplace); *see also* Whitmire v. Wal-Mart Stores Inc., 359 F. Supp. 3d 761 (D. Ariz. 2019) (noting that Arizona's Medical Marijuana Act prevents adverse employment action based solely on the presence of marijuana in a lawful user's system, and holding that Walmart could not fire an employee merely because marijuana metabolites were found in her urine; to establish lawful termination, Walmart would have had to present evidence of on-the-job impairment).

60. C.G.S.A. § 31-51x(a).

61. 16 DEL. C. § 4907A.

62. 410 ILCS 130/50(f).

63. MINN. STAT. ANN. § 152.32 subd. 3(c)(2).

64. NRS 613.333.

65. NMSA 1978, § 26-2B-9.

66. N.Y. PUB HEALTH LAW § 3369(1)–(2).

67. OKLA. STAT. tit. 63, § 427.8(H).

68. UTAH CODE ANN. § 26-61a-111(2)(b).

69. R.I. GEN. LAWS ANN. § 21-28.6-4(e)(1)(i), (2).

70. *See, e.g.,* 26 M.R.S.A. § 682(6); R.I. GEN. LAWS § 28-6.5-1.

71. Because impairment is largely undefined, employers may find it more attractive to have no drug-testing policy (or a policy not requiring testing for cannabis at any point). However, employers risk liability in these situations if an impaired employee causes harm to property, employees, or third parties.

another employee provide a second opinion before requiring the impaired employee to take a drug test. Such steps will help document the indicia of impairment so that employers can defend against a claim that any adverse action was based solely on a positive drug test for cannabis.

Employers who choose or are required to accommodate the use of medical cannabis use may also require employees to verify their medical cannabis card in the case of a positive drug screening result. Accommodating medical cannabis users are discussed in the following section, Section 3.4 Accommodating Cannabis Use.

Even in states that legalize cannabis use, employers may be permitted to take adverse action against employees who test positive for cannabis use without signs of impairment if the employee holds a job position or the employer is in an industry that is exempted from the state's statutes. These exemptions are discussed in further detail later in this chapter, in Section 4 Carve-Outs from State Cannabis Laws.

3.4 Accommodating Cannabis Use

3.4.1 Accommodating Cannabis Use under the Americans with Disabilities Act

Under federal law, employers have no obligation to accommodate employees who use cannabis—even employees who are using cannabis to address a physical or mental impairment that might constitute a disability under the Americans with Disabilities Act (ADA). Though physicians may recommend cannabis to treat an ADA-qualifying disability, the ADA exempts from its protections employees using drugs that are illegal under federal law.[72] Because cannabis users, including those using in states authorizing them to do so, are "current"[73] drug users under the ADA, they are not "qualified

---

72. The ADA provides qualified individuals protection against employment-related discrimination that is based on a disability. 42 U.S.C. § 12112(a). However, the "terms disability and qualified individual with a disability do not include individuals currently engaged in the illegal use of drugs, when the covered entity acts on the basis of such use." 29 C.F.R. § 1630.3(a); *see also* James v. City of Costa Mesa, 700 F.3d 394 (9th Cir. 2012) (affirming federal district court's decision to deny plaintiffs' application for preliminary injunction relief "on the ground that the ADA does not protect against discrimination on the basis of marijuana use, even medical marijuana use supervised by a doctor in accordance with state law, unless that use is authorized by federal law"). Notably, because cannabis use is not protected, employers generally do not have to keep positive marijuana drug tests confidential. However, an employer must nonetheless keep the results confidential if the results reveal the presence of a drug that can be lawfully prescribed, the employee's genetic information, an employee's disability, or other employee medical information. Employers should therefore keep drug test results separate from personnel files, as they would do for an employee's other medical records. Further, failing to keep drug test results confidential could result in employee defamation claims.

73. Importantly, "current" drug use does not necessarily have to occur on the same day as the adverse employment action. Whether drug use is "current" is defined on a case-by-case basis, looking to whether the drug use occurred recently enough to justify

individuals with disabilities" entitled to reasonable accommodations.[74] Stated differently, an employee using an illegal drug, including cannabis, has no protection from discrimination and no right to accommodation under the ADA, even if an employer takes an adverse employment action against the employee or refuses to accommodate the employee based entirely on that conduct.

Though *current* cannabis users are not protected from discrimination or entitled to accommodation under the ADA, employees recovering from *past* cannabis use or addiction may be entitled to reasonable accommodation under the ADA if the addiction may be considered a substantially limiting impairment.[75] And some courts have found that adverse actions against

---

an employer's reasonable belief that drug involvement is an ongoing problem. EEOC Technical Assistance Manual on the ADA § 8.3.

74. 42 U.S.C. § 12112(b)(5)(A); 29 C.F.R. § 1630.3(b); Baustian v. State of La., 910 F. Supp. 274 (E.D. La. 1996) (The court granted a motion to dismiss plaintiff's ADA claims on the grounds that use of marijuana disqualified him from being classified as a qualified individual with disabilities. Plaintiff was terminated seven weeks after being caught with marijuana while driving an assigned state vehicle. He claimed that his disability was an addiction to marijuana and that he was a recovering marijuana user. The court found that the "roughly seven weeks period between his being caught with the drugs and being terminated simply [was] not a sufficiently long enough time to avoid being classified as current drug use." The court also found that being drug-free for seven weeks was insufficient to classify the plaintiff as a recovering drug user under the safe-harbor provisions of the ADA.); Johnson v. City of Columbus, No. C2-99-531, 2001 WL 605040 (S.D. Ohio May 29, 2001) (granting defendant's motion for summary judgment against plaintiff for employment discrimination. Plaintiff was terminated from his job with the City of Columbus after testing positive for marijuana in violation of the city's drug and alcohol testing policy for commercial drivers. Plaintiff was a long-time marijuana user and sought protection under the ADA as a "qualified individual with a disability." In dismissing the case, the court found that current use of drugs is excluded from the definition of disability under the ADA.); *see also* Zenor v. El Paso Healthcare Sys., Ltd., 176 F.3d 847 (5th Cir. 1999) (affirming district court decision denying plaintiff's claim for employment discrimination after being terminated for cocaine use. The court held plaintiff was not a "qualified individual" under the ADA because his drug use was current. Further, plaintiff's self-reported drug use did not qualify him under the ADA's safe harbor provision); *but see* Kamakeeaina v. Armstrong Produce, Ltd., No. 18-CV-00480-DKW-RT, 2019 WL 1320032, at *5 (D. Haw. Mar. 22, 2019) (permitting an ADA failure-to-hire claim to proceed past the motion to dismiss stage because there was not alleged current drug use where the plaintiff alleged he informed the employer during his interview that he was registered under Hawaii's Medical Cannabis Program, where the employer told the plaintiff that if his drug test was positive, it would withdraw its offer of employment, and where the plaintiff said, he was 'prepared to have the offer taken off the table'").

75. *See* EEOC Technical Assistance Manual on the ADA § 8.5; *see also* Hartman v. City of Petaluma, 841 F. Supp. 946, 949 (N.D. Cal. 1994) (there must be "some indicia of dependence" to be considered substantially limiting a major life activity); Strausser v.

applicants or employees who test positive for cannabis could be considered a pretext for disability discrimination.[76]

Separately, although a cannabis user has no guaranteed rights or remedies under the ADA, he or she still may be entitled to rights guaranteed by other federal laws. For example, an employee may take authorized leave under the Family and Medical Leave Act for a condition that may be treated with cannabis.

3.4.2 Accommodating Medical Cannabis Use under State Law

Although federal law does not require accommodation of cannabis use for qualifying disabilities, state laws have tackled these issues in various ways. Although no state currently requires an employer to accommodate on-duty use or being under the influence of cannabis while on the job,[77] employers may need to accommodate an employee's lawful off-duty use of cannabis. States fall in different camps: (1) some jurisdictions expressly require accommodation of off-duty medical cannabis use; (2) some jurisdictions expressly do not require accommodation of off-duty medical cannabis use; and (3) some jurisdictions are silent on the issue. Each will be addressed in turn as follows.

(a) Jurisdictions Requiring Employers to Accommodate Medical Cannabis Use

Though the ADA offers no protections for the use of medical marijuana, as of the date of publication of this treatise, three states expressly require

---

Gertrude Hawk Chocolate, Inc., 2018 WL 1470796 (M.D. Pa. 2018) (stating that "in order for plaintiff to have a 'regarded as' claim under the ADA, defendant must have regarded or 'treated' him as suffering from an impairment listed in 42 U.S.C. 12102(2)(A) or 42 U.S.C. 12102(2)(B)." The court found that the employer's knowledge that plaintiff was in rehab for use of synthetic marijuana was not sufficient to "lead to the conclusion that the [employer] regarded him as impaired at the time he was terminated.").

76. *See, e.g.*, James v. City of Costa Mesa, 700 F.3d 394 (9th Cir. 2012) (holding that the ADA does not protect medical marijuana users claiming discrimination on the basis of their marijuana use, but also holding that a medical marijuana user may still be protected under the ADA if he or she has a condition that meets the ADA's definition of a disability); EEOC v. The Pines of Clarkston, Inc., 2:13-cv-14076 (E.D. Mich. 2015) (EEOC arguing that employer's stated reason for terminating employee, because he tested positive for marijuana, was pretext for disability discrimination).

77. *See* Section 3.1 On-Duty Use or Possession of Cannabis Products.

employers to accommodate an employee's off-duty use of medical cannabis: Massachusetts,[78] Nevada,[79] and New York.[80]

Employers with employees in these states should engage in the inter-
active process as they would for any applicant or employee with a disability to determine whether the employee has a disability, whether the
employer can accommodate the applicant or employee's medical cannabis use and the reasonable accommodations the employer can provide, and whether the accommodation would present an undue hardship
on the employer. Such accommodations may include permitting lawful
off-duty use of medical cannabis, excusing a positive drug test for cannabis where there were no signs of impairment at work, permitting an
employee to start work later or end a shift earlier to accommodate the
employee's need to use medical cannabis, and permitting the employee
to engage in microdosing so long as the employee is not under the influence while on duty.[81]

Note that Massachusetts[82] and Nevada[83] have recreational cannabis
statutes that appear to permit employers to have zero tolerance drug-free
workplace policies, and it is unclear how courts may interpret the accommodation requirements when such a policy is in place.

**(b) Jurisdictions in Which Employers to Do Not Need to Accommodate
Medical Cannabis Use**

The following states expressly do *not* require employers to accommodate
employees' off-duty medical cannabis use, either by statute or case law:

---

78. Allowing off-site use of medical marijuana may be a reasonable accommodation if it
does not cause an undue hardship on the employer's business. *See* Barbuto v. Advantage
Sales & Mktg., LLC, 477 Mass. 456, 78 N.E.3d 37 (2017) (court concluded that the
plaintiff "may seek a remedy through claims of handicap discrimination in violation of
G. L. c. 151B, and therefore reverse[d] the dismissal of plaintiff's discrimination claims").
79. NRS 453A.800.
80. N.Y. Pub Health Law § 3369(2).
81. Vince Polito & Richard J. Stevenson (2019), *A Systematic Study of Microdosing Psychedelics*,
14 Plos One e0211023 (2018) (generally explaining the concept of microdosing);
Samoon Ahmad, *The Paradoxical Power of Medicinal Microdosing*, Psychology Today
(Apr. 23, 2019), https://www.psychologytoday.com/us/blog/balanced/201904
/the-paradoxical-power-medicinal-microdosing (explaining the concept of microdosing
cannabis); Jennifer Alsever, *What Employers Need to Know about Employees Micro-dosing
Cannabis at Work*, Fortune (Apr. 23, 2020), https://fortune.com/2020/04/23/micro
-dosing-cannabis-at-work/ (exploring the possibility of whether microdosing cannabis
should be permitted at work).
82. Note that Massachusetts's recreational cannabis statute contains the provision and
not the medical cannabis statute. M.G.L. c. 94G § 2(e).
83. NRS 613.333.

California,[84] Colorado,[85] Georgia,[86] Hawaii,[87] Montana,[88] Ohio,[89] Oregon,[90] Utah,[91] and Washington.[92] In these states, employers do not need to accommodate the employee's medical cannabis use and can likely rely on federal law when taking adverse actions against employees/applicants who use medical cannabis or who test positive for cannabis. Employers should take care, nonetheless, that any adverse action based on medical cannabis use is not a proxy for disability discrimination or others forms of unlawful discrimination. Employers may need to offer alternate accommodations for employees with disabilities.

(c) Jurisdictions Silent on Accommodating Employee's Off-Duty Medical Cannabis Use

The remaining jurisdictions that permit medical cannabis use do not address whether employers must accommodate employees' off-duty medical cannabis use: Alaska, Arizona, Arkansas, Connecticut, Delaware, Florida,

---

84. Ross v. RagingWire Telecommunications, 174 P.3d 200 (Cal. 2008) (holding California's Compassionate Use Act does not require employers to accommodate medical marijuana use).

85. Colorado law provides that employers do not need "to accommodate the medical use of marijuana in any workplace, "Colo. Const. art. XVIII, § 14(10)(b), and courts have held that employers also do not need to accommodate off-duty use. *See* Coats v. Dish Network, LLC, 2015 CO 44, 350 P.3d 849 (employer may terminate employee due to "his state-licensed use of medical marijuana at home during nonworking hours"); Curry v. MillerCoors, Inc., No. 12-CV-02471-JLK, 2013 WL 4494307 (D. Colo. Aug. 21, 2013) ("a positive test for marijuana, whether from medical or any other use, is a legitimate basis for discharge under Colorado law").

86. O.C.G.A. § 16-12-191(g).

87. Lambdin v. Marriott Resorts Hosp. Corp., No. 16-cv-00004, 2017 WL 4079718, at *8–9 (D. Haw. Sept. 14, 2017) ("A state law decriminalizing marijuana use does not create an affirmative requirement for employers to accommodate medical marijuana use.").

88. Mont. Code Ann. § 50-46-320(4)(b); *see also* Johnson v. Columbia Falls Aluminum Co., 213 P.3d 789 (Mont. 2009) (employer has no duty to accommodate employee's use of medical marijuana); Carlson v. Charter Commc'ns, LLC, 2017 WL 3473316 (D. Mont., 2017) (stating that "[c]lear limitations in the unambiguous language of the [Montana Medical Marijuana Act] bar both Plaintiff's claims for wrongful discharge and for discrimination grounded in what is alleged to be his lawful marijuana use").

89. Ohio R.C. 3796.28.

90. Or. Rev. Stat. § 475.340; *see also* Emerald Steel Fabricators, Inc. v. Bureau of Labor & Indus., 230 P.3d 518 (Or. 2010).

91. Utah Code § 26-61a-111(4).

92. RCW 69.51A.060(4); RCW 69.51A.060(7); *see also* Swaw v. Safeway, Inc., C15-939 (W.D. Wash. Nov. 20, 2015) (employer can terminate employee for using marijuana even if employee is an authorized medical marijuana user and only used marijuana outside the workplace); *see also* Roe v. TeleTech Customer Care Mgmt. (Colo.), 247 P.3d 586, 591–92 (Wash. 2011) (state's Medical Use of Marijuana Act does not provide a civil cause of action for wrongful termination based on employee's authorized medical marijuana use).

Illinois, Louisiana, Maine, Maryland, Michigan,[93] Minnesota, Missouri, New Hampshire, New Jersey, New Mexico, North Dakota, Oklahoma, Pennsylvania, Rhode Island, Vermont, Washington, D.C., and West Virginia.

In these states, employers should analyze whether they are permitted to enforce zero-tolerance drug-free workplace policies[94] and regularly review relevant case law and pending legislation to gain an understanding of whether employees can credibly argue that the employer is required to accommodate their medical cannabis use.

3.4.3 Accommodating Recreational Cannabis Use under State Law

Although an employer may have an obligation to accommodate a medical cannabis user, there is an open question about whether an employer needs to accommodate an employee with a qualified disability who uses recreational cannabis to treat the disability and does not go through a state-sanctioned medical cannabis program. Employers likely do not need to accommodate this use where a health care provider is not recommending treatment with recreational cannabis.

4. Carve-Outs from State Cannabis Laws

Many state statutes exempt certain job positions and industries from their cannabis laws and protections.

4.1 Safety-Sensitive Positions

Many states have carve-outs for employees in "safety-sensitive" job positions; thus, employers have greater latitude to enforce zero-tolerance drug-free workplace policies with respect to employees in these positions. However, states vary as to which job positions qualify as "safety-sensitive" and when employers may enforce a zero-tolerance policy for those positions.[95] There are no guiding rules for legislators to review and consider when exempting certain "safety-sensitive" policies.[96] And, Connecticut, Hawaii, and Nevada

---

93. At least one case has held that an apartment manager did not need to accommodate the use of medical cannabis in the apartments by tenants as Michigan's was preempted by the Controlled Substances Act. *See* Forest City Residential Mgmt., Inc. *ex rel.* Plymouth Square Ltd. Dividend Hous. Ass'n v. Beasley, 71 F. Supp. 3d 715, 732 (E.D. Mich. 2014).

94. *See* Section 3.2 Off-Duty Use of Cannabis Products.

95. **Arkansas**: Ark. Const. amend. XCVIII, § 2(25); **Nevada**: Nev. A.B. 132.; **New Mexico**: N.M. Stat. Ann. § 26-2B-9 (b)(2), N.M. Stat. Ann. § 26-2B-3(Y); **New York City**: N.Y.C. Admin. Code § 9-107(31)(b)(1), N.Y.C. Admin. Code § 9-107(31)(b)(2)(C); **Oklahoma**: Okla. Stat. Ann. tit. 63, § 427.8(H)(2)(c), Okla. Stat. Ann. tit. 63, § 427.8(K)(1).

96. The National Safety Council is calling on employers to restrict marijuana use for those in safety sensitive positions, which it defines as those that impact the safety of the employee and the safety of others as a result of performing that job. National Safety Council, *Cannabis Impairment in Safety Sensitive Positions*, NSC.ORG (Oct. 21, 2019), https://www.nsc.org/in-the-newsroom/nsc-no-level-of-cannabis-use-acceptable-for-those

deny protections to medical cannabis users where the use would jeopardize health and safety.[97] It appears that Pennsylvania, Rhode Island, and West Virginia attempted to implement a safety-sensitive carve-out; however, ultimately, such statutes only relate to on-duty conduct and may be duplicative of other provisions.[98]

There are some positions that are by-and-large considered "safety sensitive," regardless of the jurisdiction. For example, employees working with children, school bus drivers, and health care workers often will be subject to a zero-tolerance policy and be unable to possess a medical marijuana card or engage in legal off-duty use of cannabis products.

In Arkansas, Nevada, New Mexico, and Oklahoma, employers may make the final call as to whether a certain position is "safety-sensitive."[99] In these instances, employers should document their analysis.

4.2 Exception for Compliance with Federal Law, Contracts, Funding, or Licensing Requirements

Laws prohibiting discrimination against cannabis users frequently include an exception for employers who would be in violation of a federal law, or who would lose a federal contract, funding, or licensing by complying with state law.[100]

-who-work-in-safety-sensitive-positions (follow "policy position" hyperlink). Similarly, The American College of Occupational and Environmental Medicine (ACOEM), an international society of more than 4,000 occupational physicians and associated professionals supports legislation permitting employers to prohibit employees in safety-sensitive positions from working while under the influence. American College of Occupational and Environmental Medicine, *Legalization of Marijuana—Implications for Workplace Safety*, ACOEM.ORG (Oct. 3, 2019), https://acoem.org/acoem/media/PDF -Library/Public_Affairs/Marijuana-Position-10-3-2019.pdf. This organization recommends that, until impairment is better defined, employers should set a period of time between the use of marijuana and the performance of safety-sensitive work. They also recommend that a position is safety-sensitive if impairment would: increase safety and health risks; adversely affect the environment through potential contamination; jeopardize the community through property damage or public peril; or involve the use of firearms, emergency response, and/or judgment that has an immediate impact on the life and health of others. *Id.* at 2.

97. *Id.*

98. **Pennsylvania**: 35 P.S. § 10231.510(4); **Rhode Island**: 21 R.I. Gen. Laws Ann. § 21-28.6-4(e)(1)(ii-iii); **West Virginia**: W. Va. Code §§ 16A-5-10(4).

99. *See* footnote 93.

100. **Arizona**: Ariz. Rev. Stat. Ann. § 36-2813(B); **Connecticut**: Conn. Gen. Stat. Ann. § 21a-408p; **Delaware**: Del. Code Ann. tit. 16, § 4905A(a)(3); **Illinois**: 410 Ill. Comp. Stat. Ann. 130/40(a)(1), 410 Ill. Comp. Stat. Ann. 130/50(d), 410 Ill. Comp. Stat. Ann. 705/10-50(g); **Maine**: Me. Rev. Stat. tit. 22, § 2430-C(3); **Massachusetts**: 935 MA ADC 501.840(2)(f); **Minnesota**: Minn. Stat. Ann. § 152.32(3)(c); **New Jersey**: N.J. Stat. Ann. § 24:6I-6.1(c)(2); **New Mexico**: N.M. Stat. § 26-2B-9 (A); **New York**: N.Y. Pub. Health Law § 3369(2); **New York City**: N.Y.C. Admin. Code § 9-107(31)(b)(2);

However, employers have had a difficult time using these exceptions to their advantage in litigation. For example, employers with federal contracts or who are the recipients of grants must comply with the Federal Drug-Free Workplace Act (DFWA).[101] The DFWA requires federal contractors and grant recipients to prohibit the "unlawful . . . use of a controlled substance" by employees in their workplace as a condition of employment. But, the DFWA does not require federal contractors to conduct drug testing for cannabis use,[102] and courts have rejected arguments that the DFWA imposes such a condition on federal contractors and grant recipients when trying to defend against claims of discrimination based on cannabis use. For example, in *Noffsinger v. SSC Niantic Op. Co., LLC, d/b/a Bride Brook Nursing & Rehab. Ctr.*, the employer argued that, as a federal contractor, it was exempt from Connecticut's anti-discrimination provision, relying on the medical cannabis statute's provision that allows employers to refuse to hire medical cannabis users if "required by federal law or required to obtain funding."[103] As a government contractor, the employer was obligated to comply with the DFWA, which, it argued, makes it unlawful for an employer to allow employees to use illegal drugs. On review, Connecticut U.S. District Court rejected the employer's arguments, concluding that the DFWA neither requires drug testing in the workplace nor regulates an employee's off-duty marijuana use.[104] The district court also rejected the employer's argument that the federal False Claims Act barred it from hiring the plaintiff, where the employer argued its employment of someone who uses medical cannabis in violation of federal law would amount to a defrauding of the federal government.[105]

Oklahoma: OKLA. STAT. ANN. tit. 63, § 425(b), OKLA. STAT. ANN. tit. 63, § 427.8(H); **Oregon**: OR. REV. STAT. ANN. § 475B.020(3)-(5); **Pennsylvania**: 35 PA. STAT. ANN. § 10231.2103(b)(3); **Rhode Island**: 21 R.I. GEN. LAWS ANN. § 21-28.6-4(e)(2); **Utah**: UTAH CODE ANN. § 26-61a-111(2); **West Virginia**: W. VA. CODE ANN. § 16A-15-4(b)(3).

101. 41 U.S.C. §§ 8101–8106.

102. *See, e.g.*, Harris v. Aerospace Testing All., No. 1:07-CV-94, 2008 WL 111979, at *4 (E.D. Tenn. Jan. 7, 2008) ("The language of the statute does not support the theory the act requires or regulates drug screening."); Santiago v. Greyhound Lines, Inc., 956 F. Supp. 144, 152 (N.D.N.Y. 1997) ("The Drug–Free Workplace Act requires federal contractors and grant recipients to discourage and punish drug use amongst employees. Although the Act does not mandate drug screening . . . it is fair to say it encourages it . . ."); Parker v. Atlanta Gas Light Co., 818 F. Supp. 345, 347 (S.D. Ga. 1993) ("The statute establishes no requirement for drug testing.").

103. Noffsinger v. SSC Niantic Operating Co., LLC, 338 F. Supp. 3d 78, 84 (D. Conn. 2018).

104. *Id.*

105. *Id.* The District Court ultimately granted the plaintiff's discrimination claim due to the employer's refusal to hire plaintiff (a medical marijuana user) after she tested positive for cannabis. *Id.* at 86.

Employers have also argued that complying with state cannabis laws would cause them to violate the Controlled Substances Act. Most courts have held that no such violation exists.[106]

4.3 Job Positions Regulated by Federal Agencies

Some positions may be regulated by federal agencies, and individuals in these positions (and their employers) may be required to abide by the safety standards imposed by such agencies. For example, the U.S. Department of Transportation (DOT)'s Drug and Alcohol Testing Regulation for safety-sensitive transportation employees does not allow medical or recreational marijuana use that is legal under state law to serve as a valid medical explanation for a positive drug test that would otherwise be disqualifying for transportation safety-sensitive positions.[107] Similarly, the U.S. Department

---

106. Lewis v. Am. Gen. Media, 355 P.3d 850, 858 (N.M. Ct. App. 2015) (finding New Mexico's medical marijuana act was not preempted by the CSA); Vialpando v. Ben's Auto. Servs., 331 P.3d 975, 976 (N.M. Ct. App. 2014) (same); Chance v. Kraft Heinz Foods Co., No. CV K18C-01-056 NEP, 2018 WL 6655670, at *3–4 (Del. Super. Ct. Dec. 17, 2018) ("[T]he CSA itself explicitly confirms Congress's intent that the statute not preempt a state law 'unless there is a positive conflict between that provision of this subchapter and that State law so that the two cannot consistently stand together.' Therefore, the Court finds that conflict preemption does not apply because the anti-discrimination provisions of the DMMA do not pose an obstacle to the objectives of Congress nor do they render compliance with both federal and state law impossible. The DMMA does not require employers to participate in an illegal activity (the unauthorized manufacture, dissemination, dispensing or possession of controlled substances) but instead merely prohibits them from discriminating based upon medical marijuana use."); Hager v. M & K Construction, 2020 WL 218390, at *8 (N.J. Super. A.D. 2020) (finding New Jersey's medical marijuana act was not preempted by the CSA); *but see* Bourgoin v. Twin Rivers Paper Company, LLC, 187 A.3d 10, 22, 2018 ME 77, ¶¶ 29–30 (Me. 2018) (CSA preempted Maine's medical cannabis act when an employer was subject to a workers' compensation order that required it to subsidize an employee's acquisition of medical marijuana).

107. 49 C.F.R. § 40.151(e). The Department of Transportation has reiterated that "the state initiatives will have no bearing on the Department of Transportation's regulated drug testing program. The Department of Transportation's Drug and Alcohol Testing Regulation—49 C.F.R. pt. 40—does not authorize the use of Schedule I drugs, including marijuana, for any reason. Therefore, Medical Review Officers (MROs) will not verify a drug test as negative based upon learning that the employee used "recreational marijuana" when states have passed "recreational marijuana" initiatives. We also firmly reiterate that an MRO will not verify a drug test negative based upon information that a physician recommended that the employee use "medical marijuana" when states have passed "medical marijuana" initiatives." U.S. DOT Office of Drug and Alcohol Policy and Compliance Notice, https://transit-safety.fta.dot.gov/DrugAndAlcohol/Regulations/Interpretations/RecreationalMarijuana/Default.aspx.

of Energy,[108] U.S. Nuclear Regulatory Commission,[109] U.S. Department of Defense,[110] Federal Aviation Administration,[111] Pipeline Hazardous Materials Safety Administration,[112] and Federal Railroad Administration[113] require mandatory drug testing that includes testing for cannabis, and disqualify a person from holding the job position if the person tests positive for cannabis. Employers should also check with state law to determine whether employers in certain industries, like public transportation, are required to drug test employees for cannabis use.

5. Related Topics Associated with Cannabis Use and Employment

Additional employment-related topics important for employers and their counsel to consider in conjunction with cannabis use and the workplace include eligibility for workers' compensation benefits and unemployment benefits.

5.1 Workers' Compensation Benefits

Ordinarily, state workers' compensation laws and benefits provide the exclusive remedies for employees who have suffered workplace injuries or illnesses; however, employees who are injured at work while "under the influence" of cannabis may be denied benefits in some states.[114]

Workers' compensation benefits typically include payment for medical treatment associated with work-related injuries. Arizona,[115] Louisiana,[116] Oklahoma,[117] Rhode Island,[118] and Vermont,[119] however, have statutes that expressly state employers and their worker's compensation insurers are not

---

108. 10 C.F.R. § 707.11; The U.S. Department of Energy has reiterated that "[t]he Mandatory Guidelines identify marijuana as a Schedule I drug under the Controlled Substance Act. As such, all DOE contractors covered by 10 CFR 707 will continue to be tested for marijuana at the established cut off levels noted in the Mandatory Guidelines. Therefore, any use of marijuana is illegal under federal law, regardless of state law." Energy. gov Offices, *Policy Flash—Recent State Initiatives on "Recreational" Marijuana use*, https://www.energy.gov/ehss/downloads/policy-flash-recent-state-initiatives-recreational-marijuana-use (last visited Apr. 19, 2020).
109. 10 C.F.R. §§ 26.31(c), (d); *id.* § 26.185(j)(6).
110. 48 C.F.R. 252.223-7004(b)-(c); *id.* 25.223-7004 § 252.223-7004(a)(2).
111. 14 C.F.R. § 120.107; *id.* § 120.109.
112. 49 C.F.R. § 199.105.
113. *Id.* § 219.701(a).
114. *See, e.g.,* Cal. Lab. Code § 3600(a)(4); Cal. Lab. Code § 5705(b).
115. A.R.S. § 36-2814 (A)(1).
116. La. Stat. Ann. § 40:1046(J).
117. Okla. Stat. tit. 63, § 427.8(I)(2).
118. R.I. Gen. Laws § 21-28.6-7(b)(1).
119. 18 V.S.A. § 4474c(b)(4).

required to pay for medical marijuana. And, state courts have reached differing opinions on whether employers and their workers' compensation carriers must reimburse an employee for medical marijuana costs.[120]

5.2 Unemployment Benefits

Many states allow employers to challenge claims for unemployment benefits in cases where the claimant was terminated for misconduct. Illegal drug use or violation of a drug-free workplace policy could, in some circumstances, constitute misconduct. However, at least one appellate court overturned the denial of unemployment benefits to employees and held that employees who carried registered medical marijuana identification cards and used the drug in accordance with the state's medical cannabis law, but were terminated after testing positive for cannabis, were entitled to unemployment benefits.[121] Yet, another appellate court held that an employee's use of medical cannabis was prohibited under the employer's zero-tolerance drug policy prohibiting "illegal drugs," and, thus, the former employee was properly denied unemployment benefits.[122] Further, Ohio's medical cannabis statute (the only one to do so) expressly states that a person whose employment was terminated for using medical cannabis in violation of an employer's zero-tolerance drug-free workplace policy will not be entitled to unemployment benefits.[123] These examples highlight that the determinations of whether an employee's lawful use of cannabis will result in a denial of unemployment benefits is state-specific and still developing.

---

120. *Compare* Vialpando v. Ben's Auto. Servs. & Redwood Fire & Cas., 331 P.3d 975 (N.M. Ct. App. 2014) (holding held that an employer and its workers' compensation carrier must reimburse an employee for medical marijuana costs) *with* Bourgoin v. Twin Rivers Paper Co., LLC, 187 A.3d 10 (Me. 2018) (holding employer not required to pay for workers' compensation claimant's medical marijuana because that would conflict with federal law).

121. Braska v. Challenge Mfg. Co., 307 Mich. App. 340, 365 (2014).

122. Beinor v. Indus. Claim Appeals Office, 262 P.3d 970, 977–78 (Colo. App. 2011).

123. Ohio R.C. 3796.28(B); Ohio R.C. 4141.29(D).

5

Cannabis and Real Property

Jaci McNally, Neva Wagner

As the cannabis industry continues to grow in all areas, from medicinal and recreational marijuana to hemp and its derivatives, everyone from investors and banks to insurance companies and landlords is noticing this market's potential. However, operating, contracting with, or providing services to a cannabis-related business is not without risks, and participants in the commercial real estate industry may find more questions than answers as they contemplate the merits and disadvantages of opening their doors to the cannabis industry. This chapter provides an overview of some real estate issues to be considered when acquiring, developing, financing, and leasing real property for use in the cultivation, processing, retail sale, or storage of cannabis products.

1. Acquisition of Real Property for Cannabis-Related Uses

1.1 Real Estate Broker Issues

In non-cannabis transactions, the real estate broker (broker) typically plays an integral role from start to finish. However, brokers have reason to be concerned when the property to be acquired, leased, or sold involves the cultivation, manufacturing, storage, or sale of cannabis products. As a general rule, brokers owe certain fiduciary duties to their clients, including duties of loyalty, disclosure, obedience, reasonable care and diligence, confidentiality, and accounting. Determining the exact scope and applicability of these duties can be complex and, in some states, depends heavily on the written agreement between the broker and the seller or buyer (or both). For example, does a broker have a duty to research and/or disclose all local laws, ordinances, and other risks that may impact an owner of a building used for the sale of recreational marijuana? If so, would that duty differ if the owner planned to sell just medicinal marijuana? What happens if the broker discloses certain information but fails to disclose a recently passed amendment to an ordinance? Can that broker be liable for a breach of fiduciary duty? The answers are currently unclear, and, therefore, brokers need to carefully weigh the risks versus the rewards when working with cannabis companies and properties. That said, for brokers who are not deterred by these uncertainties, the reward can be substantial, as the demand for property to be used for cannabis-related business is on the rise. In fact, according to a fall 2019 study by the National Association of Realtors, in states in which medicinal and recreational marijuana use is legal, brokers reported a (1) 34 percent to 42 percent increase in demand for warehouses, (2) 18 percent to 19 percent increase in demand for storefronts, and (3) 16 percent to 21 percent increase in demand for vacant land.[1] Similarly, most brokers did not report any system-wide decreases in the value of land surrounding dispensaries or grow facilities.[2]

1.2 Financing Issues

Cannabis companies may struggle to finance their real estate acquisitions, as investors and banks are wary of such transactions due to the divergence between state and federal law. Although the budding industry has a promising future in states that have authorized medicinal and/or recreational use, federal laws and regulations leave financiers exposed to increased liabilities.

1.2.1 Investors

Investors may be reluctant for a number of reasons. First, investors may face federal criminal charges for aiding and abetting a marijuana business by financing it.[3] Between 2013 and January 2018, state-legal marijuana businesses have relied on the Cole Memo, in which the Department of Justice would not enforce the federal prohibition in states with strong and effective regulation, except for situations in which a lack of enforcement would undermine the DOJ's eight federal priorities. In January 2018, U.S. Attorney General Jeff Sessions rescinded the Cole Memo and thereby eliminated the slight, but express, protection it offered. Despite this rescission, DOJ policy has remained consistent in practice since 2013.

Investors may also be deterred from selecting cannabis companies as an investment vehicle, because such companies are subject to higher effective tax rates than companies in other industries. Pursuant to Internal Revenue Code 280E, cannabis companies cannot deduct their ordinary and necessary business expenses related to the sale of marijuana. As a result, the

---

1. National Association of Realtors, *Marijuana and Real Estate: A Budding Issue* (February 2020).
2. *Id.*
3. Hilary Bricken, *Funding and Financing a Marijuana Business*, 13 SCITECH LAW 6 (2017).

effective tax rate would exceed the corporate tax rates paid by most other businesses,[4] and therefore, the return for investors is less tempting.

Third, most legalized cannabis states require disclosure of investors' identities and state approval of the investors. As with liquor licensing, the extensive nature of these disclosures can make investors hesitant. Additionally, in some states, all investors must also be in-state residents, which further limits the pool of prospective investors, and those states that do not have a residence requirement often give in-state residents an easier approval process.

1.2.2 Banks and Other Financial Institutions

Financial institutions are also leery of working with cannabis companies, because doing so increases the institution's administrative burden and exposes them to certain regulatory risk. Both Department of Treasury regulations and case law[5] provide that banks cannot facilitate criminal activity. As the possession and sale of marijuana is illegal under federal law, most banks (excluding some state cooperative and local banks) are hesitant to do business with cannabis-related companies. Most loan agreements, mortgages, deeds of trust, and related security agreements require that borrowers keep the subject property in compliance with all applicable laws and prohibit use of the property for illegal activities. Although hemp and hemp derivatives are not treated the same under federal law as marijuana, which contains higher levels of tetrahydrocannabinol (THC), the risk-adverse nature of the financial industry tends toward a cautious approach, as more fully discussed in the final paragraph of this subsection.

In addition to lending issues, banks are also reluctant to provide customary banking arrangements like bank accounts and credit card process to cannabis companies, as banks want to comply with strict federal requirements to minimize risk exposure. Banks that desire to do business with cannabis companies must comply with the Financial Crimes Enforcement Network (FinCEN) 2014 regulations. These regulations establish a number of due diligence requirements as a precondition to opening accounts and conducting business with cannabis companies, including (1) verifying that the business is state licensed and registered; (2) reviewing the license application documents; (3) requesting state enforcement authorities provide information about the business; (4) developing an understanding of the type of business activity, including products sold and customers served; (5) monitoring publicly available sources for adverse information regarding the business; (6) monitoring of suspicious activity; and (7) updating diligence materials on a regular basis. Due to their cash-only operations, cannabis companies are subject to suspicious activities reports (SARs),

---

4. *Id.*
5. *See* Fourth Corner CU v. Fed. Reserve Bank of Kansas City, No. 15-CB-01633 (D. Colo. 2016).

which provide that cash deposits in excess of $10,000 must be disclosed to FinCEN. Thus, SARs increase scrutiny from federal regulators and require a significant amount of due diligence, all of which increases the bank's costs. Thus, most banks find the FinCEN regulations and the SARs requirements to be too onerous and the risk too great.

1.2.3 Hemp and Hemp Derivatives

Fortunately, for prospective investors and financial institutions, not all cannabis companies have the same risk profile. CBD, hemp, and hemp-derivative companies offer a lower risk option for investors thanks to the 2018 Farm Bill (the Farm Bill).

The Farm Bill removes hemp from the Controlled Substances Act, creating new opportunities for lawful cultivation, possession, sale, and distribution. Pursuant to the Farm Bill, hemp's distinguishing characteristic is its lower concentration of THC (no more than 0.3 percent on a dry weight basis). However, the Farm Bill still places stringent compliance requirements on companies. For example, the Farm Bill requires land registration, annual testing of the plants/products, and a hemp disposal procedure. Thus, hemp companies still need to jump through a number of regulatory hoops. Further, although negligent violations of the Farm Bill do not have criminal repercussions, violating hemp producers still face serious consequences, including increased reporting requirements and a five-year prohibition on its hemp production, all of which could be a serious concern for financial backers.

Therefore, although the Congress hoped the Farm Bill would bring stability to the industry, it has had limited success bringing comfort to commercial real estate financiers. Furthermore, while some hemp and hemp-derivative companies have succeeded in securing loans through regional banks, these are exceptions rather than the rule, as many financial institutions continue to limit their involvement with the hemp industry.[6] In one example, U.S. Bank's subsidiary, Elavon, has opted to no longer offer payment processing services to hemp farmers and CBD companies.[7] However, the hemp industry may change rapidly as major companies, like Edward Jones, are analyzing the provisions of the 2018 Farm Bill, state laws, and the related regulations to determine what spectrum of banking, investment, insurance, and financial planning services is lawful and appropriate for hemp and hemp-derivative companies.[8] Furthermore, in the 2020 crop

---

6. Nick Thomas, *Hemp Companies Left Looking for Banking Alternatives*, Hemp Industry Daily (Apr. 15, 2019), https://hempindustrydaily.com/hemp-companies-left-looking-for-banking-alternatives/.
7. *Id.*
8. *Id.*

year, hemp producers may qualify for FSA farm loans; however, the details of these FSA farm loan programs are not yet available.[9]

1.3 Title Insurance Issues and Real Estate Due Diligence

In a standard real estate transaction, a title insurance company is engaged to, among other duties, issue a title insurance policy to the buyer. Generally, the title insurance policy will insure that the buyer has good title to the underlying real estate, subject to any matters of record. Unfortunately, in light of the conflict between federal and state law regarding the legality of cannabis, title insurance companies have limited their involvement in cannabis-related transactions, including refusing to (1) insure title to real property being used for a cannabis business, (2) act as an escrow agent for parties conducting a cannabis business, and (3) handle the transfer of funds or otherwise act as a depository of funds derived from cannabis operations.[10] In fact, Chicago Title Insurance Company and Fidelity National Title currently include the following language in their title commitments:

> Notice: Please be aware that due to the conflict between federal and state laws concerning the cultivation, distribution, manufacture or sale of marijuana, the Company is not able to close or insure any transaction involving Land that is associated with these activities.

For hemp and hemp-derivative companies, title companies are still hesitant to facilitate a hemp transaction and will review proposed transactions on a case-by-case basis.[11] One of the risks is that the title company may be unable to distinguish a hemp operation from that of other forms of cannabis, as the two look substantially similar on the surface. Additionally, although hemp is legal, it is remains subject to some significant restrictions, including land registration, annual testing, and disposal procedures, as set forth in the Farm Bill. Thus, title companies are acutely aware of the regulatory hoops through which their prospective insured would need to jump.[12]

Due to the unavailability of title policies to provide protection against title-related claims, prospective buyers should obtain title searches, an

---

9. U.S. Dep't of Agriculture, *Hemp and Farm Programs*, FARMERS.GOV, https://www.farmers.gov/manage/hemp.

10. Wendy S. Goffe, Planning for Unique and Regulated Assets: Art, Guns, Wine, Planes and Cannabis, The American Law Institute Continuing Legal Education, June 17–21, 2019; TITLE COMPANIES AND MARIJUANA BUSINESS IN OREGON, TICOR TITLE, http://www.ticornw.com/wp-content/uploads/2016/11/Title-Companies-and-Marijuana-Business-OR-.pdf (last accessed Apr. 22, 2020); *What Property Owners Need to Know About Title Insurance and Marijuana Facilities*, https://www.fraserlawfirm.com/blog/2017/10/could-property-owners-or-tenants-who-grow-process-or-sell-marijuana-make-their-property-tough-to-sell/ (last accessed Apr. 22, 2020).

11. Steve Tjaden, *Marijuana and the Title Industry*, OLD REPUBLIC TITLE (Apr. 17, 2019), https://www.oldrepublictitle.com/blog/marijuana-and-the-title-industry.

12. *Id.*

updated survey, and otherwise perform thorough due diligence of the contemplated real estate. In particular, cannabis companies must be keenly aware of any private restrictions on the use of their property. Although some of these use restrictions may be straightforward (e.g., a CC&R[13] that states that the property "shall not be used for the sale of intoxicating substances, including alcohol and cannabis"), others may be less clear (e.g., a CC&R that forbids "any unlawful use" in a state that has legalized recreational cannabis). Further, in certain instances, older and/or outdated private restrictions may need to be modified to clarify the permissibility of cannabis uses on the subject property.

1.4 Property Insurance

Property insurance reimburses a property owner if the owner's real or personal property is damaged, and the reimbursement process can become much more complicated when the property is used for a cannabis-related business. One such complication can arise if a court interprets the federal cannabis ban as supporting a public policy against insuring losses suffered by a cannabis business.[14] For example, a federal court in Hawaii held that "an insured growing cannabis for personal use in compliance with state law could not recover under her homeowners policy because the federal public policy against cannabis trumps the express terms of an insurance policy."[15] However, other federal courts have taken a different approach. In Colorado, a federal court required an insurance carrier to cover an insured's losses where the policy was written for a state-legal cannabis company and expressly covered "inventory" but excluded "contraband."[16] Thus, courts wield wide discretion in their interpretation of property insurance coverage for this industry.

2. Commercial Leasing for Cannabis-Related Uses

Commercial landlords may be tempted to lease to cannabis companies for many reasons, including high demand and the ability to charge above-market rent. In fact, it is not uncommon for the rent under a marijuana lease to be two to three times higher than the rent charged to other tenants in the same market or even the same building.[17] In addition, leasing

---

13. When used in this article "CC&R" refers to any private document (i.e., which has been recorded in the public record) that creates covenants, restrictions, or easements.

14. Francis J. Mootz III & Jason Horst, *Cannabis and Insurance*, 23 Lewis & Clark L. Rev. 893 (2019).

15. *Id.* at 901.

16. *Id.* at 902–03.

17. Mark S. Hennigh & Benton B. Bodamer, Cannabis and Commercial Real Estate: Business Opportunity and Legal Conundrum, 2019 U.S. Shopping Center Law Conference, October 25, 2019 ("Cannabis & Comm. Real Estate").

to cannabis companies can help overcome the low occupancy challenges that many landlords face as traditional retailers continue to close many of their brick and mortar locations. It should be noted, however, that the risks associated with CBD, hemp, and hemp derivatives are notably different from other cannabis products, particularly because hemp is not a controlled substance under the Controlled Substances Act.

Notwithstanding the potential advantages just highlighted, landlords that lease to cannabis companies may be subject to federal criminal and civil penalties. Pursuant to section 856(a)(1-2) of the Controlled Substances Act, it is illegal to:

> (1) knowingly open, lease, rent, use, or maintain any place, whether permanently or temporarily, for the purpose of manufacturing, distributing, or using any controlled substance; [or] (2) manage or control any place, whether permanently or temporarily, either as an owner, lessee, agent, employee, occupant or mortgagee, and knowingly and intentionally rent, lease, profit from, or make available for use, with or without compensation, the place for the purpose of unlawfully manufacturing, storing, distributing, or using a controlled substance.[18]

Criminal penalties for violation of this section include up to 20 years' imprisonment and a fine of not more than $500,000 for an individual, or a fine of $2 million for a company. The civil penalty for violation of this section is a fine of not more than the greater of $250,000 or two times the gross receipts, known or estimated, from each violation of the section. This risk cannot be contracted away or shifted to a tenant.

In addition to the possibility of federal liability, landlords face several other risks and unique challenges when leasing to cannabis companies, including (1) forfeiture (as discussed in Section 3), (2) property insurance issues (as previously discussed), (3) payment of rent in cash, (4) mortgage loan restrictions, (5) reluctant buyers of the real estate, (6) environmental concerns related to the storage and disposal of cannabis products, (7) lengthy tenant occupancy delays due to licensing issues, (8) private and public use restrictions, (9) tarnished image of the establishment, and (10) refinancing issues. Most of these risks and considerations apply equally to both hemp-related companies and other cannabis company tenants.

2.1 Leasing Due Diligence and Loan Document Review

Due diligence is essential for both landlord and tenant when properties are leased for cannabis-related purposes. Not only can local and state laws create issues, but private use restrictions contained in the chain of title and a CC&R may present issues for both landlords and tenants. This is especially

---

18. 21 U.S.C. § 856.

true if the terms and conditions related to the restrictions are unclear. For instance, if a CC&R includes the requirement that the property is to be used exclusively as a "first class" business operation, the landlord must consider the possibility that a cannabis company may not be a "first class" business operation. Therefore, it is imperative that landlords conduct the same level of property-level due diligence that a buyer of real estate would conduct.

Additionally, landlords must be cautious to not violate the terms of existing loan agreements, mortgages, and similar financing instruments to which it is a party. Landlords should carefully review such documentation to ensure that leasing the property for cannabis operations will not (1) breach any of the representations made by the landlord in the loan documents, (2) violate any ongoing operating covenants that the landlord agreed to undertake in the loan documents, or (3) trigger a default under the loan documents.

2.2 Enforcement Issues

Generally, a lease made for an illegal purpose is considered unenforceable.[19] Although this is less likely to be an issue in state courts in jurisdictions where cannabis is not illegal, a landlord or tenant may face challenges to the validity of a lease when seeking to enforce the agreement in a federal court if the tenant's permitted use includes cannabis products that are subject to the Controlled Substances Act. Therefore, in an attempt to reduce the risk that the lease will be unenforceable due to the federal prohibition on cannabis, the parties should choose the state in which the real property is located for both the governing law and the forum selection clauses of the lease. However, it is important to note that contracts for an illegal purpose are not always unenforceable. For example, if the contract can be enforced in a way that does not require illegal conduct, the court may provide relief.[20]

2.3 Drafting Considerations

Since the risks and requirements of leasing for cannabis-related uses (including hemp and hemp-derivative uses) can differ significantly from other commercial tenants, leases with cannabis tenants need to be tailored to include certain lease provisions or clauses that are not found in standard commercial lease forms. Some examples are highlighted next.

2.3.1 License Contingency or Condition Subsequent Clause

Some states, like California, require a prospective operator to obtain a signed lease or other authorization from the landlord to operate a cannabis business on the premises before the state will issue a cannabis

---

19. *See* Marshall E. Tracht, *Leasing: Marijuan Dispensary Leases in Question,* 47-JUL REAL ESTATE L. REP. NL 5 (July 2017).
20. *Id.*

license.[21] This requirement creates an issue for landlords who must enter into a lease agreement with a company that is not yet authorized to engage in the permitted use of the property. As a result, landlords should be sure that the lease includes a license contingency, which provides the landlord with a unilateral termination right (or both parties a mutual termination right) if the tenant fails to obtain the required licenses and permits within a specified period of time.[22]

2.3.2 Permitted Use

The use clause within a cannabis lease needs to be narrowly tailored, and the parties should address the tenant's anticipated use and any restricted activities that could be considered ancillary uses if not expressly forbidden. Additionally, landlords should consider including requirements that tenants permitted use be in compliance with the licenses/permits that are issued to the tenant, and that a failure to maintain such licenses/permits in good standing is a violation of the lease agreement. At a minimum, the use clause should specify (1) whether the property will be used for CBD, hemp, hemp derivatives, or medical or recreational marijuana (or a combination thereof); (2) whether the property will be used for cultivation, processing, transporting, storage, or selling of cannabis; and (3) that the tenant will comply with state and local laws. Furthermore, landlords may desire the ability to review a hemp tenant's records related to the annual testing of its products in order to confirm that such tenant is not violating its permitted use due to the THC content of its products (i.e., confirm that a hemp tenant's plants or products contain no more than 0.3 percent THC).

Lease Examples:[23]

- The Premises shall be used by Tenant to carry out a lawful cannabis business in accordance with [State Cannabis Law and Regulations] for the following uses and for no other purpose: [List permitted uses].
- Permitted Use: Agricultural growth, propagation, processing and dispensing of agricultural materials (including cannabis), industrial and office space, in accordance with current zoning for the Premises and in accordance with Applicable Laws. Permitted Use shall include the cultivation, propagation, and processing of cannabis plant parts and resins into products, the storage of same for transport, operation of a registered cannabis dispensary, and such other related use or uses permitted under Applicable Laws.

---

21. David W. Wensley & Amir Sadr, *Space to Grow: Legalization of Marijuana Presents Significant Opportunities for Property Owners Looking to Cash in on California's Budding Cannabis Industry*, 40 L.A. Law. 20 (Feb. 2018).

22. *Id.*

23. Cannabis & Comm. Real Estate, *supra* note 17; Scot Crow & Douglas Praw, Blowing Away the Smoke: Financial Opportunities in Marijuana/Hemp Real Estate Deals, 2019 U.S. Shopping Center Law Conference, October 23, 2019 ("Blowing Away the Smoke").

- This is a non-smoking premises. No smoking, including medical or recreational marijuana, inside or on the Premises is permitted. However, consuming medical marijuana with a vaporizer or in cannabis edibles, tonics, or concentrates is permitted.
- Tenant shall at all times during the term of the Lease or any extensions thereof, have a copy of Tenant's state-issued marijuana license at the Premises and shall be available during working hours to present such license, which shall be in good standing with the applicable state governmental regulating authority. Upon each renewal of Tenant's state-issued marijuana license, Tenant shall provide a copy to Landlord within twenty-four (24) hours of receipt.

2.3.3 Applicable Laws/Compliance with Laws

Most commercial lease forms define laws broadly; however, due to the divergence of state, local, and federal law, the definition needs to be adjusted for marijuana leases to limit the defined term to carve-out the federal Controlled Substances Act and similar laws.

Lease Examples:[24]

- "Applicable Laws" means all federal (to the extent not in direct conflict with applicable state, municipal or local cannabis licensing and program laws, rules and regulations), state, municipal and local laws, codes, ordinances, rules and regulations of governmental authorities, committees, associations, or other regulatory committees, agencies or governing bodies having jurisdiction over (a) the Premises, or any portion thereof, (b) Landlord or (c) Tenant, including both statutory and common law, hazardous waste rules and regulations and state cannabis licensing program laws, rules and regulation.
- Tenant's obligations hereunder shall include (i) all state and local laws and regulations from any governmental authority with jurisdiction over Tenant's use, including but not limited to [State Cannabis Laws and Regulations] and local zoning ordinances, and (ii) all federal laws to the extent those laws are not inconsistent with state and local laws allowing Tenant to use the Premises for the specified permitted uses. This covenant encompasses all applicable laws that become effective before and during the Lease term (collectively, the "Mandates"), regardless of the cost of such compliance. Tenant's inability to comply with the Mandates shall be grounds for termination of this Lease.

---

24. *Id.*

2.3.4 Rent and Form of Payment

Landlords should require cannabis tenants pay rent and any other amounts due in the form of wire transfer, check, or cashier's check, because this may protect landlords from being subject to SARs. Also, landlords should not accept percentage rent or similar revenue-based payments because the appearance of percentage rent in the lease undermines any innocent landlord defense to forfeiture (i.e., percentage rent could be interpreted as sharing in the profits of an illegal enterprise).[25] Despite this, landlords may desire to have audit rights as a method of confirming the tenant's financial status.

2.3.5 Security and On-Site Cash

Many cannabis companies operate as cash-only businesses, and thus leasing to cannabis tenants can create greater premises security demands. Some landlords may try to shift these demands onto the cannabis tenant by requiring that such tenant either directly provide additional security measures or reimburse the landlord for the landlord's actual costs to hire additional security. If a tenant provides security guards for the premises, the landlord may want the right to approve the security company or specify whether the guards are armed. Similarly, lease agreements should limit the amount of cash allowable on the premises, provide for armored car pickups, and limit tenant's ability to have an ATM on-site to reduce security risks.

Lease Example:[26]

- Tenant shall use its best efforts to ensure that patients, customers, employees, agents, and owners of Tenant and Tenant's dispensary neither loiter, nor use, smoke, vape, dab, consume, in any form or fashion, any THC and/or CBD marijuana product in the Premises or Building, on the Property or in any adjacent properties. Tenant shall remove cash from the Premises at the end of each day, so that at no time shall Tenant have an excess of [$___] on the Premises. Tenant shall provide Landlord with Tenant's daily cash transfer schedule and procedures and shall update such information to Landlord within twenty-four (24) hours of any changes to Tenant's cash transfer schedule and procedures.

2.3.6 Landlord's Access

To ensure that the terms of the lease are being complied with, landlords should require a general right to enter and inspect the premises. However, since state and local laws tend to restrict access to areas where cannabis is stored, sold, or processed, leases with cannabis companies should address

25. Michael N. Widener, *Medicinal Cannabis Entrepreneurs as Commercial Tenants: Assessment and Treatment*, 46 REAL PROP. TR. & ES. L.J. 377 (Fall 2011) ("Medicinal Entrepreneurs").
26. Cannabis & Comm. Real Estate, *supra* note 17; Blowing Away the Smoke, *supra* note 23.

both a landlord's right to access and inspect the premises and a tenant's ability to restrict such access to sensitive areas. In some jurisdictions, landlord access to sensitive areas is restricted by state law, and landlords must obtain approval from a regulatory body before it can access these areas. If such restrictions are in place, landlords should require tenants to cooperate in obtaining the necessary approvals.

Lease Examples:[27]

- If approval of the [state and local regulators] or any other governmental authority is necessary for Landlord or any mortgagee to inspect the Premises, Tenant shall use best efforts to support obtaining such approvals for inspection, time being of the essence. If Landlord's access to certain space in the Premises is conditioned on Landlord being accompanied by a member of Tenant's management team, Tenant shall provide such access to the Premises as soon as reasonably possible, after Landlord request.
- Landlord shall have the right, at any time that any portion of the Premises is occupied by Tenant's principals, agents, or contractors, including at times when the Premises is not open for business to the public, to enter the Premises for the purposes of ensuring compliance with the terms of this Lease. In accordance with state licensing rules, Landlord must be accompanied by authorized Tenant personnel while inspecting limited access areas. Landlord may photograph or video-record in any medium the activities of Tenant, subject to privacy restrictions under HIPAA and state laws and so long as such visual recordings are not provided to anyone with an interest in possessing Tenant's trade secrets (other than government entities).

2.3.7 Tenant Improvements

State and local laws often prescribe specific criteria for the layout/buildout of marijuana facilities. Landlords should require tenants to obtain any necessary governmental consents or assurances regarding the proposed design prior to commencing any construction. Similarly, landlords may be unwilling to reimburse tenants for the cost of any improvements that are unique to marijuana operations with no value to subsequent tenants, and landlords may ask tenants to remove such improvements at tenant's expense upon expiration or earlier termination of the lease.

2.3.8 Common Areas/Odors/Etc.

Most landlords desire to limit the impact that a tenant has on the common areas and the premises leased to other tenants, including preventing odors from the use of cannabis products. To preserve the appearance of the

---

27. *Id.*

property, landlords may restrict where, if, and what type of cannabis products can be consumed and require the tenant to take steps to help mitigate odors, such as the installation of additional ventilation.

2.3.9 Utilities and Operating Expenses

Cannabis tenants may consume more utilities than traditional tenants. This is particularly true with regard to warehouse spaces used for cultivation of cannabis, which require additional lighting and increase water consumption significantly. In fact, the water consumed by cannabis cultivation had a significant enough impact that the California State Water Resources Control Board adopted the Cannabis Cultivation Policy to control water usage by cannabis companies.[28] Landlords should require cannabis tenants to pay for excessive utility consumption and any additional other services that landlords provide that exclusively benefit the cannabis tenants.

2.3.10 Environmental Concerns

The lease agreement should address the proper procedures for disposal and storage of herbicides, pesticides, fertilizers, and any other hazardous substance. Some landlords may also request that tenants disclose the substances that will be used and stored on the premises. Generally, these provisions can be similar to those used for a paint store, dry cleaner, or automobile mechanic.[29]

2.3.11 Insurance and Indemnification

Insurance policies for cannabis tenants tend to be very expensive and contain numerous carve-outs. Landlords should require that tenants obtain adequate insurance coverage; however, landlords must also be aware that certain coverage is not available to cannabis companies regardless of the company's efforts. Similarly, landlords should be aware that leasing to cannabis tenants may increase the landlord's premiums for owner's and liability insurance coverage.

In light of the foregoing, a lease's typical hold harmless and indemnity covenants may be insufficient protection for landlords. As such, landlords should request that the indemnity cover damage to the building and other tenant's premises and property arising from the operation of the cannabis business, including criminal activity that targets the premises.[30] Similarly, the indemnity provision should address potential environmental hazards

---

28. *See* Cannabis Cultivation Policy: Principals and Guidelines for Cannabis Cultivation, State Water Resources Control Board (Feb. 5, 2019), https://www.waterboards.ca.gov/water_issues/programs/cannabis/docs/policy/final_cannabis_policy_with_attach_a.pdf.
29. Medicinal Entrepreneurs, *supra* note 25.
30. *Id.*

unique to marijuana operations. Finally, landlords could request an indem-
nification for losses in connection with forfeiture proceedings (temporary
or permanent) caused by the cannabis company's operation.[31]

2.3.12 Surrender and Other End-of-Term Provisions

Landlords should seek restoration of the premises and removal of mari-
juana-specific improvements deemed undesirable by the landlord upon
expiration or earlier termination of the lease. Similarly, the lease should
provide for the removal and handling of any cannabis products and related
materials (e.g., soil, fungicides, pesticides, etc.) and address the need, if
any, for odor elimination or sterilization of the premises.

Lease Example:[32]

- Tenant shall remove, coordinate, and/or destroy, as permitted and
  directed by the applicable governmental authorities, all medical marijuana products remaining in the Premises upon expiration or earlier
  termination of the Lease.

3. Forfeiture

Forfeiture is based on the fictional notion of "guilty property," which finds
that the property, through illegal activity or use, has become corrupt.
Therefore, a property owner may be party to a forfeiture action regardless
of the property owner's guilt or innocence. Real property may be seized by
the U.S. Attorney General and forfeited to the United States if the federal
government has "probable cause to believe that the real property is being
used 'to commit, or to facilitate the commission of a felony.'"[33]

Forfeiture can arise in both criminal and civil contexts; however, civil
forfeiture presents a greater risk for landlords. Criminal forfeiture is an *in
personam* (against the person) action that is limited to the property interests
of the defendant.[34] A criminal forfeiture may only be sought as a part of a
criminal prosecution and may not be ordered until the defendant is con-
victed.[35] Additionally, for criminal forfeitures pursuant to the Controlled

---

31. *Id.*

32. Cannabis & Comm. Real Estate, *supra* note 17; Blowing Away the Smoke, *supra* note 23.

33. Cielo Fortin-Camacho, *Red-handed Without a Defense: Avoiding Civil Forfeiture When
Leasing to Lawful Marijuana Tenants*, 3 Tex. A&M J. Prop. L 91 (2016).

34. Internal Revenue Manual, Internal Revenue Service, Part 9, Chapter 7,
Section 3, https://www.irs.gov/irm/part9/irm_09-007-003 (last accessed Apr. 22, 2020)
("IRM"); Types of Forfeiture, U.S. Dept. of Just., https://www.justice.gov/afp/types
-federal-forfeiture (last accessed Apr. 22, 2020).

35. *Id.*

Substances Act, there is an ancillary hearing where third parties (e.g., a landlord) have their interests addressed.[36] Therefore, the actions of a tenant will not cause a landlord to lose its fee interest, and a landlord may assert a desire to terminate the defendant's leasehold estate at the ancillary hearing. Civil forfeiture is an in rem (against the property) without regard for who the owner may be and can occur regardless of whether a Controlled Substances Act violation has been criminally prosecuted. Clearly, forfeiture, particularly civil forfeiture, presents a real threat to cannabis companies that seek to own property and landlords seeking to lease their property to cannabis tenants.

There are limited defenses to civil forfeiture. The most common nonconstitutional defense is the "innocent-owner" defense, which was hinted at in dicta by the Supreme Court in 1974 and later codified by Congress.[37] Pursuant to section 881(a)(7) of the Comprehensive Drug Abuse Prevention and Control Act, an owner's real property will not be forfeited if the owner can establish that the act leading to the forfeiture was committed without the owner's knowledge or consent. The other common defense to civil forfeiture is a constitutional due process claim relating to the seizure. However, this claim also hinges heavily on whether the illegal activity was done without the property owner's knowledge or consent and whether the property owner had done what was reasonably expected to prevent such use on the property. Thus, both the statutory innocent-owner defense and a due process claim are greatly affected by the property owner's involvement with and acquiescence to the conduct.

4. Use Restrictions

Although a state may permit hemp, hemp derivatives, medicinal, and/or recreational cannabis, not all real property within the state can be used for the cultivation, processing, storage, and sale of hemp and cannabis products. In addition to license-related requirements and the private use restrictions discussed in Section 1.3 of this chapter, cannabis companies also need to be aware of public use restrictions (such as zoning ordinances).

Public use restrictions related to the cannabis industry can exist at both the state and local levels. For example, New Mexico restricts nonprofit dispensaries from operating within 30 feet of any school, church, or day care center, and any cannabis must not be visible from the street or public

---

36. IRM, *supra* note 34.
37. *Id.*

areas.[38] Similarly, some states have caps on the number of licenses that may be issued.[39]

Additionally, many states have given municipalities significant discretion over the operations of cannabis businesses. Due to this discretion, some counties and municipalities have passed moratoriums on the cultivation, manufacture, or sale of cannabis products within their boundaries.[40] For example, a local ordinance may limit the number of plants that can be located in a cultivation facility or the hours of operation for a dispensing facility.[41]

Although these restrictions may seem daunting, these cannabis-related land-use laws share many similarities to liquor control laws.[42] In particular, regulations relating to location, size, setback, hours, signage, security, goods sold, and taxes paid echo those implemented to control liquor sales and consumption. Thus, cannabis companies should research not only state laws that may impact its operations but also any applicable local rules, regulations, and ordinances.

5. Conclusion

The cannabis industry has caused an increased demand for commercial real estate; however, not everyone is willing to take on the risks associated with cannabis. Although the risks may vary between hemp and marijuana, neither type of cannabis company represents a low-risk option. As a result, many in the commercial real estate industry are currently reluctant to take on the risk associated with a cannabis company. That said, in light of this rapidly growing industry, these same entities will likely continue to re-evaluate the risks and rewards of being a part of the cannabis business for many years to come.

---

38. Patricia E. Salkin & Zachary Kansler, *Medical Marijuana Meets Zoning: Can You Grow, Sell, and Smoke That Here?*, 62 PLANNING & ENV. L. 3, No. 8 (Aug. 2010) ("Marijuana Meets Zoning").

39. Valerio Romano, *Land Use Considerations for Cannabis Business Development*, MASSACHUSETTS CANNABIS LAW MANUAL (2019).

40. *See* Marijuana Meets Zoning, *supra* note 38; Laura Drotleff, *Hemp in California: Counties, Cities Remain Divided on Production*, HEMPINDUSTRY DAILY (Sept. 30, 2019), https://hempindustrydaily.com/hemp-in-california-california-counties-cities-split-on-hemp-production (last accessed Jan. 20, 2020).

41. Marijuana Meets Zoning, *supra* note 38.

42. Donald J. Kochan, *Incumbent Landscapes, Disruptive Uses: Perspectives on Marijuana-Related Land Use Control*, 3 TEX. A&M J. PROP. L. 35 (2016).

6

Tax Law Issues

Robert L. Mahon and Daniel A. Sito

Regardless of legal status under federal, state, and local law, cannabis businesses—like everyone else—must pay taxes. Unfortunately, the mixed legal status of cannabis businesses creates unique and challenging tax issues. Tax provisions enacted in the 1980s to combat drug trafficking have been zealously used by the Internal Revenue Service (IRS) against cannabis businesses that are operating in compliance with state and local laws. Onerous federal tax provisions coupled with high state and local taxes place significant tax burdens on the cannabis industry.

Most of this chapter is devoted to the unique tax issues faced by businesses producing and selling marijuana and marijuana-derived products. Businesses producing and selling hemp and hemp-derived products like non-marijuana cannabidiol (CBD) face fewer industry-specific tax issues.

1. Federal Income Tax Issues

1.1 General Principles

Like other businesses, the federal income taxation of cannabis businesses and their owners will depend on the legal form chosen to conduct business.

Corporations (except closely held corporations electing to be taxed as a pass-through entity under Subchapter S of the Internal Revenue Code) and certain other entities electing to be taxed as corporations currently pay a corporate income tax equal to 21 percent of their taxable income.[1] For a business engaged in the sale of goods, the computation of taxable income generally starts by subtracting the "cost of goods sold" from the business's gross receipts or sales.[2] This "gross profit" is increased by adding

---

1. I.R.C. § 11(b).
2. I.R.S. Form 1120 (U.S. Corporate Income Tax Return) (2019), lines 1a through 3.

other sources of income (e.g., rents, royalties, capital gains) and deducting expenses (e.g., salaries and wages, rent, taxes, interest, depreciation, advertising, employee benefits).[3] Thus, at a very simplified level, federal corporate income tax is computed as follows:

>   Gross receipts
> −   Cost of goods sold
>   Gross profit
> +   Other income
>   Total income
> −   Deductions
>   Taxable income

Pass-through entities (including S corporations, partnerships, and most multi-member limited liability companies) compute taxable income in a manner similar to corporations.[4] The significant difference is that pass-through entities generally do not pay federal income tax at the entity level.[5] Instead, as the label suggests, the owners of a pass-through entity include their share of the entity's taxable income on their tax returns in the year earned by the entity whether or not that income is distributed by the entity to the owners.[6]

In contrast to the owners of pass-through entities, owners of corporations (other than S corporations) are not subject to federal income tax on business income unless or until the corporation distributes after-tax income to owners as a dividend.[7] The individual income tax paid on corporate dividends represents a second level of federal income tax.

Sole proprietors, including owners of single-member limited liability companies that do not elect to be taxed as a corporation, report income from their business on their individual income tax returns.[8] Sole proprietors compute business income in a manner similar to corporations and pass-through entities: gross receipts or sales less cost of goods sold plus other income less deductions.[9] This business income is then included as part of the individual's total income, which is subject to the individual's adjustments and deductions to arrive at taxable income.[10]

---

3. *Id.* at lines 3 through 30.

4. I.R.S. Instructions for Form 1065 (2019); I.R.S. Instructions for Form 1120-S (2019).

5. I.R.C. §§ 701, 1363(a).

6. *Id.* §§ 702, 1366.

7. Boris I. Bittker & James S. Eustice, Federal Income Taxation of Corporations and Shareholders ¶ 1.03 (7th ed. 2015), Thompson Reuters Checkpoint (database updated April 2020).

8. I.R.S. 2019 Instructions for Schedule C.

9. I.R.S. Schedule C (Form 1040 or 1040-SR) (Profit or Loss From Business (Sole Proprietorship)) (2019).

10. I.R.S. Form 1040 (U.S. Individual Income Tax Return) (2019), lines 7a through 11b.

1.2 Internal Revenue Code Section 280E—Operating Expenses Not Deductible

Businesses are generally entitled to deduct operating expenses in arriving at taxable income. However, the Internal Revenue Code (IRC) specifically denies a deduction for

> any amount paid or incurred . . . in carrying on any trade or business if such trade or business (or the activities which comprise such trade or business) consists of trafficking in controlled substances (within the meaning of schedule I and II of the Controlled Substances Act) which is prohibited by Federal law or the law of any State in which such trade or business is conducted.[11]

Internal Revenue Code section 280E was enacted in response to a 1981 U.S. Tax Court decision permitting a taxpayer to deduct the ordinary and necessary expenses (home office, packaging, telephone, and automobile) of his illegal cocaine, amphetamines, and marijuana selling business.[12] Congress's reaction was swift and strong. As explained in the legislative history to section 280E:

> There is a sharply defined public policy against drug dealing. To allow drug dealers the benefit of business expense deductions at the same time that the U.S. and its citizens are losing billions of dollars per year to such persons is not compelled by the fact that such deductions are allowed to other, legal, enterprises. Such deductions must be disallowed on public policy grounds.[13]

1.2.1 "Trafficking"

Internal Revenue Code section 280E applies to the trade or business of "trafficking" in controlled substances. The IRC does not define the term "trafficking." Despite the significant negative connotation of "trafficking," courts have held that cannabis businesses operating legally under state and local law are drug traffickers for purposes of federal tax law if they regularly buy or sell cannabis or other controlled substances.[14] This includes medical marijuana dispensaries distributing marijuana in exchange for membership fees or donations.[15]

---

11. I.R.C. § 280E.

12. Edmondson v. Comm'r, 42 T.C.M. (CCH) 1533 (T.C. 1981).

13. S. Rept. 97-494 (Vol. 1) at 309 (1982).

14. Patients Mutual Assistance Collective Corp. v. Comm'r, 151 T.C. 176 (2018); N. Cal. Small Bus. Assistants, Inc. v. Comm'r, 153 T.C. 4 (2019); Californians Helping to Alleviate Med. Problems, Inc. v. Comm'r, 128 T.C. 173, 182 (2007).

15. Californians Helping to Alleviate Med. Problems, Inc. v. Comm'r, 128 T.C. 173, 182–83 (2007).

It is unclear the extent to which other taxpayers that do business with cannabis businesses might be considered "trafficking" by virtue of facilitating the purchase or sale of cannabis. The U.S. Tax Court has held that a management company was "trafficking" under IRC section 280E because its employees engaged in the purchase and sale of cannabis products for a dispensary client.[16] The court concluded, "We do not read the term 'trafficking' to require [the taxpayer] to have had title to the marijuana its employees were purchasing and selling."[17]

1.2.2 "Controlled Substances"

Marijuana is currently a controlled substance under schedule I of the Controlled Substances Act and is accordingly covered by IRC section 280E.[18] This is true even when sold by a business operating legally under state and local law and when used for medical purposes at the direction of a physician or medical professional.[19]

Internal Revenue Code section 280E does not require a criminal conviction under the Controlled Substances Act.[20] The IRS has "statutory authority to determine, as a matter of civil tax law, whether taxpayers have trafficked in controlled substances" without a criminal investigation or conviction.[21]

1.2.3 Application to Non-Cannabis Lines of Business

Section 280E denies deductions incurred in a "trade or business" that "consists of trafficking in controlled substances." The U.S. Tax Court has held that a trade or business "consists of" trafficking in controlled substances even if the taxpayer conducts activity other than trafficking a controlled substance.[22] For example, a medical dispensary that sold marijuana as well as shirts, hats, books, rolling papers, lighters, and other non-marijuana

---

16. Alt. Health Care Advocates v. Comm'r, 151 T.C. 225, 241 (2018).

17. *Id.*

18. Alpenglow Botanicals, LLC v. United States, 894 F.3d 1187, 1192 (10th Cir. 2018); 21 U.S.C. § 812(c), Schedule I(c)(10). The Agricultural Improvement Act of 2018, P.L. 115-334, removed "hemp" from the list of controlled substances. "Hemp" is "the plant Cannabis sativa L. and any part of that plant, including the seeds thereof and all derivatives, extracts, cannabinoids, isomers, acids, salts, and salts of isomers, whether growing or not, with a delta-9 tetrahydrocannabinol concentration of not more than 0.3 percent on a dry weight basis." 7 U.S. § 1639o(1).

19. Alpenglow Botanicals, LLC v. United States, 894 F.3d 1187, 1192 (10th Cir. 2018); Californians Helping to Alleviate Med. Problems, Inc. v. Comm'r, 128 T.C. 173, 181 (2007) (citing United States v. Oakland Cannabis Buyers' Coop., 532 U.S. 483, 121 S. Ct. 1711, 149 L. Ed. 2d 722 (2001)).

20. High Desert Relief, Inc. v. United States, 917 F.3d 1170, 1186 (10th Cir. 2019); Green Sol. Retail, Inc. v. United States, 855 F.3d 1111, 1121 (10th Cir. 2017) ("But § 280E has no requirement that the Department of Justice conduct a criminal investigation or obtain a conviction before § 280E applies.").

21. 894 F.3d at 1197.

22. Patients Mut. Assistance Collective Corp. v. Comm'r, 151 T.C. 176 (2018).

inventory was a business that "consists of trafficking in controlled substances" and was subject to IRC section 280E.[23]

Although a trade or business that consists of trafficking is subject to section 280E, courts have recognized that a taxpayer may have more than one trade or business, and that only the trafficking trade or business is subject to section 280E.[24] Unfortunately, for taxpayers, determining whether various business activities are separate trades or businesses depends on the facts and circumstances of each taxpayer. Courts and the IRS primarily consider "the degree of organizational and economic interrelationship of various undertakings, the business purpose which is (or might be) served by carrying on the various undertakings separately or together . . . and the similarity of the various undertakings."[25] Although the IRS generally accepts a taxpayer's characterization of its activities as a single or multiple trades or businesses, "[t]he taxpayer's characterization will not be accepted, however, when it appears that his characterization is artificial and cannot be reasonably supported under the facts and circumstances of the case."[26]

Several court cases have addressed whether a taxpayer that engaged in trafficking controlled substances and also conducted other activities was engaged in a single trade or business (and thus prohibited from deducting any expenses) or multiple trades or businesses (and thus allowed deductions for ordinary and necessary expenses from its non-trafficking trade or business). In *Californians Helping to Alleviate Med. Problems, Inc. v. Comm'r*, the U.S. Tax Court held that a taxpayer that provided caregiving services and also dispensed marijuana had two trades or businesses because "the taxpayer's primary purpose was to provide caregiving services, and that those services were both 'substantially different' from and 'stood on . . . [their] own, separate and apart' from dispensing marijuana."[27] In contrast, in subsequent decisions, the U.S. Tax Court has concluded that marijuana dispensaries that sold non-marijuana products were a single trade or business because the sale of such products "had a 'close and inseparable organizational and economic relationship' with and was 'incident to' [the taxpayer's] primary business of selling marijuana."[28] Likewise, the Tax Court has held that the provision of complementary services (e.g., therapeutic services, yoga, tai chi, classes, counseling, addiction treatment) did not cause

---

23. *Id.*

24. Californians Helping to Alleviate Med. Problems, Inc. v. Comm'r, 128 T.C. 173, 183 (2007).

25. Treas. Reg. § 1.183-1(d)(1); Patients Mut. Assistance Collective Corp. v. Comm'r, 151 T.C. 176, 198 (2018) (quoting Treas. Reg. § 1.183-1(d)(1)).

26. Treas. Reg. § 1.183-1(d)(1).

27. 151 T.C. at 198 (discussing and distinguishing Californians Helping to Alleviate Med. Problems, Inc. v. Comm'r, 128 T.C. 173, 183 (2007)).

28. 151 T.C. at 199 (citing and quoting Olive v. Comm'r, 139 T.C. 19, 41 (2012), *aff'd*, 792 F.3d 1146 (9th Cir. 2015)).

a dispensary to have a second trade or business.[29] Factors relevant to the Tax Court's analysis of the independence of a dispensary business's non-marijuana activities as a separate trade or business include whether the separate activities are conducted on the same premises; share books and records, management, or professional services; or are operated for the economic benefit of the dispensary business.[30]

1.2.4 Application to Internal Revenue Code Section 199A

Enacted as part of the Tax Cuts and Jobs Act of 2017, IRC section 199A provides owners of certain pass-through business entities (partnerships, LLCs, and S-corporations) a deduction of up to 20 percent of their allocable share of the business's "qualified business income" (QBI).[31] At the time of this writing, no IRS or case law authority has addressed whether the statutory language of IRC section 280E, which prohibits a deduction for "any amount paid or incurred" in carrying on a drug trafficking business, would prohibit the owner of a pass-through cannabis business from claiming the 20 percent QBI deduction under section 199A, and the final Treasury Regulations published under section 199A did not address this question despite industry and practitioner requests for comment. Although practitioners have argued that section 280E should not apply to the QBI deduction as it is not an expense deduction for amounts "paid or incurred," the outcome of such a position is unclear given the expansive view of the scope of section 280E taken by the U.S. Tax Court in recent decisions.[32]

1.2.5 Constitutional Issues—Eighth Amendment

Courts have uniformly rejected arguments that section 280E is a penalty that violates the prohibition on excessive fines under the Eighth Amendment. A "penalty" is generally "an exaction imposed by statute as punishment for an unlawful act."[33] In contrast, deductions from gross income are "pure acts of legislative grace, the prudence of which is left to Congress."[34] Courts have concluded that "disallowance of a deduction is not an exaction imposed as punishment" because deductions are not a matter of right and do not turn on equitable consideration.[35]

---

29. 151 T.C. at 199. *See also* Olive v. Comm'r, 792 F.3d 1146 (9th Cir. 2015) (holding that a medical marijuana dispensary that sold marijuana and provided free caregiving services had only a single trade or business—"trafficking in medical marijuana").

30. Trupp v. Comm'r, T.C. Memo 2012-108 (listing case law factors).

31. I.R.C. § 199A(a).

32. *See, e.g.*, N. Cal. Small Bus. Assistants, Inc. v. Comm'r, 153 T.C. 4 (2019) (holding that the scope of I.R.C. § 280E is not limited to business expense deductions under I.R.C. § 162).

33. United States v. La Franca, 282 U.S. 568, 572, 51 S. Ct. 278, 75 L. Ed. 551 (1931).

34. 153 T.C. 4.

35. *E.g.*, Alpenglow Botanicals, LLC v. United States, 894 F.3d 1187, 1202 (10th Cir. 2018); Green Sol. Retail, Inc. v. United States, 855 F.3d 1111, 1121 (10th Cir. 2017).

1.2.6 Constitutional Issues—Fifth Amendment
Courts have rejected arguments that the burden of defending an IRS audit
of a cannabis business violates the taxpayer's privilege against self-incrim-
ination under the Fifth Amendment. First, taxpayers that are not natural
persons have no Fifth Amendment privilege.[36] Even for natural persons, the
Tenth Circuit Court of Appeals has held that the burden of defending a tax
audit or assessment is not "a form of compulsion equivalent to a statute that
imposes criminal liability for failing to provide information subjecting the
party to liability under another criminal statute."[37] "Taxpayers must choose
between providing evidence that they are not engaged in the trafficking of
a controlled substance or forgoing the tax deductions available by the grace
of Congress."[38]

1.2.7 Constitutional Issues—Sixteenth Amendment
The Sixteenth Amendment grants Congress the power to "lay and collect
taxes on incomes, from whatever source derived."[39] Although Congress is
generally viewed as having broad power in implementing the income tax,
some taxpayers have argued that section 280E's categorical denial of *all*
deductions violates the Sixteenth Amendment. Although this view has been
rejected by the U.S. Tax Court, two dissenting members of the court concluded that "[t]his wholesale disallowance of all deductions transforms the
ostensible income tax into something that is not an income tax at all, but
rather a tax on an amount greater than a taxpayer's 'income' within the
meaning of the Sixteenth Amendment."[40]

1.3 Reductions to Gross Income—Internal Revenue Code Section 471 (Cost of Goods Sold)
Although Congress has prohibited marijuana businesses from deducting
expenses in computing taxable income, the U.S. Constitution prohibits Congress from taxing taxpayers on a return of a taxpayer's basis in capital assets
or cost of goods sold in inventory. As noted earlier, the Sixteenth Amendment grants Congress the power to "lay and collect taxes on incomes, from
whatever source derived."[41] As interpreted by the U.S. Supreme Court, the
right to tax "income" extends to "*gain* derived from capital, from labor, or

36. Braswell v. United States, 487 U.S. 99, 104–05, 108 S. Ct. 2284, 101 L. Ed. 2d 98
(1988); High Desert Relief, Inc. v. United States, 917 F.3d 1170, 1188 (10th Cir. 2019).
37. Feinberg v. Comm'r, 916 F.3d 1330, 1336 (10th Cir.), *cert. denied*, 140 S. Ct. 49, 205
L. Ed. 2d 199 (2019).
38. *Id.*
39. U.S. Const. amend. XVI.
40. N. Cal. Small Bus. Assistants, Inc. v. Comm'r, 153 T.C. 4 (2019) (Gustafson, J.,
dissenting in part).
41. U.S. Const. amend. XVI.

from both combined," but not the return of capital.[42] Thus, the IRS and courts are generally aligned that Congress may not, as a matter of constitutional law, deny cannabis businesses a reduction in their gross income for the cost of goods sold.[43]

Taxpayers generally prefer deductions to reductions in gross income because deductions are taken in the year incurred whereas the recovery of costs of goods sold is deferred until the property is sold. This is generally a timing issue. Cannabis businesses need to carefully consider the permissible costs of goods sold. Computations of the cost of goods sold depend on whether the taxpayer is a "reseller" or a "producer."

1.3.1 Resellers

A reseller's cost of goods sold is generally the "invoice price" of the inventory, less trade and other discounts, plus "transportation or other necessary charges incurred in acquiring possession of the goods."[44] Cannabis businesses are not entitled to capitalize and include in cost of goods sold "indirect costs" of inventory as required of other businesses. Internal Revenue Code section 263A was enacted in 1986 to require most taxpayers to include formerly deductible "indirect costs" in cost of goods sold (thus deferring the tax benefit of these expenses).[45] However, section 263A does

---

42. Doyle v. Mitchell Brothers Co., 247 U.S. 179, 187, 38 S. Ct. 467, 469–470, 62 L. Ed. 1054 (1918); New Colonial Ice Co. v. Helvering, 292 U.S. 435, 440 (1934).

43. I.R.S. Chief Couns. Adv. Memo. 201504011 at 2 (Jan. 23, 2015); Alpenglow Botanicals, LLC v. United States, 894 F.3d 1187, 1199 (10th Cir. 2018) ("To ensure taxation of income rather than sales, the 'cost of goods sold' is a mandatory exclusion from the calculation of a taxpayer's gross income."); Patients Mut. Assistance Collective Corp. v. Comm'r, 151 T.C. 176, 209 (2018). Congress recognized this limitation to its power when enacting I.R.C. § 280E. See S. Rept. 97-494 (Vol. 1) at 309 (1982) (explaining that "[t]o preclude possible challenges on constitutional grounds, the adjustment to gross receipts with respect to effective cost of goods sold is not affected by [Section 280E]."). However, in Beck v. Comm'r, T.C. Memo 2015-149, the U.S. Tax Court held that the owner of a marijuana dispensary could not include in his cost of goods sold the value of inventory assets seized by the Drug Enforcement Agency in an enforcement action. Although the court based its holding on the taxpayer's failure to substantiate which specific assets were seized and the cost paid to acquire the seized assets, in dictum, the court stated that even if the taxpayer had provided sufficient substantiation, the seized inventory would still not be allowable in cost of goods sold, because the inventory was confiscated and not sold. Id. Although an unpublished memorandum decision, the existence of the Beck opinion illustrates that the ability of a cannabis business to fully recover its inventory costs in all cases is not free from doubt and could be subject to challenge by a taxing authority.

44. Treas. Reg. § 1.471-3(b); I.R.S. Chief Couns. Adv. Memo. 201504011 at 6 (Jan. 23, 2015) (noting that for a marijuana reseller these costs would be "the invoice cost of the marijuana purchases, less trade or other discounts, plus transportation or other necessary charges incurred in acquiring possession of the marijuana.").

45. I.R.C. § 263A.

not apply to indirect costs that would not have otherwise been deductible under IRC section 280E.[46] As the Tax Court colorfully described the interplay of sections 263A and 280E, "Section 263A makes taxpayers defer the benefit of what used to be deductions—it does not shower that as grace on those previously damned."[47]

1.3.2 Producers

The computation of a producer's cost of goods sold is more complicated than for a reseller. A producer's cost of goods sold is generally:

> (1) the cost of raw materials and supplies entering into or consumed in connection with the product, (2) expenditures for direct labor, and (3) indirect production costs incident to and necessary for the production of the particular article, including in such indirect production costs an appropriate portion of management expenses, but not including any cost of selling or return on capital, whether by way of interest or profit.[48]

For a cannabis production business, the direct costs would include costs for marijuana seeds or plants and labor for planting, cultivating, harvesting, and sorting cannabis.[49] Indirect costs would include costs for repairs, maintenance, utilities, rent, supervisory labor, uncapitalized tools, and quality control but "only to the extent . . . incident to and necessary for production or manufacturing operations or processes."[50] A cannabis production business's cost of goods sold would not include costs for marketing, advertising, selling, distributing, research and development, interest, and other expenses to the extent not incident to or necessary for the production of cannabis or cannabis products.[51]

1.4 Reductions to Gross Income—Internal Revenue Code Section 164 (Taxes)

Cannabis businesses generally are prohibited from deducting state and local taxes because of the prohibition of deductions from gross income in IRC section 280E. However, IRC section 164 provides that certain state and local taxes are not deductible but are instead required to be "treated as part of the cost of the acquired property or, in the case of a disposition,

---

46. I.R.C. § 263A(a)(2). *See also* I.R.S. Chief Couns. Adv. Memo. 201504011 at 1 (Jan. 23, 2015) (advising that "[a] taxpayer trafficking in a Schedule I or Schedule II controlled substance determines COGS using the applicable inventory-costing regulations under § 471 as they existed when § 280E was enacted").

47. Patients Mut. Assistance Collective Corp. v. Comm'r, 151 T.C. 176, 208 (2018).

48. Treas. Reg. § 1.471-3(c).

49. *See* Chief Couns. Adv. Memo. 201504011 at 6 (Jan. 23, 2015).

50. Treas. Reg. § 1.471-11(2)(i).

51. Treas. Reg. § 1.471-11(2)(ii).

as a reduction in the amount realized on the disposition."[52] Thus, cannabis businesses can reduce their gross income for taxes that are (1) not real property, personal property, income, war, or excess profits taxes and (2) are paid or accrued "in connection with an acquisition or disposition of property."[53]

For example, the IRS Chief Counsel's Office has advised that Washington state marijuana excise taxes should be treated as a reduction in gross income (and not a deduction from gross income prohibited by IRC section 280E) because the excise tax is paid or accrued in connection with the disposition of property (marijuana).[54]

1.5 Internal Revenue Code Section 501(c)—Exempt Organizations

The IRS has determined that marijuana dispensaries cannot qualify for tax-exempt status under IRC section 501(c)(3) because they are engaged in a criminal enterprise and, thus, are not operated exclusively for charitable purposes.[55] Likewise, the IRS has concluded that a marijuana dispensary was not exempt under IRC section 501(c)(4) because it was operated in a commercial manner similar to a for profit company.[56]

2. State Tax Issues

State and local taxes vary widely by jurisdiction. As with federal taxes, cannabis businesses must generally pay applicable state and local taxes regardless of the legal status of the business under state and local law. In addition to generally applicable taxes, many state and local governments have enacted specific taxes on cannabis products and businesses.

2.1 Income Taxes

Forty-four states and the District of Columbia impose some form of net income tax. Although details vary significantly, most states rely heavily on the Internal Revenue Code in computing taxpayers' state income tax liability. Many states conform to the IRC on a rolling basis, which means that changes to the IRC become part of state law without action by the state legislature. Many other states conform to the IRC as of a specific date. A smaller number of states conform selectively to portions of the IRC. Whatever their

---

52. I.R.C. § 164(a).
53. *Id.*
54. I.R.S. Chief Couns. Adv. Memo. 201531016 at 4 (June 9, 2015).
55. E.g., Priv. Ltr. Rul. 201224036 (June 15, 2012).
56. Priv. Ltr. Rul. 201941028 (Oct. 11, 2019). *But see* Benjamin Moses Leff, *Tax Planning for Marijuana Dealers*, 99 Iowa Law Rev. 523 (2014) (suggesting the use of I.R.C. § 501(c)(4) to avoid the impact of I.R.C. § 280E and resolve the federalism issues raised by the conflict between state law and federal tax law).

level of conformity, states are free to decouple from the IRC with respect to specific provisions.

As described in detail earlier, IRC section 280E prohibits taxpayers that traffic in marijuana or other controlled substances from deducting their expenses in computing their taxable income. States that generally conform to the IRC generally incorporate the same prohibition into their state income taxes unless or until they decouple or make a state-specific modification to their income tax statutes. Specific state provisions vary widely by state and tend to evolve with the state's approach to legalization. The following sections illustrate approaches taken by several states to address the deductibility of cannabis business expenses for state income tax purposes as of the writing of this chapter.

2.1.1 California

Since January 1, 2020, and through at least 2024, licensed cannabis businesses are permitted to deduct business expenses for California personal and corporate income tax purposes.[57] Prior to 2020, California's state income tax treatment of cannabis businesses expenses depended on whether the business was organized as a corporation or a pass-through entity.

Cannabis businesses taxed as corporations have historically been permitted to deduct ordinary and necessary business expenses because California has a standalone corporate income tax that does not incorporate IRC section 280E.[58] Although California has a state law analog to IRC section 280E that applies to corporations, California may only deny deductions after a final determination by a court in a criminal or civil court proceeding to which the state or political subdivision is a party "on the merits of the legality of the activities of the taxpayer."[59]

In contrast to corporations, owners of cannabis businesses organized as pass-through entities were historically not permitted to deduct ordinary and necessary business expenses of a cannabis business for California income tax purposes because the state's individual income tax conformed to IRC section 280E. At least for 2020 through 2024, California has decoupled from IRC section 280E and individual owners of pass-through entities are able to deduct business expenses associated with licensed cannabis businesses.[60]

2.1.2 Colorado

Although Colorado generally conforms its state income tax to the federal income tax, licensed marijuana businesses may, in computing state income, deduct "an amount equal to any expenditure that is eligible to be claimed

---

57. CAL. REV. & TAX. CODE § 17209(a).
58. Cal. Franchise Tax Bd., "Medical Marijuana – State and Federal Income Tax Law" (Apr. 12, 2016).
59. CAL. REV. & TAX CODE § 24436.1(b).
60. *Id.* § 17209(a).

as a federal income tax deduction but is disallowed by section 280E of the internal revenue code because marijuana is a controlled substance under federal law."[61]

2.1.3 Illinois

Illinois generally conforms to the Internal Revenue Code and has not modified or decoupled its state income tax from IRC section 280E.[62] As a result, Illinois cannabis businesses are not entitled to deduct ordinary and necessary business expenses even if the business is operating legally under state and local law.

2.1.4 Oregon

Between 1998 and 2015, medical marijuana businesses could operate legally in Oregon but were not able to deduct their business expenses because state income law conformed to IRC section 280E.[63] However, in connection with Oregon's legalization of recreational marijuana in 2015, Oregon decoupled from IRC section 280E to allow a subtraction in computing Oregon income for "[a]ny federal deduction that the taxpayer would have been allowed for the production, processing or sale of marijuana items authorized under [state law] but for section 280E of the Internal Revenue Code."[64] Taxpayers operating outside the legal market continue to be disallowed state income tax deductions for business expenses.[65]

2.2 Other General Business Activity Taxes

Numerous states impose other business activity taxes instead of or in addition to income taxes. These include gross receipts taxes (e.g., Delaware gross receipts tax, Ohio commercial activity tax, Nevada commerce tax, Washington business and occupation tax), modified gross receipts taxes that allow some deductions (e.g., Texas franchise tax, Oregon commercial activity tax), and capital stock or net worth taxes (e.g., Massachusetts net worth tax, Tennessee franchise tax). These business taxes will generally apply to cannabis businesses in the same manner as other businesses.

Because gross receipts taxes are measured by gross receipts with few or no deductions, cannabis businesses are not generally impacted by limitations on deductions. However, states may elect to deny cannabis businesses preferential tax rates or exemptions permitted to growers, manufacturers, or sellers of other products. For example, Washington's legalization

---

61. COLO. REV. STAT. §§ 39-22-104(4)(r), 39-22-304(3)(m).
62. ILL. COMP. STAT. ch. 35, §§ 5/1501(a)(11), 5/203.
63. Wakefield v. Oregon Dep't of Revenue, 2020 WL 905739 (Or. Tax Mag. Div. 2020).
64. OR. REV. STAT. § 316.680(1)(i).
65. *Id.* §§ 316.680(1)(i), 317.363.

of cannabis was coupled with amendments to its gross receipts tax to deny numerous tax preferences to cannabis businesses.[66]

2.3 General Retail Sales Taxes

Forty-five states[67] and the District of Columbia impose generally applicable retail sales taxes. Although details vary significantly, the taxes generally apply to the sale of tangible personal property. In the absence of an exemption, these taxes would reach the sale of cannabis and cannabis products to consumers.

2.3.1 "Sales"

Sales taxes generally apply to the "sale" of tangible personal property for consideration. Cannabis businesses in some states have argued—generally unsuccessfully—that they are not making "sales" subject to sales tax because of their form of doing business. For example, Washington has held that the transfer of medical marijuana in exchange for a "donation" or "contribution" was a sale subject to sales tax. The state concluded that customers paid money to receive marijuana and not for gratuitous purposes.[68]

2.3.2 Exemptions

(a) Prescription Medicine

Many states have sales tax exemptions for sales of prescription medicines. Some states have extended sales tax exemptions to sales of medical marijuana and others have not. For example, California specifically exempts medicinal cannabis, medicinal cannabis concentrate, edible medicinal cannabis products, or topical cannabis from sales tax when sold to individuals with a medical marijuana identification card issued by the California Department of Public Health.[69] Massachusetts has interpreted its sales tax exemption for "sales of medicine . . . on prescription" to apply to "sales of marijuana and products containing marijuana to a qualifying patient or the patient's personal caregiver pursuant to a written certification by a licensed physician."[70] Washington specifically excludes "marijuana,

---

66. Wash. Rev. Code § 82.04.213.

67. Alaska does not have state sales and use taxes, but cities and boroughs within the state may impose local sales and use taxes.

68. Green Collar Club v. Dep't of Revenue, 3 Wash. App. 2d 82, 413 P.3d 1083 (2018); Wash. Dep't of Revenue, Determination No. 16-0209, 36 Wash. Tax Det. 052 (2016). However, Washington now exempts sales of medical marijuana by statute. Rev. Code Wash. § 82.08.9998(1).

69. Cal. Rev. & Tax. Code § 34011(f).

70. Mass Gen. L. ch. 64H, § 6(l); Mass. Dep't of Revenue Directive No. 15-1 (June 19, 2015).

useable marijuana, or marijuana-infused products" from its general prescription drug exemption[71] but has enacted a separate medical marijuana
exemption.[72]

(b) Food Products
Many states have sales tax exemptions for sales of food products or groceries. However, cannabis and cannabis products are generally excluded from
such sales tax exemptions.[73]

2.3.3 Business Inputs Exemptions or Incentives
(a) Agricultural Incentives
Many states provide sales tax exemptions for inputs purchased by farmers.
States have taken different approaches to applying those exemptions to
cannabis businesses. For example, California has advised that cannabis cultivators may qualify for a partial sales tax exemption for farm equipment
and machinery.[74] In contrast, Washington expressly excludes marijuana
producers from a host of sales tax exemptions generally available to farmers and horticultural businesses.[75]

(b) Manufacturing Incentives
Many states provide sales tax exemptions for purchases of machinery and
equipment used in manufacturing or research and development. States
have taken different approaches to applying those exemptions to cannabis
businesses. For example, California has advised that cannabis businesses
may qualify for California's partial sales tax exemption for machinery and
equipment used in manufacturing and research and development.[76] In

---

71. Rev. Code Wash. § 82.08.0281(4)(b). *See also* Green Collar Club v. Dep't of Revenue,
3 Wash. App. 2d 82, 413 P.3d 1083 (2018) (holding that sales of medical marijuana were
not exempt from sales tax as prescription drugs for periods before the explicit exclusion).
72. Rev. Code Wash. § 82.08.9998(1) (exempting sales of "marijuana, marijuana
concentrates, useable marijuana, marijuana-infused products" if (1) the product has
been identified by the Department of Health as being beneficial for medical use, (2) the
seller is a marijuana retailers with a medical marijuana endorsement, and (3) the buyer is
a "qualifying patients or designated providers who have been issued recognition cards.").
73. *E.g.*, Cal. Rev. & Tax Code § 7284.10(f) (excluding "cannabis" and "cannabis
products" from the definition of exempt "groceries"); Mass Gen. L. ch. 64H, § 6(h)
(excluding "marijuana products" from the definition of exempt "food products"); Rev.
Code Wash. § 82.08.0293(1) (excluding "marijuana, useable marijuana, or marijuana-
infused products" from the definition of exempt "food and food ingredients").
74. Cal. Dep't of Tax & Fee Admin., *Tax Guide for Cannabis Businesses*, https://www.cdtfa
.ca.gov/industry/cannabis.htm#Cultivators (last visited Apr. 11, 2020). *See also* California
State Board of Equalization, Special Tax Notice, No. L-421 (Oct. 1, 2015).
75. See Wash. Rev. Code § 82.04.213 (excluding "marijuana, useable marijuana, and
marijuana-infused products" from the definition of "agricultural product" and, thus,
from a host of sales tax exemptions generally available to farmers and agricultural and
horticultural businesses).
76. *Tax Guide for Cannabis Businesses*, *supra* note 74.

contrast, Washington excludes from its machinery and equipment exemption "machinery and equipment used directly in the manufacturing, research and development, or testing of marijuana, useable marijuana, or marijuana-infused products."[77]

(c) Resale Exemptions

The sale of cannabis and cannabis products for resale or for use as an ingredient in a new product will generally not be subject to a state's general retail sales tax because of state resale exemptions.[78] For example, California has advised that sales tax "does not apply to a cultivator's purchase of immature plants, clones, and seeds when the products grown from them will be resold as part of the cultivator's regular business activities."[79]

2.4 Cannabis Excise Taxes

In addition to the generally applicable taxes paid by cannabis businesses (e.g., income taxes, other business activity taxes, sales taxes, property taxes), states and local governments have an array of taxes targeted at the cannabis industry. Many of these taxes were adopted as the quid pro quo for legalization; others have histories dating back to state stamp taxes imposed on the sale or possession of illegal drugs. State taxes vary widely on the taxable incidence (e.g., retail sale, wholesale sale, cultivation or manufacture) and measure (e.g., selling price, weight).

2.4.1 Weight-Based Excise Taxes

Several states have enacted weight-based excise taxes on cannabis businesses. To date, these weight-based taxes have been imposed upstream on cultivators. For example, California imposes a cannabis cultivation tax on all harvested cannabis that enters the commercial market.[80] The tax is imposed on the cultivator and collected by the distributor or manufacturer.[81] The cannabis cultivation tax is measured by dry-weight ounces by product category. The current rates are $9.65 per dry-weight ounce for cannabis flower, $2.87 per ounce for cannabis leaves, and $1.39 per ounce for

---

77. Rev. Code Wash. § 82.08.02565(3).

78. *E.g.*, Cal. Dep't of Tax and Fee Admin. Pub. No. 557, *Guide to California Sales and Use Tax and Cannabis Tax Laws* (Feb. 1, 2018) (advising that "[t]he sale of cannabis for resale is not subject to sales tax"); 830 Code Mass. Regs. § 64N.1(3)(c)(1) (providing that a "marijuana establishment" may claim a resale exemption for sales to other marijuana establishments).

79. Cal. Dep't of Tax and Fee Admin., *Information for the Cannabis Industry: How Tax Applies to Immature Plants, Clones, and Seeds* (June 25, 2018).

80. Cal. Rev. & Tax. Code § 34012.

81. *Id.* at § 34012(h).

fresh cannabis plants.[82] These rates are adjusted annually for inflation.[83] Alaska and Maine also impose weight-based excise taxes on cultivators.[84]

2.4.2 Price-Based Excise Taxes

A more common approach to state taxation is to impose price-based excise taxes. However, such taxes vary widely.

Price-based excise taxes tend to be paid downstream at the retail sale. For example, Washington imposes a 37 percent marijuana excise tax on the selling price of each retail sale of marijuana concentrates, useable marijuana, and marijuana-infused products.[85] Rates in other states are lower but vary considerably.[86]

However, some states impose price-based excise taxes at the wholesale level or at both the retail and wholesale levels. For example, Colorado imposes a 15 percent marijuana excise tax on wholesale sales of marijuana by cultivators and a 15 percent retail marijuana sales tax on the retail sale of marijuana and marijuana products by retailers.[87] Similarly, Nevada imposes a 15 percent excise tax on the wholesale sales of marijuana and a 10 percent excise tax on retail sales of marijuana.[88]

Finally, some states impose priced-based excise taxes but vary the rate by product. For example, Illinois imposes a cannabis purchaser excise tax on the retail sale of cannabis with a rate that varies by product category (10 percent on marijuana with THC levels of 35 percent or less; 25 percent

---

82. See https://www.cdtfa.ca.gov/taxes-and-fees/tax-rates-stfd.htm (last visited Apr. 14, 2020).

83. Cal. Rev. & Tax. Code § 34012(b).

84. Alaska Stat. § 43.61.010 (imposing an excise tax on marijuana cultivation facilities equal to $50 per ounce of mature bud, $25 per ounce of immature or abnormal bud, and $15 per ounce for other parts of the plant sold or transferred to retailers or manufacturers); Me. Rev. Stat. tit. 36, § 4923 (imposing an excise tax on marijuana cultivation facilities equal to "$335 per pound . . . of marijuana flower or mature marijuana plants" and "$94 per pound . . . of marijuana trim" sold to other licensees).

85. RCW 69.50.530(1)(a). This tax is in addition to the general sales tax, which also applies to retail sales of marijuana and marijuana products.

86. *E.g.*, Cal. Rev. & Tax. Code § 34011(1)(1) (15 percent cannabis excise tax on retail sales); Mass. Gen. Law, ch. 64k, § 2 (10.75 percent excise tax on retail sales of marijuana or marijuana products, plus local option taxes); Mich. Comp. Laws § 333.27963 (10 percent excise tax on retail sales of marijuana); Or. Rev. Stat. § 475B.705 (17 percent tax on the retail sale of "marijuana items," including usable marijuana, immature plants, and cannabinoid edibles, concentrate, extract, and other cannabinoid products).

87. Colo. Rev. Stat. §§ 39-28.8-202, 39-28.8-302(1). Unlike some states, Colorado's retail marijuana sales tax is in lieu of its general sales tax.

88. Nev. Rev. Stat. § 372A.290. These taxes are in addition to the general sales tax. Nev. Rev. Stat. § 372A.290(3)(b).

on marijuana with THC levels above 35 percent; 20 percent on cannabis-infused products).[89]

2.4.3 Stamp Taxes

Many states impose controlled substance or stamp taxes on the possession of controlled substances. These stamps raise relatively little revenue—perhaps not surprisingly. Dealers and consumers of illegal drugs are generally unlikely to purchase tax stamps from government officials for their illegal goods. Instead, such taxes have been used to supplement more traditional drug crimes with civil and criminal tax penalties. For example, Alabama imposes a drugs and controlled substances tax that requires dealers to pay tax on acquisition or possession of marijuana or other controlled substances and affix a stamp evidencing payment of the tax.[90] The tax on marijuana is $3.50 per gram.[91] Failure to pay the tax and affix the stamps carries a 100 percent penalty (in addition to the tax due) and is a felony punishable under the Alabama Criminal Code.[92]

2.5 Non-Marijuana Forms of Cannabis (Hemp and CBD)

Most states tax non-marijuana forms of cannabis such as hemp and non-marijuana CBD in the same manner as other tangible personal property. For example, California does not impose its cannabis excise tax on industrial hemp or CBD products made from industrial hemp even if those products contain trace amounts of tetrahydrocannabinol (THC).[93] However, the sale of hemp and hemp products would generally be subject to California's general sales tax unless the purchase qualifies for an exemption. Colorado similarly does not impose its marijuana excise tax or marijuana sales tax on sales of "industrial hemp" or products derived from industrial hemp.[94]

---

89. 410 ILL. COMP. STAT. 705/65-10. Illinois also imposes a 7 percent cannabis cultivation privilege tax measured by the first wholesale sale of cannabis. *Id.*

90. ALA. STAT. § 40-17A-11.

91. *Id.* § 40-17A-8(1). The rate for marijuana is considerably lower than the $200 per gram rate for other controlled substances.

92. *Id.* § 40-17A-9; Murray v. State, 922 So. 2d 961 (Ala. Crim. App. 2005) (affirming a ten-year sentence for failing to affix a tax stamp).

93. CAL. REV. & TAX. CODE § 34010 (defining "cannabis" by reference to CAL. HEALTH & SAFETY CODE § 11018 and, accordingly, excluding "industrial hemp"); CAL. HEALTH & SAFETY CODE § 11018.5 (defining "industrial hemp" as "types of the plant Cannabis sativa L. having no more than three-tenths of 1 percent tetrahydrocannabinol (THC) contained in the dried flowering tops, whether growing or not; the seeds of the plant; the resin extracted from any part of the plant; and every compound, manufacture, salt, derivative, mixture, or preparation of the plant, its seeds or resin produced therefrom").

94. COLO. REV. STAT. § 39-28.8-101(7) (defining "retail marijuana").

Although uncommon, states may impose specific excise taxes on non-marijuana CBD. For example, Louisiana imposes a 3 percent excise tax on the retail sale of "industrial hemp-derived CBD products."[95]

---

95. La. Rev. Stat. § 47:1693(A).

7

Marketing

Amanda Beane, Jared Bryant, and Jason Howell

1. Marketing Cannabis Products in the United States

Companies of every size are increasingly marketing a wide assortment of cannabis and cannabis-derived products. However, many sellers are advertising such products illegally, given the nuanced differences in treatment under the law between cannabis plants and cannabis derivatives, and the relatively complex and ever-evolving regulatory scheme that governs them. Section 1 explains the differences among these products and describes at a high level the applicable regulatory scheme as it relates to advertising.

1.1 Cannabis, Marijuana, and Hemp

It is important to note that while "marijuana" and "hemp" both belong to the *cannabis* genus of plants, they are highly distinguishable from a legal perspective. This is in part due to their comparative levels of THC (tetrahydrocannabinol, the compound in cannabis most known for causing a "high" in its users). Under federal law, and for the purposes of this chapter, "hemp" is defined as any cannabis plant containing 0.3 percent or less THC by dry weight.[1] The Agriculture Improvement Act of 2018, commonly known as the 2018 Farm Bill, made hemp and hemp-derived products federally legal (see discussion in Chapter 1). Conversely, "marijuana" is defined as any cannabis plant that contains more than 0.3 percent THC by

---

1. Generally, Cannabis plants containing 0.3 percent or less THC by dry weight do not contain enough THC to generate a "high."

dry weight.[2] Some states have legalized recreational marijuana, but it is not legal at the federal level.

1.2 Cannabis Derivatives

Cannabis plants (both hemp and marijuana) produce derivative ingredients, including cannabidiol (CBD), which has experienced increased popularity with marketers due to its suspected therapeutic applications. On a molecular level, CBD looks the same whether it is sourced from hemp or marijuana. However, only hemp and hemp derivatives were federally legalized by the 2018 Farm Bill. Therefore, products containing CBD derived from hemp are generally legal at the federal level (see later in this chapter for a discussion of the exceptions), but products containing CBD derived from marijuana are illegal, even if they contain 0 percent THC.

Furthermore, federal law prohibits the inclusion of hemp derivatives like CBD in certain products such as foods, drugs, and dietary supplements, even when containing 0 percent THC.[3] And although advertising hemp-derived CBD in certain products is legal under federal law, selling those products may ultimately be illegal in certain states. For example, recreational marijuana is legal in Washington state, but placing hemp-derived CBD in foods and beverages there is illegal.[4]

1.3 Legality of Advertising Cannabis Products

The legality of advertising marijuana and marijuana derivatives largely depends on state laws, as such advertising is generally illegal under federal law but permitted in certain states when done in accordance with their regulations (see "Marijuana and Marijuana Derivative Advertising," Section 5 of this chapter). Although the laws governing the advertising of hemp products not intended for consumption are generally the same as for any other product, the advertising of hemp derivatives intended for consumption is more of a gray area.

For example, some states like Iowa still treat hemp and hemp derivatives as controlled substances and prohibit their manufacture, delivery, or possession for nonmedical purposes.[5] And although, so far, it does not appear

---

2. Some marijuana plants contain as much as 30 percent THC, more than enough to generate a "high."

3. See U.S. Food & Drug Administration, *What You Need to Know (And What We're Working to Find Out) About Products Containing Cannabis or Cannabis-derived Compounds, Including CBD,* https://www.fda.gov/consumers/consumer-updates/what-you-need-know-and-what-were-working-find-out-about-products-containing-cannabis-or-cannabis ("It is currently illegal to market CBD by adding it to a food or labeling it as a dietary supplement.").

4. *See* Washington State Dep't of Agriculture, *Restrictions on the Use of Hemp CBD as a Food Ingredient,* https://agr.wa.gov/departments/food-safety/food-safety/hemp-cbd-in-food (last visited Apr. 21, 2020).

5. *See, e.g.,* IOWA CODE ANN. § 124.401(1); IOWA CODE ANN. § 124.204(m), (u); Thomas J. Miller, Attorney General's statement on hemp and CBD products, https://idph.iowa.gov/Portals/1/userfiles/234/Files/hemp_statement_A8AFF8F160A43.pdf.

that the mere act of advertising those products (without actually manufacturing, selling, or possessing them in state) would violate those states' laws (as would be the case for advertising marijuana or marijuana derivatives under federal law), companies should still exercise caution doing so in states where those products are illegal until the legal landscape develops further.

Therefore, this chapter primarily focuses on the advertising of consumable products containing hemp derivatives, the most prominent of which is currently CBD.

2. Regulatory Framework for Hemp and Hemp Derivative Advertising

2.1 Federal Advertising Laws

Under federal law, hemp and hemp derivative marketing is subject to the overlapping jurisdictions of the Federal Trade Commission (FTC) and the U.S. Food and Drug Administration (FDA). To date, the FTC and FDA have primarily enforced hemp marketing through individually or jointly sending warning letters to manufacturers, sellers, and advertisers making unsubstantiated health claims about their hemp-derived (mostly CBD) products.

2.1.1 FTC

Section 5 of the Federal Trade Commission Act (FTC Act) prohibits unfair or deceptive acts or practices.[6] "Deceptive" practices involve a material "representation, omission or practice that is likely to mislead [a] consumer acting reasonably in the circumstances, to the consumer's detriment."[7] A practice is "unfair" if it "causes or is likely to cause substantial injury to consumers which is not reasonably avoidable by consumers themselves and not outweighed by countervailing benefits to consumers or to competition."[8] The FTC holds jurisdiction over all matters regulating the truth or falsity of advertising for hemp products under the FTC Act. The FTC may bring enforcement actions against unfair, deceptive, and misleading advertising, with penalties that include injunctive relief, damages, and civil fines. In determining whether advertising is unfair, deceptive, or misleading, the FTC is guided by truth-in-advertising and unfairness standards that apply to advertising claims.

---

6. 15 U.S.C. § 45.

7. *See* Letter from James C. Miller III, Chairman, FTC, to Hon. John D. Dingell, Chairman, House Comm. On Energy & Commerce (Oct. 14, 1983), *appended to In re Cliffdale Associates., Inc.*, 103 F.T.C. 110, 174 (1984) (decision & order), https://www.ftc.gov/system/files/documents/public_statements/410531/831014deceptionstmt.pdf.

8. 15 U.S.C. § 45(n).

2.1.2 Lanham Act

Separate from government enforcement, private businesses who compete with or do business with companies selling hemp products may also challenge the unfair, deceptive, or misleading advertising practices of these businesses under the Lanham Act.[9] Businesses bringing suit need to show that they have been harmed in some way or are likely to be harmed by the advertising. To state a claim for a false advertising violation of the Lanham Act, the plaintiff must allege that (1) the defendant made a false or misleading statement of fact in commercial advertising or promotion about its or another's goods or services; (2) the statement actually deceives or is likely to deceive a substantial segment of the intended audience; (3) the deception is material in that it is likely to influence purchasing decisions; (4) the defendant caused the statement to enter interstate commerce; and (5) the statement results in actual or probable injury to the plaintiff.[10]

2.1.3 Federal Food, Drug, Dietary Supplements, and Cosmetics Regulation

The 2018 Farm Bill removed hemp as a controlled substance but preserved the FDA's authority to regulate (1) food, (2) drug, (3) dietary supplement, and (4) cosmetic products infused with cannabis and cannabis-derived compounds under the Federal Food, Drug and Cosmetic Act (FD&C Act) and section 351 of the Public Health Service Act. Penalties for violation of the FD&C Act can include the issuance of warning letters, seizure of goods, injunctions, and criminal prosecution imposing fines and/or imprisonment.[11]

2.2 State Laws

2.2.1 Mini-FTC Acts and Consumer Protection Laws

The consumer protection laws of many states do grant private rights of action for violations, and they are often consistent with the FTC Act and FD&C Act. For example, in California, violations of the FD&C Act constitute violations of California Health and Safety Code section 110100, which parallels the FD&C Act. And numerous states, California included, have "mini-FTC Acts" that parallel many of the misleading advertising prohibitions of the FTC Act.[12]

---

9. *Id.* § 1125(a)(1).

10. *See, e.g.,* Zenith Elecs. Corp. v. Exzec, Inc., 182 F.3d 1340, 1348 (Fed. Cir. 1999).

11. *See* U.S. Food & Drug Administration, *Types of FDA Enforcement Actions,* https://www .fda.gov/animal-veterinary/resources-you/types-fda-enforcement-actions (last visited Apr. 21, 2020).

12. *See, e.g.,* CAL. BUS. & PROF. CODE § 17500.

2.2.2 State Hemp and Hemp Derivative Laws

Although some states have laws regulating the sale of products containing hemp derivatives, particularly CBD,[13] few states have laws specifically regulating the *advertising* of such products.[14] Instead, in states where the sale of hemp derivative–infused products is legal, the advertising has typically generated liability under the state laws that are generally consistent with the FD&C Act and FTC Act referenced earlier.

2.3 National Advertising Division

The National Advertising Division (NAD), part of the Better Business Bureau's National Programs, monitors and evaluates truth and accuracy in national advertising directed to consumers age 12 years and older. NAD is a self-regulatory body through which consumers, competitors, and the division itself can bring complaints against advertisers across various industries. Participation in NAD proceedings is voluntary, and, although NAD issues injunctive-style recommendations, its decisions are nonbinding. However, NAD touts a compliance rate of about 90 to 95 percent with its decisions,[15] largely because if a company refuses to comply, NAD will refer the matter to the FTC (or other applicable regulator) for investigation. Because FTC and regulatory actions can carry significant monetary and other legal

---

13. For example, Massachusetts and Michigan. *See, e.g.,* Massachusetts Dep't of Agricultural Resources, *Policy Statement Regarding the Sale of Hemp-Derived Products in the Commonwealth,* https://www.mass.gov/files/documents/2019/06/12/MDAR%20Policy%20Statement%20Sale%20of%20Hemp.pdf (last visited Apr. 21, 2020); Michigan Dep't of Licensing & Regulatory Affairs, Issued Joint Guidance Regarding CBD (Cannabidiol) and Industrial Hemp, https://www.michigan.gov/lara/0,4601,7-154-89334_79571_78089-493382-,00.html (last visited Apr. 21, 2020). Other states permit the sale of CBD-infused food products (e.g., Maine and Colorado). *See Maine Agency Guidelines for Enforcement of Pl 2019 c. 528[LD 1749],* https://www.maine.gov/dacf/php/hemp/documents/HEMPPL2019c.528DLW10.19.pdf (last visited Apr. 21, 2020); Colorado Dep't of Public Health & Environment, *Hemp in Food,* https://www.colorado.gov/pacific/cdphe/industrial-hemp-food (last visited Apr. 21, 2020). California, where the manufacture and sale of cannabis (including cannabis edibles) and non-food CBD infused items like lotions has been made legal, nevertheless prohibits the sale of hemp-derived CBD-infused foods. *See* California Dep't of Public Health, *FAQ—Industrial Hemp and Cannabidiol (CBD) in Food Products,* revised July 6, 2018, https://www.cdph.ca.gov/Programs/CEH/DFDCS/CDPH%20Document%20Library/FDB/FoodSafetyProgram/HEMP/Web%20template%20for%20FSS%20Rounded%20-%20Final.pdf.

14. Apart from labeling laws for cannabis-infused products, which are discussed in Chapter 13, and laws regulating the advertising of cannabis, which are discussed in Section 5 of this chapter.

15. BBB National Programs, Inc., "BBB National Programs' National Advertising Division Launches NAD Fast-Track SWIFT, an Expedited Challenge Process for Certain Digital Advertising Claims," news release, April 2, 2020, https://bbbprograms.org/media/details/bbb-national-programs-national-advertising-division-launches-nad-fast-track-swift-an-expedited-challenge-process-for-certain-digital-advertising-claims.

penalties, participation in NAD proceedings is generally encouraged, as it often allows advertisers to correct illegal advertising claims before a regulator takes more aggressive enforcement action.

For example, in April 2018, as part of its routine monitoring program, NAD requested substantiation from That's Natural, LLC, a CBD hemp seller, for its website claims that "CBD makes cancer cells commit 'suicide' without killing other cells."[16] After That's Natural refused to participate in the proceeding, NAD referred the matter to the FTC.[17] Then, within two months after being contacted by the FTC, That's Natural removed all health-related claims from its websites, social media accounts, and print materials.[18]

3. Advertising Basics

This section covers the basics of advertising law, including an introduction to advertising claims, the concept of nonactionable puffery in claims, strategies for sufficiently making advertising disclosures, and claim substantiation.

3.1 Identifying an Advertising Claim

Advertising claims are express and implied messages that a reasonable consumer would understand to be communicated by an advertisement, and advertisers are responsible for the truth and accuracy of such claims.[19] Express claims are communicated directly by the text or audio of an advertisement; implied claims are messages communicated indirectly by an advertisment (e.g., by the advertisement as a whole given the net impression made by all of its components, such as sounds, images, and text) and can arise even when not intended by the advertiser.[20] For example, if an advertiser states that "for hundreds of years cultures have used cannabis believing it to have healing properties," the express claim conveyed to the consumer may be that *others* believe cannabis products have healing properties. But the arguably implied claim is that cannabis does, in fact, have healing powers that can help one's health issues, something that would require adequate substantiation.

---

16. *See That's Natural, LLC (CBD Hemp Oil)*, Report #6173, NAD/CARU Case Reports (Apr. 2018).

17. *Id.*

18. *See* Devin Willis Domond, *FTC Staff Letter: That's Natural, LLC (CBD Hemp Oil), Response to NAD*, June 14, 2018, https://www.ftc.gov/system/files/documents/public _statements/1385953/thats_natural_resolution_letter_6-14-18.pdf.

19. *See, e.g., In re* Kraft, Inc., 114 F.T.C. 40, 120–21 (1991).

20. *See, e.g., id.; In re* Pom Wonderful LLC, 2013-1 Trade Cas. P 78220, Final Order, 2013 WL 268926, at *5 (F.T.C. Jan. 16, 2013) ("The [FTC] may undertake a net impression analysis and find implied claims when it can 'conclude with confidence after examining the interaction of all the different elements in [an advertisement] that they contain a particular implied claim.'").

It is important to know what claims are communicated by an advertisement because claims must be true, not misleading,[21] and, in some cases, they must also be substantiated by competent and reliable scientific evidence (we discuss claim substantiation later).[22] Therefore, advertisers should always consider all reasonably implied claims when creating or reviewing advertisements, particularly when cannabis and cannabis derivative ads have *any* potential to communicate messages regarding a product's ability to affect physical or mental health.

3.2 Puffery

"Puffery" is, generally speaking, a vague or unverifiable claim that no reasonable consumer would be likely to take at face value. Puffery often takes the form of (1) an exaggerated, blustering, and boastful statement upon which no reasonable buyer would be justified in relying; or (2) a general claim of superiority over comparable products which is so vague that it can be understood as nothing more than a mere expression of opinion.[23] Because statements that qualify as mere puffery are not false or deceptive, they do not require substantiation.[24]

Determining whether a claim is actionable or mere puffery often requires a nuanced analysis and is typically heavily affected by the context of an ad. For example, describing a product as "better" may constitute puffery in one context but an actionable and verifiable claim in another context.[25]

3.3 Disclosures

As discussed earlier, an express claim can easily communicate an implied claim with a substantially different meaning. As a result, the express claims in an advertisement may be true and substantiated while the implied claims are not. One way to address this issue is to modify the express claim itself so that it no longer conveys a misleading implied claim. Alternatively, this can often be addressed by adding an appropriate qualification or disclosure to the express claim. Disclosures are helpful in clarifying the intended meaning of an ambiguous claim to avoid communicating inaccurate or unsupported implied claims.

Disclosures are also often used to ensure that customers are not misled by a claim. However, although disclosures can sometimes correct merely misleading claims, they are typically insufficient to correct false express

---

21. 15 U.S.C. § 1125(a).
22. *See, e.g.,* POM Wonderful, LLC v. F.T.C., 777 F.3d 478, 500 (D.C. Cir. 2015).
23. Pizza Hut, Inc. v. Papa John's Int'l, Inc., 227 F.3d 489, 496 (5th Cir. 2000).
24. U.S. Healthcare, Inc. v. Blue Cross of Greater Phila., 898 F.2d 914, 922 (3d Cir. 1990).
25. *Compare, e.g.,* Papa John's International (Papa John's Pizza), Report #3450, NAD/CARU Case Reports (Mar. 1998) ("Papa John's Better Ingredients. Better Pizza" found to be puffery) with *Pizza Hut*, 227 F.3d 489 (finding that the phrase "Papa John's Better Ingredients. Better Pizza" when used by itself was puffery, but when used in a different context might become misleading and actionable).

claims.[26] In other words, disclosures should not be used to directly contradict the claims being conveyed by an advertisement. Given the higher risks for making cannabis-related health claims, advertisers should be wary of using disclosures to counteract the risk of conveying such claims. For example, a claim that a cannabis-infused product has a certain health benefit is still inappropriate even when accompanied by a clear disclosure that there is insufficient scientific evidence to support that claim.[27]

Disclosures must be made in a clear and prominent manner. Clarity and prominence are evaluated based on the overall impressions that a reasonable customer would glean from the advertising. Use the following principles when drafting disclosures in online and offline mediums:

Proximity and Placement: Place disclosures near the claims that they qualify.

Prominence: Make disclosures noticeable to customers (e.g., factor in size, color, and contrast).

Distractions: Evaluate how the visuals fit together and ensure that other parts of the ads do not get in the way of necessary disclosures.

Language: Use simple, easy-to-understand language.

Repetition: Repeat disclosures as needed (e.g., repeat when claims are made across multiple web pages or in a long video).

Platform/Medium: Take into account the various devices and platforms on which the disclosures will appear, including mobile phones and small screens.

---

26. *See, e.g.,* Federal Trade Commission, *.com Disclosures: How to Make Effective Disclosures in Digital Advertising* (March 2013) https://www.ftc.gov/sites/default/files/attachments/press-releases/ftc-staff-revises-online-advertising-disclosure-guidelines/130312dotcomdisclosures.pdf ("A disclosure can only qualify or limit a claim to avoid a misleading impression. It cannot cure a false claim. If a disclosure provides information that contradicts a material claim, the disclosure will not be sufficient to prevent the ad from being deceptive. In that situation, the claim itself must be modified."); *Matter of Warner-Lambert Co.,* 86 F.T.C. 1398 (1975) (holding *pro forma* statements of no absolute prevention followed by promises of fewer colds did not cure or correct the false message that Listerine will prevent colds); *Cf.* Beneficial Corp. v. F.T.C., 542 F.2d 611, 618 (3d Cir. 1976) (Court reversed the FTC's opinion that no qualifying language could eliminate the deception stemming from use of the slogan "Instant Tax Refund").

27. *See, e.g.,* Edmundo Garcia Jr., *Herbal Healer Academy, Inc. Warning Letter,* U.S. Food & Drug Administration (September 12, 2019), https://www.fda.gov/inspections-compliance-enforcement-and-criminal-investigations/warning-letters/herbal-healer-academy-inc-570957-09122019 (Statement "FDA will not allow us to say this can be used as an antiviral supplement, however, extensive research in Israel has proven it is effective and should be supplemented with viral illness . . ." resulted in FDA warning letter).

3.4 Substantiating Advertisement Claims

3.4.1 Generally

As mentioned earlier, both express and implied advertisement claims must be substantiated, that is, supported by at least a "reasonable basis" based on credible, objective evidence prior to publication. Claims may be misleading if they lack a reasonable basis or if they are false.[28] The type and amount of evidence needed will vary depending on the nature of the claim, but, generally, claims must be supported by the amount, type, and quality of evidence that experts in the relevant field would find sufficient.[29] However, for establishment claims, that is, claims conveying that a specific level of substantiation exists, advertisers must possess the specific substantiation claimed.[30] For example, a claim that "9 out of 10 users agree . . ." would need to be supported by a reliable survey demonstrating those results.

3.4.2 Scientific Claims

Certain claims, such as those relating to health, safety, environmental benefit, and research findings, require a higher level of substantiation in the form of competent and reliable scientific evidence.[31] Scientific evidence is considered competent and reliable if it is supported by credible tests, studies, or other evidence conducted by qualified people in the field using procedures generally accepted by the scientific community to yield accurate and reliable results.[32] Advertisers must obtain appropriate substantiation, verify that such substantiation is sufficient, and save such substantiation in the company files before a claim is communicated to the public.

For health claims regarding hemp-derived products that are marketed in interstate commerce, the FTC requires "well-controlled human clinical studies, substantiating that the claims are true at the time they are made,"[33] and one FDA commissioner has stated that "controlled clinical trials testing the safety and efficacy of a drug, along with careful review through the

---

28. In the Matter of Ecm Biofilms, Inc., A Corp., Also d/b/a/ Enviroplastics Int'l, No. 9358, 2015 WL 6384951, at *39 (MSNET Oct. 19, 2015); *see, e.g., POM Wonderful,* 777 F.3d at 490 (citing *In re Pfizer Inc.,* 81 F.T.C. 23 (1972) ("In order to have had a reasonable basis, the tests must have been conducted prior to, and actually relied upon in connection with, the marketing of the product in question.")).

29. *Id.*

30. *Id.*

31. *See, e.g., id.* (affirming FTC's holding that competent and reliable scientific evidence consisting of randomized, well-controlled human clinical testing is needed for disease-related claims).

32. *Id.*

33. *See* Donald D. Ashley & Mary K. Engle, *PotNetwork Holdings, Inc. Warning Letter,* U.S. Food & Drug Administration, Federal Trade Commission (Mar. 28, 2019), https://www .ftc.gov/system/files/attachments/press-releases/ftc-joins-fda-sending-warning-letters -companies-advertising-selling-products-containing-cannabidiol/potnetwork_holdings _inc_warning_letter.pdf.

FDA's drug approval process, is the most appropriate way to bring mari-juana-derived treatments to patients."[34]

Ingredients that have historically been legal are more likely to have been through scientific testing regarding their short- and long-term impacts on human health. However, due to its previously illegal status as a Schedule I drug (see Section 5.1, "Federal Law"), cannabis is only now starting to be subjected to such testing. It may be some time before claims about the health benefits or safety of cannabis in general, let alone its derivatives as they behave in specific types of products, will have sufficient substantiation to pass regulatory muster. In sum, recent warning letters sent by the FTC and FDA create a general impression of skepticism about whether the type of evidence needed to support scientific claims regarding hemp and hemp-derived products yet exists.[35]

---

34. U.S. Food & Drug Administration, *FDA Approves First Drug Comprised of an Active Ingredient Derived from Marijuana to Treat Rare, Severe Forms of Epilepsy*, news release, June 25, 2018, https://www.fda.gov/news-events/press-announcements/fda-approves-first-drug -comprised-active-ingredient-derived-marijuana-treat-rare-severe-forms.

35. *See, e.g.*, Donald D. Ashley & Mary K. Engle, *Advanced Spine and Pain, LLC Warning Letter*, U.S. Food & Drug Administration, Federal Trade Commission, March 28, 2019, https://www.fda.gov/inspections-compliance-enforcement-and-criminal-investigations /warning-letters/advanced-spine-and-pain-llc-565256-03282019; *see, e.g.*, Donald D. Ashley & Mary K. Engle, *Nutra Pure LLC Warning Letter*, March 28, 2019, https://www.ftc.gov /system/files/attachments/press-releases/ftc-joins-fda-sending-warning-letters-companies -advertising-selling-products-containing-cannabidiol/nutra_pure_llc_warning_letter.pdf; *see, e.g.*, William A. Correll Jr. & Mary K. Engle, *PotNetwork Holdings, Inc. Warning Letter*, U.S. Food & Drug Administration, Federal Trade Commission, March 28, 2019, https:// www.fda.gov/inspections-compliance-enforcement-and-criminal-investigations/warning -letters/potnetwork-holdings-inc-564030-03282019; *see, e.g.*, Donald D. Ashley & Mary K. Engle, *Rooted Apothecary LLC Warning Letter*, U.S. Food & Drug Administration, Federal Trade Commission, October 10, 2019, https://www.fda.gov/inspections-compliance -enforcement-and-criminal-investigations/warning-letters/rooted-apothecary-llc -585312-10102019; *see, e.g.*, Steven E. Porter Jr., *Signature Formulations, LLC Warning Letter*, U.S. Food & Drug Administration, July 31, 2018, https://www.fda.gov/inspections -compliance-enforcement-and-criminal-investigations/warning-letters/signature -formulations-llc-545017-07312018; *see, e.g.*, Edmundo Garcia Jr., *Herbal Healer Academy, Inc. Warning Letter*, U.S. Food & Drug Administration, September 12, 2019, https:// www.fda.gov/inspections-compliance-enforcement-and-criminal-investigations/warning -letters/herbal-healer-academy-inc-570957-09122019; *see, e.g.*, Donald D. Ashley, *CDRL Nutritional, Inc. Warning Letter*, U.S. Food & Drug Administration, November 22, 2019, https://www.fda.gov/inspections-compliance-enforcement-and-criminal-investigations /warning-letters/cdrl-nutritional-inc-593398-11222019; *see, e.g.*, Donald D. Ashley, *Curaleaf, Inc. Warning Letter*, U.S. Food & Drug Administration, July 22, 2019, https://www.fda .gov/inspections-compliance-enforcement-and-criminal-investigations/warning-letters /curaleaf-inc-579289-07222019.

3.5 Health Claims

To date, the greatest source of both federal enforcement and state lawsuits relating to advertising hemp-derived products stems from making health-related claims about the product. For this reason, we address health claims on their own in this section.

3.5.1 Generally

Health claims about hemp derivative–infused products typically convey that the products can help improve one's physical or mental health; can treat, cure, mitigate, or prevent any type of physical or mental health issue (a "health-benefit" claim); or are generally not detrimental to human health (a "healthy" claim). Simply put, if an advertisement even *implies* that use of a hemp derivative–infused product is safe or might have *any* sort of physical or mental impact on its users (e.g., improves sleep, reduces stress, relieves pain, encourages good health, or treats an illness), it likely conveys a health claim.

For example, if a CBD product is advertised as "safe for children," it constitutes a "healthy for children" claim that must be substantiated with competent and reliable scientific evidence (which, as discussed earlier, does not yet exist for CBD and cannabis products). And if a cannabis product is advertised as, for example, "promoting relaxation" or "helping treat pain," in addition to still needing competent and reliable scientific evidence to avoid violating the FTC's substantiation rules, it also communicates a drug claim. One of the issues surrounding health claims is that they risk implicating FDA compliance requirements for drugs, as discussed in later in Section 3.6.1.

3.5.2 Examples of Prohibited Health Claims

Health claims can be communicated in a number of ways, such as through descriptions of the product, the product's name, the name of the website where the advertisement or promotional copy appears, and via consumer and expert endorsements.[36]

If a hemp derivative–infused product communicates health claims, the advertisement may violate federal laws governing hemp derivative–infused product advertising. Various approaches have tried to address the lack of scientific substantiation for health-related claims, including using qualified language, displaying the reviews and testimonials of consumers (rather than statements from the advertiser), citing the results of cannabis-related studies, characterizing claims as general knowledge, and mentioning the way others have historically used cannabis or cannabis derivatives. Nevertheless, many of these claims have still resulted in warning letters from the

---

36. *See, e.g.*, Mary K. Engle, *4Bush Holdings, LLC Warning Letter*, Federal Trade Commission, Sept. 9, 2019, https://www.ftc.gov/system/files/documents/foia_requests/foia-2019 -01289_warning_letters_sent_to_cbd_companies_9-30-19.pdf.

FDA and/or FTC as well as class action lawsuits. Following are examples of advertising language that has triggered FDA and/or FTC warning letters on the basis that they conveyed healthy or health-benefit claims:

- "For hundreds of years, people have used preparations made from C. Sativa, including CBD for a variety of disorders, including gout, rheumatism, malaria, pain, and fever."[37]
- "Many people have reported relief from crippling arthritis in just 30 days using this product."[38]
- Customer testimonial stating "Cetyl Myristoleate helps with my fibromyalgia!"[39]
- "In other words, it is becoming more and more clear that in terms of a safe and effective treatment for PTSD, CBD oil could be the answer."[40]
- "A 2014 study showed that participants who received CBD oil experienced anti-anxiety and anti-depression effects from the oil."[41]
- "CBD is known for its anti-anxiety properties that can promote relaxation and stress relief."[42]
- "Increasing evidence suggests that CBD oil is a powerful option for pain . . . anxiety . . . and autism. . . . It seems like an attractive and safe option for children."[43]
- "The compounds present in CBD are found to have anti-inflammatory effects. . . . Psoriasis is an inflammatory disease."[44]

3.6 Advertising Issues Regulated by the FDA

The FDA regulates foods, drugs, dietary supplements, and cosmetic products infused with hemp derivatives under the FD&C Act and section 351 of the Public Health Service Act. And because the *way* in which a product is advertised can cause a product to qualify as one of these regulated items,[45]

---

37. Steven E. Porter Jr., *Signature Formulations, LLC Warning Letter*, U.S. Food & Drug Administration, July 31, 2018, https://www.fda.gov/inspections-compliance-enforcement-and-criminal-investigations/warning-letters/signature-formulations-llc-545017-07312018.

38. *Herbal Healer Academy, Inc. Warning Letter, supra* note 35.

39. *Id.*

40. Donald D. Ashley, *CDRL Nutritional, Inc. Warning Letter*, U.S. Food & Drug Administration, November 22, 2019, https://www.fda.gov/inspections-compliance-enforcement-and-criminal-investigations/warning-letters/cdrl-nutritional-inc-593398-11222019.

41. *Curaleaf, Inc. Warning Letter*, supra note 35.

42. *Id.*

43. *Rooted Apothecary LLC Warning Letter*, supra note 35.

44. *Nutra Pure LLC Warning Letter*, supra note 35.

45. *See, e.g.*, U.S. Food & Drug Administration, *Is It a Cosmetic, a Drug, or Both? (Or Is It Soap?)* https://www.fda.gov/cosmetics/cosmetics-laws-regulations/it-cosmetic-drug-or-both-or-it-soap#Intended_use (last visited Apr. 21, 2020).

the FDA has been active in enforcing advertising regulations related to hemp derivative–infused products.

As of the writing of this chapter, the FDA takes the position that hemp-derived CBD specifically cannot be used as an ingredient in a food, drug, or dietary supplement, but it can be included as an ingredient in cosmetic products.[46] However, the FDA has not explicitly addressed the legality of including other hemp derivatives like cannabigerol (CBG) in food, drugs, and dietary supplements.[47] Therefore, while the FDA continues developing enforcement policies for hemp derivatives such as CBD under the FD&C Act,[48] it is generally a good practice to approach all hemp derivatives advertised as foods, drugs, or dietary supplements as if they were CBD.

3.6.1 Drug Advertising

Under the FD&C Act, "drugs" are articles "intended for use in the diagnosis, cure, mitigation, treatment, or prevention of disease" and "articles (other than food) intended to affect the structure or any function of the body of man or other animals."[49] In determining a product's "intended use," the FDA analyzes (1) claims included on product labeling, *in advertising, on the Internet, or in other materials promoting the product*; (2) consumer perception; and (3) its ingredients (i.e., the presence of certain ingredients in a product that have a well-known therapeutic use associated with a drug).[50]

Using this approach, the FDA can determine that a product qualifies as a misbranded or unapproved drug if even a single advertisement (or

---

46. *See* U.S. Food & Drug Administration, *FDA Regulation of Cannabis and Cannabis-Derived Products, Including Cannabidiol (CBD)*, https://www.fda.gov/news-events/public-health-focus/fda-regulation-cannabis-and-cannabis-derived-products-including-cannabidiol-cbd (last visited Apr. 21, 2020) ("Certain cosmetic ingredients are prohibited or restricted by regulation, but currently that is not the case for any cannabis or cannabis-derived ingredients.").

47. *See, e.g.*, U.S. Food & Drug Administration, *FDA Regulation of Cannabis and Cannabis-Derived Products, Including Cannabidiol (CBD)*, https://www.fda.gov/news-events/public-health-focus/fda-regulation-cannabis-and-cannabis-derived-products-including-cannabidiol-cbd (last visited Apr. 21, 2020, ("Ingredients that are derived from parts of the cannabis plant that do not contain THC or CBD might fall outside the scope of this exclusion, and therefore might be able to be marketed as dietary supplements.").

48. *See* U.S. Food & Drug Administration, "FDA Advances Work Related to Cannabidiol Products with Focus on Protecting Public Health, Providing Market Clarity," news release, March 5, 2020, https://www.fda.gov/news-events/press-announcements/fda-advances-work-related-cannabidiol-products-focus-protecting-public-health-providing-market ("we are currently evaluating issuance of a risk-based enforcement policy that would provide greater transparency and clarity regarding factors the agency intends to take into account in prioritizing enforcement decisions").

49. FD&C Act, 21 U.S.C. § 321(g)(1).

50. U.S. Food & Drug Administration, *Is It a Cosmetic, a Drug, or Both? (Or Is It Soap?)*, https://www.fda.gov/cosmetics/cosmetics-laws-regulations/it-cosmetic-drug-or-both-or-it-soap#Intended_use.

even a single claim within an advertisement) communicates that a product containing a hemp derivative is intended for use in the diagnosis, cure, mitigation, treatment, or prevention of disease[51] or is otherwise intended to affect the structure or any function of the body (i.e., a "health-benefit" claim). Therefore, any type of claim about the benefits of hemp and its derivatives to one's health will likely communicate one of those messages and cause the FDA to regulate the product as a drug. While simply stating that a CBD product is "healthy" may not qualify as a drug claim (because that merely conveys that the product will not cause bad health rather than conveying that it can improve health), it would still constitute a health claim that requires competent and reliable scientific evidence. As discussed earlier, because such competent and reliable substantiation in the form of scientific evidence does not yet exist, the FTC could find such a claim to be unsubstantiated and misleading. See Chapter 13 for further discussion of the FDA's regulation of hemp derivatives as drugs.

3.6.2 Dietary Supplement Advertising

Advertisers can communicate that a product is a dietary supplement expressly or by implication. Because the FDA defines the term "dietary supplement" as being a product that is "intended for ingestion,"[52] hemp derivative–infused products that use a delivery method other than ingestion—for example, CBD oil that is taken "sublingually" (under the tongue), CBD patches, CBD vape pens, and CBD tinctures (which can be either ingested or delivered topically)—do not meet the FDA's definition of supplement and should never be advertised as such.[53] The advertising of a product as a dietary supplement has been cited as a cause of action by the FDA under the FD&C Act as well as by class action plaintiffs suing CBD advertisers under state laws.[54]

3.6.3 Food Product Advertising

This section briefly discusses how food and beverage laws intersect with advertising law.[55] Currently, it is illegal under 301(ll) of the FD&C Act (21 U.S.C. § 331(ll)) to advertise or market in interstate commerce any food

---

51. It is important to note that the term "disease" is extremely broad ("a condition . . . that impairs normal functioning and is typically manifested by distinguishing signs and symptoms" MERRIAM-WEBSTER) and has been interpreted as such by the FDA (i.e., as encompassing practically any sort of physical or mental issue including pain, hunger, poor sleep, anxiety, pneumonia, a hurt toe . . .).

52. *See* 21 U.S.C. § 321(ff).

53. *See, e.g.,* Donald D. Ashley, *Advanced Spine and Pain, LLC, Warning Letter,* U.S. Food & Drug Administration, March 28, 2019, https://www.fda.gov/inspections -compliance-enforcement-and-criminal-investigations/warning-letters/advanced-spine -and-pain-llc-565256-03282019.

54. *Id.; see, e.g.,* McCarthy v. Elixinol LLC, case no. 5:19-cv-07948-LHK (N.D.C.A.).

55. See Chapter 13 for an in-depth discussion of food and beverage laws.

(intended for human or animal consumption) to which THC or CBD has been added.[56]

For some hemp derivative–infused ingestible products like oil and gummies, predicting the regulatory approach of the FDA may be difficult. Although some courts have stayed class actions filed against the sellers of ingestible CBD products until the FDA completes rulemaking on the marketing of such products, other courts have denied motions to stay in similar cases.[57] FDA warning letters to CBD marketers and manufacturers indicate that simply marketing a product that comes in a form commonly associated with conventional foods (e.g., "CBD Organic Gummy Bears"[58]) may be enough to violate the FD&C Act. And describing ingestible products as conventional human foods through the use of terms like "snack," "treat," "delicious," and "tasty," or otherwise marketing them for their taste or including a nutritional fact panel with the product, appears to increase this risk.[59]

3.6.4 Cosmetic Advertising

FDA guidance has specified that cannabis and cannabis-derived ingredients are currently not restricted or prohibited from being included as ingredients in cosmetic products.[60] Cosmetic products and ingredients are also not subject to premarket approval by the FDA (except for most color additives).[61] Therefore, companies may generally advertise cosmetic products containing hemp and hemp derivatives as long as they do so truthfully and the products are not "adulterated," "misbranded," or advertised as "drugs."

---

56. *See* U.S. Food & Drug Administration, *FDA Regulation of Cannabis and Cannabis-Derived Products, Including Cannabidiol (CBD)*, 10. *Is it legal, in interstate commerce, to sell a food (including any animal food or feed) to which THC or CBD has been added?*, https://www.fda.gov/news-events/public-health-focus/fda-regulation-cannabis-and-cannabis-derived-products-including-cannabidiol-cbd#food (last visited Apr. 21, 2020).

57. *Compare* Snyder v. Green Roads of Florida, Case No. 0:19-cv-62342-UU (S.D. Fla.) with Potter v. PotNetwork Holdings, Inc., No. 19-cv-24017 (S.D. Fla.).

58. Donald D. Ashley, *Noli Oil, LLC Warning Letter*, U.S. Food & Drug Administration, Nov. 22, 2019, https://www.fda.gov/inspections-compliance-enforcement-and-criminal-investigations/warning-letters/noli-oil-llc-593497-11222019.

59. *See, e.g., id.* Donald D. Ashley, *KOI CBD LLC Warning Letter*, U.S. Food & Drug Administration, Nov. 22, 2019, https://www.fda.gov/inspections-compliance-enforcement-and-criminal-investigations/warning-letters/koi-cbd-llc-593391-11222019; *CDRL Nutritional, Inc. Warning Letter, supra* note 35.

60. *See* U.S. Food & Drug Administration, *FDA Regulation of Cannabis and Cannabis-Derived Products, Including Cannabidiol (CBD)*, 13. *What is FDA's position on cannabis and cannabis-derived ingredients in cosmetics?*, https://www.fda.gov/news-events/public-health-focus/fda-regulation-cannabis-and-cannabis-derived-products-including-cannabidiol-cbd (last visited Apr. 21, 2020).

61. *Id.*

3.6.5 Unapproved New Animal Products

Including hemp derivatives as ingredients in animal food products and advertising a hemp derivative–infused animal product as a drug (see Section 3.6.1) are both violations of the FD&C Act.[62] The FDA has issued multiple warning letters to the advertisers of pet products containing CBD as an ingredient.[63]

4. Special Advertising Issues

Although drug, dietary supplement, food product, cosmetic, and animal product claims have been the subject of many FTC and FDA enforcements and warning letters since hemp and its derivatives were federally legalized, the same issues of advertising law that are applicable to historically legal products and services still apply to hemp advertisers. This section discusses common issues in advertising, including use of endorsements and testimonials, comparative advertising, and price advertising, as well as contests, sweepstakes, and other promotions.

4.1 Endorsements and Testimonials

Many cannabis advertisers tout the benefits of their products through endorsements and testimonials from customers, celebrities, social media influencers, doctors, and other professionals, or from companies, groups, and institutions. But a common misconception among advertisers is that they can avoid liability for advertising claims when those claims are communicated via the endorsements, testimonials, quotes, or reviews of others, rather than from the advertiser directly. By adopting these communications in advertising (e.g., by posting them on a product web page, responding to reviews in a way that emphasizes or validates them, or exercising control over reviews), or by having a material connection (discussed later) with the endorser, advertisers lose that means of avoiding liability.[64] The FTC guidelines make clear that advertisers must possess adequate substantiation for

---

62. *See, e.g.*, Donald D. Ashley, *Mr. Pink Collections, LLC Warning Letter*, U.S. Food & Drug Administration, November 22, 2019, https://www.fda.gov/inspections-compliance -enforcement-and-criminal-investigations/warning-letters/mr-pink-collections-llc -593395-11222019.

63. *See, e.g., id.*; *Curaleaf, Inc. Warning Letter, supra* note 35; *Advanced Spine and Pain, LLC Warning Letter, supra* note 35.

64. *Compare* Mary K. Engle, *Ocanna Co., Warning Letter*, Sept. 9, 2019, https://www .ftc.gov/system/files/documents/foia_requests/foia-2019-01289_warning_letters_sent _to_cbd_companies_9-30-19.pdf (citing to customer testimonials displayed on the CBD product's webpage as lacking substantiation), *with Advanced Purification Engineering Corporation (Water Filter Systems)*, Report #6238, NAD/CARU Case Reports (Jan. 2019) (finding that the advertiser's actions, or lack thereof, did not make it liable for the "Made in USA" claims in customer reviews on its products' Amazon webpage).

claims conveyed through such endorsements.[65] And when endorsements represent, directly or by implication, that an individual is an expert with respect to the message (e.g., a doctor endorsing the health benefits of a CBD product), the endorser's real-world qualifications must accurately reflect the level of expertise claimed.[66]

Endorsements and testimonials are any advertising or promotional messages (even including verbal statements, demonstrations, or depictions of the name, signature, likeness, or other identifying personal characteristics of an individual or the name or seal of an organization) that consumers are likely to believe reflects the opinions, beliefs, findings, or experiences of a party other than the sponsoring company (even if the views expressed by that party are identical to those of the sponsoring company).[67]

In addition, endorsements must clearly and prominently disclose any material connection between the advertiser and the endorser that might affect the weight or credibility of the endorsement in the minds of consumers.[68] Material connections can exist when advertisers pay; give something free or at a discount; or have an existing contractual, employment, or family relationship with an endorser.[69]

There are no established "magic words" or required language that will always suffice to disclose a material connection, but endorsers should use simple words that clearly communicate the nature of the relationship to consumers, for example, #employee, #ad, #advertisement, "I received free product from [insert brand name] to try out," "I was paid by [insert brand name]," or "[insert brand name] Ambassador."[70]

4.2 Comparative Advertising

It is generally permitted under U.S. law to compare a product to a competitor's product (directly by name or otherwise), including by making superiority claims, as long as the claims are truthful and substantiated, and are not likely to confuse consumers into believing there is some affiliation or connection between the advertiser and the competitor or its products.

---

65. 16 C.F.R. § 255.2(a).

66. *Id.* § 255.3(a).

67. *See* FTC Guides Concerning the Use of Endorsements and Testimonials in Advertising, 16 C.F.R. § 255.0(b).

68. *Id* § 255.5.

69. *See* "The FTC's Endorsement Guides: What People Are Asking," Federal Trade Commission, accessed April 21, 2020, https://www.ftc.gov/tips-advice/business-center /guidance/ftcs-endorsement-guides-what-people-are-asking.

70. *See, e.g.,* "Disclosures 101 for Social Media Influencers," Federal Trade Commission, accessed April 21, 2020, https://www.ftc.gov/tips-advice/business-center/guidance /disclosures-101-social-media-influencers; Lesley Fair, "Mything the point: 6 (OK, maybe 7) myths about endorsements," Federal Trade Commission, September 10, 2015, https://www.ftc.gov/news-events/blogs/business-blog/2015/09/mything-point-6-ok -maybe-7-myths-about-endorsements.

However, the very nature of comparative advertising claims often puts them at higher risk of challenge by the competition, so it is important to carefully consider any advertising material that arguably conveys negative information about a third-party person or business.

Advertisers should have sufficient substantiation before publishing comparative claims and should ensure that comparisons are "apples to apples" between the respective products or services. Furthermore, to limit the risk of triggering a trademark infringement claim, advertisers should use no more of another's trademark or brand name than is necessary to communicate the comparison.

4.3 Price Advertising

Advertising claims regarding price, sales, and discounts are subject to scrutiny from regulators, competitors, and consumers. Apart from the FTC's jurisdiction over false or misleading price advertising practices, states have their own laws that apply specifically to pricing and sales.[71] Although these laws vary among states, one key principle is that all material pricing terms for promotional offers must be clearly and prominently disclosed to customers.

When comparing a cannabis product's "regular price" to its lower "sale price," the claimed "regular price" must be a legitimate bona fide price at which the product or service was offered to the public on a regular basis for a reasonably substantial period of time.[72] State-specific laws apply, too. For example, under California law, no price can be advertised as a former price unless it was the prevailing market price within the three months immediately preceding the publication of the sale price (unless the date when the alleged former price did prevail is clearly, exactly, and conspicuously disclosed).[73]

4.4 Contest and Sweepstakes Promotions

Offering an "illegal lottery," that is, a promotion that involves the three elements of prize (something of value is awarded to winners), chance (winners are selected randomly or based on a sufficient level of chance), and consideration (entrants must provide something of value or expend substantial time or effort to enter), is typically illegal under federal and state law.[74] To avoid qualifying as an illegal lottery, the promotion should be structured as a proper contest or sweepstakes. A "contest"[75] removes the

---

71. *See, e.g.*, CAL. BUS. & PROF. CODE § 17501; MICH. COMP. LAWS ANN. § 445.314.

72. 16 C.F.R. § 233.1.

73. CAL. BUS. & PROF. CODE § 17501.

74. *See, e.g.*, 720 ILL. COMP. STAT. ANN. 5/28-2(b).

75. Some states prohibit contests from having entry fees in certain circumstances (particularly when an element of chance is arguably still present), and, generally, all contest prizes should be established prior to the contest's launch, rather than being dependent on the number of entries into the contest (i.e., don't pool entry fees). *See, e.g.*, MD. CODE ANN., COM. LAW § 13-305(b); VT. STAT. ANN. tit. 13, § 2143b; FLA. STAT. ANN.

"chance" element (by determining winners based on objective measurements of skill), whereas a "sweepstakes" removes the consideration element (e.g., by providing a free method of entry).

Many of the applicable state and federal laws require contests and sweepstakes to have publicly available official rules containing certain terms (such as eligibility criteria, prize details and values, entry method details and deadlines, and odds of winning), and sponsors must disclose certain material terms in advertising for the contest or sweepstakes.[76]

Lastly, public-facing methods of entry often constitute endorsements (e.g., requiring entrants to publish a social media post calling out a particular brand), so the FTC requires entrants to use the terms #contest or #sweepstakes with the entry in such circumstances so that viewers understand the material connection and reason for the post.[77]

Before holding a contest or sweepstakes, a seller or advertiser is advised to check the laws regarding marijuana, contests, illegal lotteries, and gambling within any state whose citizens are eligible to participate.[78]

5. Marijuana and Marijuana Derivative Advertising

Although this chapter largely focuses on hemp derivative advertising and the current regulatory scheme in the wake of the 2018 Farm Bill, the principles discussed in Sections 3 and 4 herein (excluding Section 3.6) generally apply to marijuana and marijuana derivative advertising by licensed marijuana retailers as well. And because the legality of cannabis continues to change and expand state by state, we address it briefly here.

5.1 Federal Law

Under the Controlled Substances Act (CSA), publishing advertisements for cannabis products is prohibited. Marijuana currently qualifies as a Schedule I controlled substance under the CSA, which makes it illegal to "place in any newspaper, magazine, handbill, or other publications, any written advertisement knowing that it has the purpose of seeking or offering illegally to receive, buy, or distribute a Schedule I controlled substance" or "use the Internet, or cause the Internet to be used, to advertise the sale of, or to offer to sell, distribute, or dispense, a controlled substance."[79] The CSA

---

§ 849.094(2)(e); State v. Gambling Device, 859 S.W.2d 519, 523 (Tex. Ct. App. 1993) (interpreting a Texas gambling statute "to apply to contrivances that incorporate any element of chance, even if the exercise of skill also influences the outcome").

76. *See, e.g.,* Colo. Rev. Stat. § 6-1-803.

77. *See* "The FTC's Endorsement Guides: What People Are Asking," Federal Trade Commission, accessed April 21, 2020, https://www.ftc.gov/tips-advice/business-center /guidance/ftcs-endorsement-guides-what-people-are-asking.

78. *See, e.g.,* Wash. Admin. Code § 314-55-155(4) (prohibiting marijuana licensees from offering "giveaways").

79. 21 U.S.C. § 843(c)(1)–(2)(A).

likewise prohibits offering for sale drug paraphernalia, including products intended for use with controlled substances, such as marijuana.[80] Although there is an exception for companies that use the Internet to "merely advocate[] the use of a controlled substance or include[] pricing information without attempting to facilitate an actual transaction,"[81] this chapter focuses on entities attempting to facilitate an actual marijuana transaction.

Although advertising marijuana products is illegal under the CSA, to date the federal government has not taken any action against companies that publish written marijuana advertisements wholly within states where marijuana has been legalized.

5.2 State Laws

Many of the states where the sale of recreational marijuana is legal have specific laws governing cannabis advertising. Those laws continue to change, but the following examples provide a snapshot of the types of regulations governing marijuana advertising:

- All cannabis advertisements should accurately and legibly identify the seller.[82]
- Cannabis advertisements placed in broadcast, cable, radio, print, and digital communications (including specific websites) must only be displayed where at least 71.6 percent of the audience (85 percent in Massachusetts) is reasonably expected to be 21 years of age or older, as determined by reliable, up-to-date audience composition data.[83]
- Advertising involving direct communications should utilize an age-verification method to ensure the recipient is at least 21.[84]
- Do not disseminate advertisements implying that a product originates from a particular region that differs from its true source.[85]
- Do not advertise on billboards or similar devices located on interstate highways or state highways that cross the border of any other state.[86]
- Advertisements should not encourage consumption of cannabis by people under age 21.[87]

---

80. *Id.* § 863.
81. *Id.* § 843(c)(2)(C)(ii).
82. Cal. Bus. & Prof. Code § 26151(a)(1).
83. *See, e.g., id.* § 26151(b); Mass. Gen. Laws Ann. ch. 94G, § 4(a ½)(xxix).
84. Cal. Bus. & Prof. Code § 26151(c).
85. *Id.* § 26152(c).
86. *Id.* § 26152(d).
87. *Id.* § 26152(e).

- Advertisements should not include symbols, language, music, gestures, cartoon characters, or other elements and content known to appeal to children or people under 21.[88]
- Do not place advertisements within the vicinity of schools (e.g., within 1,000 feet).[89]
- Do not give away free cannabis, cannabis products, or cannabis accessories as part of a promotion.[90]
- Some states require all marijuana advertisements to include certain disclosures. For example, Washington state requires all marijuana advertising to include the following warnings: "This product has intoxicating effects and may be habit forming"; "Marijuana can impair concentration, coordination, and judgment. Do not operate a vehicle or machinery under the influence of this drug"; "There may be health risks associated with consumption of this product"; and "For use only by adults twenty-one and older. Keep out of the reach of children."[91]
- Advertisements should not specifically target people located outside the state where recreational cannabis has been legalized.[92]
- Do not promote overconsumption of marijuana.[93]

These rules (except for the rule prohibiting encouragement of consumption by persons under 21) might not apply if the advertisement is placed in a licensed cannabis store and is not visible from a public place.[94] Additional rules apply and vary across states that legalize the sale of recreational cannabis. Cannabis advertisers should therefore closely review the laws of any state where they advertise.

6. Conclusion

As the cannabis legal landscape continues to evolve, it is increasingly important for cannabis and cannabis derivative advertisers to stay abreast of the regulations applicable to their products. General truth-in-advertising standards that apply to conventional products also apply to cannabis and cannabis derivatives, e.g., claims must be truthful, non-misleading, and adequately substantiated. But additional laws may apply depending on (1) the type of cannabis or cannabis derivative included in a product, (2) the type

---

88. *Id.* § 26152(f).
89. *Id.* § 26152(g).
90. *Id.* § 26153.
91. Wash. Admin. Code § 314-55-155(6)(a–d).
92. *Id.* § 314-55-155(1)(d).
93. *Id.* § 314-55-155(1)(a)(ii).
94. *See, e.g.,* Cal. Bus. & Prof. Code § 26155(a).

of product in which the cannabis or cannabis derivative is included, and (3) the jurisdiction where the cannabis or cannabis derivative is being advertised and sold.

Licensed marijuana and marijuana derivative advertisers should comply with applicable state laws and avoid allowing their advertising to enter interstate commerce, thus triggering potential federal liability. Hemp and hemp derivative advertisers, while also complying with state laws, must comply with federal regulators such as the FTC and FDA. Finally, regardless of what type of cannabis or cannabis derivative is being advertised, health claims about cannabis products likely lack the necessary substantiation and should be scrutinized carefully.

8

Trademarks

L. Omar Cojulun and Grace Stanton

1. Federal Overview of Cannabis Trademarks

1.1 The Federal Lanham Act and the Lawful Use in Commerce Requirement

The Lanham Act, also known as the Trademark Act of 1946, is the federal statute that governs trademarks, including the procedures for federally registering a trademark.[1] To be eligible for trademark protection, the Lanham Act requires that a mark be distinctive and be used in commerce.[2] At a high level, the distinctive trademark requirement addresses a trademark's strength for indicating the source of goods or services, and its ability to allow customers to identify and distinguish goods or services of one seller from another.

Regarding the use in commerce requirement, the U.S. Patent and Trademark Office (USPTO) requires that the use of a trademark in commerce be "lawful use" to qualify for federal registration.[3] However, while the Lanham Act defines commerce as "all commerce which may lawfully be regulated by Congress," it does not explicitly require or define "lawful use."[4] Rather, the origin of the lawful use requirement is a Trademark Trial and Appeal Board (TTAB) decision issued in 1968 that reasoned it would be inconsistent to accept the flow of certain goods in commerce if there is a federal statute

---

1. *See* 15 U.S.C. § 1051.
2. *Id.*
3. *See* Trademark Manual of Examining Procedure (TMEP) § 907.
4. *See* 15 U.S.C. § 1127.

prohibiting it.[5] As such, the USPTO will refuse to register a trademark if the proposed goods or services listed in the application are illegal under federal law.

1.2 Compliance with the Controlled Substances Act

Several federal laws[6] are considered by the USPTO when determining whether certain cannabis-related goods or services may be lawfully used in commerce for the purpose of granting a federal trademark registration.[7] Until late 2018, anything related to the plant *Cannabis sativa L.*, including anything derived from hemp such as cannabidiol (CBD), were illegal under the Controlled Substances Act (CSA).[8] Specifically, the CSA prohibits the manufacturing, distributing, dispensing, or possession of cannabis and cannabis-based products and services, including selling, offering for sale, or using any facility of interstate commerce to transport cannabis.[9] Therefore, if a trademark application lists cannabis-related goods or services that appear to violate the CSA, the USPTO will issue an inquiry for more information about the intended goods or services or issue a refusal of the trademark application.

For example, in 2016, in *In re Morgan Brown*, the TTAB issued a precedential opinion refusing registration of the mark HERBAL ACCESS for "retail store services featuring herbs."[10] Notably, the TTAB stated it was proper for the USPTO to look to evidence such as the specimen of use submitted with the application and the applicant's website to determine that the applicant's retail store services for "herbs" included the sale of cannabis, which is illegal under federal law.[11]

Similarly, in 2016, in *In re JJ206, LLC, dba JuJu Joints*, the TTAB issued another precedential opinion refusing the intent-to-use based application to register POWERED BY JUJU and the use-based application to register JUJU JOINTS, both for cannabis or marijuana vaporizing devices.[12] The applications were initially rejected by the USPTO based on the applicant's lack of a bona fide intent to use the mark in lawful commerce and lack of

---

5. *In re* Stellar Int'l, Inc., 159 USPQ 48, 51, 1968 WL 8159 (1968) (finding unlawful use in commerce when a product label did not comply with the Federal Food, Drug and Cosmetic Act).

6. *See* Controlled Substances Act, 21 U.S.C. §§ 801 *et seq.*; the Federal Food Drug and Cosmetic Act, 21 U.S.C. §§ 301 *et seq.*; and the Agricultural Improvement Act of 2018, Pub. L. No. 115-334 (better known as the 2018 Farm Bill).

7. USPTO, Examination Guide 1–19, https://www.uspto.gov/sites/default/files/documents/Exam%20Guide%201-19.pdf.

8. 21 U.S.C. §§ 801 *et seq.*

9. *Id.*

10. *In re Morgan Brown*, 119 USPQ2d 1350 (TTAB 2016).

11. The TTAB also noted objective evidence in the record that marijuana is an "herb."

12. *In re* JJ206, LLC, dba JuJu Joints, 120 USPQ2d 1568 (TTAB 2016).

lawful use in commerce, respectively, under the Lanham Act.[13] The TTAB affirmed the USPTO's decision and stated that since goods "intended or designed for use in ingesting, inhaling, or otherwise introducing cannabis or marijuana into the human body" were unlawful under the CSA, the applicant could not use its trademark in lawful commerce or have the requisite bona fide intent to use the trademark in lawful commerce.[14]

The applicant in this case made two notable arguments in support of their applications, neither of which convinced the TTAB, but which illustrate the federal stance on trademark protection for cannabis trademarks. First, the applicant argued that because it promoted its goods in states such as Washington where the sale and distribution of marijuana is legal, its use and intended use was lawful use in commerce under the Lanham Act.[15] The TTAB rejected this argument, however, stating that "the fact that the provision of a product or service may be lawful within a state is irrelevant to the question of federal registration when it is unlawful under federal law."[16] The applicant also argued that because it does business in states that comply with federal directives such as the *Cole Memo*,[17] its goods should be considered lawful. The TTAB also rejected this argument, stating that the *Cole Memo* does not override the CSA as the *Memo* is merely advisory.

Also, in 2017, in *In re PharmaCann LLC*, the TTAB issued a third precedential opinion confirming that a federal trademark registration requires use of a mark in commerce that is lawful under federal law.[18] The applicant here sought a federal trademark registration for PHARMACANN and PHARMACANNIS for retail store services and dispensing of pharmaceuticals featuring medical marijuana.[19] In addition to relying on the *Cole Memo*, the applicant argued that since the Appropriations Act of 2015 prohibited the DOJ from expending funds to prevent any state that has legalized

---

13. *Id.*

14. *Id.*

15. *Id.*

16. *In re id.* (*citing In re Brown*, 119 USPQ2d 1350, 1351 (TTAB 2016) (affirming the refusal for lack of lawful use of a mark for the retail sale of herbs that included marijuana).

17. The *Cole Memo* is a U.S. Department of Justice (DOJ) memorandum issued on August 29, 2013, by U.S. Deputy Attorney General James M. Cole which urges federal enforcement efforts to focus on, among other things, preventing distribution of marijuana to minors, preventing violence and firearm use in marijuana-related activities, and preventing the movement of marijuana from states where it is legal to states where it is illegal.

18. *In re* PharmaCann LLC, 123 USPQ2d 1122 (TTAB 2017).

19. The list of services listed in the application for PHARMACANN (U.S. Serial No. 86520135) and PHARMACANNIS (U.S. Serial No. 86520138) originally covered other services, including "selling substances not banned by the Controlled Substances Act" and "dispensaries selling products that are not Schedule I substances," but both applications were later amended to only cover "dispensaries selling medical marijuana in compliance with Illinois state law," and subsequently to the services ultimately rejected by the TTAB.

medical marijuana from implementing its own laws, Congress no longer treated medical marijuana as a violation of the CSA.[20] The TTAB rejected both arguments, concluding that marijuana, whether for recreational or medical use, remains illegal under the CSA.[21]

Collectively, *In re Morgan Brown*; *In re JJ206, LLC, dba JuJu Joints*; and *In re PharmaCann LLC* define the federal landscape for cannabis trademarks. Particularly, these decisions indicate that:

- If the scope of goods or services is unclear in a federal trademark application, the USPTO will likely review the specimen of use for use-based applications, review external evidence such as the applicant's website, or request more information about the applicant's activities to determine whether the goods or services listed in an application violate the CSA;
- The USPTO will refuse to register a trademark if the proposed goods or services listed in a federal trademark application are illegal under the CSA, regardless of their status under state law; and
- Applicants cannot file an intent-to-use based federal trademark application for goods or services prohibited under the CSA for the purpose of securing a trademark until cannabis is federally legalized.

1.3 The 2018 Farm Bill and Examination Guide 1-19

As described earlier, until late 2018, anything related to the plant *Cannabis sativa L.*, including CBD and anything derived from hemp, was illegal under the CSA. However, on December 20, 2018, Congress passed the 2018 Farm Bill, which removed hemp from the CSA's definition of marijuana, effectively removing any part of the plant *Cannabis sativa L.*, including derivatives such as CBD, with a delta-9 tetrahydrocannabinol (THC) concentration of not more than 0.3 percent on a dry-weight basis from the prohibited list of controlled substances under the CSA.[22] In other words, products containing hemp and derivatives of hemp such as CBD are no longer illegal controlled substances under the CSA. Thus, marks covering hemp-derived goods or services are eligible for federal trademark registration.

In response, on May 2, 2019, the USPTO issued Examination Guide 1-19 (Examination Guide) to clarify their procedure for examining federal trademark applications for marks covering cannabis-related goods or services, including applications for hemp-derived goods or services.[23] First, the USPTO confirmed it will continue to refuse registration of marks covering

---

20. *In re* PharmaCann LLC, 123 USPQ2d 1122 (TTAB 2017).
21. *Id.*
22. Text—H.R.2—115th Congress (2017-2018): *Agriculture Improvement Act of 2018*, Congress.gov (2018), https://www.congress.gov/bill/115th-congress/house-bill/2/text (last visited Jan. 19, 2020).
23. U.S. Patent and Trademark Office, *Examination Guide 1-19, Examination of Marks for Cannabis and Cannabis-Related Goods and Services after Enactment of the 2018 Farm Bill* (2019),

cannabis-related goods or services (not derived from hemp), including CBD and other extracts of cannabis, as these goods are still illegal under federal law.[24] The Examination Guide also stated that for trademark applications filed on or after December 20, 2018 (the effective date of the 2018 Farm Bill), that cover goods or services related to cannabis or CBD, the marks are eligible for trademark registration but only if the goods are derived from hemp and the description of goods or services specifies that they contain less than 0.3 percent THC.[25]

On the other hand, for applications that had been filed before December 20, 2018, and covered goods or services related to cannabis or CBD, the USPTO stated it would refuse registration based on the applicant's lack of a bona fide intent to use the mark in lawful commerce or lack of lawful use in commerce.[26] However, the USPTO did provide these applicants the opportunity to amend their applications so they would be in compliance with federal law, including by amending the filing date of the application to December 20, 2018, amending their application to an intent-to-use based application if it was originally based on use of the mark in commerce, and amending the identification of goods or services to specify that the CBD or cannabis products listed in their applications contain less than 0.3 percent THC.[27] Alternatively, the USPTO advised that applicants could file new trademark applications.[28]

Although federal trademark protection is now available for hemp-derived goods and services, the USPTO clarified that applications for consumable products containing CBD, including CBD derived from hemp, will still be refused a federal trademark registration.[29] The use of CBD in products intended for consumption by humans and animals remains unlawful under the Federal Food Drug and Cosmetic Act (FDCA), as CBD is still undergoing clinical investigations by the Food and Drug Administration to determine its safety.[30] Therefore, trademark applications for foods, beverages, dietary supplements, or pet treats containing CBD will still be refused a federal trademark registration as unlawful under the FDCA.[31]

---

https://www.uspto.gov/sites/default/files/documents/Exam%20Guide%201-19.pdf (last visited Jan. 19, 2020).

24. *Id.*

25. *Id.*

26. *Id.* (the USPTO reasoned that applications filed before December 20, 2018 "did not have a valid basis to support registration at the time of filing because the goods violated federal law").

27. *Id.*

28. *Id.*

29. *Id.*

30. 21 U.S.C. §§ 301 *et seq.*

31. U.S. Patent and Trademark Office, *Examination Guide 1-19, Examination of Marks for Cannabis and Cannabis-Related Goods and Services after Enactment of the 2018 Farm Bill* (2019),

In summary, while the 2018 Farm Bill cleared the way for federal trademark protection for certain goods and services derived from hemp that contain no more than 0.3 percent THC on a dry-weight basis, federal trademark applications for other cannabis-related goods and services will continue to be refused by the USPTO. Therefore, when filing a federal trademark application for any cannabis goods or services, including hemp and CBD derived from hemp, expect the following:

- The goods or services listed in the federal trademark application will be examined for compliance with the CSA, the 2018 Farm Bill, and the FDCA;
- The USPTO will require applicants to specify that any CBD-related goods or services listed in a federal trademark application are solely derived from hemp with a delta-9 THC concentration of not more than 0.3 percent on a dry-weight basis;
- Since it is currently unlawful to introduce food or beverages that contain CBD into interstate commerce or to market CBD in consumable products such as foods, beverages, dietary supplements, or pet treats, expect the USPTO to issue an "FDCA Refusal" stating that the goods consist of or include items that are a per se violation of federal law; and
- For applications that recite services involving the cultivation or production of hemp, expect the USPTO to request more information regarding the applicant's authorization to produce hemp.[32]

2. Alternative Trademark Protection for the Cannabis Industry and Its Limitations

2.1 State Trademark Registrations

Although the federal prohibition against cannabis (other than hemp-derived products) just described makes clear that federal trademark protection is not available for the core goods and services offered by most cannabis companies, trademark protection is still available at the state level for cannabis companies operating in certain states. Although a state trademark registration generally offers less protection and benefits than a federal trademark registration, a state trademark registration still provides important benefits that may be valuable and useful for the protection of

---

https://www.uspto.gov/sites/default/files/documents/Exam%20Guide%201-19.pdf (last visited Jan. 19, 2020).

32. The 2018 Farm Bill requires hemp to be produced under license or authorization by a state, territory, or tribal government in accordance with a plan approved by the U.S. Department of Agriculture for the commercial production of hemp. *Examination Guide.*

most cannabis brands within the state they operate in. For example, when a trademark is registered in a state, it is listed in that state's trademark database. As a result, it functions as a public record that can be used by cannabis companies to prove the first use date associated with their trademark and/or their established prior rights to use a given trademark. In other words, a state trademark registration will provide notice to other cannabis companies in a state that a trademark is already in use for certain cannabis goods or services. Therefore, a state trademark registration can be an effective way to prevent local competitors within a state from using a trademark that is already in use.

As of January 2020, 11 states and Washington D.C. have legalized the use of recreational and medical marijuana.[33] Similarly, the use of medical marijuana *only* is legal in an additional 22 states.[34] There are also an additional 13 states where only CBD products are legal (usually required to be derived from hemp).[35] However, cannabis is still completely illegal in Idaho, Kansas, Nebraska, and South Dakota.[36]

Certain states, such as Washington, California, Oregon, Colorado, Nevada, and Michigan, specifically allow state trademark registrations for cannabis-related goods or services, including for those cannabis products that are still illegal under federal law and therefore not eligible for a federal trademark registration. For example, as of January 1, 2018, cannabis-related trademarks may be registered in California with the California Secretary of State, including trademarks for medicinal products containing cannabis extracts, trademarks for live cannabis plants, trademarks for cannabis products intended for smoking, trademarks for retail stores selling cannabis products, and trademarks for delivery of cannabis products.[37] To register a trademark, California requires (1) that the cannabis goods or services covered under a trademark be authorized under California law;

---

33. *Where Is Cannabis Legal?*, Leafly (Jan. 17, 2020), https://www.leafly.com/news/cannabis-101/where-is-cannabis-legal. The 11 states where adult use cannabis is legal are Washington, Oregon, California, Nevada, Alaska, Colorado, Illinois, Michigan, Vermont, Maine, and Massachusetts.

34. *Id.* The 22 states where only medical marijuana is legal are Montana, Utah, Arizona, New Mexico, North Dakota, Minnesota, Oklahoma, Missouri, Arkansas, Louisiana, Hawaii, Ohio, Florida, West Virginia, Maryland, Pennsylvania, New York, New Hampshire, Connecticut, Rhode Island, New Jersey, and Delaware.

35. *Id.* The 13 states where only CBD products are legal are Alabama, Georgia, Indiana, Iowa, Kentucky, Mississippi, North Carolina, South Carolina, Tennessee, Texas, Virginia, Wisconsin, and Wyoming.

36. *Id.*

37. California Cannabis Portal, *Registering Cannabis-Related Trademarks in California*, https://cannabis.ca.gov/2019/04/29/registering-cannabis-related-trademarks-in-california/ (last visited Jan. 20, 2020).

(2) that applicants obtain any local and state licenses required to conduct their cannabis activities in California; and (3) that applicants be in compliance with California state labeling and packaging requirements for cannabis products.[38] California, for example, prohibits registration of trademarks associated with products that are attractive to children.[39]

However, it is important to note that many of the benefits of a federal trademark registration are not available for state trademark registrations. First, as already mentioned, the protection offered by a state trademark registration is limited to that specific state and does not offer a national presumption of ownership of a trademark. As a result, a state trademark registration will not provide cannabis companies with the rights needed to prevent other cannabis companies operating in a different state from using the same or similar trademark. Also, most states do not accept trademark applications based on an intent-to-use basis. Accordingly, cannabis companies that are unable to extend their operations across state lines to other states where cannabis may be legal cannot simply file a trademark application in another state with the intention of blocking others from using an identical or similar trademark without actual use of a trademark in that state.

2.2 Federal Registration for Ancillary Goods or Services

In addition to state-level trademark protection, another strategy available to cannabis companies is to seek federal trademark registration for ancillary goods or services that are not directly related to the production and use of cannabis, which are illegal under federal law. Although this approach may not provide federal trademark protection for cannabis goods or services directly, the strategy seeks to protect other aspects of a company's offerings such as information services. Trademark law recognizes that companies often begin by offering a limited list of goods or services and later expand to offer additional goods or services that may be related or within the company's "zone of natural expansion."[40] Trademark law further recognizes that certain goods or services are sufficiently related such that consumers may be confused by the use of an identical or similar trademark on related goods or services. If cannabis is ever legalized at the federal level, cannabis companies may be able to leverage the "zone of natural expansion" surrounding their trademarks to assert federal trademark protection for cannabis goods or services with priority over other parties at the time of legalization. Although the federal illegality of marijuana limits the value of this indirect approach to trademark protection, this approach may nevertheless help shield cannabis companies from infringement.

---

38. *Id.*
39. *Id.*
40. 5 McCarthy on Trademarks and Unfair Competition § 26:20 (5th ed.).

Many cannabis companies offer goods and/or services that are both lawful under federal law and complementary to their core cannabis goods or services, such as a website featuring information about cannabis, hemp-derived goods or services, tobacco goods or services, non-THC-infused bakery goods, and branded merchandise. For example, Bonfire Holdings, LLC DBA Bonfire Cannabis Co., a lifestyle brand of medical and recreational products, owns a federal trademark registration for FUELING ADVENTURE THROUGH CANNABIS for clothing and stickers.[41] Similarly, THE MARIJUANA COMPANY is federally registered for various clothing[42] and LIGHTLY TOASTED is federally registered for various smokers' products.[43] Also, Ghost Management Group, LLC, which operates a website at weedmaps.com that provides consumers with information regarding cannabis products, including local retailer and brand listings and consumer education on cannabis, owns multiple federal trademark registrations for WEEDMAPS, the WEEDMAPS logo, and the WM logo for these services.[44] Similarly, NUGL, Inc., which operates an online platform available at nugl.com that features a business directory and social media and networking tools for all things cannabis, owns federal trademark registrations for NUGL and the NUGL logo that cover an app, a website, and digital and print publications.[45]

However, as with state trademark registrations, seeking federal registration for ancillary goods or services may not be a guaranteed path to registration, and may come with certain limitations. As previously discussed in the case of *In re Morgan Brown*, it is proper for the USPTO to apply additional scrutiny to a trademark application, such as by looking at a specimen of use submitted with the application or reviewing an applicant's website, to determine whether the intended use of a trademark is lawful under federal law.[46]

For example, Indus Holding Company (Indus), a cannabis holding company, owns two federal trademark registrations for ALTAI and the ALTAI logo for medical cannabis resources and cannabis public advocacy.[47] Both trademark applications were initially refused registration after the USPTO found articles online showing that Indus had its own brand of medical cannabis edibles sold under the ALTAI trademark.[48] Although the refusal was withdrawn after Indus clarified the services listed in the application and

---

41. *See* U.S. Registration No. 5879813.

42. *See* U.S. Registration No. 4732570.

43. *See* U.S. Registration No. 5871317.

44. *See* U.S. Registration Nos. 4321513, 4776082, 4943997, and 5434313.

45. *See* U.S. Registration Nos. 5965240 and 5965241.

46. *In re* Morgan Brown, 119 USPQ2d 1350 (TTAB 2016).

47. *See* U.S. Registration Nos. 5187163 and 5187164; *see* Christopher R. McElwain, *High Stakes: Marijuana Brands and the USPTO'S "[Lawful] Use" Registration Criterion* (2016), https://pdf4pro.com/cdn/christopher-r-mcelwain-37a6.pdf.

48. *See* Office Actions issued on November 5, 2015 against U.S. Registration Nos. 5187163 and 5187164.

provided confirmation that the services comply with the CSA, this example shows that a cannabis company's unlawful use of a trademark can still prevent registration of the trademark for lawful goods or services in some cases.[49]

Similarly, during the USPTO's examination of the application to register WEEDMAPS for an online community that allows users to engage in social networking in the field of medical cannabis, the USPTO requested more information, including (1) brochures or advertisements related to the services; (2) a written statement indicating whether the services identified in the application comply with the CSA; (3) confirmation whether the services involve the provision of cannabis or any other illegal controlled substances; and (4) confirmation whether the services in the application were lawful under the CSA.[50] To be sure, answering such questions may be sufficient to obtain a federal trademark registration. But the scope of protection offered by a federal registration for ancillary goods or services may be limited and not provide protection for cannabis goods or services in an infringement action while cannabis remains illegal under federal law.

For example, in *Woodstock Ventures LC v. Woodstock Routes, LLC,* the owner of the WOODSTOCK trademark for music festivals and the owner of the identical WOODSTOCK trademark for smokers' articles filed trademark infringement actions against each other, alleging that the use of the WOODSTOCK trademark for cannabis and cannabis-related products was within the "natural zone of expansion" for each of them.[51] Notably, when denying the motion for preliminary injunction filed by the owner of the WOODSTOCK trademark for smokers' articles, the U.S. District Court for the Southern District of New York stated that (1) the court could not give weight to the owner's "natural zone of expansion" argument since the sale of cannabis is illegal under federal law and (2) when WOODSTOCK for smokers' articles was registered with the USPTO, the owners represented to the USPTO that the trademark would not be used to market cannabis.[52] Although this was not a decision on the merits of the case, the court's ruling indicates that the "zone of natural expansion" argument for an ancillary goods or services trademark registration may not work while cannabis is still illegal under federal law and that statements made to the USPTO during the prosecution of a trademark application can be used against a trademark owner in the future.

Nonetheless, if cannabis is ever legalized under federal law, there may be a strong argument to make that the "zone of natural expansion" of a federal trademark registration covering ancillary goods or services extends to cannabis goods or services. Also, although cannabis remains illegal under

---

49. *Id.*
50. *See* Office Action issued on March 8, 2012, against U.S. Registration No. 4321513.
51. Woodstock Ventures LC v. Woodstock Routes, LLC, 387 F. Supp.3 d 306 (2019).
52. *Id.*

federal law, a federal trademark registration for ancillary goods or services may still provide a cannabis company with a viable enforcement strategy against infringers outside of the courtroom through demand letters and negotiated settlement agreements.[53]

3. Trademark Infringement and Dilution

3.1 Likelihood of Confusion

Adopting a trademark that uniquely identifies a cannabis company's goods and services, including strengthening those rights with a state registration or a federal registration for ancillary goods or services, is an important step in the early stages of a cannabis company's brand development. For the reasons previously discussed, the owner of a trademark for cannabis goods or services cannot directly leverage the benefits provided by a federal trademark registration. Ironically, cannabis trademarks are still vulnerable to trademark infringement claims from third parties. For that reason, cannabis companies should be cautious not to choose a trademark that infringes the rights of a third party, including a third party that may not necessarily be operating in the cannabis space.

The test for trademark infringement is whether two marks are likely to be confused by consumers, based on a multifactor test.[54] Although there are many factors that can be considered, the two key factors often considered in this analysis are (1) the similarity or dissimilarity of the marks and (2) the relatedness of the goods or services.[55] However, this does not mean that a cannabis company needs to necessarily use an identical trademark for identical goods or services for there to be a valid trademark infringement claim.

For example, in *Kiva Health Brands LLC v. Kiva Brands Inc.*, Kiva Health Brands LLC (Kiva Health), a natural foods and health supplements company, filed a federal trademark infringement lawsuit against Kiva Brands Inc. (Kiva Cannabis), a cannabis company that creates cannabis-infused chocolates and other edibles.[56] Kiva Health, which started selling their products with the KIVA trademark in 2010 and continuously since 2013 and owns multiple federal registrations for KIVA, alleged that Kiva Cannabis' use of KIVA and KIVA CONFECTIONS in connection with food containing cannabis was confusing and would likely mislead consumers to assume erroneously that Kiva Health's health foods are infused with cannabis.[57] Although Kiva Cannabis asserted that it had prior common law rights in the KIVA and KIVA CONFECTIONS trademarks in California dating back

---

53. *See* McElwain, *supra* note 47.
54. *See In re* E. I. du Pont de Nemours & Co., 476 F.2d 1357, 177 USPQ 563 (C.C.P.A. 1973).
55. *Id.*
56. Kiva Health Brands LLC v. Kiva Brands Inc., 402 F. Supp. 3d 877 (2019).
57. *Id.*

to as early as 2010, including a California state registration indicating a first use date in 2010, the Northern District of California concluded that the unlawful status of Kiva Cannabis' products under federal law rendered Kiva Cannabis unable to claim priority over Kiva Health's federal trademark registrations.[58] In other words, prior common law use of a trademark in a state, including state registrations to prove such use, provides limited rights as previously discussed and may result in a cannabis company's inability to challenge a federal trademark application filed for an identical or similar trademark. Fortunately for Kiva Cannabis, the court in this case ultimately concluded there was no likelihood of confusion due in part to finding that the goods were different.[59]

However, the same result was not realized by GG Strains LLC (GG Strains), a cannabis company that developed and marketed multiple strains of cannabis under the GORILLA GLUE trademark. In 2017, The Gorilla Glue Company (Gorilla Glue), the manufacturer of various adhesive and glue products sold under the GORILLA and GORILLA GLUE trademarks, filed a federal trademark infringement lawsuit against GG Strains alleging that their use of GORILLA GLUE and an image of a gorilla in connection with cannabis strains called Gorilla Glue #1, Gorilla Glue #4, and Gorilla Glue #5 infringed and diluted Gorilla Glue's trademark rights.[60] The parties eventually reached a settlement that required GG Strains and its licensees, among other things, to cease use of the word Gorilla, the gorilla image, and any GORILLA trademarks.[61]

In 2019, the United Parcel Service (UPS) sued a group of cannabis delivery companies for trademark infringement in the U.S. District Court for the Central District of California.[62] UPS alleged that United Pot Smokers, UPS420, and THCPlant infringed UPS' family of trademarks, including their shield logo, and "intended to capitalize off UPS's extensive goodwill and reputation" by offering delivery and logistic services for cannabis products through multiple websites, including www.upsgreen.com and www.ups420.com.[63] The court ultimately issued a consent judgment and permanent injunction that required the cannabis companies, among other

---

58. *Id.*

59. *Id.*

60. Alicia Wallace, *Gorilla Glue Adhesives Firm Reaches Settlement with Marijuana Strain,* THE CANNABIST (Nov. 7, 2017), https://www.thecannabist.co/2017/10/04/gorilla-glue -marijuana-strains-lawsuit-settlement/89321/.

61. *Id.*

62. Brian Flood, *UPS Sues Cannabis Delivery Companies for Trademark Infringement,* BLOOMBERG BNA NEWS (Feb. 14, 2019), https://news.bloomberglaw.com/ip-law/ups-sues -cannabis-delivery-companies-for-trademark-infringement.

63. *Id.*

things, to cease use of the UPS trademarks and transfer all rights in any UPS trademarks or similar intellectual property, including the websites.[64]

In another case, Ozone Group Holdings LLC DBA LeafedIn (LeafedIn) filed an application to register the trademark LEAFEDIN for "Social networking services in the field of Legal/Medical Cannabis Industry provided via a website."[65] On September 28, 2016, LinkedIn filed an opposition against LeafedIn's trademark application alleging a likelihood of confusion with LinkedIn's trademarks and that the LEAFEDIN trademark would dilute the LINKEDIN trademark.[66] LeafedIn ultimately abandoned its application to register LEAFEDIN in 2018, and it was announced in 2020 that LeafedIn changed its name to LeafedOut.[67]

The preceding cases illustrate the care that cannabis companies must take when starting a brand. Cannabis companies should strive to find a unique trademark for their brands and protect and enforce them within the limits of trademark law, such as by filing for state trademark registrations and filing federal trademark applications for ancillary goods or services. Cannabis companies must also try and avoid choosing a trademark that infringes on the rights of a third party to avoid expensive litigation and rebranding costs in the future. As an example, the founder of GG Strains stated in an interview that the dispute with The Gorilla Glue Company just described and the subsequent rebranding expenses cost about $250,000.[68] This is a sum of money that can put many companies out of business, especially cannabis companies in a new and growing industry.

3.2 Dilution by Tarnishment

In addition to being subject to a claim of trademark infringement, some cannabis companies have been sued for dilution by tarnishment. This occurs when an unauthorized use of a trademark dilutes that trademark by tarnishing or degrading positive associations of the trademark to harm the reputation of the trademark.[69] Due to the free speech protections of the First Amendment, parody can often be asserted as a defense to dilution

---

64. *See* United Parcel Service, Inc. and United Parcel Service of America, Inc. v. Brendon Kennedy, Mayumi Kennedy, United Pot Smokers, UPS420, THCPlant, B & M Marketing, LLC and DOES 1-10, Case No. 5:19-cv-00284-MWF-KK, Order Granting Stipulated Consent Judgment and Permanent Injunction (C.D. Cal. 2019).

65. *See* U.S. Serial No. 86870930.

66. *See* Opposition No. 91230331 filed against U.S. Serial No. 86870930.

67. Benjie Cooper, *LeafedIn Settles Trademark Dispute With LinkedIn*, CANDID CHRONICLE (Apr. 5, 2020), https://candidchronicle.com/leafedin-settles-trademark-dispute-with -linkedin/.

68. Alicia Wallace, *Gorilla Glue Adhesives Firm Reaches Settlement with Marijuana Strain*, THE CANNABIST (Nov. 7, 2017), https://www.thecannabist.co/2017/10/04/gorilla-glue -marijuana-strains-lawsuit-settlement/89321/.

69. "Dilution by Tarnishment," MCCARTHY ON TRADEMARKS AND UNFAIR COMPETITION § 24:89 (5th ed.).

by tarnishment if, for example, a third-party's trademark is being used to criticize, ridicule, or otherwise comment on a trademark owner's product.[70] However, in the cannabis industry, there is a fine line between using a third-party's trademark to comment on that third-party's product and using a third-party's trademark to gain recognition and increase sales for your own product.[71] Some cannabis companies have found themselves on the wrong side of that line.

For example, in July 2019, Mondelez Canada Inc. (Mondelez), the owner of the Sour Patch Kids candy brand, filed a lawsuit against Stoney Patch, the California maker of a cannabis-infused candy resembling Sour Patch Kids.[72] The complaint states that "there has been a growing trend among makers of cannabis products, including edible products infused with [THC], to market their products by copying and misappropriating the colors, flavors, names and packaging of popular snacks and candies."[73] According to Mondelez, Stoney Patch uses a name almost identical to the SOUR PATCH trademark, and are copying the appearance of the actual candy and packaging that has long been associated with Mondelez's Sour Patch Kids candy. Therefore, Mondelez alleges that Stoney Patch is, among other things, tarnishing and unfairly trading on Mondelez's rights in the SOUR PATCH trademark and violating California state law, which prohibits the use of packaging and labeling designed to be appealing to children.[74]

Similarly, in 2017, Tapatio Foods, LLC (Tapatio), the producer of the Tapatio hot sauce, filed a lawsuit against Mario Mendizabal and TCG Industries, LLC d/b/a Payaso Grow (Payaso), alleging that Payaso's use of the TRAPATIO trademark and a logo with a man in a sombrero in connection with cannabis-infused hot sauce infringed on Tapatio's federally registered trademarks for TAPATIO and a similar logo featuring a man in a sombrero.[75] The parties eventually reached a settlement agreement that required Payaso to cease use of the TRAPATIO trademark and not use a confusingly similar trademark in the future.[76] Despite this agreement, Tapatio filed another lawsuit in March 2019 alleging that Payaso's use of their new trademark, TRAPSAUCE, and the image of a man in a ski mask, continues to infringe on Tapatio's trademarks.[77] Tapatio also alleges that "by using a mark that

70. *Id.*

71. Alison Malsbury, *Pot Parody: Not So Funny After All*, CANNA LAW BLOG (Apr. 23, 2015). https://www.cannalawblog.com/pot-parody-not-so-funny-after-all/.

72. Mondelez Canada Inc. v. Stoney Patch and DOES 1-10, Case No. 2:19-cv-06245-CJC-SS (C.D. Cal. 2019).

73. Mondelez Canada Inc. v. Stoney Patch and DOES 1-10, Case No. 2:19-cv-06245-CJC-SS, Complaint (C.D. Cal. 2019).

74. *Id.*

75. Tapatio Foods, LLC v. Mario Mendizabal and TCG Industries, LLC d/b/a Payaso Grow, Case No. 2:17-cv-07530, Complaint (C.D. Cal. 2017).

76. *Id.*

77. *Id.*

evokes the TAPATIO [m]arks in connection with the sale of products that illegally contain a Schedule 1 controlled substance, [Payaso] has tarnished the reputation of the TAPATIO [m]arks."[78]

Although the Sour Patch Kids case and this new lawsuit filed by Tapatio are currently pending, both cases provide clear examples of the risk of adopting or using a trademark that may not only infringe on the trademark rights of a third party but also arguably dilute the third-party trademark by tarnishing its reputation. Therefore, while adopting or using a similar trademark that imitates or copies the well-known trademark of a non-cannabis company may seem like a clever branding opportunity for cannabis goods or services, this approach may result in unexpected legal and rebranding expenses for a cannabis company. At the same time, non-cannabis companies should be vigilant of third-party trademarks in the cannabis space that may either dilute or otherwise cause a likelihood of confusion with their trademarks.

4. Takeaways

As the cannabis industry continues to grow with the legalization of cannabis spreading across the country, the marketplace will simultaneously become more crowded with cannabis brands attempting to stand out from their competition. In most, if not all, industries, the first step in building a strong brand that will be recognized by consumers in the marketplace is choosing a unique trademark and seeking a federal trademark registration for the goods or services offered under the trademark, provided it is not a trademark that infringes or dilutes the rights of a third party. As described earlier, however, federal trademark registration remains unavailable for the core cannabis goods or services offered by most cannabis companies since cannabis remains unlawful under the CSA. The USPTO will refuse to register trademarks that are intended to be used with cannabis goods or services and will perform their own internal research and/or request more information from an applicant to determine if certain goods or services violate federal law, including the CSA, the FDCA, and the 2018 Farm Bill.

There are other strategies that cannabis companies can utilize to develop a strong cannabis trademark and protect it. First, trademark protection is still available from certain states. A state trademark registration will not grant a cannabis company exclusive rights to use a trademark across the country or provide strong proof of priority in a federal trademark infringement lawsuit, but it may dissuade local competitors from using the same or a similar trademark within the state. Further, although federal trademark protection is not available for the core cannabis goods or services, it is still available for ancillary goods and services, including hemp-derived goods and services, which were federally legalized under the 2018 Farm Bill. A

---

78. *Id.*

federal trademark registration for these complementary goods and services may provide cannabis companies with an enforcement strategy and provide proof of priority for the core cannabis goods and services if marijuana becomes legal under federal law in the future.

9

Patent Law in the Cannabis Industry

Dennis Hopkins and Danielle Grant-Keane

1. Introduction

Although the federal government continues to classify cannabis[1] as among the most restrictive classes of controlled substances, the U.S. Patent & Trademark Office (USPTO) has nonetheless issued patents in this area. Generally, a patent for an invention is the grant of a property right to the inventor for a term of up to 20 years from the date on which the application for the patent (or a previously filed application to which priority is claimed) was filed in the United States.[2] Although patents are often viewed as conferring a right to practice the invention, this is a misconception. The right conferred by such a grant is "the right to exclude others from making, using, offering for sale, or selling" the claimed invention in the United States or "importing" the invention into the United States.[3] Thus, if practicing a claimed invention would violate any laws, a patent would not affect such unlawful use. For years, the USPTO has issued cannabis-related patents,

---

1. This chapter uses the term "cannabis" and "cannabis-related" to refer to plants of the genus *cannabis* and their byproducts—which include marijuana, hemp, and derivatives such as cannabidiol (CBD) and tetrahydrocannabinol (THC)—and patents and other intellectual property related thereto.
2. *General Information Concerning Patents*, United States Patent and Trademark Office (Oct. 2015), https://www.uspto.gov/patents-getting-started/general-information-concerning-patents#heading-2.
3. *Id.*; *see also* 35 U.S.C. § 154 (contents and term of patent).

including to the U.S. government,[4] for a wide variety of utility, plant, and design patents without any indication that such patents would be treated any differently than other non-cannabis-related patents.[5]

According to data analytics firm Magic Number, the USPTO issued almost 250 cannabis patents in 2017 and 2018—more cannabis patents than those issued in the previous seven years combined.[6] And in 2017 and 2018, the USPTO received nearly 550 cannabis-related applications, which is consistent *with all* filing activity from 2010 to 2016 combined.[7] Reports project legal cannabis sales to reach $30 billion by 2025, and patent filers are looking to cash in on this.[8] Drug companies and research conglomerates have maintained a steady stream of filings covering medical treatments and pharmaceutical compositions, while others have sought patents on vaporizers, cultivation techniques, and cannabis-infused products like edible oils, chewable edibles, toothpastes, and alcoholic drinks.[9] In 2019, companies like GW Pharmaceuticals, a biopharmaceutical company, and Lunatech, a cannabis oil extraction company, led the pack as the top corporate patent filers in the United States.[10] However, the patent landscape has primarily been characterized by low-volume filings from small to midsize companies and individual inventors.[11] More than 780 entities have filed for at least one patent, and as legalization expands, cannabis patent portfolios will morph these businesses into attractive targets ripe for takeover.[12]

---

4. U.S. Patent No. 6,630,507B1 (2003 patent for "cannabinoids as antioxidants and neuroprotectants" assigned to the U.S. Department of Health and Human Services).

5. *See* Matthew Kamps, *The Number of Cannabis-Centric Patents Is Getting High*, Law360 (Oct. 10, 2019), https://www.law360.com/articles/1206064; U.S. Patent No. 4,189,491 (1980 patent for "tetrahydrocannabinol in a method of treating glaucoma"); U.S. Patent No. 9,220,294 (2015 patent for "methods and devices using cannabis vapors"); U.S. Patent No. 10,028,987 (2018 patent for "cannabis-infused milk"); U.S. Plant Patent No. PP27,475 P2 (2016 patent for "cannabis plant named 'Ecuadorian Sativa'"); U.S. Plant Patent No. PP30,639 (2019 patent for "hemp plant named 'CW2A'"); U.S. Design Patent No. D798,739 (2017 design patent for cannabis storing container with individual tear off lids); U.S. Design Patent D823,537 (2018 patent for "container for cannabis and tobacco").

6. *See* Matthew Bultman, *Cannabis Patent Activity Surges Amid Industry Gold Rush*, Law360 (Oct. 16, 2019), https://www.law360.com/articles/1203746/cannabis-patent -activity-surges-amid-industry-gold-rush.

7. *Id.*

8. *Id.*

9. *Id.*; *see also* Paul Bremmer, *As Cannabis Patent Filings Increase, Are Food and Beverage Companies Positioned to Benefit?*, IP Watchdog (Nov. 9, 2018), https://www.ipwatchdog .com/2018/11/09/cannabis-patent-filings-increase/id=102898/.

10. Bultman, *supra* note 6.

11. *Id.*

12. *Id.*; *see also* Alan Brochstein, *Mergers and Acquisitions Light Up The Cannabis Sector*, Forbes (Apr. 7, 2019), https://www.forbes.com/sites/alanjbrochstein/2019/04/07 /mergers-and-acquisitions-light-up-the-cannabis-sector/#344bc9af887e.

2. How Can the Industry Protect Its IP?

2.1 Utility Patents

Utility patents are available to anyone who "invents or discovers any new and useful process, machine, manufacture, or composition of matter, or any new and useful improvement thereof."[13] Laws of nature, natural phenomena, and abstract ideas are not patentable as these comprise "the basic tools of scientific and technological work."[14] Patent law, ultimately, seeks to strike "a delicate balance between creating 'incentives that lead to creation, invention, and discovery' and imped[ing] the flow of information that might permit, or indeed spur, invention."[15] In analyzing cannabis-related utility patents, the USPTO reviews such applications as it would any other application and grants them accordingly.

In order for an invention to be patentable, it must be new or novel as defined in the patent law, which provides that

> [a] person shall be entitled to a patent unless (1) the claimed invention was patented, described in a printed publication, or in public use, on sale, or otherwise available to the public before the effective filing date of the claimed invention; or (2) the claimed invention was described in a patent issued under section 151, or in an application for patent published or deemed published under section 122(b), in which the patent or application, as the case may be, names another inventor and was effectively filed before the effective filing date of the claimed invention.[16]

Even if the subject matter sought to be patented is not exactly found in the prior art, but rather involves one or more differences over the similar aspect already known, the USPTO may still refuse a patent if the differences would be obvious.[17]

> A patent for a claimed invention may not be obtained . . . if the differences between the claimed invention and the prior art are such that the claimed invention as a whole would have been obvious before the effective filing date of the claimed invention to a person having ordinary skill in the art to which the claimed invention pertains.[18]

---

13. 35 U.S.C. § 101.

14. Alice Corp. Pty. Ltd. v. CLS Bank Intern., 573 U.S. 208, 216 (2014) (quoting Assoc. for Molecular Pathology v. Myriad Genetics, Inc., 569 U.S. 576, 589 (2013)).

15. *Myriad*, 569 U.S. at 590 (citing Mayo Collab. Servs. v. Prometheus Labs., Inc., 566 U.S. 66, 92 (2012)).

16. 35 U.S.C. § 102.

17. *General Information Concerning Patents*, United States Patent and Trademark Office (Oct. 2015), https://www.uspto.gov/patents-getting-started/general-information-concerning-patents#heading-2.

18. 35 U.S.C. § 103.

This nonobvious requirement is the most difficult hurdle to overcome in attaining a utility patent.[19] In analyzing nonobviousness, patent examiners will review older patents and art to find similarities with the claimed invention.[20] If all features from the claimed invention can be found in a single piece of art, then it will be rejected.[21] Alternatively, the examiner may combine two or more pieces of prior art and attempt to find all of the claimed invention's features in the combined pieces.[22] If the examiner finds all the features through a combination of patents, the examiner will reject the claimed invention because it is an obvious combination of features in the prior art.[23] Only if the claimed invention overcomes the patent examiner's obviousness analysis can it complete this step toward patentability.

Unlike trademark law,[24] patent law does not explicitly prohibit the patenting of cannabis or cannabis-related products.[25] In the past, inventions that primarily served illegal purposes or were "injurious to the well-being, good policy, or sound morals of society" were deemed invalid under 35 U.S.C. § 101 due to a lack of "utility."[26] But this principal has not been enforced in recent years, nor has it been an issue with regard to cannabis-related inventions.[27] Thus, as long as a cannabis-related invention meets the novel, nonobvious, and other requirements, patentability is possible.

Utility patents in the cannabis realm "can be granted for sexually and asexually reproducing plants, seeds, plant varieties, plant parts (e.g. fruit and flowers), and processes of producing plants, plant genes, and hybrids."[28] Additionally, patents can be attained for formulations and other products

---

19. *See* Joseph Dylan Summer, *Patenting Marijuana Strains: Baking Up Patent Protection for Growers in the Legal Fog of this Budding Industry*, 23 JIPL 169, 188 (2015).
20. *Id.* at 188–89.
21. *Id.* at 189.
22. *Id.*
23. *Id.*
24. *See, e.g.*, 15 U.S.C. § 1127 (where the Lanham Act defines "trademark" to mean "any word, name, symbol, or device . . . which a person has a bona fide intention to use in commerce . . ." and requires that such commerce "may *lawfully* be regulated by Congress").
25. *See* 35 U.S.C. § 101 (which does not limit patentable inventions to those serving a legal or lawful purpose); Madison Margolin, *Future Weed: Formulations, Patents and Where Cannabis Is Going Next*, ROLLING STONE (Jan. 20, 2019), https://www.rollingstone.com/culture/culture-features/future-weed-formulations-patents-and-where-cannabis-is-going-next-781439/.
26. *See* Dunstan H. Barnes, *So Your Client Wants to Open An Illinois Cannabis Dispensary?*, 105 ILBJ 26, 30 (Oct. 2017); Juicy Whip, Inc. v. Orange Bank, Inc., 185 F.3d 1364, 1366–67 (Fed. Cir. 1999) (internal citation omitted) (describing history of illegality principle).
27. *Id.*
28. Canna Law Blog, *Cannabis Patents: The 101*, CANNA LAW BLOG (Sept. 17, 2017), https://www.cannalawblog.com/cannabis-patents-the-101/.

made from cannabis plants.[29] Cannabis-related patent applications are primarily examined by the USPTO's Technology Center 1600 given their biological and chemical properties.[30] A 2019 survey of cannabis-related patent applications revealed that the majority of granted patents focus on cannabinoid receptor targeting,[31] compositions and derivatives, and methods of treating disease.[32] These trends likely correspond to the arguable utility and potential for medical benefits within such patents.

Utility patents under the Patent Act have more stringent written description requirements for applications in comparison to plant patents.[33] However, such stringent requirements, in turn, provide broader security in comparison to other forms of protection.[34] For example, plant patents only contain a single claim defining the scope of the patent.[35] Utility patents, conversely, may have multiple claims addressing different parts of the plant or methods of using the plant which are disclosed in the patent's specification.[36]

Another difficulty in patentability, particularly for "plant parts, tissues, cells, and clones of cannabis varieties" is satisfying the USPTO's enablement requirement.[37] The USPTO requires that a "specification must be in clear, full, concise, and exact terms to enable any person skilled in the art or science to which the invention pertains to make and use the same."[38] However, enabling those skilled in the art to "make" a plant can be difficult as these inventions are less amenable to explanation through a written description.[39] As such, the USPTO permits patent applicants to deposit inventive seeds to supplement the disclosure in the specification to provide an adequate written description of the invention and to enable those

---

29. Clinton South & Brian Shortell, *Patenting Cannabis: Possibilities and Pitfalls*, IP Watch Dog (Feb. 7, 2020), https://www.ipwatchdog.com/2020/02/07/patenting-cannabis-possibilities-pitfalls/id=118615/.

30. Pauline M. Pelletier & Deborah Sterling, Ph.D., *What Cannabis Patent Applicants Can Learn from Biopharma*, Law360 (Jan. 2019), https://www.sternekessler.com/news-insights/publications/what-cannabis-patent-applicants-can-learn-biopharma.

31. *See, e.g.*, U.S. Patent No. 8,367,714 (patent for "cannabinoid receptor targeted agent"); U.S. Patent No. 9,656,981 (patent for "peripherally-acting cannabinoid receptor agonists for chronic pain"); U.S. Patent No. 8,138,216 (patent for "cannabinoid receptor antagonists/inverse agonists useful for treating metabolic disorders, including obesity and diabetes").

32. Pelletier & Sterling, *supra* note 30.

33. Canna Law Blog, *supra* note 28.

34. *Id.*

35. *Id.*

36. *Id.*

37. South & Shortell, *supra* note 29; 35 U.S.C. § 112.

38. *Nonprovisional (Utility) Patent Application Filing Guide*, United States Patent and Trademark Office (January 2014), https://www.uspto.gov/patents-getting-started/patent-basics/types-patent-applications/nonprovisional-utility-patent.

39. South & Shortell, *supra* note 29.

skilled in the art to make and use the claimed invention.[40] Inventive seeds must be deposited at a publicly accessible U.S. depository so the public may obtain samples for reproduction upon expiration of the patent.[41] The issue that arises is that cannabis' categorization as a Schedule I drug makes it impossible to legally deposit such material at a U.S. depository.[42] Consequently, applicants pursuing this route of satisfying enablement will need to deposit such samples at an international depository, like the National Collections of Industrial, Food and Marine Bacteria in Scotland, which the USPTO is obligated to recognize under the Budapest Treaty of 1977.[43] This difficulty was illustrated by the prosecution of U.S. Patent No. 9,095,554 (issued on August 4, 2015), for which the patentee ultimately overcame this enablement hurdle and attained a patent for "breeding, production, processing and use of specialty cannabis."[44]

2.2 Design Patents

Another beneficial, although less popular, component of an intellectual property portfolio is a design patent. Only 10 percent of all issued patents are design patents, and less than 1 percent of cannabis-related filings are design patents.[45] Design patents are available to anyone who "invents a new, original, and ornamental design for an article of manufacture."[46] In the cannabis industry, these patents can provide a valuable form of protection as an alternative to utility patents. A design patent only protects the look and appearance of an article and does not cover "structural or utilitarian features."[47] As such, design patent applications may only have a single claim, as opposed to utility patents, which may contain several.[48] Due to this, design patents are often cheaper and quicker to obtain, which is desirable for an ever-developing industry with cost-conscious businesses.[49] Patentees have acquired cannabis-related design patents, including a "pull

40. *Changes to Requirements for Seed Deposits at American Type Culture Collection and Advanced Notice of Change to Manual of Patent Examining Procedure*, United States Patent and Trademark Office (Mar. 1, 2019), https://www.uspto.gov/sites/default/files/documents/seed-deposit-2019.pdf.
41. *Id.; see also* U.S. Patent No. 9,095,554 at 244:15-62.
42. South & Shortell, *supra* note 29.
43. *Id.; see also* U.S. Patent No. 9,095,554 at 244:15-62.
44. U.S. Patent No. 9,095,554.
45. Matthew S. Dicke & Sana Hakim, *In The Weeds: Key Intellectual Property Takeaways for the Cannabis Industry*, THE NATIONAL LAW REVIEW (Nov. 4, 2019).
46. 35 U.S.C. § 171.
47. *Design Patent Application Guide*, U.S. Patent and Trademark Office (April 2019), https://www.uspto.gov/patents-getting-started/patent-basics/types-patent-applications/design-patent-application-guide.
48. *Id.; see also* 37 C.F.R. § 1.153.
49. Dicke & Hakim, *supra* note 45.

tab simulating a cannabis leaf cutout,"[50] a "waffle maker with cannabis leaf shape,"[51] and a "container for cannabis and tobacco."[52]

2.3 Plant Patents

Cannabis cultivators can also obtain plant patents under the Plant Patent Act.[53] The Plant Patent Act was the first piece of legislation in the world that granted patent rights to plant breeders, and affords agriculture the same opportunity to participate in the economic benefits of the patent system as had been afforded to industry.[54] But although plant patents may appear to present a logical option for patentees, these patents offer limited protections.[55]

Plant patents are available to anyone who "invents or discovers and asexually reproduces any distinct and new variety of plant, including cultivated sports, mutants, hybrids, and newly found seedlings, other than a tuber propagated plant or a plant found in an uncultivated state, may obtain a patent. . . ."[56] To be patentable, the USPTO also requires (1) that the plant is not a plant that is excluded by statute, where the part of the plant used for asexual reproduction is not a tuber food part, as with potato or Jerusalem artichoke; (2) that the inventor named for a plant patent application must be the person who actually invented the claimed plant, that is, discovered or developed and identified or isolated, and asexually reproduced the plant; (3) that the plant has not been patented, in public use, on sale, or otherwise available to the public prior to the effective filing date of the patent application with certain exceptions; (4) that the plant has not been described in a U.S. patent or published patent application with certain exceptions; (5) that the plant be shown to differ from known, related plants by at least one distinguishing characteristic, which is more than a difference caused by growing conditions or fertility levels, and so on; and (6) that the invention would not have been obvious to one having ordinary skill in the art as of the effective filing date of the claimed plant invention.[57]

However, as earlier mentioned,[58] plant patents have limited enforceability. These patents are limited to plants that are asexually produced and,

---

50. U.S. Design Patent No. D840,809.

51. U.S. Design Patent No. D869,237.

52. U.S. Design Patent No. D823,537.

53. 35 U.S.C. § 161.

54. *See* Ann K. Wooster, *Construction and Application of Plant Patent Act (35 U.S.C.A. §§ 161 et seq.)*, 135 A.L.R. FED. 273 (1996).

55. South & Shortell, *supra* note 29.

56. 35 U.S.C. § 161.

57. *General Information About 35 U.S.C. 161 Plant Patents*, United States Patent and Trademark Office (Sept. 2017), https://www.uspto.gov/patents-getting-started/patent-basics/types-patent-applications/general-information-about-35-usc-161#heading-2.

58. *See infra* Section 2.1 (discussing utility patents).

thus, cannot be enforced against producers of sexually produced plants.[59] Additionally, plant patents are limited to one claim, in comparison to utility patents, which may seek protection over multiple claims.[60] Such limitations likely contribute to the fact that less than 1 percent of currently active cannabis patents are plant patents.[61] Still, this provides a more affordable alternative to seeking a utility patent and contributes, particularly, to the horticultural body of cannabis knowledge.

2.4 Plant Variety Certifications

Cannabis cultivators can also obtain patent-like protections for novel varieties of sexually reproduced plants from the U.S. Department of Agriculture under the Plant Variety Protection Act (PVPA).[62] Congress sought to expand plant protections beyond the Plant Patent Act by creating certificates of plant variety protection, which provide intellectual property rights for seeds and other types of uncultivated, sexually reproduced plants that are not afforded protection under the Plant Patent Act.[63] Varieties seeking certification must be new, similar to the Patent Act's novelty requirement.[64] The PVPA certifies that "the breeder (or the successor in interest of the breeder), has the right, during the term of the plant variety protection, to exclude others from selling the variety or offering it for sale, or reproducing it, or importing it, or exporting it, or using it in producing (as distinguished from developing) a hybrid or different variety therefrom. . . ."[65] Generally, the term of the plant variety protection expires 20 years from the date of issue of the certificate.[66] If a certificate owner finds an infringement of plant variety protection, owners may pursue a civil action for infringement.[67] Ultimately, the PVPA aims to encourage developers of novel plant varieties to research and market new varieties for the benefit of the public.[68] However, a significant caveat to pursuing a PVPA certificate is that the act requires applicants to submit at least 3,000 seeds to a Colorado depository.[69] Despite Colorado's progressive stance on cannabis, the plant remains a

---

59. "Asexual reproduction is the propagation of a plant without the use of fertilized seeds to assure an exact genetic copy of the plant being reproduced." *General Information, supra* note 57. Acceptable modes of asexual reproduction include rooting cuttings, grafting and budding, bulbs, slips, layering, runners, tissue culture, and apomitic seeds. *Id.*

60. *Id.*; *see also* Canna Law Blog, *supra* note 28.

61. South & Shortell, *supra* note 29.

62. 7 U.S.C. §§ 2321–2582.

63. Summer, *supra* note 19, at 190; 7 U.S.C. § 2421.

64. Canna Law Blog, *supra* note 28.

65. 7 U.S.C. § 2483(a).

66. *Id.* at § 2483(b)(1).

67. *Id.* at § 2561.

68. *Id.* at § 2581.

69. *PVPO Program Requirements*, United States Department of Agriculture, https://www.ams.usda.gov/services/plant-variety-protection/pvpo-requirements.

federally controlled drug, and applicants in compliance with the program's requirements, consequently, risk criminal prosecution. The USDA has yet to issue a PVPA certificate for a cannabis plant.[70]

3. Why Is Patentability Important?

The protection of cannabis-related intellectual property in the patent space generates benefits for both patent owners and consumers. Consumers of patented cannabis strains and formulations, for example, can expect regulated and consistent dosing and psychoactivity, allowing for safer, more predictable experimentation.[71] On the other hand, patent owners can develop valuable patent portfolios protecting their inventions and distinguishing them from competitors.[72] This, in turn, promotes the advancement of science.

3.1 Marketability for Future Consolidation

Patent portfolios often fuel mergers and acquisitions, which are increasing in the cannabis industry.[73] For example, Canada's Canopy Growth Corporation had amassed more than five dozen global patents and applications by buying Ebbu Inc., a Colorado-based hemp research company with nine U.S. patent applications; Storz & Bickel GmbH & Co. KG, a German vaporizer maker; and KeyLeaf, a plant-based processing company in Saskatchewan and Illinois.[74] In January 2020, Cresco Labs, one of the largest vertically integrated multistate cannabis operators in the United States, closed its acquisition of CannaRoyalty (doing business as Origin House).[75] Cresco Labs' acquisition provides distribution, manufacturing, cultivation, and branding resources in California, where Origin House operates, and will make Cresco a leading wholesale distributor selling to over 575 dispensaries.[76] Accordingly, the surge in cannabis-related patent filings should be unsurprising.[77]

3.2 Enforceability in the Courts

Although profitable merger activity has caused patent filings to surge, it remains to be seen whether such patents are enforceable in court given

---

70. South & Shortell, *supra* note 28.

71. *See* Margolin, *supra* note 25.

72. *See* Malathi Nayak, *Cannabis Companies Gamble on Patents to Lure Possible Suitors*, BLOOMBERG LAW (Aug. 1, 2019).

73. *Id.*; *see also* Brochstein, *supra* note 12.

74. *See* Malathi Nayak, *supra* note 72.

75. *See* NCV Newswire, *Cresco Labs Closes Acquisition of Origin House*, NEW CANNABIS VENTURES (Jan. 8, 2020), https://www.newcannabisventures.com/cresco-labs-closes -acquisition-of-origin-house/.

76. *Id.*

77. Bultman, *supra* note 6.

the lack of cannabis-related patent litigation. Another potential benefit of owning a patent is the ability to enforce it against others who infringe upon its rights and seek damages in federal court. However, only one patent infringement lawsuit involving a cannabis-related patent has hit the dockets. In July 2018, United Cannabis Corporation (UCANN), a biotechnology company specializing in the development, distribution, licensing, and sale of medical cannabis products, filed a patent infringement lawsuit in the U.S. District Court for the District of Colorado against Pure Hemp Collective, alleging infringement of UCANN's U.S. Patent No. 9,730,911 (the "911 patent"), which relates to extracting cannabinoids from cannabis.[78]

The 911 patent relates "to the field of cannabinoids—various chemicals derived from the *cannabis sativa* plant—for human consumption."[79] The patent describes "the need to provide more effective and safer *cannabis* extracts for various medical uses, [and] extraction methods that provide unique active compounds that are useful to treat pain and various medical conditions.[80] The 911 patent ultimately only claims inventions related to extracts and formulations.[81]

UCANN's personnel purchased and tested Pure Hemp's Vina Bell 500 mg product, concluding that the product infringed one claim in the 911 patent—"[a] liquid cannabinoid formulation wherein at least 95% of the total cannabinoids is cannabidiol (CBD)."[82] Pure Hemp responded to the complaint with an argument that the asserted claims of the 911 patent are directed toward unpatentable subject matter.[83] The district court ultimately ruled against Pure Hemp, concluding that none of the challenged claims of the 911 patent were directed toward unpatentable subject matter.[84] But the court, separately, made a number of "preliminary observations" as well.[85]

Although Pure Hemp did not challenge the 911 patent regarding its purpose or use for any of the claimed formulations, the court evaluated the patent based on the purpose described in the specification; "the obvious thrust of the patent is a supposedly new means by which humans can consume cannabinoids so that those cannabinoids can produce the pharmacological effects they are known to have, thus (hopefully) treating or

---

78. *See* Eric Sandy, *Colorado Cannabis Patent Lawsuit Will Be Worth Watching*, Cannabis Business Times (Aug. 15, 2018), https://www.cannabisbusinesstimes.com/article/ucann-pure-hemp-patent-lawsuit-cannabis/; Jonathan Hyman, *How the 'UCANN v. Pure Hemp' IP Lawsuit Will Affect the Cannabis Industry*, Cannabis Business Times (July 29, 2019), https://www.cannabisbusinesstimes.com/article/ucann-pure-hemp-lawsuit-analysis-intellectual-property-knobbe-martens/.
79. United Cannabis Corp. v. Pure Hemp Collective, Inc., 18-cv-1922-WJM-NYW, 2019 WL 1651846, at *1 (D. Col. Apr. 17, 2019).
80. *Id.* (quoting 911 Patent at 1:32-39).
81. *Id.* at *2.
82. Sandy, *supra* note 78.
83. *United Cannabis Corp.*, 2019 WL 1651846, at *2.
84. *Id.* at *5.
85. *Id.* at *6.

ameliorating various diseases and symptoms."[86] Additionally, the court explicitly identified factors that the 911 patent does *not* claim, including processes for extracting cannabinoids from cannabis plants; required inactive ingredients within the formulation; required ratios between the cannabinoid portion of the liquid formulation and inactive ingredients; processes for ensuring that the percentage threshold has been met (as these methods "are well known in the art"); and methods for using any claimed formulation to treat any particular disease, condition, or symptom.[87] Thus, the court carefully delineated the limits of this case.

Turning to the patentability analysis, Pure Hemp argued that the 911 patent was "'directed to' the unpatentable natural phenomenon of the specified chemical compounds (cannabinoids, terpenes, and flavonoids), as if UCANN is trying to secure a monopoly on use of these compounds."[88] UCANN argued in response (1) that the liquid formulation was, itself, novel, and (2) that the "markedly different physiological characteristics" were novel.[89] The court limited its analysis to the novelty of the liquid formulation[90] and found that the claims of the patent were not directed toward patent-ineligible subject matter.[91]

Ordinarily in a patent litigation, a defendant would challenge the validity of a patent and draw on a wealth of prior art—years, sometimes decades, of academic studies, peer-reviewed articles, patents, patent applications, and other types of public information—to suggest that the patent is obvious or anticipated. But in the cannabis space, the prior art is significantly limited. Prior to progressive waves of legalization, the cannabis industry kept a relatively low profile in order to avoid prosecution and arrest. Therefore, although prior art may exist, it will take time to build a substantial body of potential prior art.

3.3 Potential for Patent Challenges via *Inter Partes* Review

Conversely, patent ownership also subjects patent owners to validity challenges through *inter partes* review (IPRs), and cannabis-related patents are not exempt from such challenges. IPR proceedings involve challenges to the validity of patents before the Patent Trial and Appeal Board.[92] In comparison to litigation, the scope of IPR proceedings are only limited to challenges based on obviousness or anticipation tied to patents and printed publications.[93] In an IPR, the parties submit evidence, including from

86. *Id.* at *6.
87. *Id.*
88. *Id.* (internal citation omitted).
89. *United Cannabis Corp.*, 2019 WL 1651846.
90. *Id.* at *7.
91. *Id.*
92. Perkins Coie, *IPR>>IRL: A Brief Guide to the Essentials of Inter Partes Reviews in Real Life* (Nov. 2019), https://issuu.com/perkinscoie/docs/2019_ipr_primer_v12_for_issue?e=15417991/70519117.
93. *Id.* at 5.

experts, and may conduct some limited discovery.[94] The Patent Trial and Appeal Board (PTAB) will conduct an oral hearing where the parties appear before a three-member panel of the PTAB to summarize their arguments and answer questions, and the PTAB will issue a final written description following the hearing.[95] This type of proceeding is often viewed as a strategic alternative to patent litigation due to the faster speed of the proceeding in comparison to other federal court venues, the technical savvy of the PTAB, and the lowered burden of proving invalidity (a preponderance of the evidence versus clear and convincing evidence).[96] On January 3, 2019, the PTAB issued the landmark IPR decision involving a cannabis patent for the use of cannabinoids in the treatment of epilepsy and, specifically, generalized or partial seizures.[97] Although the PTAB determined that claims 1 and 2 of the patent were unpatentable as obvious, the remaining 11 challenged claims were deemed valid and, thus, potentially enforceable.[98] This case illustrates that, thus far, neither the courts nor the USPTO will discriminate against cannabis patents due to their subject matter.

4. Conclusion

Ultimately, once the federal government legalizes cannabis, patent owners will no longer face uncertainty regarding enforceability and will be free to pursue their day in court against alleged infringers. Cannabis-related patents, in turn, will only increase in value.

---

94. *Id.*
95. *Id.*
96. *Id.* at 3, 8–9.
97. IPR2017-00503 at 4.
98. *Id.* at 37.

10

Cannabis Litigation: Trends and Considerations

David Biderman, Charles Sipos, and Tommy Tobin

Operating within a constantly evolving legal and regulatory landscape, cannabis businesses have been the subject of numerous civil actions. Given the relatively recent nature of these actions, the breadth of precedent in the nascent area of cannabis litigation is fairly light. Even so, existing actions provide a useful guide to the future ahead for cannabis litigation.

This chapter discusses several considerations specific to cannabis litigation practice, such as the enforceability of contracts within the cannabis industry. Additionally, an overview of some of the fundamentals of civil practice, particularly the types of claims that often affect cannabis businesses, class action basics, and common defenses to claims, is provided.

1. Cannabis and Civil Litigation

The complex network of federal, state, and even local laws applicable to cannabis businesses can result in a dizzying array of requirements to maintain compliance. Civil disputes involving cannabis businesses can take many forms, from zoning and land use challenges to disagreements between suppliers.

Consumer class actions in the cannabis industry are among the most recent and important trends in cannabis litigation, especially as cannabis use becomes more widespread. Plaintiffs' attorneys are increasingly targeting cannabis businesses on a putative class basis. Many predict a further wave of consumer litigation against these businesses, especially against cannabidiol (CBD) product manufacturers.[1] As one article noted: "additional

---

1. Diana Novak Jones, *Class Action 'Avalanche' Coming for CBD Industry*, Law360 (Oct. 30, 2019); David T. Biderman, Barak Cohen, Tommy Tobin, & Michael Bleicher, *Insight: A New Class—The CBD Lawsuit Floodgates Are Opening*, Bloomberg Law (Dec. 18, 2019).

class action litigation cases are expected, and companies should proactively mitigate potential litigation risks."[2]

As cannabis products continue to garner additional publicity and more widespread availability, the prospect of regulatory action comes into greater focus. For example, warning letters issued by the U.S. Food and Drug Administration (FDA) in November 2019 prompted several federal class action filings in California, alleging violations of state consumer protection law and arguing that the cannabis products were "illegal to sell."[3] Agency regulatory actions and warning letters often lead to putative class action filings as consumers seek redress for alleged harm related to the products under the regulator's focus.

1.1 Types of Cases

As litigation involving cannabis companies can take many forms, cannabis businesses and their counsel should be familiar with common claims affecting the industry. Given its prominence as a vehicle to get putative class plaintiffs' complaints into court, cannabis businesses should pay particular attention to state consumer protection laws. As manufacturers of consumer products, especially products that may be consumed, smoked, vaporized, rubbed, or otherwise incorporated into consumers' bodies, cannabis companies should also be aware of other laws that could create liability exposure.

1.1.1 Consumer Protection

Consumer protection laws exist in all 50 states. Generally, they protect the public against misleading and unfair business practices, such as false advertising. Many of these laws are enforceable by the state attorneys general as well as private parties.

Prior to exercising private rights of action, individuals must often first comply with procedural requirements, such as sending a pre-suit notice to the defendant.[4]

Some states, such as New York and California, have multiple consumer protection laws in the same state that are often litigated together, but they nonetheless may contain varying requirements.[5] Although the exact parameters of the applicable consumer protection law depend on the statute's text and its interpretation in the state courts, these laws generally require that (1) a consumer is (2) injured or deceived and that damage was (3) caused

---

2. Biderman et al., *supra* note 1.

3. *See id.*

4. *See, e.g.*, ALA. CODE § 8-19-10(e) (requiring advance notice); MASS. GEN. LAWS ch. 93A, § 9(3) (generally requiring pre-suit notice); Consumers Legal Remedies Act (CRLA), CAL. CIVIL CODE § 1782 (same).

5. *See* N.Y. GEN. BUS. LAW §§ 349 and 350; CLRA, CAL. CIV. CODE §§ 1750, *et seq.*; False Advertising Law, BUSINESS & PROFESSIONS CODE §§ 17500, *et seq.*; Unfair Competition Law, BUSINESS & PROFESSIONS CODE §§ 17200, *et seq.*

by (4) defendant's deceptive or misleading act or trade practice. Important distinctions exist as to the elements of consumer protection laws, and local laws must be consulted. One of the most critical distinctions is whether the laws require that a consumer relied upon the allegedly deceptive or misleading act.[6]

Unless prohibited by state law,[7] state consumer protection laws are often used as vehicles for putative class action plaintiffs to get their cases into court. Evidence drawn from the food litigation context suggests that courts in New York and California are likely to see large numbers of cannabis-related cases in the years ahead alleging consumer protection theories.[8]

State consumer protection laws can also result in the award of attorneys' fees to a prevailing consumer as well as multiple or punitive damages, especially if the violations of the laws are found to be willful or knowing.[9] Some states impose such penalties if companies do not grant relief in response to a plaintiff's pre-suit demand.[10]

False advertising is a particular concern for cannabis companies, especially where claims might outstrip available scientific evidence. In order to mitigate potential risks, companies should consider avoiding claims that are difficult or impossible to verify, such as gummies "curing cancer," and using scientific evidence to substantiate implied or express health claims.[11]

---

6. *Compare* ARK. CODE § 4-88-113(f) (requiring reliance as precondition to private right of action) *with* Odom v. Fairbanks Memorial Hosp., 999 P.2d 123, 132 (Alaska 2000) (noting that under Alaska consumer protection law, "Actual injury as a result of the deception is not required. . . . All that is required is a showing that the acts and practices were capable of being interpreted in a misleading way.").

7. *See* ARK. CODE § 4-88-113(f)(1)(B) ("A private class action under this section is prohibited unless the claim is being asserted for a violation of Arkansas Constitution, amendment 89."); LA. REV. STAT. § 51:1409(A) (consumer "may bring an action individually but not in a representative capacity to recover actual damages."); MONT. CODE § 30-14-133(1) (consumer "may bring an individual but not a class action" under state consumer protection law).

8. *See* PERKINS COIE, FOOD LITIGATION YEAR IN REVIEW 2019 at 6 (Feb. 2020).

9. *See, e.g.,* N.H. REV. STAT. § 358-A:10(1); N.J. STAT. ANN. § 56:8-19; N.M. STAT. ANN. §§ 57-12-10(B) & (C).

10. *See* MASS. GEN. LAWS ch. 93A, § 9(3) (allowing damage multiple of "up to three but not less than two [actual damages] if the court finds that . . . the act or practice was a willful or knowing violation . . . or that the refusal to grant relief upon demand was made in bad faith with knowledge or reason to know that the act or practice complained of violated" state law); N.C. GEN. STAT. § 75-16.1 (awarding fees if "(1) The party charged with the violation has willfully engaged in the act or practice, and there was an unwarranted refusal by such party to fully resolve the matter which constitutes the basis of such suit; or (2) The party instituting the action knew, or should have known, the action was frivolous and malicious.").

11. David T. Biderman, Barak Cohen, Tommy Tobin, & Michael Bleicher, *Multiple CBD Class Actions Filed with More Expected,* JD SUPRA (Dec. 5, 2019).

1.1.2 Products Liability and Negligence

Manufacturers and sellers of cannabis products should take all reasonable care to ensure that the products they make and sell are safe for consumers to use. This is especially true as cannabis products may be consumed, smoked, vaporized, rubbed, or otherwise absorbed into a person's body and these products should be safe for their intended use.

Sometimes, even though a company has exercised all reasonable care, a product might nonetheless cause damage. For example, more than 120 lawsuits were filed in 2017 alone regarding battery explosions in vape pens.[12] In such cases, for example, consumers might allege that there was a defect in the product's design, manufacturing, or warnings that contributed to it becoming unreasonably dangerous for use.[13] In order to prevail, consumers would also need to demonstrate that that defect caused the injury claimed. State laws on strict products liability have significant distinctions that should also be taken into account.

In negligence actions, plaintiffs must establish the familiar five elements of duty, breach, cause-in-fact, proximate cause, and injury. Cannabis companies should be aware that they may have a duty to exercise reasonable care in supplying goods for consumers' use, especially as that product might be consumed.[14] In terms of proximate cause, companies should consider the intended and advertised uses of the product and how consumers are likely to interact with a product. For example, it is conceivable that a consumer might inhale a product's smoke when a product is intended to be smoked.

1.1.3 California Proposition 65

California's Safe Drinking Water and Toxic Enforcement Act of 1986, also known as Proposition 65, requires businesses that sell consumer products—including food—to notify Californians about certain chemicals that are in those products that are known to the state to cause cancer or reproductive health issues. Given that California is a prime market for cannabis companies, manufacturers and sellers should take care to label products appropriately when marketing products in that state.

---

12. Izzy Kapnick, *Vape Battery Explosion Lawsuits on the Rise*, COURTHOUSE NEWS (Dec. 29, 2017) (noting concerns that "small retail vape shops, which are commonly named as defendants in the litigation alongside Chinese battery manufacturers, are not financially equipped to handle the influx of litigation"); *see also* Shelia Kaplan, *E-Cigarette Exploded in Teenager's Mouth, Damaging His Jaw*, N.Y. TIMES (June 19, 2019).

13. *See* RESTATEMENT (2D) OF TORTS § 402A.

14. *See generally* Edward C. v. City of Albuquerque, 2010-NMSC-043, 148 N.M. 646, 241 P.3d 1086 (2010) ("Two categories of legal duty are recognized: (1) an affirmative duty to conform one's actions to a specific standard of care in relation to a specific individual or group of individuals created by a specific statutory or common-law standard; and (2) a defensive duty that is the general negligence standard, requiring the individual to use reasonable care in his activities and dealings in relation to society as a whole.").

The state of California has placed Δ9-tetrahydrocannabinol, better known as "THC," and cannabis (marijuana) smoke on the list of chemicals requiring a Proposition 65 warning.[15] Products containing THC must be properly labeled regarding a risk for reproductive harm. Even though marijuana smoke was previously placed on the Proposition 65 list of recognized chemicals in 2009, the state now requires Proposition 65 warnings for marijuana products intended to be smoked that warn against both potential cancer-causing and reproductive health effects.

Because CBD may contain THC, companies should label products appropriately to comply with Proposition 65 warning mandates.[16]

Violations of Proposition 65 labeling requirements can pose substantial litigation risks, especially as Proposition 65 allows for a private right of action. Failure to comply with warning requirements can result in statutory violations of $2,500 per violation per day.

1.1.4 Contract Law

In the course of doing business, transactions are regularly handled by contract. Unfortunately, sometimes contracts are breached and litigation ensues. Cannabis companies might find themselves moving to enforce a contract's term or defending against an alleged breach.

When reviewing breach of contract claims, courts look to see whether a contract is valid and enforceable, there was a violation of the contract's terms, and damage resulted. State breach of contract elements vary somewhat.

Generally, contracts to engage in illegal activities are unenforceable as a matter of law.[17] Certain aspects of the cannabis industry, such as growing marijuana or its recreational use, may be legal under some state laws but remain illegal under federal law. This puts courts in a quandary, summed up by a recent law review article title: "Are 'Legal' Marijuana Contracts 'Illegal?'"[18]

Ultimately, the question of whether a particular contract is illegal involves an element of subjectivity as it depends on both the circumstances of the

---

15. *See* Kristine Kruger, Barak Cohen, Tommy Tobin, & Jasmine Wetherell, *Proposition 65 Labeling Obligations Anticipated for CBD Products Containing THC*, JD Supra (Feb. 15, 2020).

16. *Id.*

17. Bovard v. Am. Horse Enterprises, Inc., 201 Cal. App. 3d 832, 838, 247 Cal. Rptr. 340, 343 (1988) ("Whenever a court becomes aware that a contract is illegal, it has a duty to refrain from entertaining an action to enforce the contract."); *see also* Lee On v. Long, 37 Cal. 2d 499, 502, 234 P.2d 9, 11 (1951) (*en banc*) ("No principle of law is better settled than that a party to an illegal contract cannot come into a court of law and ask to have his illegal objects carried out; nor can he set up a case in which he must necessarily disclose an illegal purpose as the groundwork of his claim.").

18. Luke Scheuer, *Are "Legal" Marijuana Contracts "Illegal?"* 16 U.C. Davis Bus. L.J. 31 (2015).

individual case and a recognition that social mores about the purportedly "illegal" conduct at issue may change over time.[19]

At least one state, Colorado, has codified an exception to the general rule against "illegal" contracts by passing a law that expressly states that contracts pertaining to marijuana are enforceable.[20]

Nonetheless, federal courts continue to wrestle with illegality. The general trend is to find that the business interactions contemplated by the contract are severable from the cannabis-related nature of the business. For example, the Northern District of California found "even where contracts concern illegal objects, where it is possible for a court to enforce a contract in a way that does not require illegal conduct, the court is not barred from according such relief."[21] For example, a case in the Northern District of Texas found that a loan of more than $9.3 million to start a cannabis business was enforceable in federal court because repayment of that loan would not require any manufacturing, distributing, dispensing, or possession of marijuana.[22]

1.1.5 Class Actions

Class actions are of particular concern for cannabis companies from a litigation perspective.

(a) Class Action Requirements

Given the risk of exposure to consumer class actions, cannabis companies and their counsel should be aware of the requirements necessary to certify a class. Federal courts recognize that the class certification determination might sound "the death knell of the ligation."[23]

Federal Rule 23(a) provides for four key criteria for class certification. Each requirement must be satisfied.

The elements of class certification required by Federal Rule 23(a) are:

- Numerosity: The number of individuals must make individual joinder impractical.

---

19. *Bovard*, 201 Cal. App. at 838 ("The question whether a contract violates public policy necessarily involves a degree of subjectivity.").

20. CO REV STAT § 13-22-601 (2016) ("It is the public policy of the state of Colorado that a contract is not void or voidable as against public policy if it pertains to lawful activities authorized" under the state constitution and Colorado's marijuana laws).

21. Mann v. Gullickson, No. 15-CV-03630-MEJ, 2016 WL 6473215, at *7 (N.D. Cal. Nov. 2, 2016) ("even if the Notes concern an illegal object (i.e., a violation of the [Controlled Substances Act]), it is possible for the court to enforce the Notes in a way that does not require any party to engage in illegal conduct.").

22. Ginsburg v. ICC Holdings, LLC, No. 3:16-CV-2311-D, 2017 WL 5467688, at *8 (N.D. Tex. Nov. 13, 2017).

23. Chamberlan v. Ford Motor Co., 402 F.3d 952, 957 (9th Cir. 2005).

- Commonality: The members of the class must present common questions of law or fact.
- Typicality: The claims or defenses of the class representatives must be typical of those of class members.
- Adequacy: The class representatives must fairly and adequately represent the interests of the class.

(b) Securities Laws

Class actions against cannabis companies are becoming more common.[24] Material omissions or misrepresentations in public disclosures can lead to actionable controversies.

Federal securities laws are written broadly. For example, section 10(b) makes it illegal to "use or employ, in connection with the purchase or sale of any security" a "manipulative or deceptive device or contrivance in contravention of such rules and regulations as the [SEC] may prescribe."[25] The implementing regulation, known as "Rule 10b-5," makes it unlawful for any person, "*directly or indirectly,*" to:

> (a) To employ any device, scheme, or artifice to defraud, (b) To make any untrue statement of a material fact or to omit to state a material fact necessary in order to make the statements made, in the light of the circumstances under which they were made, not misleading, or (c) To engage in any act, practice, or course of business which operates or would operate as a fraud or deceit upon any person, in connection with the purchase or sale of any security.[26]

Elements of section 10(b) claims include:

- A material misrepresentation or omission;
- Made with scienter;
- Causal nexus between the material omission or misrepresentation and the purchase or sale of a security;
- Plaintiff's reliance on the material misrepresentation or omission;
- Plaintiff's economic loss; and
- Causal nexus between the economic loss suffered by plaintiff and the material misrepresentation or omission.[27]

Federal laws also create personal liability for misleading statements upon which an investor sold or purchased a security.[28] Several cases have alleged

---

24. *See* Amanda Bronstad, *Investors Targeted Lawsuits at Cannabis Companies in 2019, Report Finds,* LAW.COM (Jan. 21, 2020).
25. 15 U.S.C. § 78j(b).
26. 17 C.F.R. § 240.10b-5.
27. *See* Dura Pharms., Inc. v. Broudo, 544 U.S. 336, 341–42 (2005).
28. 15 U.S.C. § 78r(a).

that publicly traded cannabis companies violated federal securities laws by communicating material omissions or misrepresentations to investors.[29]

Given the growth of cannabis businesses, and additional listings on public stock exchanges, additional securities class action cases are expected.

(c) Americans with Disabilities Act (ADA)

Several recent class action lawsuits have targeted cannabis companies for ADA claims. The ADA prohibits places of public accommodation from discriminating "on the basis of disability in the full and equal enjoyment of the goods, services, facilities, privileges, advantages, or accommodations" of any such place.[30] Traditionally, the ADA was limited to the brick-and-mortar world. Now, courts are split on whether to include websites as "places of public accommodation."[31]

In fact, at least five class action cases have been filed against cannabis companies for an alleged inability of a blind individual to access the website. Cannabis companies should ensure their physical and digital spaces are accessible, for example, by ensuring websites use alt-text, correctly nested headings, and proper links for individuals using screen reading technologies.

(d) Privacy Laws and Cannabis

International, federal, and state privacy laws are of particular concern to cannabis companies. Because cannabis companies have to collect sensitive information, such as photo ID or date of birth, to comply with state laws, data breaches of these companies can expose customers' personal information. In January 2020, researchers found a data breach that had exposed the full names, phone numbers, dates of births, medical ID numbers, signatures, gram limits, and sales figures of 30,000 medical marijuana customers.[32]

The European Union and California have imposed stringent privacy laws that impose new restrictions on the collection, management, and use of personal information.[33] Other states are considering similar data privacy

---

29. *See, e.g.*, Samn v. India Globalization Technology, et al., No. 1:18-cv-6199 (E.D.N.Y., filed Nov. 2, 2018) (alleged failure to disclose change in business model and delisting from New York Stock Exchange); Radcliff v. Joseph D. Dowling, et al., No. A-19-794377-B (Clark Cnty. District Court, Nevada, filed May 7, 2019) (alleged failure to disclose that patent had been rejected); *In re* Curaleaf Holdings, Inc. Securities Litigation, (E.D.N.Y., filed Aug. 5, 2019) (alleged failure to disclose that cannabis products were not approved by FDA).

30. 42 U.S.C. § 12182(a).

31. *See* Gil v. Winn-Dixie Stores, Inc., 257 F. Supp. 3d 1340, 1348 (S.D. Fla. 2017) ("Courts are split on whether the ADA limits places of public accommodation to physical spaces.").

32. Jason Murdock, *Data Breach Exposes Personal Details of Over 30,000 U.S. Cannabis Users*, NEWSWEEK (Jan. 23, 2020).

33. *See generally* Laura Jehl & Alan Friel, *CCPA and GDPR Comparison Chart*, WESTLAW PRACTICAL LAW (2019) (providing comparison of California and E.U. laws regarding

proposals. Cannabis companies interacting with or marketing to European or California consumers should be mindful of what data they collect and how it is stored.

Class action cases are just starting regarding California's data privacy law, known as the California Consumer Privacy Act (CCPA), and cannabis companies should take proactive steps to mitigate litigation risk resulting from this law.

The federal Telephone Consumer Protection Act (TCPA) can, and already has, posed significant litigation risk for cannabis companies. The TCPA was enacted in 1991 to address unwanted marketing calls. It has now expanded to faxes and text messages, along with other media. Marketing practices using an auto-dialer or sending unsolicited text messages can result in class action allegations. In April 2019, a cannabis company settled a TCPA suit for $1.75 million involving more than 50,000 customers.[34] In March 2020, TCPA allegations were brought against a dispensary company along with a demand of $500 per unwanted text.[35]

Allegations continue to target cannabis companies; at least one cannabis delivery service has defeated class certification relating to TCPA claims.[36] In *Alex Derval, v. Xaler*, the Central District of California found that putative class plaintiffs had initially proposed thousands of class members, then revised that estimate to "hundreds" or "at least 20–40" in later filings.[37] At the class certification stage, the court ultimately found that there was no "support that any of those customers received unwanted text messages, revoked consent to receive messages, or continued to receive messages after revocation."[38]

1.2 Common Defenses

Cannabis companies defending lawsuits have numerous defenses available to them, which vary by particular claim and jurisdiction. Following is a review of common defenses, particularly in the class action context.

1.2.1 Pleading with Specificity

Federal Rule 9(b) requires special pleading standards in cases alleging fraud or mistake. The pleadings must state these claims with particularity. Federal courts have interpreted Rule 9(b) to require that a complaint "(1) specify the statements that the plaintiff contends were fraudulent,

---

privacy).

34. Allison Grande, *California Marijuana App to Shell Out $1.75M to end TCPA Suit*, Law360 (Apr. 2, 2019).

35. Jack Queen, *Weed Dispensary Hit with TCPA Suit Alleging Spam Text*, Law360 (Mar. 31, 2020).

36. Alex Derval, et al., v. Xaler, et al., No. 2:19-cv-01881-ODW (C.D. Cal. Jan. 28, 2020), Dkt. 38.

37. *Id.* at *4.

38. *Id.* at *5.

(2) identify the speaker, (3) state where and when the statements were made, and (4) explain why the statements were fraudulent."[39]

Cannabis companies facing allegations that consumers were misled by a purportedly fraudulent claim must have notice of what the claim was, where it was located, how the claims were communicated to the plaintiff, and why the claims are false. This information will assist the company in responding to and defending the lawsuit's allegations.

1.2.2 Reasonable Consumer

Pursuant to Federal Rule 12(b)(6), a complaint that fails to state a claim for which relief can be granted should be dismissed. At the motion to dismiss stage, a court generally accepts well-pled allegations as true, but claims must cross the line from conceivable to plausible in order to escape dismissal.[40]

In consumer class action suits, members of the public must be "likely to be deceived" by the alleged misrepresentation.[41] Courts evaluate whether the public is "likely to be deceived" under the reasonable consumer standard. Where the pleading does not plausibly allege that a reasonable consumer would be deceived, the action should not survive dismissal.[42]

Drawing upon experience in the food and beverage sector,[43] the reasonable consumer defense is an important tool for cannabis companies looking to defend consumer class action cases. Strained and implausible readings of disputed labeling terms are unlikely to survive a reasonable consumer review.[44] In a consumer class action, the individual decision maker who determines what a "reasonable consumer" might consider a reasonable reading of contested labeling ultimately remains the presiding judicial officer. Cannabis companies must recognize that certain labeling terms that are known to consumers, even those that are relatively unsophisticated, in the cannabis marketplace are not necessarily known to judicial officers. Judges, particularly at the federal level, may be unfamiliar with the legitimate cannabis industry. Based on this unfamiliarity, it is possible that some judges might be reticent to find that certain terms are "reasonable."

1.3 Preemption

Generally, preemption defenses rely on the assumption that higher legal authority, such as the federal government, binds lower authorities when

---

39. Rombach v. Chang, 355 F.3d 164, 170 (2d Cir. 2004).
40. Bell Atlantic Corp. v. Twombly, 550 U.S. 544, 570 (2007).
41. *See* Becerra v. Dr Pepper/Seven Up, Inc., — F.3d —, 2019 WL 7287554, at *3 (9th Cir. Dec. 30, 2019); *accord* Ebner v. Fresh, Inc., 838 F.3d 958, 965 (9th Cir. 2016).
42. *See, e.g.*, Painter v. Blue Diamond Growers, 757 F. App'x 517, 519 (9th Cir. 2018); Cruz v. Anheuser-Busch Companies, LLC, 682 F. App'x 583, 583 (9th Cir. 2017); Carrea v. Dreyer's Grand Ice Cream, Inc., 475 F. App'x 113, 115 (9th Cir. 2012).
43. Perkins Coie, *supra* note 8, at 9.
44. *See id.*

legal or regulatory questions arise. There are two species of preemption: express and implied.

Express preemption occurs when a higher legal authority directly and explicitly opposes the lower authority. For example, a state law prohibiting the addition of CBD to a food product sold in the state would preempt a local city ordinance allowing such a product.

On the other hand, implied preemption occurs when the higher authority's preemptive intent is implied by the structure and purpose of the relevant law.

In the cannabis litigation context, preemption may be a difficult defense given the complex array of overlapping, and often conflicting, rules governing the cultivation, manufacturing, processing, and sale of cannabis products. Nonetheless, litigants may be able to point to compliance with federal or state standards to preempt consumer protection or tort claims.

1.4 Primary Jurisdiction

The overlapping federal and state authorities governing cannabis lead to thorny issues concerning appropriate regulatory authority over certain aspects of the cannabis industry.

Primary jurisdiction is a prudential doctrine that leads courts to defer to agencies that should initially determine an issue. The primary jurisdiction doctrine applies where claims implicate a federal agency's expertise with a regulated product, and the court wishes to take advantage of the agency's expertise in order to promote uniformity and the integrity of the regulatory scheme surrounding the regulated product.[45]

Four factors guide the court's review of whether to apply the primary jurisdiction doctrine: (1) the need to resolve an issue that (2) has been placed by Congress within the jurisdiction of an administrative body that has regulatory authority (3) pursuant to a statute that subjects an industry or activity to a comprehensive regulatory scheme that (4) requires expertise or uniformity in administration.[46] The court's decision to apply primary jurisdiction and defer its decision making is discretionary.

Cannabis companies, particularly those in the CBD industry, should consider whether primary jurisdiction could present the possibility to stay pending litigation until the federal agency issues its final determination.

Following the 2018 Farm Bill, the availability of CBD has become far more widespread. In November 2019, the FDA revised its Consumer Update regarding CBD to note, "It is currently illegal to market CBD by adding it to a food or labeling it as a dietary supplement."[47] The agency's

---

45. Greenfield v. Yucatan Foods, L.P., 18 F. Supp. 3d 1371, 1375 (S.D. Fla. 2014).

46. *In re* Horizon Organic Milk Plus DHA Omega–3 Mktg. & Sales Practice Litig., 955 F. Supp. 2d 1311, 1348 (S.D. Fla. 2013).

47. U.S. Food & Drug Admin., *What You Need to Know (And What We're Working to Find Out) About Products Containing Cannabis or Cannabis-derived Compounds, Including CBD* (Nov. 25, 2020).

announcement noted that it was exploring "potential pathways for various types of CBD products to be lawfully marketed" and expected to provide an update on its "progress regarding the agency's approach to these products in the coming weeks."[48]

Recent cases suggest that the application of primary jurisdiction for CBD may be helpful to cannabis companies facing lawsuits. Two putative class action suits in the Southern District of Florida alleging similar claims against CBD companies that allegedly mislabeled the amount of CBD in the products reached opposite results on the question of primary jurisdiction.[49] In one case, the court relied on the FDA's primary jurisdiction to stay litigation pending further regulatory action by the agency: "FDA regulations currently provide little guidance with respect to whether CBD ingestibles, in all their variations are food supplements, nutrients or additives and what labelling standards are applicable to each iteration."[50] But, in the second case, decided later, the court held that further FDA action would be unnecessary to resolve the case, noting "the FDA has not expressed interest in modifying the disclosure requirements for nutrients or additives, nor have the Defendants pointed to any regulation under consideration that may affect these specific food labeling requirements and thus impact this case."[51]

2. Conclusion

As cannabis businesses grow, so, too, will the risk of high-stakes commercial litigation, especially consumer class action matters. Private party litigation targeting cannabis businesses is likely to increase substantially in the coming years as cannabis becomes more widely available and the regulatory structures continue to develop. Businesses should work proactively to mitigate potential litigation risks, and a substantial part of that process is understanding the potential claims and defenses cannabis companies are likely to encounter. Complying with relevant regulatory authority assists a cannabis company's pre-litigation preparedness, especially as agency warning letters can often prompt consumer litigation.

---

48. *Id.*; *see also* Tommy Tobin, *CBD in Food and Beverage: 3 Development to Watch in 2020*, FORBES (Dec. 31, 2019) ("After the agency's November announcement and warning letters, manufacturers of CBD products, particularly those in food and beverage categories, should watch how the FDA clarifies and enforces its position on CBD-containing products over the new year.").

49. *Compare* Snyder v. Green Roads of Fla. LLC, – F. Supp. 3d –, No. 0:19-CV-62342-UU, 2020 WL 42239, at *6 (S.D. Fla. Jan. 3, 2020) (staying case on primary jurisdiction grounds) *with* Potter v. Potnetwork Holdings, Inc., No. 19-24017-CIV, 2020 WL 1516518 (S.D. Fla. Mar. 30, 2020) (rejecting primary jurisdiction).

50. *Snyder*, 2020 WL 42239, at *7.

51. *Potter*, 2020 WL 1516518, at *6.

11

Insurance Considerations for the Cannabis Industry

Robert P. Jacobs

Insurance underwriters do not like the unknown. If they perceive there to be a risk, but they cannot quantify or assess the likelihood of the risk materializing into a loss or liability, then they may contend that it is difficult to arrive at a price for accepting that risk. But more than that, they may even contend that it is difficult to determine which type of policy properly captures the risk. This may be the case with the cannabis industry.

As a legitimate industry, it is new. Laws and regulations vary by state and, indeed, state and federal law is not in sync. The apparatus surrounding the large-scale production of cannabis products is also new, to some extent. Even more fundamentally, courts have not yet had the opportunity to provide much guidance on underlying liability issues, such as a cannabis manufacturer's duty of care with respect to its products, much less insurance issues, such as when alleged cannabis-related bodily injury takes place or whether cannabis is considered a carcinogen with respect to certain carcinogen-related exclusions.

Regardless, for companies involved in the cannabis industry that are perplexed by the insurance landscape, this chapter provides some guidance. Specifically, this chapter provides an overview of some of basic insurance products that any cannabis-related business should consider, along with the corresponding issues that might arise with respect to such insurance products.

1. Overview of Basic Insurance Products

There probably is an insurance product sold for nearly every risk. But there are five basic types of insurance that any business, including a cannabis-related business, should consider: (1) comprehensive general liability; (2) property loss and business interruption; (3) commercial crime; (4) cyber; and (5) directors and officers liability (D&O). Overviews of each are discussed next.

1.1 Comprehensive General Liability

As its name implies, Comprehensive General Liability (CGL) insurance policies are meant to provide broad coverage to protect a policyholder if its operations, including its products, are alleged to harm a third party, typically in the form of property damage or bodily injury, or both.

Most such policies are "occurrence-based" policies because the threshold requirement of coverage is that an "occurrence" has taken place, which generally is defined as "an accident, including a continuous or repeated exposure to conditions" that results in property damage or bodily injury during the policy period. If an occurrence does take place, the policy is said to be "triggered," which means merely that the threshold requirement of coverage is met, subject to other possible limitations, such as various contractual coverage exclusions.

An occurrence-based policy can be triggered regardless of when a claim might be made against the policyholder. Indeed, for such things as latent bodily injury claims (those in which a disease or other injury does not manifest itself for years after the disease process began), it is not uncommon for a claim to made against a policyholder many years after a policy period has expired. Yet, if the bodily injury can be proven to have taken place, at least in part, during the period of long-expired insurance policy, that policy is triggered and should still respond to the claim (subject, of course, to exclusions or other conditions or limitations).

Some CGL policies are triggered in other ways, such as by a claim being made against the policyholder during the policy period. Other policies are triggered by occurrence, but only if that occurrence also is reported to the insurer during the policy period. These policies are aptly called "claims-made" and "occurrence-reported" policies, respectively.

Regardless of the type of trigger mechanism, these policies also require that any alleged property damage or bodily injury be "neither expected nor intended" from the policyholder's standpoint. The so-called expected or intended concept is meant to prevent coverage for damage or injury resulting either from intentional or reckless conduct. Although that seems straightforward enough, as discussed later, the concept can be a tricky one, in terms of determining which conduct is the relevant conduct with respect to determining expectation or intent.

1.2 Property Loss and Business Interruption Insurance

This type of insurance is meant to protect a business from what are referred to as "first-party" losses. "First party" refers to a loss sustained by the policyholder itself as opposed to injury or damage that the policyholder's operations allegedly caused to someone else, that is, a "third party."

As its name implies, this insurance typically has two major components. First, it is meant to provide coverage for if the policyholder's own business property sustains physical damage, such as that which might result from a fire. Second, if any physical damage to property causes an interruption in the policyholder's business, the insurance is supposed to indemnify the policyholder for the lost revenue sustained during the period of time it takes the business to resume operations.

These policies also typically cover what is known as "contingent business interruption," which is what might happen if a policyholder's business cannot operate as a result of physical damage that shut down a supplier's operations. The policies also typically cover costs incurred in trying to mitigate a loss, such as in connection with various temporary fixes to property or in obtaining supplies from other sources at a higher price.

This insurance most commonly is written on an "all risks" basis, meaning that they cover all possible risks of property damage except those expressly excluded. For example, a common exclusion that came to light in the aftermath of Hurricane Katrina is that these policies often will expressly exclude damage caused by flooding.

1.3 Commercial Crime or Fidelity Insurance

Commercial crime insurance is meant to protect a business from financial losses resulting from crime, ranging from run-of-the mill employee theft to various forms of sophisticated electronic crime. But the reality is that this coverage is meant primarily to protect a business from crimes committed by its own employees or from vendors. In that regard, there are some crime policies that provide coverage only for employee theft, which are called "fidelity" polices because "fidelity" is commonly defined as meaning "faithfulness" or "loyalty"—attributes that all employees ideally would embody. So, simply put, these types of policies are meant to protect a business from employees that are unfaithful or disloyal because they steal.

In any event, most comprehensive commercial crime policies provide the following basic coverages:

- Theft, damage, or destruction of money, securities, or other property either on the policyholder's premises or in transit.
- Computer fraud, such as the illegal transfer of funds from the policyholder to another account.
- Forgery, particularly forging the policyholder's signature on checks or other business documents.
- Receipt of counterfeit currency.

Unlike most property policies, which provide coverage for all risks, except those expressly excluded, commercial crime policies usually provide coverage only for "named perils," meaning that the risks covered must be expressly stated.

These policies are typically triggered when the policyholder discovers a loss has occurred or when then the policyholder becomes aware of facts that would lead a reasonable person to assume that a loss has occurred. This latter concept can also be a little tricky in scenarios in which theft or computer fraud occurs gradually or in small increments in which it is not immediately obvious that criminal activity is ongoing.

Indeed, situations in which a policyholder experiences a "slow drip" of theft occurring largely under the radar can not only confound the discovery of the loss but also bring into play the issue of how to apply deductibles. Specifically, most commercial crime policies apply a deductible to each "loss," which can be an ambiguous concept if, for example, an employee's theft of money or property is a series of distinct events over time. In such circumstances where an employee is carrying out a scheme over time, most policies will allow the aggregation of all of the individual events into one "loss" so that only one deductible applies. If there are several employees, or if the scheme involves different manners of theft—for example, stealing money from a safe or cash register and also transferring money electronically out of the policyholder's account, there can be questions as to whether there is a single loss or several losses.

1.4 Cyber Insurance

Cyber risk used to be risk that most considered to be confined largely to tech companies. This, of course, is no longer the case. Now, every company (and nearly every person) faces some form of cyber risk. Accordingly, cyber insurance has now become a part of most businesses' basic insurance portfolios.

Although cyber insurance is more varied than most other lines of insurance, with less in the way of uniform language, as discussed in the following sections, most of them provide at least three basic protections: (1) network security, (2) privacy, and (3) business interruption. In that regard, cyber insurance is a hybrid line of insurance providing both first-party (network security and business interruption) and third-party liability (privacy) protections.

1.4.1 Network Security
This part of a cyber policy is meant to protect a policyholder's business from network security failures, which may include such things as data breaches, malware infections, ransomware, or other types of risks that compromise the integrity of a business's network. Again, this is first-party insurance because it covers costs that the policyholder itself incurs as a result of a network security incident. Such costs may include such things as:

- Forensic consultants
- Legal counsel
- Data restoration

- Breach notification to affected parties
- Ransomware payments
- Public relations
- Credit monitoring

In short, this component of cyber insurance is meant to both restore the business's network and deal with any of the fallout that results from such an incident.

1.4.2 Privacy

All businesses maintain some information that someone considers to be private. This can be employee information, including such things as social security numbers, addresses, phone numbers, and health insurance or medical information, among many others. For customers, it can also include credit card information, in addition to addresses, phone numbers, etc. Private information can also include a supplier's trade secrets.

Privacy can mean two things. First, it can mean secrecy—keeping confidential information protected from dissemination to third parties. Second, it can mean being left alone—being free from unwanted contact. Either one of these forms of privacy can be breached if confidential data that a business is maintaining is released through some form of breach. If that were to occur, then the business can become liable to those whose private information was released.[1]

Cyber insurance typically is meant to respond to any such liabilities by providing the following protections:

- Legal fees and expenses incurred in defending against lawsuits resulting from the breach
- Indemnifying the policyholder for any damages it must pay to third parties on account of the breach
- Costs, sometimes including fines or penalties, due to regulatory enforcement in light of the breach

Indeed, in the cyber age, the protection of private information is becoming increasingly difficult, making this type of insurance coverage particularly relevant.

---

1. California has enacted a statute—the California Consumer Privacy Act (CCPA)—that is designed to both protect consumer's privacy rights and also hold companies accountable for data breaches. The CCPA gives consumers a vehicle to sue companies if nonencrypted and nonredacted personal information is stolen in a data breach arguably as a result of the company's failure to maintain reasonable security practices and procedures. The CCPA is similar to the General Data Protection Regulation (GDPR) enacted by the European Union.

1.4.3 Business Interruption

A business's computer network can be one of the most important components of its infrastructure. If a cyber incident shuts down the business's network, business operations can come to a halt. This is also true if a supplier's network goes down, or that of any third-party vendor on which a business relies.

Similar to traditional business interruption insurance, cyber business interruption insurance is meant to provide coverage for revenue lost during the period it takes to restore whichever network has been affected. And, like traditional business interruption insurance, this should also include any expenses incurred in getting the network up and running, or to mitigate the loss.

The main difference between cyber business interruption insurance and traditional business interruption insurance is that, in the context of cyber, traditional notions of "physical" property damage do not really apply. Instead, cyber business interruption insurance usually requires some other type of event, such as a third-party hack, or some system failure such as a failed software patch or a glitch caused by simple human error.

1.4.4 Directors and Officers (D&O) Liability

The principal purpose of what is typically referred to as D&O insurance is to protect the personal assets of a company's directors and officers if they are sued by investors, employees, and others for negligence or breach of fiduciary duty in their roles as managers of the business. D&O insurance policies usually refer to such conduct as a "wrongful act." This is known as "side A" coverage. A wrongful act is typically defined fairly broadly as "any actual or alleged act, error or omission, misstatement, misleading statement, neglect or breach of duty" by a director or officer "while acting in his or her capacity as such."[2] A wrongful act definition also may include certain conduct relating to employees, such as alleged wrongful termination or discrimination, among other things.

D&O policies also provide what is known as "side B" coverage, which provides coverage to the company itself if it has to indemnify a director or officer for such wrongful acts. In that regard, most corporate bylaws require the company to indemnify directors and officers if they are sued for an alleged wrongful act. The side B coverage provides backup support for this obligation.

D&O policies also usually protect the company directly for liability arising from a "securities claim," which typically is defined as claims made against the company for violating federal or state laws or regulations relating to

---

2. D&O policies often can cover other categories of individuals beyond just directors and officers. Protected individuals are usually referred to as "Insured Persons" and may include any category of employee that serves in some management function. The scope of the Insured Person definition may be a matter of negotiation with the insurer.

the regulation of securities brought by investors or brought derivatively on behalf of the company by an investor. Securities claims are usually filed if an investor believes that directors or officers are in breach of their fiduciary duties to the company and, as a result, are mismanaging it in such a way as to cause a decrease in stock value.[3]

2. Overview of Key Risks and the Corresponding Insurance Product

The cannabis industry has many component parts, from growers to retailers (dispensaries) and everything in between. And, each component part of this burgeoning industry has its own set of risks and exposures for which it will need insurance protection. The key types of insurance that each such component business should consider are discussed in the following sections.

2.1 Product Liability

Cannabis growers need the same protections as any farmers, although there are some heightened challenges.

To begin, there obviously is some increased risk of product liability claims due to the fact that some cannabinoids—chemicals unique to the cannabis plant—are responsible for the plant's psychoactive effects. Some of these psychoactive effects can manifest themselves in loss of memory, some impact on cognition and psychomotor performance, and possibly increased anxiety, among other things. Although numerous products also can be deemed to have some adverse health effect—such as alcohol and red meat—cannabis products might attract blame for a wide range of perceived adverse health effects due to its historical reputation as a psychoactive drug and its ambiguous or at least inconsistent status with respect to legality among the states and the federal government.

In short, it is possible that users of cannabis products who sustain what they perceive to be some injury from the use of those products will blame the growers, among others, and sue them for compensation. In that regard, the point of sale may be the first point of litigation, especially if the products being sold in the dispensary do not have a readily identifiable manufacturer, such as may be the case with pure cannabis leaf (aka "flower") sold for smoking, and so on (picture a tea shop where the tea is scooped out of jars or cannisters and sold in bags, with no identifiable grower or processor). But, the manufacturers of other labeled cannabis products,

---

3. D&O policies may provide other grants of coverage as well, such as protecting directors and officers from the costs of having to comply with regulatory subpoena or participate in regulatory interview relating to an investigation into corporate malfeasance. D&O policies usually cover defense costs arising out covered clams, although such costs are usually reimbursed rather than advanced or paid directly to defense counsel.

such as tinctures or edibles, might ultimately find themselves as the central target of a broad range of claims based on such things as product purity or any allegation that a product's ingredients causes injury (e.g., heavy metals allegedly present in CBD oil).

This is the type of risk that CGL policies are meant to cover—claims alleging bodily injury from the use of a product. Although CGL policies have generally broad grants of coverage—that is, bodily injury arising out of the policyholder's product or other aspects of its operations—like all insurance policies, those broad coverage grants are then limited by exclusions. Companies engaged in the cannabis industry might find that their insurers are relying on, or at least considering, three particular exclusions that purport to exclude coverage for (1) failure to comply with applicable law, (2) health hazards, and/or (3) carcinogens. These three exclusions are all reflections of insurers' unease with what is unknown about the emerging cannabis industry.[4]

Finally, the "expected or intended" concept might come into play with respect to cannabis products. Although any insurer that sells CGL coverage to a cannabis-related enterprise should be assumed to have accepted all of the risk that comes with this industry, it is possible that an insurer will take a hard look at any particular product that is alleged to cause harm, to see if there is any basis to argue that the policyholder had any relevant warnings in that regard. This level of analysis might include any warnings or advice from a supplier to the policyholder's own studies and quality assurance to information generally available to the public, such as studies by various health organizations or governmental bodies. Although it is usually a stretch to say that any policyholder "intended" its product to cause harm, insurers usually gloss over that reality and argue merely that the policyholder either expected or should have expected that its product would cause harm. Under the laws of most jurisdictions, an insurer would have to prove that the policyholder subjectively expected or intended that its product would cause harm; an objective analysis of what the policyholder should have expected or intended is not enough.[5]

---

4. But see discussion of *Green Earth* decision later in the chapter, with respect to the issue of whether an insurer can exclude coverage for the precise risk it agrees to underwrite.

5. *See, e.g.*, Shell Oil Co. v. Winterthur Swiss Ins. Co., 12 Cal. App. 4th 715, 745–46 (1993), 15 Cal. Rptr. 2d 815, 834–35 (Cal. App. 1993), *modified*, 1993 Cal. App. LEXIS 156 (Cal. App. 1993); Hecla Mining Co. v. New Hampshire Ins. Co., 811 P.2d 1083, 1088 (Colo. 1991) (holding that "the phrase 'neither expected nor intended' should be read only to exclude those damages that the insured knew would flow directly and immediately from its intentional act"); Broderick Inv. Co. v. Hartford Acc. & Indem. Co., 954 F.2d 601, 606 (10th Cir. 1992); Queen City Farms, Inc. v. Aetna Cas. & Sur. Co.,126 Wash. 2d 50, 64–69, 882 P.2d 703, 712–14 (Wash. 1994) (en banc), amended, 891 P.2d 718 (Wash. 1995); Espinet v. Horvath, 157 Vt. 257, 259, 597 A.2d 307 (1991) (acknowledging the standard and holding that policyholder's intent to cause harm could not be inferred as a matter of law); Quincy Mut. Fire Ins. Co. v. Abernathy, 393 Mass. 81, 83–85, 469 N.E.2d 797,

2.2 Fires, Bugs, and Other Sources of Property Loss

Given the risk of fire in greenhouses, property loss and business interruption insurance should be considered. These policies typically only cover sudden, fortuitous losses arising either from "named perils" or "all risks," depending on the policy type. They are meant to cover losses arising from fires, some natural disasters, and any other mishaps that cause damage to the policyholder's property, including such things as lost power to a greenhouse or irrigation system that results in damaged crops.

These policies do, however, have some key exclusions that could limit coverage. These include exclusions for mold, mildew, bugs, and grower error; all are very real risks to a cannabis grower. In addition, the policies might exclude coverage for "contraband, or property in the course of illegal transportation or trade," an exclusion which should not ever apply, if a grower is confining its business activities to a state in which it is legal to grow cannabis.[6] This includes the transport of the crop; it must stay within a state in which it is legal. If the crop were to be transported across state lines, even if to another state in which it is legal, an insurer might argue that federal interstate commerce laws apply, under which cannabis is not legal, thereby theoretically bringing any property loss claim within the contraband exclusion's scope.

As of the present, this type of coverage can be expensive, due primarily to the fact that the insurance industry is wary that smaller growers may not be as experienced in crop protection as more established growers with respect to other types of crops.

2.3 Theft

The cannabis industry also faces heightened risks of employee theft. This might be especially true for growers and dispensaries. For growers, the risk of theft might be greatest with respect to the growing plants, from which dishonest employees can cut leaves and stems, diminishing the size of the crop. For dispensaries, the risk is the theft of cash, given that most dispensaries trade in cash as opposed to credit cards.

Commercial crime policies are meant to cover precisely these types of risks. Unfortunately, many insurers may find the risk to be too great and will refuse to underwrite them. Or, although they might be willing to sell some coverage, that coverage might be substantially limited by exclusions. For example, an insurer might exclude coverage for growing plants, which they might view as too easy to steal, and limit coverage to other property in a grower's operations, such as lights or other equipment. And, for

---

799–800 (Mass. 1984) ("Our cases have concluded that an injury is nonaccidental only where the result was actually, not constructively, intended."); Patrons-Oxford Mut. Ins. Co. v. Dodge, 426 A.2d 888, 892 (Me. 1981); Arco Indus. Corp. v. American Motorists Ins. Co., 448 Mich. 395, 404–05 (1995).

6. See discussion of *Green Earth* case later in the chapter.

dispensaries, they might try to attach an exclusion for the theft of cash but be willing to insure against the theft of the actual products being sold, provided there are strict inventory controls. Although such exclusions could gut much of the coverage, it may be better to protect some of the business than to have no coverage at all.

2.4 Improper Release of Customer Information

There is a saying in this day and age that "all companies are tech companies." That is certainly true of companies in the cannabis industry, for a variety of reasons. The most obvious tech-related risk arises from the fact that dispensaries typically collect personally identifiable information (PII) from their customers, such as that which is derived from a driver's license (name, address, birth date, etc.), phone numbers, and possibly e-mail addresses. Not only must companies that collect PII protect that information, but, in this case, there is a significant possibility that dispensary customers would be especially sensitive to the disclosure not only of their PII but also of the mere fact that they are customers at all. Accordingly, the potential exposure from a data breach is high.

This is where cyber liability insurance is supposed to step in and provide coverage for the costs of mitigating any data breach and for any liability arising from the release of customers' PII. In that regard, the trickiest part with respect to cyber liability insurance may be in its procurement. Specifically, cyber liability underwriters will be very concerned about the security controls that the prospective policyholder has in place and, if they are doing their jobs correctly, underwriters will engage in a comprehensive and rigorous review of those controls, including the types of data security professionals that the policyholder uses and the plan that the policyholder has in place for responding to a data breach.

More importantly, the prospective policyholder has to make sure that it is accurately reporting the amount of PII records it maintains or expects to maintain. This could be challenging in the retail context because it may not be possible to accurately predict this information during the policy procurement stage. Regardless, it is important for any prospective policyholder to be as diligent and forthcoming as possible in providing this information to the underwriters, because mistakes or omissions that are revealed after a breach has occurred could give the insurer grounds to either avoid providing coverage for a given incident or to rescind the policy altogether.[7]

---

7. However, rescission is an extreme measure and the insurer would bear the burden of proving that any purported omission or misrepresentation was material to the underwriting process. The concept of "materiality" means that the insurer either would not have sold the policy, or it would have sold it on different terms and conditions (including a different premium) if it had correct information. In most jurisdictions, the insurer would have to satisfy this burden of proof through documents in its underwriting files, as opposed to the mere self-serving testimony of its underwriters.

Dispensaries are among the businesses that should be most concerned about a data breach involving PII, because dispensaries require that all customers that walk through their doors divulge that data, which they then store electronically. Indeed, dispensaries require that all their customers present identification, typically a driver's license or other government-issued ID, from which they derive PII such as a customer's name, date of birth, address, driver's license number (or passport number or other equivalent), and possibly their photograph.

Even in states in which cannabis is entirely legal or in which it is legal for medical use, many customers want to keep their use of cannabis products private. This is true for at least two principal reasons. First, cannabis is not legal under federal law and, as a result, there is a possibility that knowledge of a customer's cannabis could be problematic on various levels, particularly with respect to employment. Specifically, it is possible that with respect to certain jobs that are subject to licensing—such as attorneys, medical professionals, psychotherapists, among many others—knowledge of cannabis use could pose a risk to such licensing. Second, notwithstanding its legality on the federal level, there might be a stigma associated with cannabis use, even in states in which it is legal.

In any event, it is clear that a data breach involving a dispensary could result in significant liability if customers' PII is released, particularly if any such breach affects a customer's employment. Accordingly, dispensaries need to be especially vigilant with respect to the PII that they collect, and they need to protect themselves against a breach by purchasing cyber liability insurance. And, as mentioned earlier, they need to be very careful about properly disclosing the number of PII records they maintain, or expect to maintain, when applying for cyber liability insurance.

2.5 Loss of Share Value

Almost all companies, whether private or public, have shareholders. And, a company's directors and officers owe a fiduciary duty to their shareholders to manage the company as diligently as possible to protect and hopefully increase the value of the shareholders' investments. If any perceived negligence, recklessness, or other malfeasance in the discharge of those responsibilities causes, or allegedly causes, a decrease in share value, a shareholder can bring a lawsuit against the directors and officers, or the company, seeking to hold any or all of them liable for that loss.

The cannabis industry may be especially vulnerable to such lawsuits due to both the lack of established standards regarding corporate stewardship as well as the regulatory uncertainty concerning the legality of cannabis products, among other things. For instance, if a company engages in the interstate transit of cannabis products, in disregard of the risks of doing so and without divulging that information to investors, and that company is then penalized or shut down by federal authorities, the shareholders might bring a claim alleging that the directors and officers breached their fiduciary obligations in allowing such activity. There are other recent examples of conduct particular to the cannabis industry that has formed the basis of shareholder claims.

In one instance, a publicly traded cannabis company experienced a decline in share value and was then accused by shareholders of making misleading statements ahead of its initial public offering with respect to its quality controls.[8] The shareholders brought this lawsuit after a wholesale customer—a producer of medical marijuana products—returned a large shipment of cannabis product based on quality control issues. The company responded with two main arguments: (1) it made no misleading statement in its prospectus; it was known to investors that companies that produce agricultural products face heightened quality control risks, and cannabis products are no exception; and (ii) the drop in share value was the result not of any quality control problems but, rather, it was the result of unforeseeable regulatory "headwinds."

In another instance, a shareholder lawsuit alleged a misleading stock offering with respect to a company that manufactured CBD drugs.[9] That lawsuit alleged that the directors and officers knew prior to the offering that participants in the clinical trials of one of the company's principal products had experienced adverse side effects and failed to disclose that information. Even though the company continued to pursue FDA approval for its product, the company's share price dropped 22 percent. So, in essence, the shareholders' lawsuit alleged that the directors and officers breached their fiduciary obligations by withholding from investors the fact that a key product might not receive FDA approval.

Claims such as these, in which investors are alleging a loss of share value, are the types of claims that D&O policies are meant to cover. Indeed, D&O policies cover actual or alleged "wrongful acts," and any claims alleging that a company or its directors or officers misled or otherwise neglected their responsibilities to investors should fall within the scope of that definition.

3. Judicial Guidance

Judicial law on insurance issues concerning the cannabis industry is not yet well developed. But, in just the few years since more and more states have started to make cannabis legal for both recreational or medical use, there already has been some evolution in the law.

For example, in *Tracy v. USAA Casualty Insurance Co.*,[10] the policyholder was a private citizen who grew marijuana for her own medical use, which was legal under the laws of Hawaii. Twelve of her plants were stolen, for which she made a claim under her homeowner's insurance policy. The

---

8. *See In re* Sundial Growers Inc. Securities Litigation, No. 1:19-cv-08913-ALC (S.D.N.Y.).
9. *See* Scott Whiteley, et. al v. Zynerba Pharm., et. al., No. 2:18-cv-04959-NIQA (E.D. Pa).
10. Tracy v. USAA Casualty Insurance Co., 2012 WL 928186 (D. Haw. Mar. 16, 2012).

policyholder's claim was based on the fact that the insurance policy expressly covered "trees, shrubs, and other plants."

But the insurer denied coverage on the premise that the policyholder did not have an "insurable interest" in the marijuana plants because growing such plants was still illegal under federal law. Even though growing marijuana for medical use was legal under Hawaii law, the insurer argued that state law cannot preempt federal law and, therefore, paying the policyholder for her stolen marijuana plants would be against public policy. The insurer further relied on a Hawaii statute that prohibited the enforcement of illegal contracts.

After an analysis of Hawaii's medical marijuana laws, the court concluded that, as long as the policyholder was compliant with those laws in her growing of the marijuana plants, she did, in fact, have an insurable interest in those plants.[11]

Notwithstanding that, the court still considered the question of whether it would be against public policy for the insurer to provide coverage for the stolen plants, because the growing of marijuana plants was still illegal under federal law. After analyzing certain judicial authority that reinforced the notion that federal law preempts state law on the legality of marijuana, the court ultimately concluded that the insurer did not have to pay for the stolen plants, because doing so would be "contrary to federal law and public policy."[12] In reaching this decision, the court noted that the "rule under Hawaii law that courts may decline to enforce a contract that is illegal or contrary to public policy applies where the enforcement of the contract would violate federal law."[13]

Fast forward four short years, and we find *The Green Earth Wellness Center LLC v. Atain Specialty Insurance Co* ("*Green Earth*")[14] in which the policyholder both grew marijuana plants and sold marijuana products in a medical marijuana dispensary. The policyholder sustained two distinct losses. First, there was a wildfire that the policyholder contended caused smoke and ash to damage its growing operations, including its growing marijuana plants as well as its harvested marijuana flowers and buds that were being prepared for sale. Second, the policyholder experienced a theft, in which thieves broke in and stole some marijuana plants.

The policyholder made a coverage claim for each incident under its property damage policy. The insurer denied coverage for these claims based on a variety of arguments, including the arguments that (1) growing plants were not "stock" insured under the policy; (2) the contraband exclusion barred coverage for these losses; and (3) it would be against public

11. *Id.* at *10.
12. *Id.* at *13.
13. *Id.*
14. The Green Earth Wellness Center LLC v. Atain Specialty Insurance Co., 163 F. Supp. 3d 821 (D. Colo. 2016).

policy to provide coverage for marijuana products because such products were not legal under federal law (the policyholder's business was in Colorado, where such products were legal under state law).

With respect to the insurer's first argument, the court noted the word "stock" was not defined and, therefore, it was necessary to review several dictionary definitions.[15] After careful analysis of those definitions, the court concluded that growing plants might be considered "stock," which was sometimes defined as including raw materials (the court commented that, although growing plants probably would not be considered a "raw material" under most common understandings of that term, because some definitions included references to such things as wheat being a raw material, the court could not rule out the possibility that the parties intended growing marijuana plants to be part of the policyholder's "stock").[16] The court, however, ultimately concluded that coverage for the growing plants was nevertheless barred under a policy provision that unambiguously excluded coverage for "growing crops."[17]

Having concluded that the policyholder's growing plants were not covered, the court then turned to the issue of whether there was coverage for the harvested plants that were part of the policyholder's saleable inventory. That brought the court to the insurer's second argument regarding the scope of the policy's contraband exclusion. Here, the court again noted that the word "contraband" was undefined and, therefore, again consulted a dictionary in which the word "contraband" included "goods or merchandise whose importation, exportation, or possession is forbidden."[18] Although the court accepted the fact that the possession of marijuana for distribution remained illegal under federal law, the analysis did not end there. Rather, the court noted that federal policy on marijuana had become far more nuanced over the years, such that it was not clear whether there would ever be federal enforcement action against the policyholder's operations. The court further considered the fact that the policyholder's operations were legal under Colorado law, which meant that marijuana would not be considered contraband if sold for distribution within the state.[19] Based on both the uncertainties regarding federal enforcement and the legality of the policyholder's operations under Colorado law, the court found that the contraband exclusion was ambiguous in this context.[20]

Due to that ambiguity, the court then sought to discern the parties' mutual intent through the review of extrinsic evidence. After reviewing certain underwriting materials, the court ultimately settled on the common-sense

---

15. *Id.* at 827–28.
16. *Id.*
17. *Id.* at 831–32.
18. *Id.* at 832.
19. *Id.* at 833.
20. *Id.*

reality that the insurer sold a policy to cover a marijuana business and, therefore, the parties shared a mutual intention that the policy would cover that business. In other words, the insurer could not then take the position that the policyholder's entire inventory was excluded as contraband.[21]

The insurer's third argument—that coverage should be precluded as against public policy—is related to its second argument regarding the contraband exclusion. In support of this argument, the insurer relied upon *Tracy*, discussed earlier, which had held that coverage for marijuana plants "'would be contrary to federal law and public policy.'"[22] But, with the passage of four years since that decision, the court noted that there was "a continued erosion of any clear and consistent federal policy in this area."[23] Based on that reality, the court declined to follow *Tracy*. And, the court also relied on the same observation it had made with respect to the contraband exclusion, namely, that the insurer obviously knew what it was insuring.

The takeaways from *Green Earth* are (1) policyholders that operate growing facilities and dispensaries should be aware of distinctions that might be drawn between growing and harvested marijuana; and (2) that having profited from the sale of insurance policies to cannabis-related businesses, insurers should not be allowed to avoid their contractual obligations based solely on federal law, which is in flux.

4. Conclusion

Although the cannabis industry faces the same categories of risk as many other businesses, it does have its own set of circumstances, which pose their own set of challenges. Although these challenges must be recognized and addressed, traditional insurance products should be available to cover these businesses. The key to a healthy "contractual" relationship between policyholder and insurer is an open dialogue before the coverage is bound, so that each side's intentions and expectations are openly expressed to avoid latent ambiguities and mutual mistake. As the cannabis industry becomes more mainstream through state law and ultimately federal law, and more courts have opportunities to comment on these issues, navigating insurance coverage for the risks attendant to this industry should become commonplace and, hopefully, mundane.

---

21. *Id.* at 833–34.
22. *Id.* at 835.
23. *Id.*

12

Bankruptcy

Bradley Cosman and Brian Audette

1. Introduction to Bankruptcy, Receiverships, and Assignments for the Benefit of Creditors

Bankruptcy is a product of federal law under title 11 of the United States Code, 11 U.S.C. §§ 101, *et seq.* (as amended, the "Bankruptcy Code"). The principal purpose of bankruptcy is "to grant a 'fresh start' to the 'honest but unfortunate debtor.'"[1] Indeed, bankruptcy provides financially distressed individuals and businesses an opportunity to catch their proverbial breaths to reorganize and shed certain debts.[2] The breathing spell benefits not only the debtor but also the debtor's creditors by preventing (1) a race to the courthouse, (2) the seizure of a debtor's assets by a particular creditor, and (3) a drain on a debtor's assets from defending litigation in multiple forums.

Chapters 7, 11, and 13 of the Bankruptcy Code are most commonly utilized. Chapter 7 is purely for liquidation. In Chapter 7, which is available to individuals and businesses, an independent trustee is appointed to take possession of a debtor's nonexempt assets, liquidate such assets, and

---

1. Marrama v. Citizens Bank of Mass., 127 S. Ct. 1105, 1107 (2007).

2. With certain enumerated exceptions, the commencement of a bankruptcy case generally operates as a stay against, among other things, any attempts to enforce prepetition claims against a debtor, obtain possession of a debtor's property, or continue any prepetition lawsuits against a debtor. *See* 11 U.S.C. § 362(a). This "automatic stay" has been described as "one of the fundamental debtor protections provided by the bankruptcy laws." Midlantic Nat'l Bank v. N.J. Dep't of Envtl. Protection, 106 S. Ct. 755, 760 (1986) (quoting S. Rep. No. 95-989, p. 54 (1978); H.R. Rep. No. 95-595, p. 340 (1977), U.S. Code Cong. & Admin. News 1978, pp. 5787, 5840, 5963, 6296)).

distribute the net proceeds to the debtor's creditors.[3] Although Chapter 7 is available to individuals and businesses, only an individual may obtain a discharge in Chapter 7.[4]

Chapter 13 is only available to individuals (not businesses) and even then, only those with liabilities below certain statutory thresholds.[5] In Chapter 13, a debtor with regular income retains possession of his or her assets and agrees to a repayment plan approved by the bankruptcy court.[6] An independent Chapter 13 trustee collects payments from the debtor and disburses them to creditors under terms of a plan that typically span three to five years.[7] A Chapter 13 debtor does not receive a discharge until the end of his plan period.

Chapter 11 is generally for reorganization and is available to both individuals and businesses.[8] Although the primary goal of Chapter 11 is to reorganize, it expressly contemplates liquidations.[9] A Chapter 11 proceeding typically culminates in a bankruptcy court's confirmation of a plan of reorganization, which becomes binding on the debtor and its creditors.[10] Moreover, confirmation of a plan in bankruptcy typically discharges a debtor's debts that arose prior to confirmation.[11]

Bankruptcy cases commenced under Chapters 7, 11, and 13 are subject to dismissal "for cause."[12] Cause is not defined by the Bankruptcy Code; however, Chapters 7, 11, and 13 all include non-exhaustive lists of factors

3. *See* U.S. Trustee v. Fishback (In re Glados, Inc.), 83 F.3d 1360, 1365 (1996) (stating that "[t]he purpose of a Chapter 7 case is to administer efficiently the liquidation of the estate for the benefit of the creditors").

4. *See* 11 U.S.C. § 727(a); *see also In re* Boca Village Ass'n, Inc., 422 B.R. 318, 324 (Bankr. S.D. Fla. 2009) (recognizing that "the objective of providing the honest but unfortunate debtor with a fresh start is not served in a corporate Chapter 7 case because corporate debtors are ineligible for discharge.").

5. *See* 11 U.S.C. § 109(e) (Chapter 13 is available when noncontingent, liquidated, unsecured debts total less than $419,275 and noncontingent, liquidated, secured debts total less than $1,257,850.).

6. *See id.*

7. *See* Tower Loan of Miss., Inc. v. Maddox (In re Maddox), 15 F.3d 1347, 1355 (5th Cir. 1994).

8. *See* S.N.A. Nut Co. v. The Haagen-Dazs Co. (In re S.N.A. Nut Co.), Nos. 94 B 5993, 00 C 2820, 2000 WL 988528, *4 (N.D. Ill. July 17, 2000); *see also In re* Johnson, 546 B.R. 83, 143 (Bankr. S.D. Ohio 2016) (stating that "the primary purpose of an individual Chapter 11 case is to provide the debtor with a breathing spell so that he can reorganize his debts and provide a recovery to his creditors out of his future earnings rather than a lesser recovery through liquidation.").

9. *See* Fla. Dep't of Revenue v. Piccadilly Cafeterias, Inc., 128 S. Ct. 2326, 2331 n.2 (2008).

10. *See* 11 U.S.C. § 1141(a).

11. *See id.* § 1141(d)(1)(A). A corporate debtor will not receive a discharge if the debtor is liquidated under terms of the Chapter 11 plan.

12. *See, e.g., id.* §§ 707(a), 1112(b), and 1307(c).

that may constitute cause.[13] Courts recognize that cause is a broad concept that affords bankruptcy courts flexibility in determining whether to
dismiss a bankruptcy case.[14] Under Chapter 11 of the Bankruptcy Code,
cause includes a debtor's "gross mismanagement of the estate."[15] Alternatively, a bankruptcy court may convert a Chapter 11 or Chapter 13 case to
a case under Chapter 7 of the Bankruptcy Code—depending on whether
dismissal or conversion is in the best interests of the bankruptcy estate and
creditors.[16] In Chapter 11, the bankruptcy court shall confirm a plan only
if certain enumerated requirements are met, including that "[t]he plan
has been proposed in good faith and not by any means forbidden by law."[17]

Receiverships and assignments for the benefit of creditors (ABC), on
the other hand, are creatures of equity or state law. As a result, each state
has adopted different statutory provisions governing receiverships and
ABCs, and each federal district has adopted different standards for appointment of a federal receiver. Careful attention must be paid to the particular
standards and local precedent for the jurisdiction in which the receivership or ABC is commenced. Nonetheless, despite jurisdictional nuances,
the core tenets of receiverships and ABCs are generally consistent across
jurisdictions.

As to receiverships, most states recognize two types: a "custodial receivership" covering specific assets of the debtor and a broader "general receivership" or "equity receivership" encompassing all of the debtor's assets.
Custodial receiverships are typically initiated by a secured creditor with
respect to discrete pieces of collateral. The custodial receivership ensures
the collateral is preserved and protected while the secured creditor completes a foreclosure. By contrast, the broader general receivership covers a
debtor's operations and, most often, substantially all of its assets. A general
receivership is often preferable when a secured creditor is secured by all
of the debtor's assets and those assets are worth more as a going concern.
The broader general receivership permits the receiver to assume control
of the debtor's day-to-day operations pending an orderly sale of the assets
as a going concern. Although general receiverships are often sought by
secured lenders, general receiverships may be sought by equity holders or
other stakeholders due to corporate waste, governance disputes, or grid-
lock (among other things).

ABCs are creatures of the common law: an insolvent debtor can assign all
of its assets to its chosen "assignee," who is then responsible for liquidating
the assets and distributing the proceeds to creditors much like a Chapter 7

---

13. *See* 11 U.S.C. §§ 707(a), 1112(b)(4), and 1307(c).
14. *See, e.g.,* Kelly v. Cypress Fin. Trading Co., L.P. (In re Cypress Fin. Trading Co., L.P.),
620 Fed. Appx. 287, 289 (5th Cir. 2015).
15. 11 U.S.C. § 1107(b)(4)(B).
16. *See* 11 U.S.C. §§ 1112(b)(1), 1307(c).
17. *Id.* § 1129(a)(3).

trustee in bankruptcy. In most states, ABCs remain common law, non-statutory processes, although some states have adopted ABC statutes. ABCs are in effect out-of-court Chapter 7s: the result will inevitably be liquidation of the entity.

2. Treatment of Cannabis in Bankruptcy Cases

Individuals and businesses tied directly or indirectly to the marijuana industry consistently have been unable to take advantage of bankruptcy laws and have found bankruptcy court to be an unfriendly forum—notwithstanding how "honest" and "unfortunate" they may be. Bankruptcy courts have routinely dismissed cases when the debtor has any connection to marijuana. The most common reason for dismissing marijuana-related bankruptcies has been a finding that conduct by the debtor involving marijuana remains a federal crime.[18] Indeed, in April 2017, Clifford J. White III, the director of the Executive Office for United States Trustees (the U.S. Trustee),[19] delivered a directive to all Chapter 7 and Chapter 13 trustees advising them that, among other things, "[i]t is the policy of the United States Trustee Program that United States Trustees shall move to dismiss or object in all cases involving marijuana assets on grounds that such assets may not be administered under the Bankruptcy Code."[20]

Even prior to the U.S. Trustee directive, bankruptcy courts were not tolerant of cases with even attenuated connections to marijuana. For example, a bankruptcy court held that there was sufficient cause to convert or dismiss the Chapter 11 case of a debtor that derived approximately 25 percent of its revenues from leasing warehouse space to tenants who the debtor knew were in the business of growing marijuana.[21] Even though the debtor was not directly involved in the marijuana industry, the *Rent-Rite* court found that the debtor's conduct amounted to an ongoing criminal violation of the federal Controlled Substances Act. Therefore, the court concluded that (1) the debtor had "unclean hands" and could not obtain relief from a

---

18. Debtors operating in the hemp and/or cannabidiol (CBD) oil industries do not face the same challenges as those dealing with marijuana because hemp and CBD are not illegal at the federal level.

19. The United States Trustee Program is a component of the Department of Justice that is tasked with, among other things, overseeing the federal bankruptcy process, protecting the integrity of the bankruptcy system, monitoring the conduct of parties and private trustees and ensuring compliance with applicable bankruptcy laws and procedures. *See* https://www.justice.gov/ust/about-program. Not to be confused with independent Chapter 7 and Chapter 13 trustees, United States Trustees have standing to participate in all bankruptcy cases.

20. *See* https://www.justice.gov/ust/file/marijuana_assets.pdf/download.

21. *See In re* Rent-Rite Super Kegs West Ltd., 484 B.R. 799 (Bankr. D. Colo. 2012).

court of equity,[22] and (2) there was gross mismanagement of the estate.[23] In addition, the court noted that the debtor could not confirm a Chapter 11 plan that relied on income from an illegal activity because such a plan would fail the requirement that plans must be "proposed in good faith and not by any means forbidden by law."[24]

In a later Chapter 13 case in which the U.S. Trustee moved to dismiss, the debtor grew and sold medical marijuana legally in Michigan.[25] In *Johnson*, the bankruptcy court gave the debtor a choice to either abandon entirely his connection to marijuana and obtain relief under the Bankruptcy Code or retain his marijuana business, which would result in the dismissal of his case.[26] The court—while recognizing the debtor's "dire" need for bankruptcy relief—concluded that the debtor could not continue a federally illegal enterprise while enjoying the federal benefits provided by the Bankruptcy Code.[27] The court reasoned that permitting the debtor to remain in Chapter 13 would result in the Chapter 13 trustee and the court inevitably supporting the debtor's criminal enterprise.[28]

The U.S. Trustee likewise moved to dismiss the Chapter 7 case of a marijuana grower and his wife, thereby prompting the debtors to attempt to convert their case to one under Chapter 13.[29] In *Arenas*, the court dismissed the debtors' case for cause under section 707(a) of the Bankruptcy Code—holding unequivocally that a debtor in the marijuana business cannot obtain relief in a bankruptcy court.[30] The court also opined that conversion to Chapter 13 was improper because the case would be subject to dismissal for cause under section 1307(c) of the Bankruptcy Code due to the debtors' lack of good faith and inability to confirm a Chapter 13 plan that relied upon income from growing marijuana.[31]

Bankruptcy courts have been equally harsh to *creditors* of debtors in the marijuana industry.[32] In *Medpoint*, creditors filed an involuntary bankruptcy

22. *See id.* at 806 (stating that "[t]raditionally, bankruptcy courts are regarded as courts of equity.").
23. *See id.* at 809 (citing 11 U.S.C. § 1112(b)(4)(B)).
24. *See id.* (quoting 11 U.S.C. § 1129(a)(3)); *see also In re* Arm Ventures, LLC, 564 B.R. 77, 86 (holding that conversion or dismissal is warranted when—in addition to the case constituting a bad faith filing—a debtor proposes a plan that cannot satisfy section 1129(a)(3) of the Bankruptcy Code because it is dependent on rental income from the marijuana industry.)).
25. *See In re* Johnson, 532 B.R. 53 (Bankr. W.D. Mich. 2015).
26. *See id.* at 58–59.
27. *See id.* at 59.
28. *See id.* at 56–57.
29. *See* Arenas v. U.S. Trustee (In re Arenas), 535 B.R. 845 (B.A.P. 10th Cir. 2015).
30. *See id.* at 847.
31. *See id.* at 850–51.
32. *See In re* Medpoint Mgmt., LLC, 528 B.R. 178 (Bankr. D. Ariz. 2015).

petition against a debtor in the medical marijuana business.[33] The debtor moved to dismiss the petition on the grounds that (1) a trustee may not administer marijuana assets without violating the Controlled Substances Act and (2) the petitioning creditors' had unclean hands because they likewise operate in the marijuana industry due to their dealings with the debtor.[34] The court agreed, finding there was cause to dismiss the debtor's case and that the petitioning creditors could not obtain any relief from a bankruptcy court.[35]

Debtors with more remote connections to marijuana may find at least a scintilla of solace in *Olson*.[36] In *Olson*, the bankruptcy court dismissed *sua sponte* the Chapter 13 case of a 92-year-old woman who owned a commercial property that was leased, in part, to a marijuana dispensary.[37] On appeal, the bankruptcy appellate panel reversed and remanded because the bankruptcy court did not make any findings of fact or conclusions of law to demonstrate that all elements of the Controlled Substances Act had been established.[38] Notably, the concurrence stated that: "I concur in the memorandum and write separately to emphasize (1) the importance of evaluating whether the Debtor is actually violating the Controlled Substantive Act and (2) the need for the bankruptcy court to explain its conclusion that dismissal was mandatory under these circumstances."[39] Consequently, *Olson* counsels bankruptcy courts must expressly find that the debtor is violating the Controlled Substances Act to warrant dismissal.

The momentum continued in the marijuana industry's favor when the Ninth Circuit issued its opinion in *Garvin*.[40] *Garvin* involved five real estate holding companies, one of which leased property to a marijuana grower.[41] Consequently, the U.S. Trustee moved to dismiss the case.[42] The bankruptcy court denied the motion, but with leave for the U.S. Trustee to renew its request at plan confirmation.[43] The debtor filed a reorganization plan to which the U.S. Trustee objected on the grounds that it violated section 1129(a)(3) of the Bankruptcy Code's requirement that the plan must be proposed in good faith and not by any means forbidden by law.[44] The bankruptcy court confirmed the plan over the U.S. Trustee's objection, and the

33. 528 B.R. at 180.
34. *See id.* at 182–83.
35. *See id.* at 184–87.
36. Olson v. Van Meter (In re Olson), BAP No. NV-17-1168-LTiF, 2018 WL 989263 (B.A.P. 9th Cir. Feb. 5, 2018).
37. 2018 WL 989263, *4.
38. *See id.* at *5–6.
39. *Id.* at *6.
40. Garvin v. Cook Invs. NW, SPNWY, LLC, 922 F.3d 1031 (9th Cir. 2019).
41. *See id.* at 1033.
42. *See id.*
43. *See id.*
44. *See id.* at 1034.

U.S. Trustee did not renew its motion to dismiss at that time.[45] By the time the case was heard by the Ninth Circuit, unsecured creditors had been paid in full pursuant to the debtors' plan and the secured creditor was in the process of being repaid.

On appeal, the Ninth Circuit refused to consider the U.S. Trustee's request to dismiss the debtors' case for cause under section 1112(b) of the Bankruptcy Code because the U.S. Trustee did not renew its request at plan confirmation.[46] Nevertheless, the U.S. Trustee contended that, because the debtors continued to receive rent payments from the marijuana grower, the debtors plan was "'proposed . . . by . . . means forbidden by law'" in violation of section 1129(a)(3) of the Bankruptcy Code.[47] The court—framing the issue as one of statutory construction—held that section 1129(a)(3) addresses only the *manner* in which plans are proposed as opposed to the *contents* of the plan.[48] Thus, only plans that are proposed by means forbidden by law are improper under section 1129(a)(3). Because there was no evidence that the debtors proposed their plan by means forbidden by law, the court upheld confirmation.[49] Nevertheless, the court noted that, absent waiver, courts may consider whether similar cases should be dismissed for cause under section 1112(b) of the Bankruptcy Code.[50]

But any momentum resulting from *Olson* and *Garvin* was short-lived. In *Basrah*,[51] the bankruptcy court dismissed a debtor's Chapter 11 bankruptcy for cause because the debtor leased space to a medical marijuana dispensary.[52] In dismissing the debtor's case, the court distinguished *Garvin* on the ground that *Garvin* only considered plan confirmation under section 1129(a)(3) of the Bankruptcy Code and not whether the case should be dismissed for cause under section 1112(b).[53] The court also disagreed with *Garvin's* interpretation of section 1129(a)(3).[54]

In another case decided shortly after *Garvin*, the bankruptcy court dismissed the Chapter 11 case of related entities whose business relied on selling equipment and supplies to individuals and businesses in the marijuana industry.[55] On appeal, the district court affirmed—holding, among other things, that (1) there is cause for dismissal under section 1112(b) of the Bankruptcy Code if a debtor runs a business dedicated to serving the

---

45. *See id.*
46. *See id.*
47. *Id.* at 1034–35.
48. *See id.* at 1035.
49. *See id.*
50. *See id.* at 1036.
51. *In re* Basrah Custom Design, Inc., 600 B.R. 368 (Bankr. E.D. Mich. 2019).
52. *See Basrah*, 600 B.R. at 371–72.
53. *See id.* at 381 n.38.
54. *See id.*
55. *See* Way to Grow, Inc. v. Inniss (In re Way to Grow, Inc.), 610 B.R. 338 (D. Colo. 2019).

marijuana industry; and (2) a "marijuana-based" business cannot propose a plan in good faith pursuant to section 1129(a)(3) of the Bankruptcy Code.[56]

Courts are still wrestling with these issues in 2020. For example, in *Burton*, a bankruptcy court dismissed the Chapter 13 case of individuals who owned an interest in an entity that, while not operating, had previously operated in the marijuana industry and was suing third parties for breach of marijuana-based contracts.[57] On appeal, the *Burton* court affirmed and concluded that there was sufficient cause for dismissal under section 1307(c) of the Bankruptcy Code, because any proceeds recovered from the debtors' litigation would represent profits from a business that is illegal under federal law.[58] Nevertheless, citing *Olson* and *Garvin*, the court did recognize the less stringent standard applied in the Ninth Circuit, stating:

> We believe that the stated reluctance in this Circuit to adopt per se bright-line rules requiring the immediate disposition of bankruptcy cases in which marijuana activity is present, and the flexible cause standard under § 1307(c), coupled with the abuse of discretion standard of review on appeal, give bankruptcy courts appropriate latitude to deal with these variations.[59]

Most recently, a Colorado district court addressed whether it was proper for a bankruptcy court to revoke an order reopening a Chapter 7 case because permitting the case to proceed could involve the Chapter 7 trustee's administration of a marijuana asset in violation of federal law.[60] In *Malul*, the debtor owned an equity interest in an entity that never operated but was formed to conduct business in the marijuana industry.[61] The debtor sought to reopen her case and cause the Chapter 7 trustee to abandon the debtor's claims against the marijuana entity's former principal, whom the debtor accused of misappropriating the debtor's investment.[62] The court concluded that dismissal was proper because the debtor's investment in the marijuana entity, in and of itself, was illegal and any proceeds recovered in connection with the failed investment would be proceeds derived from an illegal activity.[63]

Although case law regarding the treatment of marijuana in bankruptcy is still in its relative infancy, bankruptcy courts have been almost unanimously foreclosed to allowing debtors directly or indirectly involved in the marijuana industry. At bottom, debtors with even attenuated connections to the marijuana industry face a significant uphill battle in obtaining relief under

---

56. *See id.* at 345.
57. *See* Burton v. Maney (In re Burton), 610 B.R. 633 (B.A.P. 9th Cir. 2020).
58. *See id.* at 639.
59. *See id.*
60. *See In re* Malul, No. 11-21140 MER, 2020 WL 1486775 (D. Colo. Mar. 24, 2020).
61. *See id.* at *1.
62. *See id.* at *1–3.
63. *See id.* at *9.

the Bankruptcy Code so long as marijuana continues to be classified as a Schedule 1 substance under the Controlled Substances Act. The responsibility to amend either the Bankruptcy Code or the Controlled Substances Act rests squarely with Congress and, unless it acts, bankruptcy relief will remain largely unavailable to debtors with connections to a marijuana business.

3. Treatment of Cannabis in Receiverships and ABCs

Blocked from bankruptcy relief, distressed cannabis companies (and those who do business with them) typically resort to a receivership or ABC as the alternative vehicles for resolving financial disputes. Although receiverships and ABCs lack the same degree of precedent and much of the statutory framework of bankruptcy proceedings, receiverships and ABCs provide parties significant flexibility and can often be set up to operate as pseudo-bankruptcy proceedings.

3.1 Receiverships

Receiverships are most often initiated by lenders as a remedy for borrower defaults, but anyone can request appointment of a receiver, including business partners, trade creditors, landlords, and regulating agencies. Indeed, receiverships are frequently used to resolve deadlocks among business partners, address accounting irregularities, or address issues with departing members. Given this flexibility, cannabis companies and the parties they deal with are frequently seeking relief through receivership.

Whether based on a contractual remedy or the court's general equitable power, the receivership court must find that it possesses jurisdiction over the matter before a receiver can be appointed; mere consent by the parties may be insufficient.[64] Under any circumstance, appointment of a receiver

---

64. *See, e.g.*, Hamzavi v. Bowen, 730 A.2d 274, 276 (Md. Ct. App. 1999) ("Generally, a court of law without equity jurisdiction or statutory authority has no power to appoint a receiver."); Cty. Nat. Bank of N. Miami Beach v. Stern, 287 So. 2d 106, 107 (Fla. Dist. Ct. App. 1973) ("The appointment of a receiver is discretionary with the court, but before the court may get to the point of exercising its discretion, it must be satisfied that it has jurisdiction over the parties and the subject matter."); Huggins v. Green Top Dairy Farms, 273 P.2d 399, 406 (Idaho 1954) ("Even though the contract provided that a receiver might be appointed on the happening of certain contingencies, the statutory requisites and the jurisdiction of the court for the appointment of a receiver would have to exist before the receiver could lawfully be appointed."); Wingfoot Cal. Homes Co. v. Valley Nat'l Bank of Phoenix, 248 P.2d 738 (Ariz. 1952) (noting that "it is well stated that parties may not by contract or stipulation confer jurisdiction on a court," rather, "the right of a court to appoint a receiver must exist under the law independent of a contract in question"); *see also* 53 C.J. 52, Sec. 40; 45 Am. Jur. 101, Secs. 119 and 120; 75 C.J.S., Receivers, § 35, p. 696.

is recognized as an extraordinary equitable remedy.[65] Although "there is no precise formula for determining when a receiver may be appointed," courts weigh a variety of factors, including (but not limited to) whether (1) the parties contractually consented to the appointment; (2) plaintiff has a valid claim; (3) defendant has either engaged or is likely to engage in fraud; (4) the property is in imminent danger of dissipation; (5) available legal remedies are inadequate; (6) the harm to plaintiff by denial of receivership would outweigh injury to defendant; (7) plaintiff's probable success in the action and the possibility of irreparable injury to plaintiff's interest in the property; and (8) plaintiff's interests sought to be protected will in fact be well-served by receivership.[66] No single factor is dispositive and courts have broad discretion in appointing a receiver.[67]

Relying on the courts' broad equitable powers in defining the scope of a receivership, distressed cannabis companies have used receiverships as pseudo-bankruptcy proceedings offering many of the benefits typically associated with bankruptcy. Among other things, receiverships can be set up to subject continued operations to a budget, to provide new financing on a priming basis through receivership certificates, to reject burdensome contracts, to stay creditor actions against company assets, and to sell off company assets.[68] As such, cannabis receiverships can, in many critical respects, function as "bankruptcy lite."

Even with these quasi-bankruptcy protections, distressed cannabis receiverships—as with most receiverships—usually result in an asset sale.[69] To that end, a cannabis receivership typically involves appointment of a receiver, selected by the lender or plaintiff, to run a cannabis business while also undertaking an auction process to sell the assets.[70] An auction process is

---

65. *See, e.g.,* Canada Life Assur. Co. v. LaPeter, 563 F.3d 837, 844 (9th Cir. 2009) ("Under federal law, appointing a 'receiver is an extraordinary equitable remedy.'" (quoting Aviation Supply Corp. v. F.S.B.I. Aerospace, Inc., 999 F.2d 314. 316 (8th Cir. 1993)); Morand v. Superior Court, 38 Cal. App. 3d 347, 350–51, 113 Cal. Rptr. 281 (1974); Bero v. Name Intelligence, Inc., 195 Wn. App. 170 (Wa. Ct. App. 2016).

66. *See, e.g., Canada Life,* 563 F.3d at 844 (*citing* Aviation Supply Corp. v. R.S.B.I. Aerospace, Inc., 999 F.2d 314, 316 (8th Cir. 1993) (quotations omitted); Sterling Sav. Bank v. Citadel Development Co., 656 F. Supp. 2d 1248, 1260 (D. Or. 2009).

67. *Canada Life,* 563 F.3d at 845; *see also Sterling,* 656 F. Supp. 2d at 1258 ("that a receiver is not a matter of right or entitlement is demonstrated by the well-settled principle that the court has broad discretion in deciding whether to appoint a receiver").

68. *See, e.g.,* Cima Grp. LLV v. CWNEVADA, LLC, 2019 Nev. Dist. LEXIS 572 (Nev. June 13, 2019) (comprehensive order appointing receiver of cannabis business and assets); Order Confirming Receiver and Granting Prelim. Inj., Razuki v. Malan, No. 37-2018-00034229-CU-BC-CTL (Cal. Super. Ct. Sept. 26, 2018) (same).

69. Cannabis receiverships typically result in a sale because the statutory "cramdown" provisions available in bankruptcy to bind non-consenting creditors to a proposed plan of reorganization are not available in receivership. *See* 11 USC § 1129(b).

70. *See, e.g., Auction of Licensed California Cannabis Business Brings in $8.25 Million,* Marijuana Bus. Daily, https://mjbizdaily.com/auction-of-licensed-california-marijuana

used to ensure the receivership estate receives the highest and best price for the assets being sold.

Receivership sales raise several issues. First, some states have specific statutes, licensing requirements, or other regulations restricting who may manage and control a cannabis business or cannabis assets.[71] Parties must take such requirements into account when proposing a receiver candidate. Second, whereas section 363 of the bankruptcy code expressly empowers debtors in bankruptcy to sell estate property free and clear of all liens, claims, and encumbrances, state laws vary on whether a *receiver* can similarly sell assets free and clear of all liens, claims, and encumbrances.[72] Accordingly, buyers of distressed cannabis assets must carefully evaluate successor liability and other risks as part of their due diligence. Third, buyers and sellers in receivership sales must remember that, just like bankruptcy sales, receivership sales are subject to a secured creditor's right to credit bid.[73]

Another critical risk factor that parties seeking appointment of a receiver must take into account is that the court has broad power to apportion the administrative costs of the receivership to the parties—particularly (but not exclusively) those at whose insistence the receiver was appointed.[74]

-business-brings-in-8-25-million/ (last visited July 9, 2020) (describing the receivership sale of the business assets of The Guild San Jose, a vertically integrated cannabis business licensed in California).

71. *See, e.g.*, RCW 7.60.010 *et seq.*; OKLA. STAT. ANN. tit. 12, § 1560; OAR 845-025-1260; *see also* Yates v. Harman, 2018 Colo. App. LEXIS 303 (Colo. App. Mar. 8, 2018) (holding any receiver must possess the proper licenses under Colorado law to operate the entities).

72. *See, e.g.*, N.J. STAT. ANN. § 14A:14-7 (court may authorize receiver to sell assets free and clear of encumbrances where (1) the holders of the encumbrances receive prior notice and (2) the receiver shows that the sale "may be reasonably expected to benefit general creditors of the corporation without adversely affecting the interest of the holders of the encumbrances"); Krupnick v. Windy Ridge, Corp., 147 A.D. 3d 1247, 1249 (N.Y. Super. Ct. App. 2017) (holding that the lower court erred in approving the receiver's sale of property free and clear of encumbrances because N.Y. Bus. Corp. Law § 1206 (governing "powers of permanent receiver") does not grant a receiver "the same power that a trustee in bankruptcy has under chapter 7 of the Bankruptcy Code to dispose of real property free and clear of all liens and mortgages"); BNP Paribas v. Olsen's Mill, Inc., 799 N.W. 2d 792, 801 (Wis. 2011) (noting that under Wisconsin law, a receiver may sell assets free and clear of liens only with secured creditors' consent (citing WIS. STAT. ANN. §§ 128 *et seq.*, 409.315)); Park Nat'l Bank v. Cattani, 931 N.E. 2d 623, 626 (Ohio Ct. App. 2010) (finding that Ohio's statute providing the powers of a receiver, OHIO REV. CODE ANN. § 2735.04, grants courts "the power to authorize a receiver, under certain circumstances, to sell property at a private sale free and clear of all liens and encumbrances").

73. Secured lenders to cannabis companies are able to exercise rights under Article 9, including the right to conduct foreclosure sales and credit bid for collateral, but may be reluctant to do so due to lender liability and regulatory risks, as well as an unwillingness to be involved in actually running a cannabis business.

74. Atlantic Trust Co. v. Chapman, 208 U.S. 360, 375 (1908) ("[C]ases may arise in which, because of their special circumstances, it is equitable to require the parties, at whose

Accordingly, if the receivership assets are insufficient to cover the receiver's fees and other administrative expenses of the receivership estate, the court may effectively surcharge the parties.

3.2 ABCs

In states that have legalized marijuana, an ABC could be useful to a distressed cannabis company as an alternative to bankruptcy or a receivership. To commence an ABC, an entity will generally execute an assignment agreement whereby it assigns all its assets to a third-party assignee, who then liquidates such assets and distributes the proceeds to the entity's creditors. Once the assets are transferred to the assignee, creditors are generally unable to enforce direct remedies against the assigned assets.[75] Although an ABC most commonly results in a piecemeal liquidation,[76] nothing prevents the assignee from selling a business as a going concern if such a sale would maximize the value of the assets.[77]

ABCs are a product of state law, and state laws range in formality and flexibility. Indeed, ABCs are governed solely by common law in 11 states, and numerous other states have enacted statutes governing ABC proceedings, which may be overseen by the applicable state court. By way of example only, following is a summary of ABC laws in three states that have legalized marijuana—Illinois, Washington, and California.

Governed solely by common law without any court oversight, ABCs in Illinois provide significant flexibility and are frequently used as an alternative to bankruptcy.[78] However, certain requirements must be met to commence

---

instance a receiver of property was appointed, to meet the expenses of the receivership, when the fund in court is ascertained to be insufficient for that purpose."); Downtown Sunnyvale Residential LLC v. Wells Fargo Bank, N.A., Nos. H038572, H039024, 2015 Cal. App. Unpub. LEXIS 357, at *58 (Jan. 20, 2015) (Generally, the costs of a receivership are paid from the property in the receivership estate. However, courts may also impose the receiver costs on a party who sought the appointment of the receiver or "apportion them among the parties, depending upon circumstances.") (citing City of Chula Vista v. Gutierrez, 207 Cal. App. 4th 681, 685–86 (2012)); 2 CLARK ON RECEIVERS § 641(i) (3d ed. 1959).

75. GEOFFREY BERMAN, GENERAL ASSIGNMENTS FOR THE BENEFIT OF CREDITORS: THE ABCs OF ABCs 1–2 (2d ed. 2006).

76. Credit Managers Ass'n v. Nat'l Independent Bus. Alliance, 162 Cal. App. 3d 1166, 1169 (1984).

77. William Choslovsky & Eric Walker, *An Alternative to Bankruptcy: the ABCs of ABCs*, in THE AMERICAS RESTRUCTURING & INSOLVENCY GUIDE 2008/2009, at 90, 91 (2009), *available at* http://www.americasrestructuring.com/08_SF/p90-95%20An%20alternative%20to %20bankruptcy.pdf (("ABCs are not limited to liquidations. Just as in bankruptcy, an ABC can be used to facilitate a going-concern sale of the debtor's assets to a third-party.").

78. Edward R. Morrison, *Bargaining around Bankruptcy: Small Business Workouts and State Law*, 38 J. LEGAL STUD. 255, 257 (2009).

a valid Illinois ABC:[79] (1) the assignment must be in writing and must contain express language establishing a trust over specific property for the benefit of creditors;[80] (2) the trust agreement must set forth the powers and duties of the assignee;[81] (3) the assets must be conveyed for the benefit of *all* creditors;[82] (4) the assignment must be absolute and unqualified and constitute all of the debtor's interests in the property conveyed;[83] (5) the assignment may not attempt to compromise or discharge claims against the assignor or force creditors to accept anything less than full payment of their claims;[84] (6) the assignment may not exempt the assignee from personal liability for willful misconduct or negligence;[85] (7) the assignor may not condition or reserve any benefit or use of the assigned property;[86] and (8) the assignee must formally accept the assignment.[87]

In Illinois, creditors' claims are paid by the assignee in the following order of priority: (1) claims secured by liens or encumbrances against assets; (2) the costs of administration, including unpaid rent, insurance, utilities, the assignee's fees and costs (including attorneys' fees and costs); (3) claims of the U.S. government for taxes; (4) state and local government claims; (5) wage claims; and (6) general unsecured claims, such as trade claims.[88]

In 2004, Washington restated its ABC statute to work hand-in-hand with the Washington Receivership Act. The result is a hybrid statute providing that the assignee shall become a receiver following the execution of the assignment.[89] "In effect, [in Washington] all ABCs must now be converted after the execution of the assignment into receivership actions."[90] The surviving ABC-specific laws provide that the assignment must be for the benefit

---

79. Alan P. Solow, Bruce L. Wald, & Daniel A. Zazove, *Illinois Common Law Assignments for the Benefit of the Creditors* (2006).
80. Black v. Palmer, 15 Ill. App. 2d 207, 145 N.E.2d 797, 800 (1st Dist. 1957).
81. Illinois Bell Telephone Co. v. Wolf Furniture House, Inc., 157 Ill. App. 3d 190, 509 N.E.2d 1289, 109 Ill. Dec. 277 (1st Dist. 1987).
82. Browne-Chapin Lumber Co. v. Union Nat'l Bank of Chicago, 159 Ill. 458, 42 N.E. 967 (1896).
83. *In re* Birk & Johnson, 295 F. 510 (7th Cir. 1923).
84. Tribune Co. v. R. & J Furniture Sales, Inc., 20 Ill. App. 2d 370, 155 N.E.2d 844, 846 (1st Dist. 1959); Gessler v. Myca Co., 29 Ill. App. 2d 227, 172 N.E.2d 503 (2d Dist. 1961).
85. Robinson v. Nye, 21 Ill. 592 (1859); Finlay v. Dickerson, 29 Ill. 9 (1862).
86. Hardin v. Osborne, 60 Ill. 93 (1871).
87. MacVeagh v. Chase & Sanborn, 67 Ill. App. 160 (1st Dist. 1896).
88. Solow et. al., *supra* note 12, at 4–5.
89. RCW 7.08.030(3) ("Every assignment shall be effective when a petition to appoint the assignee as receiver has been filed by the assignor, with the clerk of the superior court in the county of assignor's residence…").
90. Marc Barreca, *Washington's Receivership Act* (Sept. 2008), http://www.klgates.com/files/upload/barreca_wareceivershipact.pdf. [Mr. Barreca, the principal drafter of the 2004 ABC and receivership statute while in private practice, is now the Chief Judge of the Bankruptcy Court for the Western District of Washington.]

of *all* the assignor's creditors in proportion to the amount of their respective claims.[91]

To commence an ABC/receivership in Washington, the assignee must file the assignment document with the clerk of the court where the assignor had its principal place of business or registered office.[92] The assignee also must file schedules of the assignor's assets and liabilities[93] and post a bond in an amount specified by the court overseeing the proceeding.[94] Once properly commenced, Washington's receivership laws provide for a 60-day stay—similar to the automatic stay under the Bankruptcy Code.[95] Also, a receiver may assume and reject executory contracts.[96] Further, the receiver may conduct sales of assets free and clear of liens.[97] Upon the liquidation of assets, the assignee/receiver satisfied claims of creditors according the following priorities: (1) secured creditors; (2) the costs of administration, including the receiver's attorneys' fees and costs; (3) wages earned within 180 days of the receiver's appointment not to exceed $10,950; (4) claims of individuals for deposits in connection with the purchase or lease of real property not to exceed $2,450; (5) unsecured claims of governmental units for unpaid taxes; and (6) general unsecured claims.[98] Because Washington ABCs are governed by the same rules as receiverships, they have a more secure statutory basis and a wider base of precedents on which to draw, although there is still a paucity of receivership precedent compared to bankruptcy.[99]

California has enacted a number of flexible statutes generally applicable to ABCs.[100] Unlike some states with statutory schemes governing ABCs,

---

91. R.C.W. § 7.08.010.

92. *Id.* § 7.08.030 (3).

93. *Id.* § 7.60.090.

94. *Id.* § 7.60.045.

95. *Id.* § 7.60.110. The stay may be (and often is) continued in effect multiple times after that initial period, but unlike the bankruptcy automatic stay it will expire during the case absent court order. *Id.*

96. *Id.* § 7.60.130; *see also* Barreca, *supra* note 90, at 4.

97. *Id.* § 7.60.260.

98. *Id.* § 7.60.230.

99. Further, Washington courts regularly use bankruptcy case law to fill in the interstices of the receivership statute. *See* JOHN KAPLAN & ALAN SMITH, STRATEGIC ALTERNATIVES FOR DISTRESSED BUSINESSES § 74:1 (2020) ("Absent available Washington case law, analogies to Federal bankruptcy law are often drawn.").

100. *See, e.g.,* CAL. CIV. PRO. CODE § 493.020 (stating that "notwithstanding any other provision of this title, the defendant may make a general assignment for the benefit of creditors"); CAL. CIV. PRO. CODE §§ 493.030–493.060 (Addresses termination of any lien of a temporary protective order or attachment if the lien was created within 90 days prior to the making of the ABC and sets out detailed instructions for the release of said property to the assignee. Such liens, however, are reinstated under certain circumstances, including if the ABC is set aside other than by the filing of a bankruptcy petition.); CAL. CIV. PRO. CODE §§ 1204–1204.5 (sets forth the order of priority in which

California does not require a public court filing to commence an ABC[101] and the ABC is not overseen by a court. Nevertheless, the following requirements must be met in connection with a California ABC: (1) the assignor and assignee must execute a written instrument creating a trust and detailing the powers of the assignee; and (2) the assignee must set a deadline for the submission of claims and serve notice of such deadline to creditors.[102] Distributions from a California ABC should be made according to the following priorities:[103] (1) secured creditors; (2) costs and expenses of the ABCs administration, including the assignee's legal fees and costs; (3) obligations owing to the United States (i.e., federal tax claims); (4) wage claims earned within 12 months of the assignment not to exceed $4,300 and contributions to employee benefit plans;[104] (5) state tax claims; (6) security deposits of individuals up to $900 in connection with the purchase or lease of real property; (7) unpaid unemployment insurance contributions; and (8) general unsecured claims.

In states that have legalized marijuana, an ABC could provide a cannabis company a desirable alternative to a Chapter 7 case.[105] Indeed, states that have a longer history with legal cannabis (i.e., Washington, Oregon, and California) have promulgated regulations to ensure that distressed cannabis businesses can utilize ABCs.[106] Moreover, with an ABC a distressed

---

creditors are paid); CAL. CIV. PRO. CODE § 1800 (discussing the right of the assignee to recover transferred property); CAL. CIV. PRO. CODE § 1802 (Requiring the assignee to give written notice of the assignment to the assignor's creditors, equity holders, and other parties in interest within 30 days after the assignment has been accepted in writing. The assignee is also required to set a bar date for filing claims between 150 and 180 days after the date of the first written notice to the creditors and parties in interest.).

101. New York City Bar Association, Committee on Bankruptcy and Corporate Reorganization, *Non-Bankruptcy Alternative to Restructurings and Asset Sales*, November 2010, https://www.nycbar.org/pdf/report/uploads/20072001-NonBankruptcyAlternativestoRestructuringsandAssetSales.pdf.

102. CAL. CIV. PRO. CODE § 1802.

103. David S. Kupetz, *Assignment for the Benefit of Creditors: Effective Tool for Selling and Winding Up Distressed Businesses*, VALLEY LAWYER (June 2013).

104. CAL. CIV. PRO. CODE § 1204.

105. Joey Peña & John Schroyer, *Auction of Licensed California Cannabis Business Brings in $8.25 Million*, (June 7, 2019), https://mjbizdaily.com/auction-of-licensed-california-marijuana-business-brings-in-8-25-million/.

106. *See, e.g.*, WA. ADMIN. CODE 314-55-137 (receiver may operate a marijuana licensee's business during a receivership period); ADMIN. R. 845-025-1260 (trustee or receiver may be issued a temporary authority to operate a licensed, recreational marijuana business for a reasonable period of time); 3 CA CR § 8206 (in the event of an assignment for the benefit of creditors, the department must be notified with ten calendar days; the department may grant a successor in interest written approval to continue operations for a specified time); Hopkins Carley, *California Superior Court Upholds Creditor's Security Interest in Cannabis Business Assets, Including Cannabis Licenses*, https://www.hopkinscarley.com/blog/client-alerts-blogs-updates/corporate-client-alerts/california-superior

marijuana business may have more control over the sale and liquidation process because it has the ability to select the assignee (as opposed to a Chapter 7 trustee randomly assigned from a panel). Further, given the general refusal of bankruptcy courts to retain cases filed by or against marijuana businesses, there will be no risk that creditors could file an involuntary bankruptcy proceeding against the troubled business either before or after commencing an ABC (as can happen in other industries).

-court-upholds-creditors-security-interest-in-cannabis-business-assets-including-cannabis -licenses (noting that a receiver had been successfully appointed to administer marijuana assets).

13

Regulation of Cannabis-Containing Products in the U.S. Food and Beverage Supply

Stephen M. Ostroff, MD

There are several ways that cannabis and cannabis-derived compounds can be used. Among the options is consuming foods or beverages to which cannabis and/or cannabis-derived compounds (especially cannabidiol, or CBD) have been added as an ingredient. Interest in the addition of cannabis to foods and beverages has increased substantially since the Agricultural Improvement Act of 2018 (usually referred to as the 2018 Farm Bill) was signed into law. The 2018 Farm Bill legalized the growth, harvest, and sale of industrial hemp (defined as cannabis that contains less than 0.3 percent tetrahydrocannabinol, or THC) in the United States by removing it from the Controlled Substances Act's Schedule I. De-scheduling of industrial hemp was designed, in part, to facilitate the availability of CBD-containing products, including foods, in the marketplace. However, the Farm Bill did not change the underlying statutory framework of food and beverage regulation. Therefore, it is important to understand how the U.S. food and beverage regulatory system operates and the pathways and options that need to be considered by anyone interested in legally bringing foods and beverages containing cannabis, CBD, or other cannabis-derived compounds to market.

1. Federal Food Safety Oversight

The United States has what is widely considered the most abundant, diverse, and nutritious food supply in the world. To protect public health, it also has some of the highest food safety standards in the world. Federal agencies have the lead role in establishing these food safety standards and ensuring the standards are met by food producers. The role of the federal government in food safety was established with the passage of the Food and Drugs Act (usually referred to as the Pure Food and Drugs Act, PFDA), along with the separate Meat Inspection Act, in 1906. Prior to that time, the U.S. food supply was mostly overseen by the states and localities, because most food was grown and processed locally and was not widely distributed. Even today, state and local authorities continue to have an important role in food safety, especially in retail establishments where food is sold. In the decades after the passage of the PFDA, the marketplace for food and drugs underwent significant changes, and in 1938 the PFDA was supplanted by the Federal Food, Drug, and Cosmetic Act (FDCA). The FDCA, the Federal Meat Inspection Act (FMIA), the 1957 Poultry Products Inspection Act (PPIA), and the 1970 Egg Products Inspections Act (EPIA) are the legal underpinnings of today's food safety regulatory system. Congress continues to periodically pass food safety legislation[1] to reflect the changing nature of the food supply and associated emerging health risks. These new laws are incorporated into the relevant chapters of the FDCA, FMIA, PPIA, or EPIA in the form of amendments or new sections, maintaining these laws as the principal framework of this country's oversight of the safety of the food supply.

The requirements in the Food, Drug, and Cosmetics Act are enforced by the U.S. Food and Drug Administration (FDA), whereas the FMIA, PPIA, and EPIA are carried out by the Food Safety and Inspection Service (FSIS) of the U.S. Department of Agriculture (USDA). This bifurcated structure has been in place since the beginning of federal oversight in 1906. FSIS has responsibility for meat and poultry products from species listed in the FMIA and PPIA (known as amenable species), processed egg products, and, most recently, catfish. All other foods, including meat from non-amenable species such as buffalo, fall under FDA's jurisdiction.

Other federal agencies also play important roles in overseeing the food supply. These include the Centers for Disease Control and Prevention (CDC), which monitors and investigates foodborne illnesses, including outbreaks, and makes recommendations about their prevention and control, but does not regulate foods; the Environmental Protection Agency (EPA), which registers pesticides, sets tolerance levels for them in the food supply and regulates other environmental contaminants that could enter the food supply; and the Federal Trade Commission (FTC), which regulates advertising of consumer products, including foods, and acts on deceptive marketing. States, territories, and localities inspect retail establishments, including restaurants and grocery stores using FDA's Food Code as guidance. In

---

1. Recent examples include the Dietary Supplement Health and Education Act of 1994 and the Food Safety Modernization Act, which was signed into law in 2011.

addition, FDA funds states to conduct, under FDA's authorities, inspections of registered human and animal food facilities and farms located in their jurisdictions.

2. Food-Related Provisions of the Food, Drug, and Cosmetics Act

The major food-related provisions of the FDCA are contained in chapter IV of the statute. This chapter defines the circumstances in which a food is considered unsafe for consumption, which is the basis for FDA to take a regulatory action. If a food does not fall into these circumstances, it is assumed to be safe and can be marketed. It is important to understand the circumstances that make food unsafe because they are relevant to adding cannabis or cannabis-containing compounds to the food supply.

These are two major principles in chapter IV that determine whether a food is unsafe to consume. One is the principle of food adulteration and the other is the principle of food misbranding.

2.1 Adulteration and Food Ingredients

Food adulteration is defined in the FDCA in section 402(a)1 as follows: "A food shall be deemed to be adulterated if it bears or contains any poisonous or deleterious substance which may render it injurious to health." This is a straightforward yet expansive definition that gives FDA a great deal of leeway in determining whether a food is adulterated or has a high likelihood of being adulterated, which is important given the complexity of the food supply. The courts have generally deferred to FDA's scientific and professional judgment regarding when the agency considers a food to be adulterated or likely to be adulterated and should not be available for consumption. The basis for adulteration can take many forms, including hazards arising from unsafe chemicals, toxins, microbial agents, filth, radioactivity, or physical agents (e.g., metal fragments).

There are two ways a food can contain a poisonous or deleterious substance. One is that the hazardous substance is a naturally occurring constituent of the food (i.e., is part of the whole food). However, the food is not intrinsically adulterated in the FDCA if the amount of the substance present in the food "does not ordinarily render it injurious to health."[2] There are many substances that are found in low levels in fruits, vegetables, grains, and other foods but at levels that do not ordinarily cause harm. Examples include caffeine in coffee, arsenic in rice, and glycoalkaloids in potatoes. In such instances, the agency can establish tolerances or action levels that if exceeded would cause the food to be considered adulterated.

The second way a food can contain a poisonous or deleterious substance is if it has been *added* to the food, either directly as an ingredient or

---

2. Section 402(a)1.

indirectly. Examples of the latter include when acrylamide is formed from the frying or roasting process, chemicals migrate into a food from a food contact surface, or mercury is absorbed into fish from the environment.

The FDCA considers a food to be adulterated if it contains an added poisonous or deleterious substance that renders the food unsafe, unless that substance is unavoidable due to the manufacturing process for the food, or its presence cannot be avoided by the application of good manufacturing processes. In the latter circumstances, analogous to naturally occurring ingredients, section 406 of chapter IV allows the agency to set tolerance levels that specify the amounts that are allowable before the food is considered unsafe due to the presence of the unavoidable added substance.

Ingredients are added to foods for functional reasons, such as acting as a flavoring agent or a flavor enhancer; for its nutritive value or to enhance nutritional quality; for texture, consistency, or quality; to make a food more palatable; as a food colorant; or to act as a preservative. Historically, hazardous food ingredients were a major source of foodborne illness and even death and were a major reason for the PFDA. As food science progressed, the complexity and volume of new food ingredients, many synthetic, increased. Yet FDA's statutory authority only allowed them to be removed from the marketplace after a food was found to be adulterated. Concerns about food ingredients of questionable safety led to the Food Additives Amendment Act of 1958, which was incorporated into the FDCA as section 409.

The food additive amendment was a major shift in regulatory oversight, because it declared that a food ingredient was de facto unsafe unless it had been approved for use by FDA. It established the food ingredient petition process for gaining agency approval with a standard of reasonable certainty that the ingredient is safe for its intended use as determined by competent scientists. The petition is granted by FDA via issuance of a regulation that lays out the conditions of use.

However, the FDCA also established a definition for a food additive, which is included in chapter II of the statute. The definition states that an ingredient is a food additive *only* if the ingredient is not generally recognized among scientific experts as having been adequately shown through scientific procedures (or experience if the ingredient was in the food supply before 1958) to be safe for its intended conditions of use. This qualification created the "generally recognized as safe" or GRAS standard for food ingredients. As presently applied, information regarding the ingredient, including its intended use, can be submitted to FDA through a GRAS notification along with the scientific evidence that the ingredient is safe for the intended use. The program can review that information and either concur with the assessment by acknowledging the determination, indicate the information submitted is insufficient to make a determination or the information raises safety concerns, or (if requested by the submitter) cease to review the notification. Alternatively, an entity can convene its own scientific experts and make its own determination that the ingredient is generally recognized as safe without notifying FDA of the determination. FDA has issued guidance to industry that strongly encourages food producers to notify the agency of a GRAS determination not only to seek the agency's view but also so that FDA has a way to track ingredients being added to food. Of note, when making a GRAS determination, the scientific experts should not only consider the specific intended use but should also take into consideration the safety of cumulative exposure to the ingredient. In addition, GRAS status can be change if new scientific information becomes available about the ingredient's safety. In 2015, FDA determined that it no longer considered partially hydrogenated oils (also known as trans fats) added to foods to be GRAS after reviewing evidence that consumption of these compounds was harmful to cardiovascular health and there was no safe level of exposure.

Today, the food additive petition process and GRAS determinations are the available pathways for adding new ingredients to foods. The scientific data that forms the basis of a GRAS determination should be widely available, and there should be consensus among experts about the safety of the ingredient. Information submitted in a food additive petition can be non-public and only available to FDA. If an ingredient is added to a food without using one of these pathways, the food is adulterated because it contains an unsafe ingredient. Of note, USDA relies on FDA's determinations regarding the safety of ingredients that may be added to USDA-regulated foods, although FDA often consults with USDA during the review.

One additional way a food can become adulterated in the FDCA is "if it consists in whole or in part of any filthy, putrid, or decomposed substance"[3] or "if has been prepared, packed, or held under insanitary conditions whereby it may have been contaminated."[4] FDA does not have to prove that the product is contaminated, only that the conditions in which it was produced or held *could* lead to contamination. Food producers must follow current good manufacturing practices (cGMPs) issued by FDA. As part of the implementation of the Food Safety Modernization Act (FSMA), modernized cGMPs for human food were developed by FDA and took effect in 2016. The first cGMPs for animal foods also were developed as part of FSMA at the same time. These cGMPs are used by the agency during inspections as a basis to determine whether foods were produced in unsanitary conditions and could therefore be adulterated. FSMA also established a new preventive controls standard for both human and animal food manufacturers. These standards require certain food manufacturers to develop a food safety plan that identifies food safety hazards in the production process that may render foods adulterated and develop preventive controls for these hazards. The manufacturer then implements the preventive controls and must verify that they are controlling the hazard.

---

3. Section 402(a)3.
4. Section 402(a)4.

2.2 Dietary Supplements

Another food category that is important to any discussion of cannabis and/ or cannabis-derived compounds in the food supply is dietary supplements. These are regulated by FDA based on provisions of the 1994 Dietary Supplement Health and Education Act (DSHEA) and are also found in chapter IV of the FDCA. Section 201(ff) defines a dietary supplement as a product meant to supplement the diet that contains one or more of a vitamin; mineral; herb or other botanical; amino acid; a dietary substance meant to increase total dietary intake; or a concentrate, metabolite, or extract of any of these substances. A dietary supplement is further defined as (1) a substance that is ingested (e.g. eaten), (2) cannot be represented as a conventional food (foods and dietary supplements are mutually exclusive categories), (3) has to be specifically labeled as a dietary supplement, and (4) cannot be the sole item of a meal or diet.

Supplements can be in the form of any food (such as a solid or liquid) and can also be in pill, capsule, or powder form. FDA has interpreted the FDCA definition to mean that a dietary supplement cannot contain a synthesized version of a compound that is present in an herb or botanical extract.

A dietary supplement also cannot contain a substance that meets the FDCA definition of either an approved or investigational drug or biologic *unless* the substance was first used as a dietary supplement before it became a drug or biologic. The reverse is not true. As a result, it is impermissible for a dietary supplement to claim that it may prevent, treat, mitigate, or cure a disease since such claims are reserved for approved drugs and biologics.

However, producers of dietary supplements are permitted to make "structure-function claims." Structure-function claims are described in section 403(r)6 of the FDCA as generalized statements about how the product affects the body. Illustrative examples are "builds muscles," "increases energy," "improves digestive health," or "strengthens the immune system," but statements such as "prevents cancer" or "improves Alzheimer's disease" are not permitted. When a structure-function claim is made, it must be accompanied by standardized wording that the claim has not been evaluated by the FDA and that the product is not intended to diagnose, treat, cure, or prevent a disease. Although FDA regulates the labeling of dietary supplements, advertising is regulated by the FTC.

Dietary supplements have their own cGMPs and, similar to GRAS standards, the manufacturer must have a scientific basis that the product is reasonably expected to be safe under the labeled conditions of use. The information that forms the basis for this determination is held by the manufacturer and is not required to be submitted to the FDA.

Dietary supplement ingredients that were present in the food supply before the 1994 enactment of DSHEA do not require notification to the

FDA. The manufacturer must have documentary evidence that the ingredient was present in the food supply before that date. An ingredient that is to be used in a dietary supplement that cannot meet the pre-DSHEA standard is considered a "new dietary ingredient," or NDI. A manufacturer intending to use an NDI must submit to FDA information on how the ingredient will be used and the scientific basis for its safety 75 days before it enters the market. If no concerns are raised by FDA in this 75-day window, the product containing the NDI may be marketed. FDA maintains a publicly available list of NDI notifications and the outcome of the review.

The adulteration provisions for conventional foods also generally apply to dietary supplements, including the presence of poisonous or deleterious substances and adherence to dietary supplement cGMPs.

2.3 Misbranding of Foods and Dietary Supplements

The FDCA includes detailed requirements regarding the labeling of food and dietary supplements to provide essential information to the consumer about the product. Any food that fails to provide or inaccurately provides the required information or otherwise has statements that are "false and misleading" is considered misbranded and cannot be marketed. The misbranding provisions of the FDCA are included in section 403 of chapter IV of the statute. Essential elements of labeling include the identity of the product, who manufactured or distributed the product, the quantity in the package, a list of ingredients, the type of flavoring (e.g., artificial or imitation), and, since 2006, whether it contains a food source from which a major allergen is derived. Since the enactment of the 1990 Nutrition Labeling and Education Act, the food must also have a Nutrition Facts Label that lists calories, amounts of specified nutrients, and serving size. In 2016, the Nutrition Facts Label was updated to reflect current nutrition science with an initial compliance date of January 1, 2020. There is a separate Supplement Facts Label for dietary supplements.

Section 201(k) defines labeling as any written, printed, or graphic matter on the container of the article or that can be seen through any wrapping or packaging that accompanies the article. Section 201(n) provides a definition of misleading in the context of whether an article is misbranded:

> If an article is alleged to be misbranded because the labeling or advertising is misleading . . . there should be taken into account not only representations made or suggested . . . but also the extent to which the labeling or advertising fails to reveal facts material . . . with respect to consequences that may result from use of the article.

Thus, a product may be misbranded if it conveys misleading information and if it fails to provide certain information about the article that is important to the user.

3. Application of Statutes and Regulations to Cannabis and Cannabis-Derived Compounds in the Food Supply and Current Status

Most of the current interest in adding cannabis and cannabis-derived compounds to the food supply is focused on cannabidiol (CBD). Before discussing CBD, it is worthwhile noting the current situation with other cannabis components with respect to the food supply.

- Hemp seed—refers to the seeds of *Cannabis sativa L.* and does not naturally contain either THC or CBD. In practice, hemp seeds may contain trace amounts of both compounds incidentally acquired from the rest of the plant during the harvesting process. The edible part of the seed is the hulled portion and is often referred to as hemp hearts. Hemp hearts have a history of usage in both conventional foods and dietary supplements. In December 2018, FDA issued "no concerns" letters in response to three GRAS notifications received from Fresh Hemp Foods for the use of hulled hemp seed, hemp seed protein powder, and hemp seed oil in food. Hemp seeds have been used for their taste, aroma, nutritional value, and for other functional purposes in both solid foods and beverages. Dietary supplements containing these items have been on the market with a variety of structure-function claims. FDA has not received any GRAS notifications related to use of hemp seed in animal foods.
- Industrial hemp—refers to *Cannabis sativa L.* plants with a THC concentration of no more than 0.3 on a dry-weight basis as well as the seeds and all derivatives and extracts from such plants. Industrial hemp was removed from Schedule 1 of the Controlled Substances Act by the 2018 Farm Bill and therefore can be legally grown and harvested in the United States. Industrial hemp contains high levels of CBD, and there is significant interest in adding CBD extracted from industrial hemp to conventional foods and dietary supplements. However, the 2018 Farm Bill preserved all of FDA's authorities to regulate the use of compounds derived from industrial hemp in products regulated by the agency. Thus, foods and dietary supplements containing compounds from industrial hemp are subject to all relevant FDA regulations. The plant itself is used for purposes such as rope and textiles, although the leaves are considered edible.
- Cannabis and THC—refers to *Cannabis sativa L.* plants (marijuana) that do not meet the criteria for industrial hemp and all compounds derived from the plants. These plants have higher levels of THC, which is the primary psychoactive component of cannabis. Cannabis and THC remain on Schedule I under the Controlled Substances Act.

FDA has not approved either cannabis or THC through a food additive petition or as a new dietary ingredient for use in dietary supplements. It would be highly unlikely that the agency would favorably review a request to use these in foods or dietary supplements given their psychoactive properties and abuse potential.

Medical marijuana is legal in the majority of states and D.C. Each state has its own specific list of medical indications and conditions of use. Some states permit edible forms to be sold in addition to inhaled forms, whereas other states do not. In addition to permitting the use of marijuana for medical purposes, 11 states and D.C. allow recreational use of marijuana, with some allowing the sale of edibles. Edibles containing marijuana or THC have taken many forms, such as brownies, cookies, candies, and beverages. Some states that permit edibles prohibit forms such as candy that might appeal to minors. Limits on the amount of THC or marijuana that is legally permitted in edibles varies by state, as does the amount that can be purchased at one time.

Two synthetic forms of THC, dronabinol and nabilone, were approved as drugs by FDA in 1985 for the treatment of AIDS-related weight loss and chemotherapy-induced nausea and vomiting. These approvals were based on clinical studies demonstrating effectiveness and benefits that outweighed risks. FDA continues to encourage researchers to conduct clinical studies that would demonstrate the safety and effectiveness of marijuana for medical use and THC for additional medical conditions, and has issued guidance on how to conduct these studies and navigate the regulatory process.

Because of these drug approvals, THC cannot be added to food that is introduced into interstate commerce. Section 301(ll) of the FDCA states the "introduction or delivery for introduction into interstate commerce of any food to which has been added a drug approved under Section 505 . . . or for which substantial clinical investigations have been instituted and for which the existence of such investigations has been made public" is a prohibited act. Section 301(ll) goes on to state this would not be a prohibited act if there was evidence THC was used in food before dronabinol and nabilone were approved or before the Investigational New Drug (IND) applications that allowed clinical trials of these drugs were approved and made public. FDA has stated that it has no evidence that THC meets this exception. Additional exceptions listed in 301(ll) are (1) if a regulation has been issued prescribing safe conditions of use of THC in food, (2) if a regulation has been issued affirming conditions under which THC is GRAS, or (3) if a GRAS determination for THC has been notified to FDA and the agency has not raised concerns through the issuance of a letter to the submitter. No regulations regarding the safe conditions of use of THC have been issued and there has been no GRAS determination for THC.

There are analogous provisions in the FDCA that make it unlawful for a dietary supplement to contain an approved or investigational drug unless there is evidence that it was used in dietary supplements before it was approved as a drug or for investigational use. These provisions are found in the definition of a dietary supplement in section 201(ff)(3)(A) of the FDCA. FDA has stated there is no evidence THC was used in dietary supplements before dronabinol or nabilone were approved for marketing or investigational use, rendering any dietary supplements that contain THC adulterated. Section 201(ff)(3)(B) permits the issuance of a regulation that allows the lawful use of an approved drug in dietary supplements, but no such regulation has been proposed or finalized for THC.

In summary, there are multiple reasons that cannabis and THC cannot at present be added to FDA-regulated conventional foods or dietary supplements. These include:

1. They are on Schedule I of the Controlled Substances Act.
2. They have not been subject to an approved Food Additive Petition or a GRAS determination.
3. Synthetic versions of THC are approved drugs.

The identification of either cannabis or THC in an FDA-regulated food or dietary supplement would make that product adulterated.

Of note, when Food Additive Petitions or GRAS notifications are submitted to FDA, the submitter indicates how the ingredient is intended to be used, including why it is being added (e.g., as a flavoring agent, nutrient, or for functional purposes such as texture). Cannabis and THC are generally used for their psychoactive properties or for a perceived therapeutic benefit, which is much different than for taste or nutritional value. When coupled with safety concerns related to cannabis and THC, it is unlikely a submission to the agency would be favorably viewed.

3.1 Cannabidiol (CBD)

Cannabidiol (CBD) is a compound that, in contrast to THC, does not have psychotropic properties and does not have similar abuse potential. It is found in all forms of cannabis. Many varieties of recreational cannabis have been developed to have high levels of THC and lower CBD content. In contrast, industrial hemp has high levels of CBD and negligible amounts of THC; varieties are being developed to maximize CBD yields. Since enactment of the 2018 Farm Bill, CBD can be legally extracted from industrial hemp, with the most common forms being CBD oil and tinctures.

CBD is purported to have a variety of therapeutic benefits in humans and pets. Some extreme examples include treatment of diseases such as diabetes and cancer. More commonly claimed uses include pain relief, sleep aid, an anti-anxiety agent, a muscle relaxant, an anti-inflammatory, relief of fatigue and depression, and an aid for opiate withdrawal. There is little substantiation for any of these claims. CBD has also been added to cosmetics for a variety of purposes.

CBD is best known for its effect on persons with seizure disorders, especially childhood seizures, and muscle spasticity. Some parents have turned to CBD oil when other therapeutic options did not adequately control their children's seizures. Many offered testimonials about how CBD oil resulted in marked improvement in their children's condition.

In 2014, FDA approved an IND application submitted by GW Pharmaceuticals to conduct clinical trials of a CBD extract for the treatment of Dravet Syndrome, which is a rare treatment-resistant form of childhood epilepsy. Those trials showed the drug was effective. In 2018, the CBD extract was approved by FDA under the trade name Epidiolex for use in children over two years of age with Dravet Syndrome and a second rare form of childhood epilepsy known as Lennox-Gastaut Syndrome. This drug has a much higher concentration of CBD than the concentrations found in commercially available CBD products.

Another GW Pharmaceuticals product, Sativex, which is a combination of THC and CBD in spray form, was approved by FDA for investigational use in 2006, even earlier than Epidiolex, initially for cancer pain and subsequently, in 2013, for spasticity in patients with multiple sclerosis. However, the drug has not been approved for marketing in the United States.

CBD oil is widely available over the Internet and in a variety of retail settings. It is legal to market in many states and was further boosted by enactment of the 2018 Farm Bill. CBD-containing cosmetics are also widely available in both retail settings and over the Internet. CBD edibles and beverages are readily found and purchased online and in retail stores. State laws vary regarding the legality of CBD edibles. In some states they are authorized, although others specifically prohibit them.

At present, CBD is not approved by FDA as an ingredient in foods or dietary supplements. But there is widespread interest, even by large food producers, in developing a federally approved pathway that would allow CBD to enter the food supply. However, many of the same issues arise with CBD as with other cannabis-derived compounds, even after enactment of the 2018 Farm Bill.

Two possible options to allow CBD to be used as an ingredient in FDA-regulated conventional foods are through a GRAS notification or a Food Additive Petition. For these options to be available, there needs to be evidence that CBD was used in food before the IND for Sativex was approved in 2006 and the IND for Epidiolex was approved and publicly announced in 2014. FDA has stated that no evidence of such use has come to the agency's attention but it would be open to receiving evidence of earlier use in foods.

In May 2019, FDA held a public hearing (also known as a Part 15 hearing) on cannabis and cannabis-derived compounds to obtain information to help inform future directions and regulatory actions. CBD was a major topic of discussion. Many presenters were supportive of CBD's use as an ingredient in foods and dietary supplements, whereas others raised concerns. Among these concerns were:

- Poor quality control of the extraction and manufacturing process, resulting in significant variability in the amount and quality of CBD.
- Variability in amounts of CBD in products when compared to the labeled quantity, including some products with no CBD whereas others contained excess amounts.
- Presence of contaminants, including heavy metals and pesticides.
- Detection of synthetic rather than natural CBD.
- Safety concerns, especially when consumed by vulnerable populations such as children and pregnant women.
- Potential for interactions with medications, alcohol, or other substances leading to adverse events.

In November 2019, FDA issued a statement that, based on currently available information, the agency was unable to conclude that CBD was GRAS for use as a food ingredient. The agency indicated this conclusion was reached both because there is evidence suggesting CBD may be harmful and because there are important data gaps related to safety.

Specific harms raised by FDA, which could be exacerbated by repeated exposure, include:

- Possible liver toxicity.
- Drug interactions that could alter the metabolism of other medications, resulting in serious side effects.
- Use of CBD with alcohol or other central nervous system depressants could result in excessive drowsiness and sedation that could lead to injuries and other problems.
- Mood changes.
- Gastrointestinal symptoms.

Safety-related data gaps include:

- Impact of cumulative exposure.
- Effects of CBD on the developing brain when children are exposed.
- Effects of prenatal exposure on the fetus and exposure to newborns via breastfeeding.
- Interactions of CBD with other herbs and botanicals.
- Potential for CBD to cause male reproductive toxicity, which has been observed in laboratory mice.

A food producer has the option to assemble its own scientific experts and make an independent GRAS determination based on widely available scientific evidence and studies. They are also not required to notify FDA of their GRAS determination. But from a practical standpoint, FDA's November

2019 statement rules out this option. FDA can request the evidentiary basis for an independent GRAS determination, which has to include widely available scientific evidence and the identity of the subject matter experts. Furthermore, the agency can request removal of a CBD-containing food from the marketplace by citing section 301 (ll), prohibiting the introduction of a food into interstate commerce that contains an approved drug.

Another possible option for a food producer would be to submit a food additive petition to allow the use of CBD as a food ingredient. The petition could contain non-public information as the basis for its safety for a specific intended use. However, FDA would certainly raise all of the safety concerns found in the November 2019 statement as a basis for denial unless somehow the petitioner adequately addressed through scientific data all of these concerns and data gaps. If somehow the petition was granted, the 301 (ll) prohibition would no longer apply as the agency would have issued a regulation specifying the safe conditions of use and other stipulations such as labeling.

The pathway for a CBD-containing dietary supplement to come to market would be through the pre-market submission of an NDI notification. Since FDA has stated it has seen no evidence that CBD was in the food supply before the GW Pharmaceuticals IND application was approved for Sativex in 2006, it could also not have been a supplement ingredient pre-DSHEA. The November 2019 FDA statement is just as relevant to dietary supplements as it is to conventional foods, possibly even more so since dietary supplements often contain mixtures of herbs and botanicals, and FDA raised concerns about possible interactions with CBD. FDA would almost certainly issue a non-concurrence for any NDI notification regarding CBD. In addition, a CBD-containing dietary supplement would violate the section 201 (ff) (3) (A) definition of a dietary supplement, which does not allow a drug to be used in a dietary supplement without evidence of its use before the IND was approved.

However, the FDCA does contain an option for FDA to issue a regulation allowing the use of CBD in dietary supplements despite it being an approved drug. But this option may be difficult unless the safety concerns and data gaps have been satisfactorily resolved.

In summary, there are challenges to using CBD as an ingredient in FDA-regulated conventional foods and dietary supplements. These obstacles exist despite the changes instituted by the 2018 Farm Bill, because it did not modify FDA's regulatory oversight.

These challenges include:

- CBD is an approved drug with no evidence of being in the food supply before clinical trials were initiated in 2014.
- FDA has stated that due to safety concerns and data gaps, CBD would at present not qualify for GRAS status.

These concerns will be difficult to resolve.

3.2 Cannabigerol (CBG)

Cannabis contains many other compounds that are referred to as minor cannabinoids because they occur in concentrations considerably lower than THC and CBD. Some are closer chemically to THC, whereas others are closer to CBD. One compound that has been extracted and is also available as an oil is cannabigerol (CBG). CBG is the progenitor to both THC and CBD. In the cannabis plant, it is enzymatically converted to either THC or CBD with the proportions of each depending on the plant variety. Because it is the parent compound and is rapidly metabolize, it is only present in cannabis in small amounts. This makes extracting it and producing CBG oil significantly more expensive than extracting either THC or CBD. However, it is available over the Internet and in some retail establishments, similarly to CBD.

Putative health benefits have been attributed to CBG, including control of glaucoma, anti-inflammatory properties (especially for bowel disease), anti-cancer properties, and anti-infective properties. None of these appear to have been well studied and there have been no FDA-approved clinical trials, nor is it an FDA-approved drug.

The 2018 Farm Bill defines hemp as any part of that plant, including the seeds thereof and all derivatives, extracts, cannabinoids, isomers, acids, salts, and salts of isomers, whether growing or not. This includes CBG if it has been derived from industrial hemp. Because it has not been approved for investigation as a drug, some of the impediments to its use as an ingredient in conventional foods and dietary supplements do not apply to CBG. FDA has issued no statements on CBG safety concerns and data gaps.

Therefore, the Food Additive Petition, GRAS determination, and NDI pathways are technically available for CBG. However, CBG has not been well studied and there is little basis for establishing its safety as an ingredient in conventional foods or dietary supplements. The scientific studies and information needed for a GRAS determination do not appear to be widely available for subject matter experts to review and reach consensus. Therefore, FDA would almost certainly raise many of the same concerns mentioned for CBD, and the data gaps for CBG are probably even wider than for CBD since this compound is not as widely used and is less available than CBD.

3.3 Animal Foods

As noted, in addition to the presence of cannabinoids in edibles for humans, they have also been added to pet treats and supplements. The FDCA does not distinguish between human and animal foods in the parts of the law previously cited. Therefore, the preceding discussions are also relevant to pet foods and supplements. There is little information available regarding safety in dogs, cats, and other species, and safety is likely to vary in different breeds and species. CBD is not an approved drug for use in animals.

4. FDA Regulatory Actions

FDA has wide latitude to take actions against products that contain cannabis or cannabis-derived compounds because they often violate multiple sections of the FDCA. To date, FDA's actions have focused on marketers of products that threaten public health by making claims to treat, cure, mitigate, or prevent serious diseases or health conditions. Such claims are reserved for drugs that have gone through the FDA regulatory process and been shown to be safe and effective with rigorous production standards. People may use these cannabinoid-containing products in the mistaken belief that they are safe and work for their disease or condition. They may use them in lieu of (or in addition to) proven therapies prescribed by their health care providers. When that occurs, not only is their disease or condition not being treated, but they also risk serious adverse reactions or drug-drug interactions with other medications they are taking.

FDA's regulatory actions have come in the form of warning letters that have been issued in each of the last five years to marketers who widely distribute their products, usually over the Internet. Eighteen warning letters were issued in 2015 to six marketers, 22 warning letters to ten marketers in 2016, four warning letters to four marketers in 2017, and one warning letter in 2018.

In November 2019, 15 warning letters were issued to 15 different marketers; each was selling a variety of CBD-containing products and all were making drug claims that made them unapproved and misbranded drugs. In addition, many of the warning letters cited food- and dietary supplement-related violations. Fourteen cited prohibited acts provisions for placing into interstate commerce human or animal food containing a drug; 13 cited adulteration provisions for both human and animal foods for containing an unapproved food ingredient (13 for animal food—including one for food-producing animals—and ten for human food); 11 cited dietary supplement provisions for containing an unapproved new dietary ingredient; and one cited misbranding of the food for not containing all required information. The warning letters were sent to marketers around the country, including states where medical marijuana, recreational marijuana, and edibles are legal.

These warning letters were given prominent visibility by FDA at the time of their release through media statements and posting on FDA's website as a means to educate the public about the risks associated with these products as well as warning the rest of the cannabis industry about activities that are likely to bring FDA scrutiny and action. A review of the warning letter recipients' web sites found that some were inactive, whereas others had removed the items or removed the drug-related claims.

6. FDA Regulatory Actions

14

Regulatory Overview of the Canadian Cannabis Industry

David Wood and Philippe Tardiff

1. Federalism and Legislative History

The Canadian cannabis industry has been federally regulated since July 30, 2001. Until the Cannabis Act[1] (the Act) came into effect, cannabis was a controlled substance scheduled to the Controlled Drugs and Substances Act[2] (the CDSA), and possession of cannabis was prohibited, with criminal penalties enforced under the CDSA and the Criminal Code.[3] The Constitution of Canada does not allow provincial jurisdiction on prohibitions or other restrictions of controlled substances. As a result, medical cannabis is, and always has been, regulated *exclusively* at the federal level in Canada, initially through iterative regulations under the CDSA implemented between 2001 and 2016 and subsequently through regulations under the Act beginning October 17, 2018. Similarly, commercial production of industrial hemp was regulated under the CDSA beginning March 12, 1998, and is now regulated under the Act. Federal regulation of the Canadian cannabis industry presents a fundamental departure from individual state industries operating under federal prohibition.

Prior to the Act coming into effect, cannabis was listed as Item 1 in Schedule 2 of the CDSA and possession of cannabis was a criminal offence. Medical access regulations under the CDSA provided exemptions from prohibition of cannabis: the Access to Cannabis for Medical

---

1. Cannabis Act, S.C. 2018, c 16 (Can.).
2. S.C. 1996, c 19 (Can.).
3. R.S.C. 1985, c C-46 (Can.).

Purposes Regulations[4] (the ACMPR) from 2016 to 2018, the Marihuana for Medical Purposes Regulations[5] (the MMPR) from 2013 to 2016, and the Marihuana Medical Access Regulations[6] (the MMAR) from 2001 to 2013. Along with the Narcotic Control Regulations[7] (the NCR), each of the MMAR, the MMPR, and the ACMPR provided for regulated access to medical cannabis. The Industrial Hemp Regulations[8] (the 1998 IHR) were also enacted under the CDSA in 1998, regulating the Canadian industrial hemp industry.

Each of the MMAR, the MMPR, and the ACMPR provided for mail-order access to "dried marihuana," with cannabis oil becoming commercially available under the MMPR following a successful court challenge that concluded with a hearing before the Supreme Court of Canada.[9] The MMAR and the ACMPR also allowed personal cultivation. Mail-order access through the MMAR was provided directly from Health Canada and fulfilled by a private entity called Prairie Plant Systems, Canada's closest analogy to the Marijuana Project at the University of Mississippi. The MMPR and the ACMPR each provided for a privatized commercial production base of "licensed producers." Licensed producers under the ACMPR became federal license holders under the Cannabis Regulations (the CR)[10] when the Act came into effect.

The Act came into effect on October 17, 2018. All provisions of the Act are predicated on unique regulation of cannabis, which was made possible by repeal of item 1 of schedule 2 of the CDSA.[11] Repeal of item 1 of schedule 2 of the CDSA meant that cannabis was no longer prohibited by default as a controlled substance. Instead, the Act, along with the CR and the Industrial Hemp Regulations[12] (the 2018 IHR), provides a framework for commercial regulation of cannabis. This controversial change in Canadian policy with respect to cannabis was made to protect public health and public safety and, in particular, to (1) protect the health of young persons by restricting their access to cannabis; (2) protect young persons and others from inducements to use cannabis; (3) provide for the licit production of cannabis to reduce illicit activities in relation to cannabis; (4) deter

---

4. SOR/2016-230, *repealed by* SOR/2018-147 § 33 (Can.).
5. SOR/2013-119, *repealed by* SOR/2016-230 § 281 (Can.).
6. SOR/2001-227, *repealed by* SOR/2013-119 § 267 (Can.).
7. C.R.C., c 1041 (Can.) (The NCR are regulations under the CDSA and, since October 17, 2018, no longer apply to cannabis).
8. SOR/98-156, *repealed by* SOR/2018-147 § 33 (Can.).
9. R. v. Smith, [2015] 2 S.C.R. 34 (Can.).
10. Cannabis Regulations, SOR/2018-144 (Can.).
11. Act, *supra* note 1, at § 204(1) ("Item 1 of Schedule II to the [CDSA] is repealed.").
12. Industrial Hemp Regulations, SOR/2018-145 (Can.).

illicit activities in relation to cannabis through appropriate sanctions and enforcement measures; (5) reduce the burden on the criminal justice system in relation to cannabis; (6) provide access to a quality-controlled supply of cannabis; and (7) enhance public awareness of the health risks associated with cannabis use.[13]

Subsections 7(c) and (f) of the Act are consistent with a robust, accessible, and engaging market for cannabis, providing a regulated alternative to the illicit market. To the extent those who use cannabis choose to purchase from the regulated market rather than the illicit market, the opportunity for the illicit market is diminished, serving the goals expressed in subsections 7(c) and (e), and servicing the goal if not the mechanism of subsection 7(d). By eroding the illicit market and supporting the regulated market, which is subject to significant restrictions on sale, promotion, packaging, and labeling, the purposes of subsections 7(a), (b), and (g) are served. Considered in recognition of the persistent and resilient illicit market for cannabis, a successful cannabis industry is critical to the success of Canada's choice to regulate rather than prohibit cannabis.

The Act and the CR regulate commercial and personal cultivation, saleable classes of cannabis, packaging, labeling, promotional activity, sale, issue of licenses, security clearances, tracking, physical security requirements, good production practices, import, export, medical access (still mail order and entirely federal), and other aspects of the cannabis industry. The Act and the Criminal Code provide criminal penalties for noncompliant commercial production and sale, with particularly strong penalties for sale to minors.

All commercial cultivation of cannabis plants is regulated under the CR and the 2018 IHR. Cannabis products that are regulated for sale must be processed from cannabis cultivated under a license issued pursuant to the CR or the 2018 IHR (in Canada, flowers from industrial hemp cannabis plants are considered "cannabis"). All cannabis products must be processed, packaged, and labeled in compliance with a license issued under the CR, and are subject to duty and stamping requirements in accordance with the Excise Act, 2001.[14]

---

13. Act, *supra* note 1, at § 7.
14. S.C. 2002, c 22 (Can.).

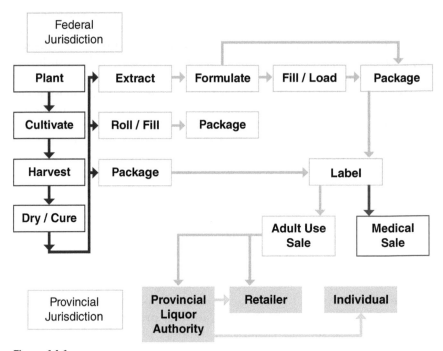

Figure 14.1

Figure 14.1 illustrates the commercial cannabis supply chain in Canada. Exclusive federal regulation of cannabis applies along the supply chain from cultivation through processing to a packaged, labeled, excise duty-stamped cannabis product. Federal jurisdiction remains over medical sale. The Act provides for provincial or territorial regulation of sale.[15] All ten provinces and all three territories have regulated adult-use cannabis sale. The Act allows provincial or territorial regulation of medical sale, but no provinces or territories have done so.

The Act regulates cultivation and processing for personal purposes in addition to commercial cultivation and processing. Residents of Canada are, subject to provincial law, entitled to cultivate up to four cannabis plants for personal use, and potentially many more with medical access through the CR. Cannabis plants cultivated for personal use (medical or adult use), and cannabis of any class prepared from those plants, cannot be sold.

2. Federally Regulated Activity

In the CDSA, cannabis was used as a blanket term, which includes dried marihuana, cannabis resin, delta-9-tetrahydrocannabinol (THC), cannabidiol (CBD), cannabinol (CBN), and cannabis seeds. The definition

---

15. Act, *supra* note 1, at § 69(1).

of "cannabis" in the Act was updated to "a cannabis plant and anything referred to in Schedule 1 but does not include anything referred to in Schedule 2."[16] *Schedule 1* includes "any part of the cannabis plant, including the phytocannabinoids produced by, or found in, such a plant." *Schedule 2* excludes from the definition of "cannabis" the following portions of a cannabis plant: (1) nonviable seed; (2) a mature stalk, without any leaf, flower, seed, or branch; (3) fiber derived from a mature stalk, without any leaf, flower, seed, or branch; and (4) the root.

The Act defines a "cannabis plant" as "a plant that belongs to the genus Cannabis" and "dried cannabis" as "any part of a cannabis plant that has been subjected to a drying process, other than seeds."[17] The 2018 IHR define "industrial hemp" as "a cannabis plant—or any part of that plant—in which the concentration of THC is 0.3% or less in the flowering heads and leaves."[18]

Unless otherwise authorized by the Act, it is prohibited for an organization to possess cannabis.[19] "Organization" is defined with reference to the Criminal Code and includes all common legal business entities.[20] Indictable offences for possession in contravention of the Act are punishable by a fine in an amount that is at the discretion of the Court[21] or a summary conviction with a fine of up to $100,000. Authorizations to possess cannabis may be issued as licenses or exemptions.[22] The CR provide for licensing broadly, with specific authorizations for cultivation, processing, sale, analytical testing, and research.[23] The 2018 IHR provide for licenses to cultivate, propagate, and process industrial hemp.[24] All applications for licenses are through a national Cannabis Tracking and Licensing System (CTLS) online portal, which is also under federal jurisdiction.[25]

The Act, and the licenses provided for in the CR and the 2018 IHR, establish a framework for commercial production of a "cannabis product," which is defined by the CR as

cannabis of only one of the classes that are set out in Schedule 4 to the Act—or a cannabis accessory if that accessory contains such cannabis—after it has been packaged and labelled for sale to a consumer at the retail level, but does not include a drug containing cannabis.[26]

---

16. *Id.* § 2(1).
17. *Id.*
18. 2018 IHR, *supra* note 12, at § 1(2).
19. Act, *supra* note 1, at ¶ 8(1)(f).
20. Criminal Code, *supra* note 3, at § 2.
21. Act, *supra* note 1, at § 8(2)(a)(iii).
22. *Id.* §§ 62(1), 140.
23. CR, *supra* note 10, at § 8(1).
24. 2018 IHR, *supra* note 12, at § 3(1).
25. Act, *supra* note 1, at §§ 81–83.
26. CR, *supra* note 10, at § 1(2).

A "cannabis accessory" is defined as

(a) a thing, including rolling papers or wraps, holders, pipes, water pipes, bongs and vaporizers, that is represented to be used in the consumption of cannabis or a thing that is represented to be used in the production of cannabis; (b) a thing that is deemed under subsection (3) to be represented to be used in the consumption or production of cannabis.[27]

2.1 Licenses Issued under the Cannabis Regulations

The Act[28] and the CR provide production licenses, including cultivation (a "Cultivation License") and processing (a "Processing License").[29] Cannabis products may be sold to provincial gambling, liquor, and cannabis authorities (a "Cannabis Control Authority") who manage access to the adult-use market in their province of jurisdiction. In some jurisdictions, sale directly to authorized retailers (retailers) or private wholesalers is possible. Alternatively, a holder of a license for sale for medical purposes (a medical sale license) may sell cannabis products directly to clients. Cultivation licenses authorize cultivation of cannabis, bulk sale of dried or fresh cannabis, and sale of cannabis plants and cannabis plant seeds to cannabis control authorities or to a medical sale license holder. Processing licenses authorize the sale of cannabis products from any classes of cannabis listed on the particular processing license to a cannabis control authority or a medical sale license holder.[30] Cultivation licenses, processing licenses, and medical sale licenses provide control over the supply chain for cannabis products, and carry considerably more stringent requirements than licenses for analytical testing (an analytical testing license) or research (a research license), or licenses issued under the 2018 IHR (a hemp license).

Security clearances are required for officers, directors, and "key personnel" of any holder of a cultivation license, processing license, or medical sale license.[31] Key personnel include the head of security, responsible person,[32] master grower (cultivation licenses only),[33] quality assurance person (QAP; processing licenses only),[34] or any alternative for any such

---

27. Act, *supra* note 3, at § 2(1). Subsection 2(3) reads: "(3) For the purposes of the definition cannabis accessory, a thing that is commonly used in the consumption of cannabis is deemed to be represented to be used in the consumption of cannabis if the thing is sold at the same point of sale as cannabis." *Id.* This would include, for example, a lighter.

28. Act, *supra* note 1, at § 61.

29. CR, *supra* note 10, at ¶¶ 8(1)(a), (b).

30. *Id.* §§ 11–16 (cultivation), 17–21 (processing).

31. *Id.* § 50.

32. *Id.* §§ 37(1), 37(3).

33. *Id.* § 12.

34. *Id.* § 19.

position. Individuals are eligible for a security clearance if they require one for a position as a license holder, including following completion of a corporate transaction (officer, director, or key personnel), or have been selected for a position as key personnel.[35] Security clearances are portable between license holders and have a term of up to five years.[36] Security clearances will be denied for reasons including reasonable suspicion of participation in trafficking of controlled substances, fraud, corruption, terrorism, counterfeiting, laundering, acts or threats of violence, membership in a criminal organization, associating with individuals involved in any of the preceding, or activities that pose a risk to the integrity of the control of production and distribution of cannabis.[37] Security clearances may be suspended or cancelled if Health Canada has reasonable grounds to believe that a risk to public health or public safety posed by the security clearance holder, including the risk of cannabis being diverted to an illicit market or activity, has become unacceptable.[38]

Physical security, visual recording, and intrusion detection systems are required for standard cultivation licenses, standard processing licenses, and medical sale licenses that authorize possession of cannabis products.[39] Micro-cultivation licenses, nursery licenses, micro-processing licenses, analytical testing licenses, and research licenses provide access to more limited amounts of cannabis and have less stringent physical security requirements, no visual recording requirements, and no intrusion detection requirements.[40]

Data retention requirements apply to all licenses for cannabis inventory, packaging, labeling, ingredient lists, transactions, offsite antimicrobial treatment, destruction, security, compliance with production standards, standard operating procedures (SOP), sanitation programs, recall control, promotion, research, compliance with micro-processing limits, import, export, and key investors.[41] Reporting to Health Canada is required for confirmation of compliance, import, export, new cannabis products, promotion, theft or loss, voluntary recalls, and adverse reactions.[42]

2.1.1 Cultivation Licenses

Cultivation licenses include standard cultivation, micro-cultivation, and nursery licenses,[43] each of which authorize cultivation and sale of cannabis.[44]

---

35. CR, *supra* note 10, at § 51.
36. *Id.* § 56.
37. *Id.* § 53.
38. *Id.* § 58.
39. *Id.* §§ 62–73, 78.
40. CR, *supra* note 10, at §§ 74, 75, 77.
41. *Id.* §§ 221–241 (not all will apply to every CR license).
42. *Id.* §§ 242–248 (not all will apply to every CR license).
43. *Id.* § 8(3).
44. *Id.* ¶ 8(1)(a) and §§ 11–16.

Standard and micro-cultivation licenses authorize cultivation of cannabis plants, and sale of cannabis plants, cannabis plant seeds, dried cannabis, and fresh cannabis to other license holders.[45] Nursery licenses carry the same authorizations other than sale of dried or fresh cannabis.[46] Cultivation license holders may sell two classes of cannabis products—cannabis plants and cannabis plant seeds—to a Cannabis Control Authority, Retailer, or Medical Sale License holder, or directly to individuals at the request of any of these authorized resellers of cannabis products.[47]

A micro-cultivation license holder is limited in that all cultivation must take place in a clearly delineated surface area that cannot exceed 200 m^2 (~2,150 square feet). This surface area is calculated taking into account multiple levels (i.e., two or more levels cannot provide a total canopy of over 200 m^2).[48] A nursery license holder is limited to a total surface area that does not exceed 50 m^2 (~530 square feet) within which all budding or flowering cannabis plants, including all parts of those plants, must be contained.[49] The nursery license holder must not possess more than 5 kg of flowering heads, with the exception of cannabis plant seeds, and must destroy any flowering heads, leaves, and branches of the cannabis plants within 30 days of harvesting.[50]

2.1.2 Processing Licenses

Processing licenses may include authorizations to manufacture cannabis products and obtain cannabis other than by cultivation.[51] "Processing license" is an umbrella term that is divided into standard processing and micro-processing licenses.[52] Processing licenses authorize sale or distribution of any class of cannabis to other license holders authorized to possess the class of cannabis, and sale of cannabis products to a cannabis control authority, retailer, or medical sale license, or directly to individuals at the request of any of these authorized resellers of cannabis products.[53]

A holder of a processing license must employ a QAP and, if necessary, an additional individual for expertise specific to edible cannabis to support the QAP.[54] The QAP is responsible for assuring quality of any cannabis before sale.[55] Each processing license lists classes of cannabis products that

---

45. *Id.* § 11.
46. *Id.* § 14.
47. CR, *supra* note 10, at ¶ 11(5)(c) (standard or micro-cultivation) or ¶ 14(5)(b) (nursery).
48. *Id.* § 13.
49. *Id.* ¶ 16(1)(a).
50. *Id.* ¶¶ 16(1)(b), (c).
51. *Id.* ¶ 8(1)(b) and §§ 17–21.
52. CR, *supra* note 10, at § 8(4).
53. *Id.* § 17(5).
54. *Id.* §§ 19(1), (1.1).
55. *Id.* § 19(2).

are authorized for sale. A processing license holder must file a notice of new cannabis product document with Health Canada at least 60 days before making a new cannabis product available for sale.[56]

A micro-processing license holder is relatively limited in terms of the total processing capacity of the processing license—up to 600 kg (~1,320 lbs) of dried cannabis or equivalent in other cannabis annually,[57] or any amount of dried cannabis or fresh cannabis that is all sourced from one micro-cultivation license located at the same site as the micro-processing license.[58] The authorizations applicable to a micro-processing license exclude synthesizing cannabis.[59]

2.1.3 Analytical Testing License

An analytical testing license authorizes possession and distribution (not sale) of cannabis to other analytical testing license holders.[60] A head of laboratory must be appointed but need not be security cleared.[61] As described further in Section 4.1, certain testing must be completed by an independent third-party lab, such as an analytical testing license holder, before a cannabis product can be authorized for sale by a QAP.

2.1.4 Medical Sale License

Medical sale licenses authorize sale of cannabis products to clients and to hospital employees. Medical sale of cannabis is entirely by mail order and is federally regulated, as was the case under the MMAR, MMPR, and ACMPR prior to the Act. Some medical sale licenses do not authorize possession of cannabis products and have reduced physical security requirements.[62]

Medical sale license holders sell cannabis products to clients. An individual is a patient of their physician or other health care practitioner, who may write a medical document for their patient. The patient may register the medical document with a medical sale license holder, becoming a client of the medical sale license holder to purchase cannabis products from the medical sale license holder.[63] Alternatively, the patient may register their

---

56. *Id.* § 244. This does not apply to cannabis products that are cannabis plants or cannabis plant seeds.

57. CR, *supra* note 10, at §§ 21(1), (2). Equivalency of dried cannabis to a variety of other forms of cannabis are provided in Schedule 3 to the Act, *supra* note 1.

58. CR, *supra* note 10, at § 21(3).

59. *Id.* ¶ 17(2)(b)(i).

60. *Id.* § 22. In addition to analytical testing license holders, the CR allow individuals to be authorized to test cannabis for the government of Canada or a provincial government operating in a laboratory. *Id.* § 4.

61. *Id.* § 23(3).

62. *Id.* §§ 26, 27. For medical sales licenses lacking possession authorization, fulfillment is through a cultivation license as described in relation to cultivation licenses, *supra* at note 47, and in relation to processing licenses, *supra* note 53.

63. *Id.* §§ 278–293.

medical document with Health Canada and receive a registration certificate from Health Canada allowing cultivation beyond the four plants ordinarily allowed to adults.[64]

A medical document is not a prescription. Cannabis has no established medical use and is not prescribed in the manner that drugs regulated under the Food and Drugs Act[65] and the Food and Drug Regulations (the FDR)[66] are prescribed. Drugs containing cannabis may be prescribed,[67] but cannabis products, even when accessed for medical purposes, are not prescribed. Rather, a medical document is "provided by a health care practitioner to support the use of cannabis for medical purposes."[68] Upon a client providing a medical document or a registration certificate to a medical sale license holder, the medical sale license holder issues a registration document to the client.[69] A registration document is a document that evidences the client's authorization to possess more than 30 g of dried cannabis or equivalent in public.

2.1.5 Research License
A research license authorizes possession, production, and transport of cannabis between sites that are set out in the research license.[70] A research license holder may also authorize sale of cannabis plants and cannabis plant seeds to a cultivation license holder or research license holder,[71] allowing breeding of new cannabis plant varieties for commercial production. However, a research license holder cannot onboard new varieties of cannabis plants from unregulated channels, as can cultivation license holders.[72]

Specific authorizations of research licenses are determined by Health Canada. Research licenses may be issued on an ongoing basis for a broad and general research program or on a project-specific basis. Palatability testing for product development may be authorized, but any evaluation of the effects of the cannabis must be completed pursuant to a clinical trial using cannabis prepared in accordance with standards outlined in the application for the research license.

---

64. *Id.* §§ 306–329.
65. Food and Drugs Act, R.S.C., 1985, c F-27 (Can.). The Food and Drugs Act is commonly abbreviated to FDA, but we have not used this acronym as it is confusing with the acronym commonly used for the U.S. Food and Drug Administration.
66. Food and Drug Regulations, C.R.C. c 870 (Can.).
67. Drugs containing cannabis and combination products are respectively regulated under Parts 8 and 9 of the CR, *supra* note 10, and also under the FDR, *supra* note 66.
68. CR, *supra* note 10, at § 264(1).
69. *Id.* § 282(2).
70. *Id.* ¶ 28(1)(a).
71. *Id.* ¶ 28(1)(b).
72. *Id.* § 10 (which authorization is not available to research license holders).

2.2 Licenses Issued under the Industrial Hemp Regulations

A hemp license may authorize cultivation of industrial hemp, sale of industrial hemp, import or export of seed or grain, and possession of grain for the purpose of processing the grain. A hemp license issued to a plant breeder may also allow propagation of industrial hemp, possession of seed or grain for the purposes of cleaning the seed or grain, and to obtain seed by preparing the seed.[73] No security clearances are required for officers or directors of a hemp license holder.

Cultivation is for commercial production of seed, grain, fiber, and "flowering tops, leaves and branches of industrial hemp" (hemp biomass). Seed is for sale to other holders of an IHR license. Grain is generally used as input material for food or natural health products and may also be processed into derivatives, such as cooking oil or natural health products. Fiber is generally used for production of textiles or paper. Hemp biomass is used only for production of cannabis products. A holder of a hemp licence authorizing cultivation may only sow pedigreed seed that is of an approved cultivar[74] identified in the hemp license.[75] The license holder must retain documents that confirm the pedigreed status of all seed sown, including the official tag, in addition to information regarding the quantity of seed of each cultivar sown and other information.[76]

Propagation is to breed new varieties and requires a qualified plant breeder on staff.[77] In addition to compliance with the Act and the 2018 IHR, a holder of a hemp licence authorizing propagation must also maintain compliance with the Seed Act[78] and the Seeds Regulations.[79]

Processing under a hemp license is restricted to processing grain and fiber. Hemp biomass may not be processed under a hemp license other than harvesting and drying for storage. A holder of a hemp license that authorizes sale of industrial hemp may sell seed, grain, or fiber to the holder of a hemp license. Hemp biomass may be sold to a processing license holder

---

73. 2018 IHR, *supra* note 12, at § 3(1); *see also* § 1(1). "Grain" means achene of industrial hemp that is not represented, sold, or used to grow a plant, and "seed" means achene of industrial hemp that is represented, sold, or used to grow a plant.

74. *Id.* 26(1); as in § 1(1). "Approved cultivar" means any variety of industrial hemp set out in the *List of Approved Cultivars*, published by the government of Canada on its website, as amended from time to time.

75. 2018 IHR, *supra* note 12, at § 33(5). "List of Approved Cultivars for the 2020 Growing Season: Industrial Hemp Varieties Approved for Commercial Production," Government of Canada, https://www.canada.ca/en/health-canada/services/drugs-medication/cannabis/producing-selling-hemp/commercial-licence/list-approved-cultivars-cannabis-sativa.html.

76. *Id.* §§ 33(5), 27(1). Documentation and retention requirements are set out in the 2018 IHR. *E.g., id.* § 33(1).

77. *Id.* § 3(1).

78. Seeds Act, R.S.C. 1985, c S-8 (Can.).

79. Seeds Regulations, C.R.C. c 1400 (Can.).

for extraction or other processing into cannabis products.[80] Sale of hemp biomass must be tracked in the CTLS by the processing license holder. Sale of grain, seed, or fiber is not tracked in the CTLS. Import and export of industrial hemp is summarized in Section 2.5 of this chapter.

2.3 National Cannabis Tracking and Licensing System

The Act provides power to Health Canada to establish a national cannabis tracking system for tracking cannabis, to prevent regulated cannabis from being diverted to an illicit market and illicit cannabis from being diverted into the regulated market, and to require reporting.[81] The CTLS is a single online platform that was created and put into effect pursuant to this power.

The Cannabis Tracking System Order (the CTLS Order)[82] requires holders of cultivation licenses, processing licenses, and medical sale licenses to report data of inventory, sale, distribution, packaging, labeling, return, destruction, loss, theft, and other points through the CTLS on a monthly basis, and for cultivation license holders, confirmation of the square footage under production.[83] The CTLS Order also requires cannabis control authorities to report inventory, sale, distribution, return, destruction, loss, theft, and other data related to cannabis products.[84] The CTLS Order requires retailers to report similar data to cannabis control authorities, who in turn will report to Health Canada as required by section 4 of the CTLS Order.[85]

In addition to tracking, the CTLS online portal is also the single point of entry through which entities apply for licenses under the CR and the 2018 IHR, and through which individuals apply for security clearances. Only the responsible person named in an application or license may access a license holder or applicant's CTLS account and correspond with Health Canada as a representative of the license holder or applicant. Each individual who requires a security clearance applies through the CTLS and may correspond with Health Canada about their security clearance application, but not about the application more broadly.

2.4 Promotional Activity

Sale of cannabis and cannabis accessories is inherently linked to promotion of cannabis and cannabis accessories. The Act and the CR include prohibitions on content, and both requirements and prohibitions on venue for promotional activity relating to cannabis, cannabis accessories, and services related to cannabis. "Services related to cannabis" are not defined in the

---

80. 2018 IHR, *supra* note 12, at § 28.
81. Act, *supra* note 1, at §§ 81–82.
82. Cannabis Tracking System Order, SOR/2019-202 (Can.).
83. *Id.* §§ 2, 3.
84. *Id.* § 4.
85. *Id.* § 5.

Act or the CR. Health Canada has published a guideline on the quantum of penalties for noncompliance with the Act, which also apply to noncompliant promotional activity.[86] The Act and the CR require retention of records relating to promotional activity for two years, which may be audited and assessed for compliance by Health Canada at any time.[87]

2.4.1 Blanket Prohibition and Specific Prohibitions on Content

In service of the purpose of protecting young people,[88] the Act includes a blanket prohibition on promoting cannabis, cannabis accessories, and services related to cannabis, with specific prohibitions on content. With respect to content, it is prohibited to promote (1) by communicating information about price or distribution; (2) in a manner that there are reasonable grounds to believe could be appealing to young persons; (3) by means of a testimonial or endorsement, however displayed or communicated; (4) by means of the depiction of a person, character, or animal, whether real or fictional; or (5) by presenting it or any of its brand elements in a manner that associates it or the brand element with, or evokes a positive or negative emotion about or image of, a way of life such as one that includes glamour, recreation, excitement, vitality, risk, or daring.[89]

The Act prohibits promoting in a manner that is false, misleading, or deceptive, or that is likely to create an erroneous impression about its characteristics, value, quantity, composition, strength, concentration, potency, purity, quality, merit, safety, health effects, or health risks.[90] The CR prohibit representations related to health or cosmetic benefits, regardless of whether the representations are false, misleading, deceptive, or likely to create an erroneous impression.[91] The CR prohibit association with alcoholic beverages, tobacco products, or vaping products.[92]

Cannabis extracts cannot be promoted as having flavors that are also prohibited for promotion in the Tobacco and Vaping Products Act (the TVPA):[93] confectionary, dessert, soft drink, or energy drink. That said, the cannabis extract may have these flavors, subject to a requirement in the Act

---

86. "Administrative monetary penalties under the Cannabis Act," GOVERNMENT OF CANADA (Sept. 23, 2019), https://www.canada.ca/en/health-canada/services/cannabis -regulations-licensed-producers/administrative-monetary-penalties.html.

87. Act, *supra* note 1, at § 43; CR, *supra* note 10, at § 245.

88. Act, *supra* note 1, at § 7(b).

89. *Id.* § 17(1).

90. *Id.* § 18. These prohibitions are similar to those applied to therapeutic products in the Food and Drugs Act, *supra* note 65.

91. CR, *supra* note 10, at § 104.12.

92. *Id.* §§ 104.15, 104.16. "Vaping products" are defined in the TVPA and do not include cannabis products.

93. *Id.* § 104.11, referencing Tobacco and Vaping Products Act, S.C. 1997, c. 13 (Can.) at Schedule 3; *see also* TVPA, S.C. 1997, c. 13 (Can.) at §§ 30.48, 30.49. Schedule 3 also includes the flavor "cannabis," which is a prohibited flavor to promote vaping products,

that no cannabis may be sold if it has a sensory attribute that there are reasonable grounds to believe could be appealing to young persons.[94]

Edible cannabis cannot be promoted by communicating information about the energy value of the edible cannabis, other than reproducing the mandatory nutrition facts table on the label.[95] Edible cannabis cannot be promoted as giving the impression that the cannabis product meets particular dietary requirements (e.g. diabetes, celiac disease, etc.) or dietary requirements of young people.[96]

2.4.2 Exceptions to Blanket Prohibition, and Requirements and Prohibitions on Venue

In service of providing for licit product, providing access to a quality-controlled source of cannabis, and enhancing public awareness of the health risks associated with cannabis use,[97] the Act includes exceptions to the blanket prohibition on promotional activity for informational promotions and brand-preference promotions, provided certain boundaries are respected through requirements on venue. Informational and brand preference promotions are each directed to adults who have already decided to purchase cannabis to help them make informed choices, in contrast with promotional activity that is directed to causing an individual to decide to purchase cannabis.

Exceptions to the blanket prohibition include promotion that is (1) in a communication that is addressed and sent to an individual who is 18 years of age or older and is identified by name, (2) in a place where young persons are not permitted by law, and (3) communicated by means of a telecommunication (e.g., social media, website, e-mail, etc.), where the person responsible for the content of the promotion has taken reasonable steps to ensure that the promotion cannot be accessed by a young person.[98] Promotion of cannabis under subsection 17(2) of the Act is restricted to persons that are authorized to produce, sell, or distribute cannabis, but promotion of cannabis accessories or services related to cannabis under subsection 17(3) is not similarly restricted.

The content prohibitions must be respected within the permissible venues, subject to an exception allowing signs at the point of sale that inform customers of prices.[99] The Act also prohibits certain venues for promotional activity. Display of a brand element in the sponsorship of a person, entity,

---

but the CR excludes "cannabis" from the prohibition applicable to cannabis extracts. CR, *supra* note 10, at § 104.11.

94. Act, *supra* note 1, at § 31.

95. CR, *supra* note 10, at § 104.13.

96. *Id.* § 104.14.

97. Act, *supra* note 1, at § 7.

98. *Id.* §§ 17(2) (cannabis), 17(3) (cannabis accessories).

99. *Id.* §§ 17(4) (cannabis), 17(5) (cannabis accessories).

event, activity, or facility,[100] and use of a brand element in the name of a sports or cultural event facility,[101] are each prohibited. Promotions must not be visible or audible from outside a venue.[102]

Promotion by displaying a brand element on a thing that is neither cannabis nor a cannabis accessory (a promotional item) is permitted. Display of brand elements on promotional items remains prohibited if the promotional item is associated with young persons, if there are reasonable grounds to believe that the promotional item could be appealing to young persons, or if the promotional item is associated with a way of life, such as one that includes glamour, recreation, vitality, excitement, vitality, risk, or daring.[103] A promotional item may include only one brand element, and the brand element must be displayed only once.[104] The brand element must be smaller than or equal to 300 cm^2 (~46.5 square inches) and no letter, character, or number may be taller than 4 cm (~1.5 inches).[105]

2.4.3 Prohibition on Inducements

Inducements of cannabis or a cannabis accessory without monetary consideration or in consideration of the purchase of any thing or service are prohibited.[106] Similarly, it is prohibited to provide or offer to provide any thing that is not cannabis or a cannabis accessory, including a right to participate in a game, draw, lottery, or contest, if it is provided or offered to be provided as an inducement for the purchase of cannabis or a cannabis accessory.[107] All license holders under the CR, or any business that sells cannabis or cannabis accessories, must report information related to any inducements through the CTLS.[108]

A combined effect of the two prohibitions is that any "two for one" or other volume discount on cannabis products or cannabis accessories, or any other benefit that can be accessed only by purchasing cannabis products or cannabis accessories, is prohibited. Similarly, these restrictions would prevent, for example, a lighter or a package of matches to be given away with a purchase of a cannabis product. These restrictions are consistent with discouraging commercial practices that incentivize individuals to purchase more cannabis than they otherwise would have.

---

100. *Id.* § 21.
101. *Id.* § 22.
102. CR, *supra* note 10, at § 104.17.
103. Act, *supra* note 1, at § 17(6).
104. CR, *supra* note 10, at § 104.18.
105. *Id.* § 104.2.
106. Act, *supra* note 1, at ¶ 24(1)(a).
107. *Id.* ¶ 24(1)(b), (c).
108. *Id.* § 43(3).

2.5 Import and Export

The Act, the CR, and the 2018 IHR together authorize import and export of cannabis only for medical or scientific purposes, or in respect of industrial hemp.[109] Restriction of import and export of cannabis to medical and scientific purposes, and to industrial hemp, is in compliance with the United Nations (UN) drug control conventions, to which Canada is a party.[110]

The CR authorize a holder of a license issued under the CR to import or export cannabis for medical or scientific purposes. An import permit or an export permit is required for each shipment of cannabis.[111] An application for a permit may be refused for a number of reasons, some of which involve discretion of Health Canada.[112] Information relevant to an import or export event must be maintained for at least two years after the information was provided.[113]

The 2018 IHR authorize a holder of a hemp license to import or export seed or grain.[114] Although a hemp license allows sale of hemp biomass to other hemp license holders or a holder of a license issued under the CR,[115] only seed and grain may be imported or exported under a hemp license. Derivatives of industrial hemp can be imported or exported without a license or permit, provided that the shipment is accompanied by a certificate of analysis stating that the product contains a concentration of 10 micrograms of THC or less.[116] A "derivative" is a product made by processing only the grain of industrial hemp and includes no CBD or other phytocannabinoids.[117]

The 2018 IHR require an import permit or export permit for each shipment of industrial hemp.[118] Information relevant to an import or export event must be maintained for at least one year after the information was recorded.[119] An importer of seed must only import seed of pedigreed status

---

109. *Id.* § 62(2); CR, *supra* note 10, at Part 10 (§§ 203–220); 2018 IHR, *supra* note 12, at §§ 8–24.
110. Single Convention on Narcotic Drugs of 1961 as amended by the 1972 Protocol, Mar. 30, 1961, 967 U.N.T.S. 14152 (entered into force 13 December 1964); Convention on Psychotropic Substances, Feb. 21, 1971, 32 U.S.T. 543, 1019 U.N.T.S. 14956 (entered into force Aug. 8, 1975); United Nations Convention Against Illicit Traffic in Narcotic Drugs and Psychotropic Substances, Dec. 20, 1988, 28 I.L.M. 493, 1582 U.N.T.S. 27627 (entered into force Nov. 11, 1990).
111. CR, *supra* note 10, at §§ 204(1) (import permit), 213(1) (export permit).
112. Act, *supra* note 1, at ¶¶ 62(7)(a), (g); CR, *supra* note 10, at § 206(b) (import), ¶¶ 215(b)(i), (ii) (export).
113. *Id.* §§ 239 (import), 240 (export).
114. 2018 IHR, *supra* note 12, at ¶ 3(1)(b).
115. *Id.* § 28.
116. *Id.* § 2(1).
117. *Id.* § 2(3).
118. *Id.* §§ 8 (import permits), 12 (export permits).
119. 2018 IHR, *supra* note 12, at § 33.

that is of an approved cultivar and is recognized under the Organisation for Economic Co-operation and Development Seed Schemes (OESS) or by the Association of Official Seed Certifying Agencies (AOSA).[120] An importer of grain must only import grain from a country that participates in the OESS or a country that has an agency that is a member of the AOSA. A plant breeder may also import seed of a variety of industrial hemp that is set out in their license, which may include varieties that are not approved cultivars.[121] In the case of seed, documents must also be provided establishing that the seed is of pedigreed status and of an approved cultivar, unless the importer is a plant breeder, in which case the breed must be set out in the plant breeder's license.[122]

In respect of cannabis plant seeds, including for approved cultivars of industrial hemp, import for commercial production must comply with the Seeds Act and the Seeds Regulations to verify that imported seeds are free of noxious weeds and meet standards for purity and germination.[123]

3. Provincially Regulated Activity

The Act allows for provincial or territorial regulation of sale,[124] provided that provincial legislation authorizes sale only of regulated cannabis products, prohibits sale to young people, requires record keeping, and includes anti-diversion measures.[125] All ten provinces and all three territories of Canada have regulated adult-use cannabis sale under provincial or territorial legislation.

In addition to regulating commercial activity, provincial and territorial governments restrict where cannabis can be used. Some provinces allow use in public ,whereas others do not, and within provinces allowing use in public, some municipalities have banned use in public. Some municipalities have also banned retailers from operating. Similarly, provincial restrictions on use in stationary vehicles, use in vehicles by passengers, and other points vary, and in some cases vary between cannabis intended for ingestion and cannabis intended for inhalation. The territory of Nunavut, which has a total population of less than 40,000 individuals, has legislation allowing onsite consumption businesses, but to the author's knowledge, no such businesses have opened as of this writing.

Cannabis products can be sold by processing license holders (and in the case of cannabis plants and cannabis plant seeds, also cultivation license holders) to liquor authorities, or in Saskatchewan and Manitoba, directly

---

120. *Id.* § 16(a).
121. *Id.* § 16(b).
122. *Id.* § 20(d).
123. Seeds Regulations, *supra* note 79, at §§ 40(1), 40(3).
124. Act, *supra* note 1, at § 69(1).
125. *Id.* § 69(3).

to retailers, for adult-use sale. Once cannabis products are sold to a liquor authority or a retailer, the cannabis products are under provincial regulation and must be sold in compliance with applicable provincial laws. A summary of all applicable provincial laws is beyond the scope of this summary. That said, there are common trends.

Adult-use consumers may purchase cannabis products online directly from liquor authorities in all provinces and jurisdictions other than Manitoba, Saskatchewan, and the Northwest Territories. In Manitoba, Saskatchewan, and the Northwest Territories, individual consumers may purchase cannabis products online directly from retailers.

Adult-use consumers may also purchase cannabis products from retail storefronts operated by retailers. In British Columbia, retailers are both privately and publicly operated. In Alberta, Saskatchewan, Manitoba, Ontario, Newfoundland, Nunavut, and the Northwest Territories, retailers are privately operated. In Québec, Nova Scotia, New Brunswick, Prince Edward Island, and the Yukon, retailers are publicly operated, with New Brunswick currently privatizing its cannabis stores.

The Act prohibits adults from possessing more than 30 g of dried cannabis or equivalent in a public place.[126] Applicable provincial and territorial laws universally prohibit sale of more than 30 g of dried cannabis or equivalent in a single transaction. Young persons are not allowed inside retailer locations. Retailers are only allowed to sell cannabis and cannabis accessories—food products, magazines, or other items that are not cannabis or cannabis accessories cannot be sold.

Closely connected with adult-use sale is promotional activity. Some provinces and territories have passed legislation restricting and limiting promotional activity related to cannabis, in some cases requiring registration of individuals who represent processing license holders. The provinces and territories have different approaches to preventing associations between processing license holders and retailers, similar to preventing establishment of tied houses in the liquor industry.

The Act permits regulation of sale at the provincial level. The Act is silent on whether such sale is for medical or adult-use markets. To date, no provincial legislation relating to medical sale has been put into effect, whether in relation to pharmacy sales or otherwise. The CR contemplate sale of cannabis through pharmacies by regulating certain aspects of pharmacy-based sale at the federal level.[127] Such sale would have to be authorized by provincial legislation and would have to be consistent with professional codes of ethics applicable to pharmacists.

---

126. *Id.* ¶ 8(1)(a).
127. CR, *supra* note 10, at §§ 337–345.

4. Cannabis Products

A "cannabis product" is defined as

> cannabis of only one of the classes that are set out in Schedule 4 to the Act—or a cannabis accessory if that accessory contains such cannabis—after it has been packaged and labelled for sale to a consumer at the retail level, but does not include a drug containing cannabis.[128]

When the Act came into effect on October 17, 2018, five classes of cannabis were listed in Schedule 4 to the Act for sale as cannabis products: dried cannabis, cannabis oil, fresh cannabis, cannabis plants, and cannabis plant seeds. On October 17, 2019, amendments to the Act[129] expanded classes of saleable cannabis to include edible cannabis, cannabis extracts, and cannabis topicals.[130] The Amending Order deletes cannabis oil from Schedule 4 to the Act effective October 17, 2020.[131] The Product Diversification Regulations allow manufacturing and sale of cannabis oil products that were approved for sale prior to October 17, 2019, to continue for one year.[132]

Each class of cannabis is defined by limitation or exclusion in terms of ingredients, amount of cannabis or THC per dosage form and per immediate container, and other details.[133] There are no limitations on CBD concentrations or amounts per dosage or per container in any class of cannabis. Cannabis products must be packaged and labeled in accordance with the CR.[134] Discrete units in an edible cannabis, cannabis extract, or cannabis topical product may vary only by flavor and color, but not size or other properties.[135] Cannabis products in these classes of cannabis must not contain less than 85 percent or more than 115 percent of the THC or CBD shown on the label.[136]

The term "cannabis product" is absent from the Act. The Act prohibits sale of cannabis including any substance listed in Schedule 5 of the Act (currently nicotine, caffeine, and ethyl alcohol).[137] Beyond these broad prohibitions, details relating to cannabis products are provided in the CR. Regardless of the class of cannabis, all cannabis products are regulated

---

128. *Id.* § 1(2).

129. Regulations Amending the Cannabis Regulations (New Classes of Cannabis), SOR/2019-206 (Can.) (the "Product Diversification Regulations"); Order Amending Schedules 3 and 4 to the Cannabis Act, SOR/2019-207 (Can.) (the "Amending Order").

130. Amending Order, *id.* § 5.

131. *Id.* § 6(2).

132. Product Diversification Regulations, *supra* note 129, at § 73.

133. CR, *supra* note 10, at Part 6 (§§ 92.1–104).

134. *Id.* at Part 7 (§§ 105–138).

135. *Id.* § 98.1.

136. *Id.* § 97(1). Edible cannabis products may vary by more than 15 percent where the amounts of phytocannabinoids per package are below 5 mg.

137. Act, *supra* note 1, at §§ 34, 151; *id.* at Schedule 5.

entirely under the CR. Neither the Food and Drugs Act nor the FDR apply to cannabis products, but the content of the Food and Drugs Act and the FDR are referenced in the Act and the CR.

The CR do not focus on cannabis accessories. It is possible that regulations specific to cannabis accessories will be issued in the future. Treatment of cannabis accessories in the CR is primarily through cannabis accessories that are part of a cannabis product. In this context, cannabis accessories most commonly include a rolling paper or wrap, concentrate cartridge or pod, concentrate pen (i.e. integral reservoir, heating element, and battery), spray bottle, beverage container, or other dispensing device from which cannabis is directly consumed.

4.1 Good Production Practices

In Canada, drugs are regulated by the FDR, and natural health products (NHPs) are regulated by the Natural Health Products Regulations[138] (the NHPR). The FDR and the NHPR require that good manufacturing practices (GMP) standards be met for drugs and NHPs marketed and sold in Canada.[139] In contrast, the CR do not require GMP standards to be met for cannabis products.

The CR require cannabis and cannabis products to be cultivated and manufactured in compliance with Good Production Practices (GPP) defined in Part 5 of the CR.[140] Commercial sale, distribution, or export of cannabis cultivated or manufactured outside of compliance with GPP is prohibited[141] and a QAP must not release cannabis products for sale without compliance with GPP.[142] Unlike GMP requirements for drug products and natural health products, GPP include no requirements for batch-to-batch consistency of amount of THC and CBD in cannabis products.

Cannabis plants must be cultivated and cannabis products manufactured in accordance with SOPs designed to ensure that GPP requirements are met.[143] Any pest control product (PCP" with which cannabis is treated must be registered for use on cannabis under the Pest Control Products Act (the PCP Act),[144] subject to exceptions for a PCP used during cooking or processing of food used in edible cannabis.[145]

---

138. Natural Health Products Regulations, SOR/2003-196 (Can.).

139. FDR, *supra* note 66, at §§ C.02.003, C.02.003.1, C.02.003.3; NHPR, *supra* note 138, at § 43.

140. CR, *supra* note 10, at Part 5 (§§ 78.1–92).

141. *Id.* § 79.

142. *Id.* ¶ 19(2)(a), § 79.

143. *Id.* § 80.

144. Pest Control Products Act, S.C. 2002, c. 28 (Can.).

145. *Id.* § 81; Pest Control Products Regulations, SOR/2006-124 at ¶ 3(1)(b)(ii) (Can.). The Pest Control Products Regulations define PCP at § 2(1) as including ". . . a product, an organism or a substance, including a product, an organism or a substance derived through biotechnology, that consists of its active ingredient, formulants and

Testing must be undertaken by all license holders in order to sell or export a cannabis product. All testing must be undertaken using established methods, and a sample from each test that is of a sufficient quantity to repeat all tests that have been applied must be maintained for at least a year.[146]

Percentages of THC, CBD, Δ9-tetrahydrocannabinolic acid (THCA), and cannabidiolic acid (CBDA) must be confirmed. Phytocannabinoid percentage testing may be carried out on the final form of the cannabis, including, where applicable, any cannabis accessory (e.g., a cartridge for cannabis extract intended for inhalation, a rolling paper for dried cannabis, etc.).[147] Chemical and microbial contaminant testing must also be undertaken. For cannabis other than edible cannabis, testing is carried out on the final form of the cannabis, including any cannabis accessory, either before or after packaging and labeling. For edible cannabis, the testing must be conducted on the final step in the production process in which a contaminant could be introduced into the edible cannabis product.[148] The tolerance limits for contaminant testing must be determined with respect to pharmacopeias or other reference documents recognized in the Food and Drugs Act.[149]

Testing for phytocannabinoid concentrations and contaminants other than PCP residue, and dissolution or disintegration testing, may be completed by the processing license holder or an affiliated company.[150] Testing for PCP residues is not specifically required in the CR. That said, the Act allows any conditions to be placed on a license as Health Canada sees fit.[151] All licenses issue with mandatory requirements for PCP testing as a condition. A Health Canada policy document requires that all PCP testing be based on a test by a third-party laboratory.[152]

---

contaminants, and that is manufactured, represented, distributed or used as a means for directly or indirectly controlling, destroying, attracting or repelling a pest or for mitigating or preventing its injurious, noxious or troublesome effects."

146. PCP Act, *supra* note 144, at § 92.

147. *Id.* § 90.

148. *Id.* §§ 91(1), (2).

149. *Id.* §§ 91(3), 93(3), 94(2).

150. "Good Production Practices Guide for Cannabis: Requirements under Part 5 of the Cannabis Regulations," at § 5.3.1.4 (Aug. 29, 2019, Health Canada), https://www.canada.ca/en/health-canada/services/cannabis-regulations-licensed-producers/good-production-practices-guide.html.

151. Act, *supra* note 1, at § 62(1).

152. "Mandatory Cannabis Testing for Pesticide Active Ingredients: Requirements," § 5.2.1 (Aug. 30, 2019, Health Canada), https://www.canada.ca/en/public-health/services/publications/drugs-health-products/cannabis-testing-pesticide-requirements.html.

4.2 Classes of Cannabis
4.2.1 Dried Cannabis and Fresh Cannabis
Dried cannabis is defined by the Act as "any part of a cannabis plant that has been subjected to a drying process, other than seeds."[153] Dried cannabis can be sold as intact flower, milled cannabis, pre-rolled cannabis, cannabis loaded into pods, or other forms. Unlike other classes of cannabis, there are no limits on the THC concentration of dried cannabis. However, dried cannabis intended for consumption by inhalation cannot be provided in a discrete unit (e.g., a rolling paper used for a pre-roll, etc.) with more than 1 g of dried cannabis.[154]

Dried cannabis products cannot include ingredients other than dried cannabis. Dried cannabis products may include microbial and chemical contaminants subject to limits established in the Food and Drugs Act and residues of a PCP subject to limits established under the PCP Act.[155] Neither THC nor THCA may be added to dried cannabis used in a cannabis product.[156]

The preceding restrictions and labeling rules also apply to fresh cannabis. Fresh cannabis is defined in the CR as "freshly harvested cannabis buds and leaves, but does not include plant material that can be used to propagate cannabis."[157] Five grams of fresh cannabis is considered equivalent to 1 g of dried cannabis.[158] As of this writing, the author is unaware of any cannabis products in the fresh cannabis class of cannabis having been made commercially available in Canada.

4.2.2 Cannabis Plants and Seeds
Cannabis plants are defined in the Act as "a plant that belongs to the genus *Cannabis*."[159] Possession of cannabis plants in a public place is limited to four cannabis plants.[160] An immediate container of a cannabis plant product must not include more than four cannabis plants, and the cannabis plants must not be budding or flowering.[161] Cannabis plant seeds are not defined in the Act, but have an equivalency factor of one seed being equivalent to 1 g of dried cannabis.[162] Cannabis plants and cannabis plant seeds sold as cannabis products may include a PCP registered for use on cannabis

---

153. Act, *supra* note 1, at § 2(1).
154. CR, *supra* note 10, at § 100.
155. *Id.* § 93.
156. *Id.* § 99.
157. *Id.* § 1(1).
158. Act, *supra* note 1, at Schedule 3.
159. *Id.* § 1(1).
160. *Id.* ¶¶ 8(1)(d), (e).
161. CR, *supra* note 10, at § 109.
162. Act, *supra* note 1, at Schedule 3.

within the maximum residue limits specified in relation to cannabis by the PCP Act.[163]

4.2.3 Edible Cannabis

Edible cannabis includes beverages and is defined in the CR as

> a substance or mixture of substances that contains or has on it anything referred to in item 1 or 3 of Schedule 1 to the Act and that is intended to be consumed in the same manner as food. It does not include dried cannabis, fresh cannabis, cannabis plants or cannabis plant seeds.[164]

Edible cannabis has an equivalency factor of 15 g solids or 70 g non-solids being equivalent to 1 g of dried cannabis.[165]

Ingredients included in edible cannabis products may only include food and food additives. Additional restrictions apply to meat, poultry, fish, food produced by the processing license holder, food additives, and vitamins.[166] Caffeine may be present in amounts of up to 30 mg per immediate container only if the caffeine is introduced through ingredients that naturally include caffeine.[167] Ethyl alcohol may be present in concentrations of up to 0.5 percent.[168] Edible cannabis products that must be stored below 4°C (39°F) when unopened are prohibited.[169]

A significant point of departure from the trend in U.S. state markets is the extremely conservative per-package limit on THC for edible cannabis products of 10 mg.[170] No activities with food regulated under the Food and Drugs Act (i.e., food without cannabis) can be undertaken in the same building as activities with cannabis.[171]

4.2.4 Cannabis Extracts and Cannabis Oil

The CR defines cannabis extract as "(a) a substance produced by (i) subjecting anything referred to in item 1 of Schedule 1 to the Act to extraction processing, or (ii) synthesizing a substance that is identical to a phytocannabinoid produced by, or found in, a cannabis plant; or (b) a substance or mixture of substances that contains or has on it a substance produced in a manner referred to in paragraph (a)" and cannabis concentrate as "a substance that has a concentration of greater than 3% w/w of THC,

---

163. CR, *supra* note 10, at § 92.2.
164. *Id.* § 1(1).
165. Act, *supra* note 1, at Schedule 3.
166. CR, *supra* note 10, at § 102.
167. *Id.* § 102.2.
168. *Id.* § 102.3.
169. *Id.* § 102.4.
170. *Id.* § 102.7.
171. *Id.* §§ 88.3(2), (3).

taking into account the potential to convert THCA into THC."[172] Cannabis extracts have an equivalency factor of 15 g solids or 70 g non-solids being equivalent to 1 g of dried cannabis, or of 0.25 g of cannabis concentrates being equivalent to 1 g of dried cannabis.[173] The immediate container of a cannabis extracts that is in a non-solid form at a temperature of 22 ±2°C must contain no more than 90 mL of cannabis extract.[174]

Cannabis extract products include cannabis products intended for use by inhalation or by ingestion.[175] In either case, the only ingredients that may be included are carrier substances, flavoring agents, and substances that are necessary to maintain the quality or stability of the cannabis product.[176] The phytocannabinoids and terpenoids must be uniformly distributed in the cannabis extract.[177] The immediate container of a cannabis extract must not permit the extract to be easily poured or drunk directly from the container, and it must include an integrated dispensing mechanism that dispenses no more than 10 mg THC per activation, unless the cannabis product includes a cannabis accessory that dispenses the cannabis extract.[178]

Substances prohibited in vaping products by the TVPA are specifically prohibited in all cannabis extracts. Sugars, sweeteners, or sweetening agents as defined in the FDR are also prohibited in all cannabis extracts. The TVPA prohibits use of vitamins in vaping products, but a vitamin may be used in cannabis extracts to the extent that the vitamin is necessary to maintain the quality or stability of the cannabis product.[179]

Cannabis extracts intended for inhalation may include ingredients necessary to maintain quality or stability where a standard for the ingredient has been defined in the Food and Drugs Act. Cannabis extracts intended for ingestion may include ethyl alcohol, provided that the total weight of the cannabis extract in each immediate container of the cannabis product does not exceed 7.5 g.[180] A container of cannabis extract intended for ingestion, such as cannabis concentrates in a tablet or capsule, may have up to 10 mg THC per dosage unit and up to 1,000 mg THC per container.[181]

Cannabis oil is defined in the CR as "an oil that contains anything referred to in item 1 or 3 of Schedule 1 to the Act and that is in liquid form at a temperature of 22 ± 2°C."[182] As described earlier, cannabis oil is a legacy

---

172. *Id.* § 1(1).

173. Act, *supra* note 1, at Schedule 3.

174. CR, *supra* note 10, at § 122.3.

175. *Id.* § 1(2) ("ingestion" includes absorption in the mouth; no definition is provided for inhalation).

176. *Id.* § 101.3(1).

177. *Id.* § 101.4.

178. *Id.* § 122.5.

179. *Id.* §§ 101.3(2), (3).

180. *Id.* §§ 101.3(5), (6).

181. *Id.* §§ 96(1), 101.2.

182. *Id.* § 1(1).

class of cannabis that will soon no longer be sold. Cannabis oil is limited to 30 mg/mL THC.[183] Cannabis oil may be provided in capsules or other dosage forms, provided that each dosage form includes no more than 10 mg of THC.[184]

In comparison to cannabis oil, cannabis extracts intended for ingestion may have concentrations over 30 mg/mL, but since 30 mg/mL is 3.0 percent, such cannabis extracts would meet the definition of "cannabis concentrate" and would be limited to 7.5 g of cannabis in each immediate container.

4.2.5 Cannabis Topicals

Cannabis topicals are defined in the CR as

> a substance or mixture of substances that contains or has on it anything referred to in item 1 or 3 of Schedule 1 to the Act and that is intended for use, directly or indirectly, exclusively on external body surfaces, including hair and nails.[185]

Although cannabis concentrates are most commonly associated with cannabis extracts, particularly cannabis extracts intended for inhalation, it is possible for a cannabis topical to exceed 3.0 percent THC and also fall within the restrictions on container size applicable to a cannabis concentrate. Cannabis topicals have an equivalency factor of 15 g of solids or 70 g of non-solids being equivalent to 1 g of dried cannabis, or of 0.25 g of cannabis concentrates being equivalent to 1 g of dried cannabis for cannabis topicals that exceed 3.0 percent THC.[186]

Cannabis topicals cannot be sold for use near the eye or for use on broken or damaged skin.[187] Phytocannabinoids and terpenoids must be uniformly distributed in the cannabis extract.[188] A container of cannabis topicals may have up to 10 mg THC per dosage unit and up to 1,000 mg THC per container.[189]

4.3 Packaging and Labeling

The Act restricts labeling and packaging of cannabis products similarly to the restrictions on promotional activity. Specifically, any packaging or labeling is prohibited (1) if there are reasonable grounds to believe the

---

183. *Id.* § 101 (as the CR read prior to October 17, 2019).
184. *Id.* § 96(1) (the CR prior to October 17, 2019, included this provision at § 97).
185. *Id.* § 1(1).
186. Act, *supra* note 1, at Schedule 3.
187. CR, *supra* note 10, at § 98. These restrictions apply regardless of the class of cannabis but most naturally fit within the topical cannabis class of cannabis. Cannabis extracts cannot be represented for use on external body surfaces, including hair and nails. *Id.* § 101.5.
188. *Id.* § 101.4.
189. *Id.* §§ 96(1), 101.2.

packaging or labeling could be appealing to young persons; (2) that sets out a testimonial or endorsement, however displayed or communicated; (3) that sets out a depiction of a person, character, or animal, whether real or fictional; or (4) that associates the cannabis or any of its brand elements with, or evokes a positive or negative emotion about or image of, a way of life such as one that includes glamour, recreation, excitement, vitality, risk, or daring.[190] The Act imposes identical restrictions on packaging and labeling of cannabis accessories,[191] but the CR do not regulate packaging or labeling of cannabis accessories. However, the CR include both additional prohibitions and prescribed requirements on packaging and labeling of cannabis products.[192]

The standardized cannabis symbol[193] is an important feature throughout all packaging and labeling requirements. The standardized cannabis symbol must be displayed on all labels and cannabis accessories intended for inhalation in a cannabis product (e.g., concentrate cartridge, disposable reservoir/heating element/battery, concentrate pod, etc.) where the cannabis product includes more than 10 µg/g of THC.[194] The standardized cannabis symbol must be at least 1.27 cm (0.5 inches) by 1.27 cm (0.5 inches), displayed with a white border of at least 2 points on all sides, and must maintain a consistent aspect ratio.[195] See Figure 14.2.

Figure 14.2

190. Act, *supra* note 1, at § 26.

191. *Id.* § 27.

192. CR, *supra* note 10, at Part 7, with §§ 108–122.5 applying to packaging and §§ 123–136 applying to labeling.

193. *Id.* § 105(1); Health Canada, "Standardized Cannabis Symbol," GOVERNMENT OF CANADA, https://www.canada.ca/en/health-canada/services/drugs-medication/cannabis/laws-regulations/regulations-support-cannabis-act/standardized-symbol.html.

194. CR, *supra* note 10, at ¶ 123(1)(f) and §§ 123.1(2), 132.34(1).

195. *Id.* §§ 123.1(3), 130(5), 132.34(2).

4.3.1 Packaging

An immediate container must be opaque or translucent, prevent contamination of the cannabis, include a tamper-evidence security feature, meet the FDR requirements of a child-resistant package, and must not contain more than 30 g of dried cannabis or equivalent.[196]

The CR include several features that provide a "plain packaging" approach to cannabis products. Subject to authorizations or requirements in the CR indicated in respect of a label, no container may include any brand element or other image.[197] A bar code may be displayed only once on any container, must be rectangular, and must be printed in black and white.[198] The interior and exterior surfaces must each be one uniform color, but each surface may be a different color. Metallic or fluorescent colors, and colors that fail to contrast with the yellow background of the health warning message or with the standardized cannabis symbol are prohibited.[199] The interior and exterior surfaces must have a smooth texture without raised features, embossing, decorative ridges, bulges, or other irregularities, other than to facilitate opening the container or to assist the visually impaired.[200] Hidden features are prohibited unless for prevention of counterfeiting.[201] Where an immediate container is small, it may include a peel-back or accordion panel that includes the label.[202]

4.3.2 Labeling

The CR require labeling on all cannabis products to identify the cultivation license holder or processing license holder that manufactured the cannabis product.[203] The label must also identify the class of cannabis, brand name, lot number, recommended storage conditions, packaging data, a statement that no expiry date has been established or the expiry date, and the warning "KEEP OUT OF REACH OF CHILDREN / TENIR HORS DE LA PORTÉE DES ENFANTS."[204]

All labels must also include one of several health warning messages published by the government of Canada, which must be rotated to maintain equal display of each warning message across all containers for a given

---

196. CR, *supra* note 10, at §§ 108–110.
197. *Id.* §§ 111, 112.
198. *Id.* § 122. It is likely that by "rectangular," the legislature intended to write "rectilinear," and that a square bar code would also be acceptable.
199. *Id.* § 113.
200. *Id.* § 115.
201. CR, *supra* note 10, at § 116.
202. *Id.* § 132.27.
203. *Id.* ¶ 123(1)(a).
204. *Id.* ¶¶ 123(1)(b)–(d).

cannabis product.[205] The label of any cannabis product including more than 10 µg/g of THC must include the standardized cannabis symbol.[206]

The CR require that all information included on a label be in both English and French, other than the International Nomenclature of Cosmetic Ingredient (INCI) name for topical cannabis products. The CR include font size requirements limiting the font size of the brand name, defining a minimum size of the standardized cannabis symbol, defining a minimum font size for the health warning message, defining minimum spacing requirements, requiring a yellow color for the background of the health warning message, requiring black or white text other than the brand name and brand element, and prohibiting metallic or fluorescent colors in the brand name and brand element.[207] Any brand element that may be mistaken for the standardized cannabis symbol is prohibited.[208] Information related to health benefits, cosmetic benefits, energy value or nutrition (other than on the nutrition facts table), dietary requirements (e.g., diabetic, celiac, etc.), association with alcoholic beverages, and association with tobacco and vaping products are all prohibited.[209]

The label on any dried cannabis, fresh cannabis, cannabis extracts, or cannabis topical product must include the net weight in grams of cannabis.[210] All cannabis products other than dried cannabis must include a statement of equivalency to grams of dried cannabis,[211] or the number of cannabis plants or cannabis plant seeds that are in the cannabis product.[212] Where cannabis is divided into discrete units, the label must include the number of units and the weight of each unit.[213] The label must also include the THC and CBD per unit or per gram.[214] Other than dried or fresh cannabis that is not in discrete units (e.g., intact or milled flower, etc.), the intended use of the cannabis product must be indicated.[215] Cannabis extracts or cannabis topicals must include a list of ingredients and the identity of the cannabis product in terms of its common name or function, and in the case of cannabis extracts only, the name of any food allergen that is present in

---

205. *Id.* ¶ 123(1)(e), § 123(4).
206. *Id.* ¶ 123(1)(f).
207. CR, *supra* note 10, at §§ 130(1)–(4).
208. *Id.* § 131.
209. *Id.* §§ 132.28–132.33.
210. *Id.* ¶¶ 124(1)(a), 132.1(1)(a), 132.12(1)(a), and §§ 124.1(a), 125(a), 132.11(a), 132.15(a), 132.16(a).
211. *Id.* ¶ 123(1)(g), with reference to § 2(4) of the Act, *supra* note 1.
212. CR, *supra* note 10, at §§ 128–129.
213. *Id.* ¶¶ 124(1)(b), 124(1)(c), 132.1(1)(b), 132.1(1)(c), and §§ 124.1(b), 124.1(c), 132.11(b), 132.11(c), 132.15(b), 132.15(c).
214. *Id.* ¶¶ 124(1)(d)–(g), 132.1(1)(d)–(g), 132.12(1)(b)–(e), and §§ 124.1(d)–(g), 125(b)–(e), 132.11(d)–(g), 132.15(d)–(g), 132.16(b)–(e).
215. *Id.* ¶¶ 124(1)(h), 132.1(1)(k), 132.12(1)(j), and §§ 124.1(h), 132.11(k), 132.15(j), 132.16(h).

the cannabis extract.[216] No label of a cannabis extract may include brand elements or other features indicating that the cannabis extract may have a flavor set out in Schedule 3 of the TVPA.[217]

Cannabis products that are edible cannabis must include a label with the net weight in grams of solid form edible cannabis and in any other case the net volume in milliliters.[218] Where the cannabis is divided into discrete units, the label must also include the number of units.[219] The label must also include the THC and CBD per unit, and also in the entire edible cannabis product where the edible cannabis product includes discrete units.[220] The label must also include a list of ingredients, the source of any food allergen or gluten, sulphites in excess of 10 ppm, a nutrition facts table, the common name of the cannabis product, and information related to irradiation.[221] Additional rules apply to listing ingredients, nutrition facts, presenting sources of food allergens, and declarations of risk of cross-contamination with food allergens or sulphites.[222]

5. Corporate Finance

The legalization of cannabis in Canada gave rise to a new industry in need of capital. The ability of cannabis businesses to access capital, privately or from the public markets, has been an important factor in their growth. Canadian and international issuers alike have accessed Canada's capital markets and sought listings on one of Canada's stock exchanges. This section reviews the principal Canadian regulatory requirements applicable to corporate finance, and to mergers and acquisitions transactions involving public companies operating in the cannabis industry.[223]

5.1 Distribution of Securities in Canada

Securities regulation in Canada is a provincial and territorial matter (rather than a federal matter) subject to exception in the case of systemic risk.[224] Under the umbrella of the Canadian Securities Administrators (CSA),

---

216. *Id.* ¶¶ 132.1(1)(h)–(j), 132.12(1)(g)–(i), and §§ 132.11(h)–(j), 132.15(h), (i), 132.16(f), (g).

217. CR, *supra* note 10, at § 132.13(1), referencing the TVPA, *supra* note 93, at Schedule 3; *see also* TVPA, *supra* note 93, at §§ 30.48, 30.49. Schedule 3 also includes the flavor "cannabis," which is a prohibited flavor to promote vaping products, but the CR exclude "cannabis" from the prohibition applicable to cannabis extracts. CR, *supra* note 10, at § 132.13(1).

218. CR, *supra* note 10, at ¶¶ 132.18(1)(a), 132.19(1)(a).

219. *Id.* ¶ 132.18(1)(b).

220. *Id.* ¶¶ 132.18(1)(c) (j), 132.19(1)(b)–(e).

221. *Id.* ¶¶ 132.18(1)(k)–(q), 132.19(1)(f)–(l).

222. *Id.* §§ 132.21–132.25.

223. Securities Act, R.S.O. 1990, c. S.5 (Can.).

224. *Reference re Pan-Canadian Securities Regulation* [2018] 3 S.C.R. 189 (Can.).

provincial and territorial securities regulatory authorities have harmonized a number of regulations and administrative processes.[225] Trades in securities, including distributions of securities for capital raising purposes, are subject to regulation under Canadian securities legislation. One of the key requirements applicable to a distribution of securities is the prospectus requirement, as further discussed next.

5.1.1 Prospectus and Other Disclosure Requirements Applicable to Cannabis Companies

In order for an issuer to distribute securities to the public in Canada it must, unless an exemption is available, first file with, and obtain a receipt for both a preliminary prospectus and a final prospectus, from the local provincial and territorial securities authorities in each Canadian jurisdiction where the offering is being made.[226]

A prospectus is a comprehensive disclosure document that is required to contain full, true, and plain disclosure of all material facts concerning the securities being offered for sale. In addition, the prospectus must include all of the prescribed information required under the applicable prospectus form, including audited annual financial statements and unaudited interim financial statements for interim periods subsequent to most recent year-end. [227]

An issuer (through the intermediary of a securities dealer) is permitted to market an offering of securities and solicit expressions of interest from potential purchasers (but not binding commitments) once the preliminary prospectus has been filed and a receipt for it has been issued by applicable securities regulatory authorities. The preliminary prospectus must be delivered to any prospective investor who is contacted. When the final terms of the offering have been settled and the regulatory authorities' comments regarding the preliminary prospectus have been satisfied, the issuer may file a final prospectus. Once the receipt for the final prospectus has been issued, the underwriters may accept subscriptions from potential investors.[228]

---

225. Canadian Securities Administrators, "CSA Business Plan 2019-2022," CSA-ACVM (May 28, 2019), https://www.securities-administrators.ca/uploadedFiles/General/pdfs/CSA_Business_Plan_2019-2022.pdf.

226. Securities Act, *supra* note 223, at § 53.

227. Financial statements included in a prospectus or filed by a reporting issuer pursuant to applicable continuous disclosure obligation must be prepared in accordance with International Financial Reporting Standards (IFRS), subject to certain compliance including for "SEC Registrants" in respect of which financial statements may be prepared in accordance with U.S. Generally Accepted Accounting Principles (US GAAP). "National Instrument 52-107- Acceptable Auditing Standards and Accounting Principles," Ontario Securities Commission, https://www.osc.gov.on.ca/en/13530.htm.

228. However, an investor may withdraw from a purchase during a period of two days from the date on which the investor, or a dealer acting on behalf of the purchaser,

Although cannabis companies are not subject to prescribed disclosure requirements applicable expressly to the cannabis industry, the CSA has provided guidance on its expectations in respect of disclosure by cannabis companies, in particular "reporting issuers," including in prospectuses and other disclosure documents. These are summarized as follows.

In its *Staff Notice 51-352* (published in 2017), the CSA comments that the political and regulatory circumstances regarding how cannabis-related activity is treated in the United States remain uncertain.[229] As a result, the CSA have set out specific disclosure expectations for all issuers with direct or indirect cannabis operations in the United States. The CSA have indicated that they will continue to permit financings in Canada by such issuers provided that specific risk disclosure requirements are included in prospectuses, annual information forms, marketing materials, and management discussion and analyses (MD&As). The CSA notice outlines disclosure expectations specifically for U.S. cannabis issuers premised on the assumption that activities are conducted in compliance with local laws. The extent of the expected disclosure varies based on the nature of operations of the issuer. The CSA notice refers to four categories of issuers, namely (1) all issuers with U.S. marijuana-related activities, (2) U.S. marijuana issuers with direct involvement in cultivation or distribution,[230] (3) U.S. marijuana issuers with indirect involvement in cultivation or distribution,[231] and (4) U.S. marijuana issuers with material ancillary involvement.[232]

In its *Staff Notice 51-357* (published in 2018), the CSA expresses guidance aimed at improving the disclosure in the financial statements and MD&As. In addition, the CSA notes that improved risk factor disclosure was expected of issuers with U.S. operations.

---

receives a copy of the final prospectus. Securities Act, *supra* note 223 at 71(2). Once a final prospectus has been filed in a CSA jurisdiction or listed on a recognized stock exchange, the issuer becomes a "reporting issuer", and therefore subject to prescribed disclosure requirements. *See id.* at § 1(1), for the definition of reporting issuer; *see generally*, "National Instrument 51-102—Continuous Disclosure Obligations," Ontario Securities Commission, https://www.osc.gov.on.ca/en/SecuritiesLaw_51-102.htm.

229. Canadian Securities Administrators, "CSA Multilateral Staff Notice 51-352—Issuers with U.S. Marijuana-Related Activities," CSA-ACVM (Oct. 16, 2017), https://www.osc .gov.on.ca/documents/en/Securities-Category5/csa_20180208_51-352_marijuana -related-activities.pdf.

230. Direct industry involvement arises when an issuer, or a subsidiary that it controls, is directly engaged in the cultivation or distribution of marijuana in accordance with a U.S. state license.

231. Indirect industry involvement arises when an issuer has a non-controlling investment in an entity who is directly involved in the U.S. marijuana industry.

232. Ancillary industry involvement arises when an issuer provides goods and/or services not limited to financing, branding, recipes, leasing, consulting, or administrative services to third parties who are directly involved in the U.S. marijuana industry. CSA Multilateral Staff Notice 51-352, *supra* note 229.

In its *Staff Notice 51-359* (published in 2019), the CSA provides supplemental guidance for disclosure in regard to cannabis issuers. In this notice, the CSA highlights the requirements relating to disclosure of financial interests in transaction documents, and of the independence of board members.[233]

A number of exemptions from the prospectus requirements are available for the distribution of securities in Canada, including a number of exemptions relating to capital raising transactions. The principal prospectus exemption available to companies undertaking a capital raising transaction is the "accredited investor exemption."[234]

In connection with a private placement, issuers may make available to investors an "offering memorandum."[235] Cannabis issuers should include the type of information contained in the CSA staff notices referred to earlier to the extent relevant.

5.2 Canadian Stock Exchange Requirements

Canada's four principal stock exchanges are the Toronto Stock Exchange (TSX), the TSX-Venture Exchange (TSX-V), the Canadian Securities Exchange (CSE), and the NEO Exchange (NEO).

Listing requirements generally applicable to operating businesses apply equally to issuers involved in the cultivation, processing, and selling of cannabis in the cannabis industry. However, as discussed later, the approach to cannabis issuers with operations in the United States varies depending on the stock exchange.

5.2.1 TSX and TSX-V

A cannabis issuer that operates entirely domestically, or in other jurisdictions where the activities have been legalized, may apply to list as a technology company, research and development company, or an industrial company depending on its stage of development.[236]

233. Canadian Securities Administrators, "CSA Multilateral Staff Notice 51-359- Corporate Governance Related Disclosure Expectations for Reporting Issuers in the Cannabis Industry," CSA-ACVM (Nov. 12, 2019), https://www.osc.gov.on.ca/documents/en/Securities-Category5/csa_20191112_51-359_reporting-issuers-in-the-cannabis-industry.pdf.
234. "National Instrument 45-106- Prospectus Exemptions," 32 OSCB at 2.3(1), Ontario Securities Commission (Sept. 18, 2009), https://www.osc.gov.on.ca/en/SecuritiesLaw 45-106.htm; Securities Act, *supra* note 223 at § 73.3(2). A report of trade on Form 45-106F1 must be filed with the relevant Canadian securities regulator within 10 days of the completion of a distribution of securities pursuant to the "accredited investor exemption."
235. Certain prescribed information must be included in an offering memorandum, namely a description of statutory rights of action in the case of a private placement to all accredited investors. "Offering memorandum" is a term defined by Securities Act, *supra* note 223 at § 1(1).
236. Part III of TSX Company Manual (Jun. 4, 2020), https://qweri.lexum.com/w/tsx/tsxcme-en; "Policy 2.1- Initial Listing Requirements," TSX Venture Exchange (Aug. 14,

In its *Staff Notice 2017-0009* issued in October 2017, the TSX advised that listed issuers "with ongoing business activities that violate U.S. federal law regarding marijuana are not complying with applicable listing requirements." The notice clearly states that "ongoing business activities" would be interpreted broadly. The type of activities identified by the TSX, resulting in the delisting of a listed issuer, include (1) direct or indirect ownership of, or investment in, any entity engaging in activities related to the cultivation, distribution, or possession of cannabis in the United States (a U.S. Cannabis Business); (2) commercial interests or arrangements with a U.S. Cannabis Business that are similar in substance to ownership or investment; (3) providing services or products that are specifically designed for, or targeted at, a U.S. Cannabis Business; and (4) commercial interests or arrangements with entities providing such services or products to a U.S. Cannabis Business.[237]

The TSX-V commented that even though many states had regulated cannabis use in some form, due to cannabis remaining a "Schedule 1 narcotic" under the U.S. Controlled Substances Act, any revenue derived from cannabis-related activities in the United States would be considered proceeds of crime.[238]

5.2.2 Canadian Securities Exchange (CSE)

Approximately 173 companies (31 percent) listed on the CSE were involved in the cannabis industry as of October 31, 2019,[239] including companies with operations in the United States and other countries where the cultivation, research, and sale of cannabis and cannabis-related products is legal. A cannabis issuer that meets the listing requirement set out in Policy 2 may apply to list its securities on the CSE.[240] On August 4, 2017, the CSE released guidance relating to listings of cannabis companies with assets or operations in the United States, indicating that such companies may remain listed on the exchange as long as they provide a complete risk disclosure for investors, including a comprehensive discussion of the current legal framework.[241]

2013), https://www.tsx.com/resource/en/421. Part III of TSX Company Manual, *supra* note 236.

237. "TSX Staff Notice 2017-0009," Toronto Stock Exchange (Oct. 16, 2017), https://decisia.lexum.com/tsx/sn/en/454533/1/document.do. The preceding restrictions have been applied by the TSX-V.

238. "TSX-V Notice to Issuers," TSX Venture Exchange (Oct. 16, 2017), https://www.tsx.com/resource/en/1609.

239. "CSE Cannabis List," Canadian Securities Exchange, https://thecse.com/sites/default/files/CSE_Cannabis_List.pdf.

240. "Policy 2—Qualifications for Listing," Canadian Securities Exchange (Aug. 2018), https://webfiles.thecse.com/resource/CSE_Policy_2_-_Qualification_for_Listing.pdf?77Sm_PQ18oZeuBLH7VgACGX9dmE5OLvj.

241. "Notice 2017-014—Industry Guidance—Issuers with Assets or Operations in the U.S. Cannabis Industry," Canadian Securities Exchange (Aug. 4, 2017), http://thecse

5.2.3 NEO Exchange

Cannabis issuers that meet the listing requirement set out in Part II of the NEO Listing Manual may apply to list their securities on the NEO.[242] In addition, securities listed on the TSX, TSX-V, and CSE may also be traded on the NEO. The NEO has not adopted specific listing requirements or limitations for issuers with U.S. cannabis operations. A number of issuers with U.S. cannabis operations are listed on the NEO.[243]

5.3 Compliance with Proceeds of Crime Legislation

The Canadian Proceeds of Crime (Money Laundering) and Terrorist Financing Act (PCMLTFA) is administered by the Financial Transactions and Reports Analysis Centre of Canada (FINTRAC). The PCMLTFA and its associated regulations applies to various entities (reporting entities) such as securities dealers, credit unions, banks, and money services businesses. These reporting entities are required to conduct their own risk assessments of their own activities. In response to the legalization of cannabis, FIN-TRAC has provided guidance for assessing risks for dealings with cannabis businesses.[244]

Reporting entities are expected to assess and document any and all risks involved when doing business with legal cannabis-related enterprises, and appropriate measures must be taken in order to mitigate risks.

In addition to the PCMLTFA, the Canadian Criminal Code has a number of provisions regarding money laundering and proceeds of crime. The Criminal Code applies to all entities, including cannabis businesses.[245]

6. Regulatory Approvals Relevant to Mergers and Acquisitions in the Cannabis Industry

Summarized in this section are certain key regulatory approvals relevant to the acquisition of a Canadian cannabis producer. The acquisition of a Canadian reporting issuer is also subject to a number of requirements

---

.com/en/about/publications/notices/notice-2017-014-industry-guidance-issuers-with -assets-or-operations-in.

242. NEO Listing Manual at Part III, NEO EXCHANGE INC. (Feb. 6, 2020), https:// www.aequitasneo.com/documents/en/listings/aequitas-neo-exchange-listing-manual -april-11-2019.pdf.

243. "Market Activity," NEO EXCHANGE INC., https://www.aequitasneo.com/en/exchange /market-activity.

244. "Risk Assessment of a Legal Cannabis Business," FINANCIAL TRANSACTIONS AND REPORTS ANALYSIS CENTRE OF CANADA (Oct. 17, 2018), posting to *FINTRAC Policy Interpretations: Compliance Regime*, https://www.fintrac-canafe.gc.ca/guidance-directives /overview-apercu/FINS/2-eng?s=4.

245. *Criminal Code, supra* note 3 at § 354(1) (possession of property obtained by crime) and § 462.31 (laundering of proceeds of crime).

under applicable securities legislation. These requirements are beyond the ambit of this chapter.

6.1 Health Canada Notices and Approvals

The licensing regime under the Cannabis Act (Canada) is relevant to mergers and acquisitions transactions involving a licensed entity as a result of the implications of a change of control to the licensing entities. Notice to Health Canada is required in connection with a change of control transaction. Any individual who exercises (or is in a position to exercise) direct control over a cannabis license holder must hold a security clearance before assuming the duties of the position.[246] In addition, changes to the board of directors of a licensee may require approval of Health Canada. Moreover, licenses under the Cannabis Act (Canada) are not transferable.[247]

Key personnel (officers, directors, and key persons (e.g. master growers)) require federal level security clearances in correlation with the CR.[248] At the provincial level, background checks (or similar vetting/due diligence) are required by the relevant province's provincial gaming, liquor, or cannabis authorities for licensed retail operations.

6.2 Foreign Investment Review

The legalization of the Canadian cannabis industry has triggered significant interest in investments by Canadian and non-Canadian investors alike. The Investment Canada Act (ICA) provides for the review of acquisitions of control of a "Canadian business" by non-Canadians to ensure they are of net benefit to Canada.[249] Non-Canadians must file either a notification or an application for review, depending on the value of the Canadian assets or the enterprise value of the Canadian business being acquired and the industry involved.

A non-Canadian includes any entity that is not controlled or beneficially owned by Canadians. Notification must be filed by non-Canadians each time they either start a new business activity in Canada or acquire control of an existing Canadian business where the establishment or acquisition of control is not a reviewable transaction.

A notification must be given by the non-Canadian making the investment at any time before or within 30 days after implementation of the investment.

An investment involving an acquisition of control by a non-Canadian is reviewable (as opposed to being merely notifiable) if the asset value or the

---

246. "Security Clearances under the Cannabis Act and Regulations," Government of Canada (Oct. 15, 2018), https://www.canada.ca/en/health-canada/services/cannabis-regulations-licensed-producers/security-clearances.html.

247. CR, *supra* note 10, at Part II.

248. *Id.* at Part III (§§ 49–61) as discussed earlier at Section 2.1.

249. Investment Canada Act (R.S.C., 1985, c. 28 (1st Supp.)) (Can.).

enterprise value of the Canadian business being acquired exceeds one of the following thresholds: (1) if the investor is from a World Trade Organization (WTO) member country but is not a state-owned enterprise (SOE), any direct investment in a business not engaged in cultural industries in excess of an enterprise value of C$1.075 billion;[250] (2) if the investor is from a WTO member country but is an SOE, any direct investment in excess of the 2020 threshold of C$428 million (adjusted annually), based on the book value of assets of the Canadian business being acquired; (3) if the investor is from a country that is not a member of the WTO, any investment over C$5 million for a direct acquisition or over C$50 million for an indirect acquisition. However, the C$5 million threshold applies for an indirect acquisition if the asset value of the Canadian business being acquired exceeds 50 percent of the asset value of the global transaction.

The investor cannot generally complete the proposed investment until the minister has made a positive determination that the transaction will be of net benefit to Canada.

6.3 Canadian Competition Law Considerations

Competition law is another important consideration when pursuing an acquisition transaction involving a Canadian producer. A proposed acquisition transaction generally requires notification to the Competition Bureau under the Competition Act (Canada) where both of the following two thresholds are exceeded:[251]

Size-of-the-parties test. The parties to the transaction, together with all of their affiliates, collectively have assets in Canada or gross annual revenues from sales in, from, or into Canada that exceed C$400 million.

Size-of-the-transaction test. The aggregate value of the assets (or assets of the target being acquired) in Canada being acquired or the gross annual revenues from sales in or from Canada generated by those assets exceeds a certain threshold. For 2019, the threshold was CA$96 million.[252]

---

250. For investments involving Canadian (non-cultural) businesses by investors from the European Union, Australia, Chile, Colombia, Honduras, Japan, Mexico, New Zealand, Panama, Peru, Singapore, South Korea, the United States, or Vietnam, the threshold for premerger reviews under the ICA has increased to C$1.568 billion effective January 1, 2019. This list encapsulates bilateral free trade agreement partner countries (now defined in the ICA as a "Trade Agreement Investor"), and as soon as Brunei and Malaysia implement the "Comprehensive and Progressive Agreement for Trans-Pacific Partnership," this threshold will also apply to investors from those countries.

251. Competition Act, R.S.C., 1985, c. C-34 (Can.).

252. The size of transaction threshold is adjusted annually by regulation, and the figure referred to in this note is for 2019.

Where a proposed transaction is notifiable, the transacting parties, including the target, must each file certain prescribed documentation as part of the pre-merger notification filing.

The focus on the Bureau's substantive review of any proposed merger is to determine whether the transaction will result in a substantial lessening or prevention of competition in Canada in the relevant product and geographic markets. The analysis in the context of the Cannabis industry has been focused on whether an acquisition may result in a significant lessening of competition. In light of the significant number of producers and retail outlets, none of the acquisitions of Canadian cannabis companies have been restricted by the Competition Bureau.

About the Editors

Barak Cohen, Perkins Coie LLP, Washington, D.C.,
BCohen@perkinscoie.com

Barak Cohen is chair of the Perkins Coie law firm's Cannabis Industry Group, which he helped establish; co-chair of the firm's Veterans' Resource Group, which he also helped establish; Commercial Litigation Lead for the firm's Washington, D.C., office; and a partner in the firm's White Collar & Investigations practice. He is also a member of the policy council for the National Cannabis Industry Association (NCIA) and a vice-chair of the ABA's Committee on Cannabis Law and Policy. Barak has significant experience representing companies in the cannabis, CBD, CBG, and hemp industries, including companies seeking to do business in the food and beverage industry, and with investment banks, financial payment processors, and dispensaries, among others. Barak identified the growth potential in the cannabis industry at an early stage and has been a go-to attorney for companies in the space. Barak is a former Army officer and prosecutor in the U.S. Department of Justice.

Michael C. Bleicher, Perkins Coie LLP, Washington, D.C.,
MBleicher@perkinscoie.com

Michael Bleicher is an associate in Perkins Coie's commercial litigation group, where he focuses his practice on matters involving privacy, data security, and First Amendment issues for clients in the technology and communications industries. Additionally, Michael has experience advising established finance and investment banking companies involved in the cannabis industry (including marijuana, CBD (cannabidiol), CBG (cannabigerol), and hemp products and services) on entering the food and beverage market. Michael earned his BA from Brown University and JD from Harvard Law School.

Chapter Authors

Brian A. Audette, Perkins Coie LLP, Chicago, BAudette@perkinscoie.com

Amanda J. Beane, Perkins Coie LLP, Seattle, ABeane@perkinscoie.com

David T. Biderman, Perkins Coie LLP, San Francisco,
DBiderman@perkinscoie.com

Michael C. Bleicher, Perkins Coie LLP, Washington, D.C.,
MBleicher@perkinscoie.com

Jeannil D. Boji, Perkins Coie LLP, Chicago, JBoji@perkinscoie.com

Samuel D. Boro, Perkins Coie LLP, Washington, D.C.,
SBoro@perkinscoie.com

Jared H. Bryant, Perkins Coie LLP, Seattle, JBryant@perkinscoie.com

Barak Cohen, Perkins Coie LLP, Washington, D.C.,
BCohen@perkinscoie.com

L. Omar Cojulun, Perkins Coie, LLP, Seattle, LCojulun@perkinscoie.com

Bradley A. Cosman, Perkins Coie LLP, Phoenix,
BCosman@perkinscoie.com

Sara Davey, Perkins Coie LLP, Chicago, SDavey@perkinscoie.com

Danielle Fortier, Perkins Coie LLP, Denver, DFortier@perkinscoie.com

Danielle S. Grant-Keane, Perkins Coie LLP, Chicago,
DGrantKeane@perkinscoie.com

Dennis C. Hopkins, Perkins Coie LLP, New York City,
DHopkins@perkinscoie.com

Jason S. Howell, Perkins Coie LLP, Seattle, JHowell@perkinscoie.com

Robert P. Jacobs, Blank Rome LLP, Washington, D.C.,
RJacobs@blankrome.com

Lauren M. Kulpa, Perkins Coie LLP, Dallas, LKulpa@perkinscoie.com

Robert L. Mahon, Perkins Coie LLP, Seattle, RMahon@perkinscoie.com

Jaclyn A. McNally, Perkins Coie LLP, Chicago, JMcNally@perkinscoie.com

Dr. Stephen Ostroff, Former Acting Commissioner of the U.S. Food and Drug Administration, S. Ostroff Consulting, sostroff@verizon.net

Ann Marie Painter, Perkins Coie LLP, Dallas, AMPainter@perkinscoie.com

Aimee Raimer, Perkins Coie LLP, Dallas, ARaimer@perkinscoie.com

Charles C. Sipos, Perkins Coie LLP, Seattle, CSipos@perkinscoie.com

Daniel A. Sito, Perkins Coie LLP, Seattle, DSito@perkinscoie.com

Grace Han Stanton, Perkins Coie LLP, Seattle, GStanton@perkinscoie.com

Dana V. Syracuse, Perkins Coie LLP, New York City, DSyracuse@perkinscoie.com

Philippe Tardiff, Borden Ladner Gervais LLP, Toronto, PTardif@blg.com

Thomas J. Tobin, Perkins Coie LLP, Seattle, TTobin@perkinscoie.com

Neva N. Wagner, Perkins Coie LLP, Chicago, NWagner@perkinscoie.com

David Wood, Borden Ladner Gervais LLP, Calgary, DWood@blg.com

Index